CIVIL MILITIA

Civil Militia
Africa's Intractable Security Menace?

Edited by
DAVID J. FRANCIS
University of Bradford, UK

Routledge
Taylor & Francis Group

LONDON AND NEW YORK

First published 2005 by Ashgate Publishing

Published 2017 by Routledge
2 Park Square, Milton Park, Abingdon, Oxfordshire OX14 4RN
711 Third Avenue, New York, NY 10017, USA

First issued in paperback 2017

Routledge is an imprint of the Taylor & Francis Group, an informa business

British Library Cataloguing in Publication Data
Civil militia : Africa's intractable security menace?
    1. National security - Africa 2. Militia movements - Africa
    3. Civil war - Africa 4. Africa - Politics and government -
    1960-
    I. Francis, David J., 1965-
    355'.03306

Library of Congress Cataloging-in-Publication Data
Civil militia : Africa's intractable security menace? / edited by David J. Francis.
    p. cm.
    Includes bibliographical references and index.
    ISBN 0-7546-4452-9 (alk. paper)
    1. National security--Africa. 2. Militia movements--Africa. 3. Civil war--Africa.
    4. Africa--Politics and government--1960- I. Francis, David J., 1965-

    UA855.C58 2005
    322.4'2'096--dc22

                    2005011873

ISBN 13: 978-1-138-25332-2 (pbk)
ISBN 13: 978-0-7546-4452-1 (hbk)

Contents

List of Tables

About the Authors

Dr Joe A.D. Alie is Head of the Department of History and African Studies and Acting Dean of the Faculty of Arts at Fourah Bay College (FBC), University of Sierra Leone.

Dr Cage Banseka is a Political Analyst in the Political Affairs Division, African Union, Addis Ababa, Ethiopia.

Dr David J. Francis is Director of the Africa Centre for Peace and Conflict Studies, Department of Peace Studies, University of Bradford UK.

Dr Belachew Gebrewold is a Lecturer of International Relations at the University of Innsbruck/Austria.

Dr Jeremy Ginifer is Senior Research Fellow at the Centre for International Co-operation (CICS), Department of Peace Studies, Bradford University UK.

Professor Macharia Munene is Professor of History and International Relations at the United States International University, Nairobi, Kenya.

Dr Kenneth Omeje is Research Fellow in the Africa Centre, Department of Peace Studies, University of Bradford UK.

Dr Hooman Peimani is Senior Research Fellow at the Centre for International Cooperation and Security (CICS), Department of Peace Studies, University of Bradford UK.

Dr Archangel Byaruhanga Rukooko is a Senior Lecturer and Deputy Dean, Faculty of Arts, Makerere University, Kampala, Uganda.

Usman Tar is a Doctoral Researcher at the Department of Peace Studies, University of Bradford UK.

Ruben Thorning is currently Affiliate Researcher with the Nordic Institute for Asian Studies (NIAS) in Copenhagen, Denmark.

Dr Gani Joses Yoroms is Senior Research Fellow at the Africa Centre for Strategic Studies, National War College Abuja, Nigeria.

Dr Istifanus S. Zabadi is Director, Centre for Peace Research and Conflict Resolution, National War College Abuja, Nigeria.

Acknowledgements

The publication of this book would not have been possible without the technical expertise and patience of Eriko Otaki and Yuki Hashido, Research Assistants in the Africa Centre. To them we are indebted. We would also like to acknowledge the support and encouragement of our Nigeria colleagues in motivating us to undertake this project, in particular, the staff at the Centre for Peace and Conflict Resolution at the National War College in Abuja. In addition, we would like to thank our Commissioning Editor, Kirstin Howgate and Editorial Administrator, Carolyn Court, for their remarkable understanding and tolerance in the publication of this book. To Daniel Tamoũi and Ella Agnes, my sincere thanks for the joys and immeasurable happiness you have given me. Your constant, though welcomed distractions, made the editing of this project easier to endure.

List of Abbreviations

ACOTA	African Contingency Operations Training and Assistance
ACRF	African Crisis Response Force
ACRI	African Crisis Response Initiative
AFL	Armed Forces of Liberia
AFRC	Armed Forces Revolutionary Council
ANC	Armée Nationale Colongaise
APC	All Peoples Congress
ASEAN	Association of South-East Asian Nations
AU	African Union
BMATT	British Military Advisory and Training Teams
BPST	British Peace Support Team
Brahimi Report	Report of the Panel on United Nations Peace Operations
CDF	Civil Defence Force
CEAO	West African Economic Community (Communauté Economique de l'Afrique Occidentale)
CIS	Commonwealth of Independent States
CIVPOL	Civilian Police
CMRRD	Commission for the Management of Strategic Resources, National Reconstruction and Development
CPEs	Complex Political Emergencies
DDR	Disarmament, Demobilisation and Reintegration
DOMREP	Mission of the Representative of the Secretary-General in the Dominican Republic
DPA	Department of Political Affairs
DPKO	Department of Peacekeeping Operations
DRC	Democratic Republic of the Congo
E10	Elected 10 (ten non-permanent members, selected regionally and on the recommendation of the General Assembly for two-year terms)
ECOMIL	ECOWAS Mission in Liberia
ECOMOG	ECOWAS Monitoring Group
ECOWAS	Economic Community of West African States
E-IMET	Expanded version of the IMET
EU	European Union
FAS	Federation of American Scientists
FLN	National Liberation Front – Algeria (Front de Libération Nationale)

FRELIMO	Liberation Front of Mozambique (Frente de Liberacão de Mozambique)
FRY	Federal Republic of Yugoslavia
FUNCINPEC	United National Front for an Independent Neutral, Peaceful and Cooperative Cambodia
GAFCSC	Ghanaian Armed Forces Command and Staff College
ICJ	International Court of Justice
ICTY	United Nations International Criminal Tribunal for the Former Yugoslavia
IFOR	Implementation Forces in Bosnia
IGAD	Inter-Governmental Authority on Development
IGNU	Interim Government of National Unity
IMAT	The British International Military Assistance and Training
IMATT	The International Military Advisory and Training Team
IMET	International Military Education and Training
INGO	International Non-Governmental Organisation
INTERFET	Australian-led International Force in East Timor
ISAF	International Security Assistance Force
JCET	Joint/Combined Exchange Training
KFOR	Kosovo Force
KPLNF	Khmer People's National Liberation Front
LNTG	Liberian National Transitional Government
LURD	Liberians United for Reconciliation and Democracy
MICIVIH	International Civilian Mission in Haiti, OAS/UN (Mission Civile Internationale en Haïti, OEA/ONU)
MINUCI	United Nations Mission in Côte d'Ivoire (Mission des Nations Unies en Côte d'Ivoire)
MINURCA	United Nations Mission in the Central African Republic (La Mission des Nations Unis en République Centrafricaine)
MINURSO	United Nations Missions for the Referendum in Western Sahara (Missions des Nations Unies pour l'Organisation d'un Referendum au Sahara Occidental)
MISAB	Inter-African Mission to Monitor the Bangui Accords (Mission Interafricaine de Surveillance des Accords de Bangui)
MNF	Multinational Force in Haiti
MNCs	Multinational Corporations
MODEL	Movement for Democracy in Liberia
MONUA	United Nations Observer Mission in Angola
MONUC	United Nations Mission in the Democratic Republic of Congo (Mission des Nations Unies en République démocratique du Congo)

MOJA	Movement for Justice in Africa
MPLA	Popular Movement for the Liberation of Angola (Movimento Popular de Liberacão de Angola)
MSC	Military Staffs Committee
NATO	North Atlantic Treaty Organisation
NPFL	National Patriotic Front of Liberia
NPRA	National Patriotic Reconstruction Assembly
NPRC	National Provisional Ruling Council
OAS	Organisation of American States
OAU	Organisation of African Unity
OMIB	OAU observer mission to Burundi
ONUC	United Nations Operation in the Congo (Opération des Nations Unies au Congo)
ONUMOZ	United Nations Operation in Mozambique (Misión de Mantenimiento de Paz de las Naciones Unidas para Mozambique)
OSCE	Organisation for Security and Co-operation in Europe
P5	Permanent Five (China, France, Russia, UK, and US)
PAIGC	African Party for the Independence of Guinea Bissau and Cape Verde (Partido Africano de Indepencia de Guine e Capo Verde)
PDD 25	Presidential Decision Directive 25
PDK	Party of Democratic Kampuchea
PKO	Peacekeeping Operation
POLISARIO	Frente Popular Para La Liberación de Seguia El-Hamra y Rio de Oro: Army of Western Sahara
PMCs	Private Military Companies
PSC	Protracted Social Conflict
PSI	Pan-Sahelian Initiative
PSO	British Peace Support Operation
PSTC	Peace Support Training Centre
RECAMP	Reinforcement of African Peace-keeping Capacities (Renforcement des Capacités Africaines au maintien de la paix)
RENAMO	Mozambican Resistance Organisation (Resistëncia Nacional Moçambicana)
RoE	Rules of Engagement
RPF	Rwanda Patriotic Force
RUF	Revolutionary United Front
SADC	Southern African Development Community
SFOR	Stabilisation Forces in Bosnia
SHIRBRIG	UN Standby High Readiness Brigade
SLPP	Sierra Leone Peoples Party
SMC	Standing Mediation Committee

SOC	Government of the State of Cambodia
SRSG	Special Representative of the Secretary-General
STTTS	Short-Term Training Teams
SWAPO	South West African People's Organisation
TRC	Truth and Reconciliation Commission
ULIMO	United Liberian Movement for Democracy in Liberia
UN	United Nations
UNAMET	United Nations Mission in East Timor
UNAMIR	United Nations Assistance Mission for Rwanda
UNAMSIL	United Nations Mission in Sierra Leone
UNASOG	United Nations Aousou Strip Observer Group
UNAVEM I	United Nations Angola Verification Mission I
UNAVEM II	United Nations Angola Verification Mission II
UNAVEM III	United Nations Angola Verification Mission III
UNDOF	United Nations Disengagement Observer Force
UNDP	United Nations Development Programme
UNEF I	First United Nations Emergency Force
UNEF II	Second United Nations Emergency Force
UNFICYP	United Nations Peacekeeping Force in Cyprus
UNHCR	United Nations High Commissioner for Refugees
UNICEF	United Nations Children's Fund
UNIFIL	United Nations Interim Force in Lebanon
UNITA	Uniâo Nacional para a Independência Total de Angola
UNITAF	US-led Unified International Task Force in Somalia
UNIPOM	United Nations India-Pakistan Observer Mission
UNMEE	United Nations Mission in Ethiopia and Eritrea
UNMIBH	United Nations Mission in Bosnia and Herzegovina
UNMIH	United Nations Mission in Haiti
UNMIK	United Nations Interim Administration Mission in Kosovo
UNMIL	United Nations Mission in Liberia
UNMOGIP	United Nations Military Observer Group in India and Pakistan
UNMOT	United Nations Mission of Observers in Tajikistan
UNOCI	United Nations Operation in Côte d'Ivoire
UNOGIL	United Nations Observation Group in Lebanon
UNOMIG	United Nations Observer Mission in Georgia
UNOMIL	United Nations Observer Mission in Liberia
UNOMSIL	United Nations Observer Mission in Sierra Leone
UNOMUR	United Nations Observer Mission Uganda-Rwanda
UNOSOM	United Nations Operation in Somalia
UNOSOM I	United Nations Operation in Somalia I
UNOSOM II	United Nations Operation in Somalia II
UNPREDEP	United Nations Preventive Deployment Force

UNPROFOR	United Nations Protection Force
UNSAS	United Nations Standby Arrangements System
UNSCOP	United Nations Special Committee on Palestine
UNSF	United Nations Security Force in West New Guinea
UNTAC	United Nations Transitional Administration in Cambodia
UNTAES	United Nations Transitional Authority in Eastern Slavonia, Baranja and Western Sirmium
UNTAET	United Nations Transitional Administration in East Timor
UNTAG	United Nations Transition Assistance Group (in Namibia)
UNTSO	United Nations Truce Supervision Organisation
UNYOM	United Nations Yemen Observer Mission
WASP	West African Stabilisation Programme
WEU	Western European Union

Chapter 1

Introduction

David J. Francis

The pro-government Arab militias, the *Janjaweed*, in Sudan are responsible for what the United Nations has described as the 'world's worst humanitarian crisis' in the Darfur region. From Sudan to Sierra Leone, Nigeria to Somalia, Zimbabwe to Rwanda, and Uganda to the Democratic Republic of Congo (DRC), the story is the same. Civil militias have emerged as the most vexing security problem faced by contemporary Africa. The problems, challenges and implications posed by civil militias have converted them into Africa's intractable security menace. The national and human security problems posed by civil militias are far worse than the current concerns and threats from terrorism in Africa. What is also worrying is the fact that academic and policy-relevant debate on civil militiarism in conflict-prone, war-torn and post-conflict societies is scanty, or at best, half-hearted.

Defining and Conceptualising Civil Militias

How do we define and conceptualise civil militias? Are they primarily an African phenomenon? Why and how do civil militias emerge in weak, failed and collapsed states, or why do they proliferate in situations of complex political emergencies? The term 'militia' has a Latin origin meaning 'soldiery', from the word 'miles' meaning soldier. The term has evolved over time to mean auxiliary or reserve military force. A popular definition of a civil militia presents the view that it is a 'A citizen army made up of free men between the ages of sixteen and sixty who performed occasional mandatory military service to protect their country, colony, or state. Also armed and trained bands of locals who could arm themselves on short notice for their own defence'.[1] From an academic perspective, Maurice Duverger defines militia as 'a kind of private army whose members are enrolled on military lines, are subjected to the same discipline and the same training as soldiers, like them, wearing uniforms and badges, ready like them to meet the enemy with weapons in physical combat. But these members remain civilians, in general, they are not permanently mobilised nor maintained by the organisation, they are simply obliged to meet and drill frequently. They must always be ready to hold themselves at the disposal of their leaders' (Duverger, 1967, pp.36-37). These definitions constitute what we describe as the First Generation interpretation and conceptualisation of militias. The First Generation definition of militias presents the view that these are an organised group of citizens mobilised to provide military service; that they are trained as soldiers, but not part of a regular army, and are regarded as a supplementary force or reserve army organised by the state or government. In addition, they are composed of non-professional soldiers, retired, expelled or trained soldiers, often called upon in cases of emergency or crisis, or to protect governments or communities. As an irregular or reserve force, their role is to undertake an emergency support task, often of a military nature. This traditional interpretation of civil militias is based on several assumptions. Firstly, that enlistment is voluntary, though some state constitution or legislation provides for a mandatory military service. The US Constitution, for example, provides the power to call for a militia comprising physically able civilians eligible by law for military service. Secondly, it assumes that since militias are established by states, they are, therefore, regulated and accountable to the state, implying that the state has monopoly over the threat, or the use, of force within its territory. Thirdly, since they are established by the state for a specific purpose, civil militias are based on a state-centric interpretation of security, with the state as the primary security provider with militias never intended to usurp the role of the regular forces, or contest the dominance of the state.

The traditional or First Generation understanding of civil militias has several limitations when applied to the context of complex political emergencies and conflict-prone and weak states in Africa and other developing regions of the world. The changed conflict and international security environment of the post-Cold War period limits the applicability of the traditional interpretation of militias, with reference to the multiple security challenges in contemporary world politics. We have, therefore, developed a new conceptual interpretation of militias described as Second Generation civil militias. This contemporary interpretation is built on some of the elements of the traditional description of civil militias, but the main difference is that it is context specific and applies to conflict-prone, war-torn, post-conflict or transition societies, and, in general, weak and failed states. The Second Generation militias comprise citizens, including young people and unemployed youths, marginalised and dissatisfied with the prebendal state. Civil militias, according to this interpretation, are organised by a diverse group of interest and stakeholders, including governments or regimes in power, mostly with no constitutional provision or legislation legalising their existence. This type of militia could be categorised as state or government sponsored. Other diverse interests include non-state and sub-national group militias (sometimes referred to as ethnic militias) and what Ruben Thorning describes as 'civil security forces'. Whilst those specifically established as pro-government auxiliary or reserve forces have some form of military training, those organised by other interest groups often do not have any military training provision, and even when they do have, it takes the form of basic training sometimes limited to the use of small arms and light weapons. These types of militias mushroom in weak, failed and collapsed states, where the authority and legitimacy of the government or the state is contested, and where the state does not have control or monopoly of the threat or the use of force. Situations of complex political emergencies provide environments conductive to the emergence and proliferation of these types of civil militias, hence regarded as Africa's intractable security menace. Furthermore, the Second Generation civil militias also share the normative underpinning and ethos for the establishment of the First Generation militias, i.e., as a force for good, to provide public goods by defending and protecting the state and people. But in the situation of weak states, underwritten by prebendal governance, the normative ethos for the establishment of civil militias is often subverted and privatised to serve particular vested interests. The demonstrable efficacy of some of these civil militias in crime and war fighting has led to the situation whereby they usurp the security provision of the state and even undermine the effectiveness of the security functions of the state. However, this is not to say that the traditional civil militias were not susceptible to politicisation and manipulation. It becomes evident that the Second Generation conceptualisation of militias conveys the notion of a pluralist conception of the state and security. Barry Buzan therefore posits that we have to 'look to individuals and sub-state units for the most meaningful security referents' (Buzan, 1991, p.101). For the purpose of this edited volume, the focus is on the contemporary Second Generation interpretation of civil militias.

At this stage, there is a need for further conceptual clarification of terminology. The terms ethnic militia, armed vigilante group, religious militia, civil defence force, and separatist militia have been used to describe the phenomenon of civil militias in Africa and other parts of the world. These labels are unhelpful because they do not objectively reflect their origins, motivations, or rationales for creation, not their modes of operation, activities and socio-political objectives. Nnamdi Obasi has outlined a helpful categorisation of civil militias into: i. vigilante organisations; ii. militia organisations; and, iii. separatist movements.[2] However, this kind of labelling presents several problems. Firstly, it simplifies the emergence of this phenomenon and hence inevitably buys into the often simplistic and pigeonhole analysis of African conflicts and security problematic, i.e., about tribalism, ethnicity or religion. Secondly, it has led to ill-defined solutions and inappropriate policy responses by development and conflict interveners in conflict-prone and complex political emergency situations. Thirdly, the labels convey the fact that these disparate armed groups have emerged from civil society for a variety of reasons and motivations as a self-help response to insecurity. For conceptual clarity and consistency we have settled for the all-embracing terminology of civil militias, but different contributors to this book have used other terms to convey the same meaning.

Public-Private Continuum

Both the First and Second Generation definitions and conceptualisations of militias illustrate a public-private continuum. Legitimate militias are public 'institutions' regulated by and under the control of the state. They are however private in the sense that they are drawn from the civilian populace, a citizen self-help force to provide security and defence, and to be called upon in times of emergencies. As a private force, they can protect the state and people, but could also resist the legitimate exercise of the authority of the state or even challenge the status quo, especially in marginalised and polarised societies (Bristol, 1998). As a private citizens' group, where interests or perceptions or misperceptions of exclusion from the political and economic processes of the state are contested, civil militias could attempt to overthrow the oppressive power structures and social relations, and are prepared to use armed violence to achieve their objectives, or even to deconstruct state legitimacy. Basil Davidson, therefore, argues that;

> The consciousness, which triggers social mobilisation, could also provide the constant measures for raising ethnic soldiers or ethnic militias for the purpose of defending a collective cause of struggle, and often ignorant of rudimentary rules of warfare. However, consciousness is the first basis for mobilisation and training. They engage gradually in political education alongside military, for the actualisation of their objectives and goals (Davidson, 1969).

To some extent, this perception of militias conveys the notion of a revolutionary or emancipatory force, drawn from society. The view is that militias capitalise on collective grievances to mobilise and militarise disaffected groups. Insurgency and liberation groups have similar origins. Since they are drawn from society, they take on different forms such as civil society militias (including ethnic, religious and ideological groups), armed vigilante groups, and political party militias – the armed wing of political parties.

Distinguishing the Context of Civil Militias

For the purposes of analytical and conceptual clarity, it is also important to distinguish the context of civil militiarism. Firstly, there is the context of conflict-prone societies where decades of patrimonial decline, underdevelopment and state weakness provides the environment for the emergence and proliferation of civil militias. These militias emerge to protect and serve a variety of vested interests, often not established by government or state, and lack any legal or constitutional mandate, for example the context of Nigeria and Indonesia. In this context, governments are forced, by their inability to provide security, to outsource security provision to private agencies, armed vigilante groups and quasi-military outfits, for example, the Bakassi Boys in Nigeria. The ruling and governing elites also have a dominant role in the creation and proliferation of these militias. Secondly, there is the context of war-torn and post-conflict transition societies where violent and bloody civil war and state collapse or situations of complex political emergencies lead to the emergence of either pro-government civil militias or people's self-help civil defence forces, for example: Sierra Leone, Liberia, Uganda, Somalia, Sudan, Congo Brazzaville and DRC. In this context, the pro-government militias, such as the Janjaweed militias, fight a proxy war for the government and often serve as an instrument of regime consolidation and survival. An important dimension is that whether the militias are established by government or not, governments end up not being in control of the militias because militias develop lives of their own, taking on the predatory and prebendal instincts of the society and government. The militias therefore become hydra-headed monsters, difficult to tame or contain, hence an intractable security menace.

Characteristic Features of Civil Militias

We have already highlighted some of the features of militiarism. We will now focus on what produces civil militias, i.e. what kind of socio-political environment and state? For the purposes of our focus on the Second Generation interpretation of civil militias, we concentrate on the nature of the state and the state system in Africa, and how this has provided the context for the emergence and proliferation of civil militias in Africa.

The African State, Complex Political Emergencies, and Production of Civil Militias

The *Oxford Dictionary of Politics* defines the state as a 'distinct set of political institutions whose specific concern is with the organisation of domination, in the name of the common interest, within a delimited territory'.[3] This definition embraces both the broad and specific dimensions of the state and is thus bound to be not only an essentially unsatisfactory definition for some people, but also problematic in terms of application in some societies or polities. The state broadly defines a set of institutions as possessing the means of legitimate coercion, without monopoly over the use of force, exercised over a defined territory and population. The state as the authoritative decision making entity with jurisdiction over territory is vested with the responsibility to provide a variety of essential functions including the provision of welfare for its citizenry, peace, order and security for its people. Three interrelated functions of the state are evident. Firstly, the state as the sovereign authority, the recognised and accepted source of authority to organise decision-making. Secondly, the state as an institution vested with the authority for decision-making and hence an intangible symbol of identity; and thirdly, the state as primary security provider for a populated territory (Zartman, 1995, p.5). The state exercises control over rule making within its territory through the medium of organised government. The terms 'state' and 'government' are sometimes used colloquially or interchangeably to mean the same thing. Government, as distinct from the state, describes the process of governing, exercise of power by structure, and people who occupy the positions of authority in a state. Government describes the conditions of 'ordered rule', the manner, method or system of governing a society, and the structures and arrangements of offices as they relate to the governed. Government is said to constitute three distinct branches of power including legislature, executive (sometimes referred to as 'the government'), and the judiciary (UNDP, 1997, p.20).

Statehood, according to Barry Buzan, is a social construct, i.e. the 'idea of the state' is 'constructed' in the minds of those who form and govern the state (Buzan, 1983, pp.44-53). This constructed idea of the state provides legitimacy in a variety of forms. It provides territorial legitimacy, i.e. the consent of a population to live within a demarcated territory because of shared values and identities, and the right of the state to exercise authority and control over all the territory allocated to it by international law. In addition, it provides governmental legitimacy in that it serves as the basis for constituted authority, and the right to act on behalf of its citizens through agreed constitutional means. But this idea of governmental authority differs considerably between states and within states, in terms of the concept of the 'rulers' and the 'ruled'. The idea of the state, according to Christopher Clapham (1996), also provides external legitimacy, i.e. international recognition of the state as a legal and equal member of the international community of states. The exercise of external legitimacy or juridical sovereignty makes it possible for states to participate in international relations and transactions in an increasingly interdependent modern world. Clapham, therefore, argues that 'The power of rulers derives not only from the material resources and ideological support of their own people, but equally from their ability to draw on the ideological and material resources provided by other states – and also non-states, such as transitional religious organisations or business corporations'.

The application of the different definitions and conceptions of the state in Africa has been problematic. According to Clapham, the attributes ascribed to state by the mythology of statehood do not reflect the reality of statehood in Africa (Clapham, 1996, p.21). Each and every attribute of the state has either been contested, appropriated or subverted by the different elements or institutions or sets of institutions within the state. For instance, in much of Africa, there is a huge gap between the exercise of external sovereignty and domestic sovereignty. Robert Jackson describes this phenomenon as quasi-statehood, in that these are states which are recognised as sovereign independent entities by other states, within the international system, but which cannot exercise the demands of 'empirical' or domestic statehood that require them to have the capacity to exercise effective power within their own territories and be able to defend themselves from external attack (Jackson, 1986, 1990). Such states have 'negative' or juridical sovereignty, in that sovereignty is ascribed to them by other states and they only exist by the fiat of the international system. They do not possess the 'positive' sovereignty, which derives from effective control of the state (Clapham, 1996, p.15). Jackson, therefore, argues that the sovereignty regime became a device for weak states in Africa and other parts of the world to protect themselves against strong states or domestic contestations of the state. The sovereignty regime has been used, subverted and abused to serve the vested interests of those who control the official state. It is in these quasi-states that the Second Generation civil militias emerge and proliferate.

It is important to recognise that the state, as it has come to exist and operate in post-colonial Africa, is different from the conventional Western-centric understanding. Post-colonial states in Africa are sets of entities or institutions struggling for survival in the international system (Clapham, 1996). Leonardo Villalón and Phillip Huxtable therefore outline five different faces that characterised African states: a client status; a personalised identity or monopoly status; a centralised or overdeveloped morphology; a prebendal or rentier nature; and an extractive impulse (Villalon and Huxtable, 1998, p.11).

Why is the state what it is in Africa? Put simply, why has the state system failed to work in Africa or has it simply failed to function according to the traditional Westphalian expectations? At independence, it was blindly assumed by liberal theorists and neo-Marxists that everyone knew the direction in which the 'post-colonial state and society would develop: that of modern, secular frameworks with all the familiar functional check-and-balances and appropriate administrative technologies' (Doornbos, 2001, p.182.). The state was 'decorated' with high expectations as the main channel of development. In Clapham's words, 'African independence launched into international politics a group of the world's poorest, weakest and most artificial states' (Clapham, 1998). There was little awareness about how unclear, uncertain, and precarious were the efforts of the post-colonial African state to define and develop its role and position in relation to society. These high expectations were to be accompanied by painful disillusionment about the role and capacity of the state in Africa. The distinctive features of the African state are that almost all, excluding Liberia and Ethiopia (briefly colonised by Italy), are former colonies; they are the latest entrants to the state system and as such are at the earliest stage of state formation and nation building; they are the most evidently challenged domestically and most peripheral members of the global economic system (Clapham, 1998, p.1). A dominant feature of the post-colonial state in Africa is that the continent is littered with small states (both in terms of size and population), that are faced with, or are critically challenged by, a vast array of security vulnerabilities and threats. Some of these micro-states were carved out primarily to serve the political, economic and strategic self-interests of the colonial powers and, at independence, were granted the 'legal fiction' of sovereign statehood. These states include The Gambia, Lesotho, Swaziland, Botswana, Namibia, Cape Verde, Djibouti, Gabon, Equatorial Guinea, Sao Tome and Principe and Guinea Bissau. These micro-states have a demonstrated increasing vulnerability to security risk and some are not able to cope with or manage diverse security threats.[4] However, some of these micro-states have records of political stability, economic growth, sustainable development and social progress. Media commentators and some political analysts often portray the view that all states in Africa are weak, failed and underdeveloped. Neil MacFarlean asserted in the 1980s that 'There is hardly a state in black Africa which appears more viable today than it did on the eve of independence' (MacFarlean, 1984, p.131). The assertions made by analysts such as MacFarlean do not reflect objective reality because there are examples of viable, strong and modern states in Africa such as Botswana, Tunisia, South Africa, Egypt, and Namibia. These generalisations and assertions gloss over or deliberately underestimate the problems and challenges of state formation and nation building in Africa, which is barely six decades old.

Nearly six decades after independence, state formation and state-building[5] remain problematic in Africa. We have seen the evolution of some African states from weakness to disintegration and collapse. It is important to recognise that state collapse is not a phenomenon peculiar to Africa. It exists in different forms in Third World regions, for example, the former Soviet Union and Eastern Europe. But it is in Africa that the state formation[6] process has been most problematic, hence the emergence of different kinds of states. According to Leonardo Villalón and Phillip Huxtable, the African state is at a 'critical juncture' (Villalón and Huxtable, 1998). But what explains the crisis of the African state and how do we characterise the state system in Africa? A variety of external and internal factors are responsible for the contemporary nature and position of the African state. They range from colonial legacy, the fiction of juridical sovereignty and Cold War politics, to the over-extended role of the African state and the nature of domestic politics and patrimonial decline.

The state in Africa is a creation of European colonialism. European colonialism and its legacies bequeathed to African 'proto-states' a crumbling foundation for the creation of a post-colonial political order. Mohamed Ayoob argues that colonialism led to the creation of administrative units by the imperial powers without regard for the population's pre-colonial affinities and loyalties. The arbitrary and cavalier construction of colonial political boundaries in the mid-1880s cut across ethnic, tribal, religious and linguistic ties, dismembered established political units; and lumped diverse pre-colonial political entities in uneasy administrative unions (Ayoob, 1995). Ayoob further argues that colonial rule delayed the transformation of African colonies from backward into modern economies, through what would have been natural processes of economic development; stunted the growth of social classes, especially the commercial and industrial bourgeoisie; and derailed the evolutionary process of economic development by introducing discontinuities in the economic spheres through a shift from food to cash crops production. This colonial capitalist exploitation set the stage for the way and manner in which post-colonial African states were to be integrated into the global market economy. The colonial inheritance, therefore, provided the recipe for the eventual disintegration and fragmentation of the post-colonial state in Africa, because the 'state' in Africa is a product of a different history, a history of conquest (Mamdani, 1998).

Post-colonial African leaders, therefore, inherited a colonial state system predicated on control based on extraction of resources and domination of society. With limited options and in a haste to consolidate their grip on state power, the independence leaders merely replicated the colonial bureaucratic authoritarian control. The imposed state system in Africa and its associated Western-style institutions, such as parliament, political parties and bureaucracies have brought spectacular difficulties for African governments. They find it difficult to measure up to the standards for the exercise of political control propounded by Montesquieu, Rousseau, Locke or Weber. Therefore, in most African countries, the post-colonial state has not been able to overcome some of its colonial legacies. It could be argued that Africa's underdevelopment can be traced to the fact that the state-system imposed was flawed. Therefore, policies, no matter how correctly designed, were bound to face problems in terms of the state institutions responsible for their implementation (Clapham, 1996).

Whilst state building has evolved over centuries in Europe, the Westphalian project imposed on Africa at independence is not yet six decades old and has evolved in a very different and changed international environment. The processes of state building and national integration have been constrained by limited time and lack of a free hand to persuade and coerce diverse peoples and nations to accept the legitimacy of political authority, institutions and state boundaries. State building in post-colonial Africa is not different from what was obtained in the early stages of state building in Western Europe. Charles Tilly argues that the 'building of states in Western Europe cost tremendously in death, suffering, loss of rights, and unwilling surrender of land, goods and labour. Most of the European population resisted each phase of the creation of strong states' (Tilly, 1975, p.71). The state building process, after four centuries, emerged in Western Europe as strong states enjoyed the 'habitual obedience of their populations, secure in the legitimacy of their borders and institutions (although borders were never entirely free from challenge), and, therefore, positioned to respond to societal demands since those demands no longer ran counter to the accumulation of power in the hands of the state' (Ayoob, 1995, p.29). This was not to be the case in post-colonial African states. African states cannot afford the luxury of time and contemporary demands of the international society as they strive to compete and co-operate with established modern states. Ayoob, therefore, posits that systemic pressures and demonstration effects make it obligatory for African states to establish viable political communities within the shortest possible time or risk international ridicule and permanent marginalisation within the international system (Ayoob, 1995, p.30). Whilst Western nation-states in their evolution over centuries, were given the time to solve some of the difficult and complex problems of state building before they faced the challenges of mass politics, post-colonial African states had no such time and luxury. The process of decolonisation engendered mass politics. The difficult task of state building went hand in hand with pluralistic politics and all their diverse demands on the polity and its new leaders. The state was to provide the space for participatory politics, generate economic development and at the same time maintain social and civil order and exercise political control over its territory. The demands and expectations of state building, both domestic and international, within such a short period of time in post-colonial Africa are almost impossible to accomplish. Whilst the evolution of the state in Western Europe was slow, post-colonial African states at independence were called upon to exercise all aspects of modern sovereignty immediately. It would be difficult to see how Western modern states could have achieved their level of statehood and positive sovereignty in less than six decades. History shows that they could not have. If anything, post-colonial African states have done relatively well, in terms of the efforts at state building, in just a few decades. Sixty years of state building in Africa have seen an overload of the political, socio-economic and military functions and capabilities of the state because of the speed with which the state responded to domestic and international pressures to demonstrate both empirical and juridical statehood. It could be argued that the present malleability, disequilibrium, collapse and fragmented nature of the state system is partly the result of the enforced process of state formation in Africa. Ayoob argues that this 'disequilibrium lies at the root of the chronic instability that we witness in most Third World states today. Instability in turn, engenders violence and insecurity, as state-making strategies, adopted by state elites to broaden and deepen the reach of the state, clash with the interests of counter-elite and segments of the population that perceive the extension of the state authority as posing a direct danger to their social, economic, or political interests' (Ayoob, 1995, p.32). But the fundamental question is how to explain the relatively successful process of state building in countries such as South Korea and Taiwan in less than five decades? Is limited time the most serious factor hindering state formation and nation building in Africa?

An important feature is that African states were born into the Cold War politics of the 1950s, 1960s and 1970s. Independence converted Africa into a battleground for East-West Cold War rivalry. This affected the nature and performance of post-independence African states because their policy options and alternatives became limited, and were constrained by an international system in which they were pawns and, as such, could play only a marginal role.[7] The Cold War ideological rivalry between the communist East and the capitalist West had a considerable impact on Africa as it divided the continent into 'hostile' ideological camps. Cold War politics and the ideological divide also made it possible for external interventions in Africa in the form of proxy wars such as in Congo, Angola, and Mozambique. These proxy or limited wars, fuelled by the superpowers and their allies, became a common feature of the continent during the decades of the Cold War period.

Furthermore, the interests of the superpowers and their allies effectively established a stranglehold on the newly independent African states because of their strategic minerals. The exploitation of strategic minerals such as cobalt, uranium, copper, gold, diamond, chrome ore, iron ore, bauxite, zinc, manganese ore, rock phosphate, rutile (titanium dioxide), chromium, platinum, nickel and oil converted Africa into a battleground for Cold War politics and external interventions. These were minerals of strategic interest to the survival of the automobile, aircraft, satellite and telecommunications, weapons and nuclear industries in both the East and West. The availability of these strategic minerals and their industrial outputs created not only huge employment opportunities, but also vulnerabilities due to scarcity or lack of access to these raw materials. This led to the establishment of 'client states' propped up by the superpowers and their allies. But beneath the ideological rivalry between the superpowers in Africa was the intense economic and commercial rivalry to secure access to and control of Africa's strategic minerals. The Cold War conflict and competition in Africa was also about proxy wars for resources, and Africa, in the process, paid the high price of disunity and underdevelopment.

Another aspect of the sovereignty regime and Cold War politics is that the international community paid little attention to the state's treatment of its population and this often had significant bearing on its international position. The recognition of the inviolability of state boundaries removed incentives for ethnic accommodation where force was a justified means to crush secessionist and separatist threats and civil disorder. The disassociation between post-colonial African states' economic and political performance and their sovereign status, as recognised by the international community, amounted to a ridiculous pretence when poor and extremely weak and fragmented states continued to be accorded sovereign legitimacy. Cold War politics conferred on post-colonial African states a disproportionate level of juridical statehood, which did not reflect the domestic reality.

External factors played a considerable role in the crisis of state formation and nation building in Africa. But what have Africans themselves done to the state system? We may blame external factors for Africa's underdevelopment and instability, but what about characters such as Idi Amin of Uganda, Charles Taylor of Liberia, Foday Sankoh of Sierra Leone, Emperor Bokasa of the Central African Republic, Mobutu of Zaire, and Savimbi of Angola, – though propped up by Cold War politics, these characters are Africans who have brought misery and destruction on their own peoples. Internal factors are, therefore, important explanatory variables in understanding the state in Africa. The standard expectation that post-colonial African states will gradually develop features of modern Westphalian statehood, through the process of development, has not come to pass (Sorensen, 2001, p.268). Instead, we have seen a plethora of collapsed, disintegrated, fragmented, soft and weak states in Africa, largely due to the struggle for control of state power by the ruling and governing elites. Max Weber's sociological conception of state, according to Jackson and Rosberg, is that of 'a corporate group that has compulsory jurisdiction, exercises continuous organisation, and claims a monopoly of force over a territory and its population' (Jackson, 1990, p.12; Jackson and Rosberg, 1982). The majority of post-colonial African states can be described in Weber's term of 'statelessness' because they do not have a monopoly of the use of force throughout their territorial jurisdiction. Persistent internal instability, the emergence of insurgency movements, civil militias, and warlord politics clearly demonstrate that they do not pass the test of empirical sovereignty.

In the struggle to control state power and consolidate regime survival, political authority in post-colonial Africa became increasingly personalised rather than institutionalised. Ethnic and religious divisions have often produced political tensions and conflicts, which affect national integration, political and civil order, and the capacity of governments to exercise control. With hardly any viable pre-colonial tradition of statehood, and underdeveloped state institutions, coupled with the fact that the colonial institutions erected were insufficiently viable to withstand the pressures of transition to independence, state power thus became personalised in post-colonial Africa. Personalised rule became predicated on patron-clientelistic networks and patrimonial accumulations, in which the leader or strongman controls a web of informal networks within which resources emanating from the command of state apparatus are distributed to supporters. Access to state power and its patrimonial resources became the basis for the acquisition of political office. Corruption, graft, nepotism and personal accumulation became the norm for those in control of the state (Thomson, 2004, pp.108-128; Bayart, Ellis and Hibou, 1999). Control of government in the major part of post-colonial Africa became less preoccupied with public good, but served instead as a reservoir for patrimonial enrichment, power and prestige. Most of the post-colonial regimes have survived largely due to their control over means of private accumulation through patronage networks. This personalised rule did not maintain any distinction between the public and private realms of the state for example, Moi's Kenya, Kamusu Banda's

Malawi, Mobutu's Zaire, Houphouët-Boigny's Côte d'Ivoire, Stevens' Sierra Leone etc. In effect, the public face of state building became subverted by state elites serving their private interests. Clapham argues that the practical experience of the transfer of the Westphalian state system to Africa has seen the subversion of sovereignty to serve the private agendas of the state elites in that 'The state, and the ideology of sovereignty which upheld it, became in effect the playthings of those who ran it ...' (Clapham, 1996, pp.4-5). In view of the fact that in most post-colonial African states there was hardly any viable basis for the establishment of a Weberian system of rational-legal bureaucratic governance, it was inevitable that post-independence leaders, lacking any real source of power, would subvert the public face of state sovereignty in order to serve their private interests. The 'state' as represented by a select few or predatory class became a 'vampire', 'sucking the resources' of the nation with impunity.

The demands for political participation and economic redistribution have further complicated the process of state building because of the pressures and strains it puts on post-colonial states. Ayoob posits that 'This contrasts with the situation of early state makers in Europe, who could single-mindedly pursue their goals of accumulating power and extracting resources without being distracted by demands for economic redistribution and political participation, except by small segments of the privileged strata of society' (Ayoob, 1995, p.39). Thus, Charles Tilly argues that 'The European state-makers constructed, then imposed, strong national governments before mass politics began' (Tilly, 1975, p.69). In the new states in Africa, both processes, with all their inherent tensions and contractions, occurred simultaneously. The classic dilemma then was how to satisfy popular demands and the imperatives of state building at the same time, and how to use coercive authority to maintain domestic political and social order without it being unacceptable to a population influenced by notions of human rights, political participation and social justice (Ayoob, 1995, p.40). The governance dilemma predisposed many African leaders towards pleasing or placating the urban population because they posed a serious threat to political stability and regime survival. Rural constituencies were encouraged to be loyal to the regime through the informal patron-clientelistic networks.

The African state, privatised in such a fashion, can hardly be expected to demonstrate any semblance of empirical statehood. Domestic politics became characterised by the establishment of prebendal or rentier states, wherein the ruling and governing class creates clientelistic networks to ensure regime survival. The extractive basis of the economies of post-colonial African states (mineral and natural resources) incorporated them into the international patron-clientelistic networks of the global market economy. Extractive states such as Sierra Leone (diamond), Nigeria (oil), Angola (diamond and oil), Niger (uranium), Zaire (diamond and copper) concentrated development on extractive activities whilst failing to build the capacity for economic development and infrastructural integration. The malleability, 'inversion of the state' and disintegration can be partly attributed to the nature of domestic politics and the privatisation of the state by the ruling and governing elites.[8] In an attempt to survive the harsh realities of the international system, African leaders have to invent strategies for domestic and international survival. Clapham, therefore, argues that 'the evident weakness of the African states did not reduce them to a state of inertia, in which their fate was determined by external powers. On the contrary, it impelled them to take measures designed to ensure survival, or at least improve their chances of it' (Clapham, 1996, p.4).

The combination of both internal and external factors has led to the failure and collapse of some states in Africa. State collapse, according to Zartman, is when the basic functions of the state can no longer be performed, and the authoritative decision making and organising body becomes paralysed and inoperative, losing its powers of control over society, no longer able to provide security and welfare functions for its citizens. It has not only lost its political legitimacy and right to rule, but also its socio-economic apparatus is destroyed. This breakdown of governance, law and order, and loss of control over political and economic space is accompanied by societal fragmentation. Therefore, state collapse is not 'a short-term phenomenon; not a crisis with few early warnings; nor simply a matter of a coup or a riot. State collapse is a long-term degenerative disease' (Zartman, 1995, pp.5-8). But state failure and collapse are not new phenomena in Africa. Early versions of state collapse include Congo in the 1960s, Uganda and Ghana in the late 1970s and early 1980s, and Chad in the early 1980s. However, the crises of the African state system have become more apparent in the post-Cold War period as demonstrated by countries such as Somalia, Liberia, Sierra Leone, DRC etc. The prolonged economic crises experienced by many African states, and their repercussions for government revenue bases and provision of social services, the proliferation of arms and the militarisation of marginalised groups in society, the decline of international rentier resources and the outbreak of civil wars, reveals the degree of failure and fragmentation of the post-colonial state. Herbst argues that the international community, in its response to failed states in Africa, has refused to acknowledge the structural factors at work, even though empirical evidence abounds that loss of sovereignty is becoming a pattern in much of Africa. The classic response is that there is no alternative to the current state system. Reconfiguration of the political order and establishment has been the favoured response by the international community to state disintegration in Africa. Post-Cold War Africa is, therefore, poised between 'disintegration and reconfiguration' (Villalón and Huxtable, 1998, p.8).

The international response to failed and collapsed states in Africa has focused primarily on reconstituting, resurrecting and saving them. In West Africa, we have seen the 'reconstitutive intervention' of external forces such as ECOMOG in Liberia, Sierra Leone, Guinea Bissau and now Côte d'Ivoire; the American-led UN intervention in Somalia; and the Zimbabwean-led SADC intervention in former Zaire. All these are attempts to save and resurrect failed and collapsed members of the international society as a means of maintaining the conservative international system and the state-centric status quo. We are yet to see any revolutionary response to state failure in Africa that will change the prevailing fixation upon maintaining existing units and norms of international society.

The rationale for the reconstruction of failed and collapsed states is primarily to maintain the status quo of the international society which, according to

Christopher Clapham, needs effective and viable states for smooth operation and for the maintenance of international co-operation, something which the international community, African governments and populations also desire (Clapham, 1998, p.8). Reconstructing or reconfiguring the state is therefore a mechanism to strengthen the pillars, i.e. order, representation, protection and development, on which the public justification for Westphalian sovereignty had been based. Such reconstruction has often focused on reconstituting national politics to the national territory and restoring national economic flows throughout the territory (Zartman, 1995, p.9). The pivotal role of the state in the politics and development of African countries explains why it is difficult, even in the most abject cases of political fragmentation and chaos there is still the tendency to recognise such disintegrated political communities as states. Villalón and Huxtable in fact conclude that there is no obvious alternative to the Africa state and as far as they are concerned, 'In whatever form, the state seems here to stay' (Villalón and Huxtable, 1998, p.24). They argue that African states have left their marks on their populations, giving a measure of reality to their artificial existence'. The conclusion, both in theory and practice seems to suggest that there is no obvious alternative to the state system.

Linked to our analysis of the state in Africa and how it produces civil militias is the conceptualisation of complex political emergencies. Second Generation civil militias have emerged and proliferated in situations of complex emergencies. There is, therefore, a need to define and conceptualise complex emergencies. Complex political emergencies (CPEs) is one of the fashionable terminologies that emerged in the 1990s. It was coined by the UN to describe the proliferation of major crises, the majority of which were intra-state conflicts, that emerged after the end of the Cold War. It describes this 'new' category of conflicts of the 1990s as multi-causal, requiring multi-dimensional international responses including a combination of military intervention, peacekeeping and peace support operations, humanitarian relief programmes, high-level political intervention and diplomacy.[9] The majority of the wars and armed conflicts in Africa are described as complex political emergencies and are characterised by large-scale human suffering and civilian casualties, and the crisis itself is multi-dimensional. Often, the root causes of the conflict are embedded in political and socio-economic grievances (i.e. human-instigated conflicts), and sometimes complicated by natural disasters such as drought, famine and floods. The conflict is often followed by or triggers state failure and collapse, with societal fragmentation, large-scale destruction of infrastructural facilities, forced migration and internal displacement, weakness or collapse of state governing institutions. The multiple crises creates a humanitarian emergency and hence the imperative for international intervention to save lives and alleviate or ameliorate human suffering. However, state collapse also triggers complex political emergencies. The method of warfare in CPEs is a clear departure from conventional military security forces and involves civil militias, child soldiers and paramilitary forces. Often it is a war of attrition, which becomes not only an 'extension of politics by other means' (i.e. struggle to gain access and control over state power), but also an extension of economics by other means (i.e. exploitation of war economies and struggle for access and control over state resources). The majority of these conflict-torn societies are peripheral economies, and the inefficient political and economic management of the state has undermined the capacity of the state to provide welfare and security. Therefore, complex political emergency is a continuum describing the conditions immediately before, during, and after conflict or escalations of hostility, requiring immediate intervention or response. The intervention often takes the form of humanitarian relief, security and military operations and a range of nation-building intervention programmes. [10] In war-ravaged and post-conflict transition societies, often described as CPEs, civil militias emerge as part of the problems and challenges of the war-to-peace transition. To reinforce this point, Barry Buzan *et al* argue that:

> When the state fails . . . militias, mafias, clans and gangs come to the fore. Some still speak in the name of the state, but others become self-seeking and self-referencing security entities. (Buzan, 1998)

As already pointed out, in the context of shadow states and CPEs (Reno, 1995), it is difficult to make a distinction between the illegitimate and governmental civil militias. The governmental militias come in different forms, such as presidential guards or palace guards, and paramilitary outfits, with quasi-'official' state roles. Since they often lack constitutional mandate, they disappear with either change in government or the end of the regime. Prebendal underdevelopment and the politics of decline have contributed to the emergence of civil militias, in that, because of the loss of confidence and trust in the ability of the state to provide security and welfare and to defend its citizens, the civilian populace resort to self-help mechanisms to defend and protect themselves. It is a return to the days of the wild west of the American frontiers.

Civil Militias: A Security Menace in Africa?

We have alluded to the threats posed by civil militias to national and human security, and how they have emerged as a potentially 'clear and present' security menace. But what kind of security is referred to and how do we define security?[11] Security itself is a 'contested concept' in terms of definition, interpretation and specification. Barry Buzan outlines twelve different definitions of security to illustrate the problematic nature of the concept. Put simply, security is a condition of being or feeling safe from harm or danger' (Terriff, Croft, James and Morgan, 1999, p.1). The interpretation and specification of the 'condition' of 'being safe' from who or what, and the nature and type of 'danger' and the normative elements, are part of the problematic of the conceptualisation of security. Other international relations' theorists perceive security as the defence, protection and preservation of 'core values' and the 'absence of threats to acquired values' (Wolfers, 1962). But even at the height of the Cold War in the 1980s, the limited traditional conception of security focusing on national security, interests and power, with the state as the primary referent object of security, the condition of anarchy in the international system, and the military use or threat of force, was criticised by various scholars as not reflecting the nature and complexity of security (Buzan, 1982, Ullman, 1983). The emerging sources of threats to security could not be explained within the framework of the traditional conception of security, for example, the OPEC (Organisation of the Petroleum Exporting Countries) oil price rises in 1973, due to the Arab-Israeli war, brought to the fore the relevance of economic security and the role of strategic resources to national security. Richard Ullman was critical of the militarisation of the concept of security, and, together with other scholars, in particular with the end of the Cold War, has advocated a redefinition of the concept of security and the broadening and deepening of the security agenda to take on board the non-military dimensions of security, such as the environment, migration, disease, transnational crime, natural disasters, the global wealth and poverty divide, ethno-religious and nationalist identities, and the dangers of cybercrime and terrorism. The non-military/non-traditional threats to security have led to the broadening of the reference object of security to include individuals, non-state actors and sub-national groups.[12]

In Africa, non-military dimensions of security, such as environmental degradation, poverty, resource scarcity, ethno-religious and nationalist identities, crime, drugs, diseases such as HIV/AIDS and malaria, natural catastrophes like drought, famine and flood, and mass migration of people, have all threatened individual and societal security and survival, and even national security. These non-traditional sources of threat to security affect life, health, status, wealth and freedom of individuals, societies and states, and, in some cases, have created the conditions for conflict and violence in societies and polities in Africa. The non-military security threats are largely internal rather than external. What is important about these emerging non-military challenges to security and stability is that they emanate from a range of non-state, sub-state actors and factors that are trans-state in character. Also, the dangers and challenges posed by these non-traditional military security threats are not confined to a particular state or geographic region. Terriff *et al*, therefore, assert that these new security challenges cannot be managed by the traditional use of force and defence policies alone. Their management will require a range of non-military approaches as well. Their conclusion is that, the 'Non-traditional challenges, ... represent dangers which are diffuse, multidimensional and multidirectional ... these new concerns suggest that individuals as well as states are endangered' (Terriff et al., 1999, pp.115-6).

It is, therefore, not surprising that non-military challenges and threats to security in Africa are increasingly emerging as a key focus for policy, decision-makers,·and analysts. The African Leadership Forum asserted that 'The concept of security goes beyond military consideration. It embraces all aspects of society including economic, political and social dimensions of individual, family, community, local and national life' (African Leadership Forum, 1992, p.9). As Africa is the least developed region of the world it is understandable why the non-traditional sources of threats to security, within the context of widespread wars and conflict, are increasingly attracting the attention of national, regional and international leaders. The UNDP *Human Development Report 2004* gives depressing development, economic and social indicators. During the 1990s, the number of people living in extreme poverty in SSA rose from 242 million to 300 million. In comparison, extreme poverty was halved in South Asia during the 1990s (UNDP, 2003, p.10). The estimated propotion of people living on $1 a day by the end of the 1990s was 46.7% (UNDP, 2003). Per capita income shrank by 0.3% in SSA in the 1990s, while there was appreciable increase in annual growth in per capita income of 3.3% in South Asia. But it is important to note that within Africa there are different sub-regional dimensions of threat to security, for example, desertification in North Africa and famine, drought, and flooding in the Horn and southern Africa. Desertification in parts of West Africa, the Horn and southern Africa is threatening human security. In addition, deforestation and overgrazing undermine land productivity, on which the livelihood of the people depends. Scarce water and land resources in some parts of Africa undermine the security and the very survival of peoples and the preservation of core values of these communities. In addition, Africa is emerging as the world's 'soft-underbelly' for global terrorism, as witnessed by the Al Qaeda bombings of the US embassies in Kenya and Tanzania in 1998, and terrorist attacks in Mombassa, Kenya in 2002, Morocco in 2003, and Islamic fundamentalist bombings in South Africa. The conflict zones, state failure and collapse, weak law and state governing institutions, porous borders, the corruption and 'privatisation' of the security and banking institutions, and the radicalisation of disaffected populations, have made Africa a safe-haven and recruiting ground for terrorist organisations (Harmon, 2003). Therefore, terrorism, whether state-sponsored, group or individual, is a serious threat to human, societal and national security.

Civil Militias, Occult Practice and the Spirit World: Military Psychology or 'Retreat from Modernity'?

A common feature of contemporary civil militias is the link between the activities and *modus operandi* of militias and the 'belief' in supernatural powers and occult practice. Kenneth Omeje and Joe Alie's contributions have extensively discussed and analysed this phenomenon.[13] The hallmark and driving force for the putative efficacy of civil militias in security provision is their claim to supernatural powers through the use of oracular deities, secret societies, and claims of 'invincibility' or being 'inoculated' against bullets and light weapons. Civil militias such as the Bakassi Boys in Nigeria and the Kamajors in Sierra Leone have made claims that they derived their war fighting prowess from the spirit world, and they routinely dished out so-called 'war medicines' and charms to their fighters and recruits. They went through particular initiation ceremonies, officiated by high priests, that would, supposedly, make them invincible and 'protected' from enemy bullets during any war fighting or security operations. Based on extensive research, we have discovered that these militias believe that all success attributed to their operations is based on their occult practice and the efficacy of the spirit world. However, there is a serious military and security psychology associated with the purported belief of the militias in spiritism and occult practice. The use of charms and initiation ceremonies have a strategic military and war fighting purpose because they make the recruits brave, with a die-hard belief in their cause. These charms are supposed to ward off fear and develop the psychology of invincibility and valour.

Some media commentators and political analysts have dismissed the link between civil militiarism and the spirit world as a retreat from modernity and have associated this dimension with a part of the extreme reaction to the failure of development in postcolonial Africa. Rather than simply dismiss this dimension, as mere primitive mysticism, it is important to explore the implications. Why is this happening in Africa? Understanding of the sociological development of traditional Africa shows that belief in the spirit world and occult practice has been common in Africa. Newspapers in Africa are replete, on a daily basis, with stories of occult rituals, ritual murders and *Muti* practices, not only by traditional Africans but, interestingly, by some members of the ruling and governing elites, and the so-called intellectuals and aspiring intellectuals.[14] Some members of the army and state security agencies, liberation forces and guerrilla fighters have dabbled in occult practice and the spirit world in the pursuit of their military and security functions. RENAMO in Mozambique, the RUF in Sierra Leone, and the NPFL in Liberia popularised the phenomenon of 'Juju Warriors' by establishing the link between war fighting, occult practice and belief in the spirit world. The link between war fighting and the spirit world further highlights a much neglected feature of contemporary asymmetrical warfare or so-called 'new wars'. From a military and strategic perspective, the use of oracular deities and the spirit world show that in the context of asymmetrical warfare, when the 'weak' are faced with the superior or preponderant military power of the 'strong', the weak will resort to other unconventional military and psychological tactics, to harass, humiliate, demoralise and defeat the 'strong'. The use of oracular deities, Juju warriors and the spirit world by contemporary civil militias should also be understood from the perspective of the military and the psychological dimension of asymmetrical warfare.

To a sceptical western audience, this dimension of the spirit world and oracular deities is pure and simple fiction because it defies all rational explanation and scientific logic. But this does not mean that just because a particular phenomenon – and an alien one at that – fails to conform to all 'civilised' standards of rationale and scientific explanation, that it is not happening or that it does not exist.[15] This brief overview illustrates an important feature of civil militiarism.

Re-inventing Civil Society in Complex Political Emergencies

What does this tell us about civil society? Civil society, by definition, is a contested concept and subject to diverse interpretations. Civil society defines the realm of the private sphere in which social movements become organised, representing diverse interests and agendas. The concept of civil society has its origins in the western liberal democratic tradition and, as such, its application to Africa is often problematic. Civil society and grassroots social movements could be broadly categorised into socio-political organisations, developmental groups, and civil society security and defence forces. The dominant western literature, underpinned by the conventional understanding of civil society, has come to regard the activities of local community groups and grassroots social movements as less significant than the actions and interventions of the middle class elitist and often professional organisations. From this perceptive, therefore, academics and analysts such as Jeanette Hartman have argued that 'civil society in Africa is not sufficiently developed to manage its affairs and become independent of the state. If the state were to collapse then the civil society could also disintegrate'. Similarly, Jeff Haynes shares the view that countries racked by civil war and state fragmentation have a corresponding weakness in civil society (Hartman, 1999, p.199; Haynes, 1997, pp.3, 32-3).

But the context of conflict-prone, war-torn and post-conflict transition societies in Africa clearly refutes the arguments presented by Hartman, Haynes and others. There is no denying the fact that state collapse and civil war have a devastating impact on civil society but, not withstanding, it has also led to the resurgence and resilience of civil society, and in some cases even usurps or supplants the security and welfare functions of the weak or collapsed states. The positive role and activities of some of the security/defence and socio-developmental civil society forces and organisations in war-torn and transition societies demonstrate that, far from disintegrating, civil society in these complex political emergencies have shown remarkable resilience in providing public goods for the community and even necessities for existence. It is therefore in these conflict-prone and transition societies that the emancipatory and transformatory potential of civil society is more prominent. Civil society in Africa has not degenerated into what Robert Fatton described as 'conflict ridden and prone to Hobbesian war of all against all' (Fatton, 1995, pp.67-99). What is emerging in these war-torn and transition societies is a new kind of symbiotic state-society relationship, which does not readily fit into the traditional conception of civil society. In conflict-prone and transition societies, civil society represented in different forms, such as civil militias, has generated collective solidarity with a capacity for providing public goods, and even mitigated the potential for outbreak or relapse into further conflict.

Challenges Posed by Civil Militias

If the creation of civil militias has normative underpinnings, why and how do they become an intractable security menace? James Otto's descriptive article presents the powerful image that the use of civil militias in conflict-prone and war-torn societies is like 'using fuel to put out a fire'. To understand this imagery, it is necessary to look briefly at some of the challenges posed by civil militias. A major challenge is that their very existence is illegal and unconstitutional. The exercise of law and order, and the provision of security and protection of the state and people is the constitutional responsibility of the state. In the majority of African countries there is no legislation or constitutional provision governing the existence and operation of civil militias. This constitutional vacuum has created situations conducive to the emergence and proliferation of militias. According to Obasi, the attempt by some State governments in Nigeria to employ the services of and support for civil militias in policing and law enforcement operations is unconstitutional under Section 4 of the Police Act, Cap. 359 of the Laws of the Federation (Obasi, 2002, p.91). It is argued that the activities of civil militias pose a 'clear and present' danger to peace and national stability, and threaten democratic governance. The operations of militias in conflict-prone and transition societies threaten to replace the rule of law and the ballot box with gun law and armed violence.

By all indications, militias undermine and erode the western-based justice systems and the rule of law provisions of the state, and perpetually challenge democratic consolidation and sustainable peace. This book gives a detailed outline of how the activities and operations of civil militias violate basic human rights and fundamental freedoms. Civil militias do not only subvert the rule of law, but their methods of 'justice' are a gross violation of human rights. The majority of their members and recruits are complete strangers to the very basic norms of human rights and international law relating to the conduct of warfare. International organisations have documented cases of human rights abuses perpetuated by civil militias, in particular how they have 'dished out' extra-judicial killings and arbitrary execution, to persons suspected of involvement in criminal activities or perceived to be an 'enemy fighter'. But it is worthy of note that state military and security agencies in Africa also have a record of gross violations of human rights and extra-judicial executions. Civil militias, however, are only accountable to their interest groups, therefore they raise serious questions relating to accountability and transparency. Perhaps the most serious and perpetual threat posed by civil militias is to national security. In conflict-prone and transition societies, civil militias threaten public order, and societal cohesion and stability. They not only contribute to the further polarisation of already bitterly divided societies, but also aggravate ethnic tensions and intra-communal violence. In a multi-ethnic country, polarised by decades of patrimonial decline, civil militias threaten public order and efforts at peacebuilding. Due to the spillover of domestic conflicts, civil militias threaten regional peace and security as some of these militias such as the Kamajors, Mayi Mayi and Interahamwe have been involved in civil wars in neighbouring countries. Civil militias therefore effectively erode the capacity of the state to exercise domestic or empirical sovereignty and undermine the monopoly of the state over the use of force. The erosion of the states' monopoly over the use of force has led to the privatisation of security and violence, thereby presenting the perpetual image of these countries as being unstable and ungovernable. But we argue that the majority of these weak states never had the capacity to exercise domestic sovereignty in the first place.

In addition, the nature of domestic politics, based on political clientelism and patrimonialism, has created the situation whereby, even though some of these militias have been established as a 'force for good' or to provide public goods, they have been subverted, politicised, and manipulated by the ruling and governing elites and other vested interests. Political parties, ethnic and religious groups, warlords and other diverse interest groups, have organised, trained, equipped and managed civil militias to use or display physical force to achieve their specific objectives. Furthermore, the activities and operations of civil militias undermine the attainment of the goals of human security. The perpetual climate of fear and instability threaten not only access to existential necessities such as food, shelter, clothing and health care, but also qualitative aspects of human security such as freedom and participation in the decisions that affect the lives of the people. The debate is more forceful in the context of war-torn and transition societies in that civil militias are regarded as posing a serious challenge to disarmament, demobilisation and reintegration (DDR), security sector reform (SSR) and post-war democratic consolidation and governance. They do not only undermine the achievement of development goals but have also been involved in exploitation of war economies and criminal enterprises.

But the debate on the challenges posed by civil militias is unresolved. Some perceive militias, in particular situations, as a positive force in the provision of security in complex political emergencies. Opinion is divided and attitudes and responses vary amongst the populace as to whether, in fact, militias play a positive or negative role in national development and the maintenance of peace and security. The contributions to this edited volume have critically engaged with this issue, but it is left to the informed reader to arrive at their own conclusions. The sub-title of the book raises a question as to whether, in fact, civil militias constitute an intractable security problem in contemporary Africa.

Outline of the Book

Civil Militia: Africa's Intractable Security Menace? is the first publication to critically engage with the problematic posed by militias in contemporary Africa. The contributions are drawn from outstanding Africanists who live and experience, on a daily basis, the reality and challenges posed by militias in their respective countries. The book is divided into 11 further chapters. Gani Yoroms' conceptual chapter on 'Militias as a Social Phenomenon: Toward a Theoretical Construction' locates the emergence of the phenomenon of civil militias within the theory of social contract and state formation. In an attempt to provide analytical understanding of militiarism, Yoroms outlines three theoretical interpretations, namely, state, non-state, and fluid theories. The chapter gives an in-depth overview of the rise of civil militias in Africa, with a comparative insight into the historical development of militiarism, drawing on empirical cases of the United States, Soviet Union, European States and England in the 16th-19th Centuries, and South East Asia.

In Chapter 3, Joe Alie's 'The Kamajor Militia in Sierra Leone: Liberators or Nihilists?' attempts a serious analytical discussion of a specific type of civil militia in the context of war-torn and post-conflict Sierra Leone. This chapter brings to the fore the emerging debate and conceptualisation of Second Generation civil militias. The Kamajor militias and other civil defence forces and in particular the context of Sierra Leone, illustrate all the critical elements relevant to the re-conceptualisation of civil militias and how they have emerged as an intractable security menace. This chapter critically interprets the political history, economy and civil war and how these developments produced and proliferated civil militias in war-ravaged Sierra

Leone. This chapter also reveals how the collapse of the state and the inability of the regimes in power to prosecute the civil war, led to the situation where the people had to usurp the security functions of the state by organising citizens' defence forces that became a pro-government, war-fighting force. A key focus of Alie's Chapter is the analysis of the origins of the Kamajors, *modus operandi*, war activities and the military/security alliance built with pro-government mercenary and Private Military Companies (PMCs), and the ECOMOG peacekeeping and intervention forces, and how in the post-war period, they now pose serious challenges to the state, SSR, DDR, democratic consolidation and peace and stability.

Kenneth Omeje's contribution on 'The Egbesu and Bakassi Boys: African Spiritism and the Mystical Re-traditionalisation of Security' explores the link between African spiritism and the security sector. Using the specific example of two civil militias in conflict-prone Nigeria, Omeje establishes how prebendal politics and failure of postcolonial development have led to exclusion, deprivation, and marginalisation of some sectors and groups in society. In an attempt to survive, these marginalised sub-national groups and societies have developed alternative strategies of using armed violence, supported by mystical powers and occult practice, to achieve their objectives – what Omeje describes as a 'collective retreat to security re-traditionalisation'. After exploring the historical, sociological and political economy context of security retraditionalisation, the chapter analytically engages with how civil militias such as the Bakassi and Egbesu Boys are now filling the security vacuum created by corrupt patrimonialism and state weakness. An important focus of this chapter is how these civil militias challenge state legitimacy, the rule of law, democracy, public order and national stability and the collective impact on the protection of and respect for human rights and fundamental freedoms.

To illustrate that the phenomenon of civil militias is not unique to Africa, Ruben Thorning's contribution gives an insightful comparative perspective on civil militias in the context of Indonesia and Nigeria. Thorning situates the discussion of the militarisation of society and the emergence of organised civil society militias, usurping the security functions of the state or challenging state legitimate authority, as a global phenomenon – a 'social phenomenon with a possible global reach'. The chapter examines the emergence, organisation and operational activities of 'civil society militias' in both Nigeria and Indonesia. The comparative approach is important for several reasons. Firstly, it affirms that civil militiarism is a global phenomenon. Secondly, that the militarisation of states and the crisis of state formation and nation building are not unique to Africa. In addition, the comparison demonstrates that marginalised societies and groups, whose basic survival are threatened, will potentially react in diverse ways, and one such response is armed violence or civil militiarism to protect their interests. The chapter further evaluates how the privatisation of security and armed violence effectively erodes the state's monopoly over the use of force – a monopoly, in the case of both Nigeria and Indonesia, the state never fully enjoyed. The chapter's conceptual framework of the public-private militia continuum provides useful insights for the understanding of other case studies.

Istifanus Zabadi's contribution examines the regional dimension of the threats and challenges posed by civil militias in West Africa through the prism of the war-torn countries of Sierra Leone, Liberia, Côte d'Ivoire and Guinea Bissau. The chapter explores how state collapse, civil wars and complex political emergencies have produced and proliferated civil militias in West Africa. In particular, how militias pose a serious and perpetual threat to national, regional and human security. Zabadi argues that the conflict situation in West Africa has created an environment conducive to the privatisation of security, attracting all manner of armed groups and fighting forces including mercenaries, Private Military Companies (PMCs), security outfits and paramilitary groups. An important contribution of Zabadi's chapter is that it attempts to provide an understanding of the phenomenon of civil militias, both in the context of war-torn/ post-conflict, and in conflict-prone societies.

Usman Tar's chapter on 'Counter-Insurgents or Ethnic Vanguards? Civil Militia and State Violence in the Darfur Region, Western Sudan' critically assesses the emergence, role and challenges posed by the pro-government Arab militias, the Janjaweed, in Sudan. Tar's outline of the political history, economy and civil wars in Sudan, and his conflict analysis, reveals that the emergence of diverse armed groups and civil militias is the result of a combination of complex domestic and international factors. The civil war in the Darfur region of Western Sudan, and the humanitarian crisis it has generated, are products of the failure of patrimonial governance, racial, resource and identity based conflicts, including religion and ethnicity. Just as the pro-government Interahamwe was responsible for the genocide in Rwanda, so the pro-Khartoum Janjaweed militias are accused by the international community of perpetuating genocide in Darfur. To understand these complex issues, Usman Tar gives a detailed outline of the heterogeneity, civil wars and perpetual instability in Sudan, the perverse manifestations of civil militias in contemporary Sudan, the organisation and *modus operandi* of the Janjaweed militias, and how they posed a challenge to the recently concluded Naivasha Peace Agreement between the Sudan Peoples Liberation Army (SPLA) rebel movement and the Khartoum government. The chapter raises the wider issues of how militias threaten peace, security and stability in complex emergency situations, and in particular, the regional implications.

Cage Banseka's contribution on 'The Anti-Gang Civil Militia in Cameroon and the Threat to National and Human Security' examines the phenomenon of urban militias conceptualised from a security perspective. Banseka locates the emergence of civil militias and the threat posed to national and human security, within the context of the political history and the nature of domestic politics in Cameroon. Decades of neo-patrimonial governance have impoverished and marginalised sections of the civil populace, who in turn, have responded in diverse ways, including armed violence, to contest the dominance of the state and the ruling class. Banseka's chapter further highlights the specific context and case study of urban-based civil militias in a conflict-prone country, and the diverse, and sometimes, contradictory responses of the civilian populace and government to this phenomenon.

An important dimension of Belachew Gebrewold's contribution on 'Civil Militias and the Militarisation of Society in the Horn of Africa' is the explanation of the regional dimensions of civil militias. The majority of the countries in the Horn have been challenged by diverse forms of intra-state and interstate wars and armed conflicts and, in the process, have produced scores of civil militias, and even provided the environment for the recruitment and proliferation of armed vigilantes. After examining the contexts and crisis of state formation and nation building, security challenges and armed violence in the Horn, Gebrewold explores the specific cases of Ethiopia, Eritrea, Sudan and Somalia, and how these have produced not only civil militias, but also radical and fundamentalist Islamic groups and terrorist outfits. Gebrewold presents the view that the militarisation of society and the proliferation of small arms have taken on a trans-border dimension, locking the countries of the Horn into a complex security situation whereby conflicts potentially spill over into neighbouring countries.

A. Byaruhanga Rukooko's chapter focuses on two important developments in Uganda that are at the heart of this book. Firstly, how the political history and protracted conflicts and instability in post-colonial Uganda have created a variety of civil militias and armed groups. Secondly, how the context of a violent and bloody civil war, and the inability of the government to end the war, have led to the funding and establishment of pro-government militias to help prosecute that civil war. Rukooko's chapter shares similar generic themes with the contribution of Joe Alie on Sierra Leone. To illustrate the distinguishing features of the specific context of Uganda, Rukooko focuses on the emergence and consolidation of President Museveni's National Resistant Movement/Army and its auxiliary forces (local Defence Units), how Museveni's government has institutionalised militiarism in Uganda through the Kalangala Action Plan, and other civil defence groups such as the Anti-stock theft unit and the Nyekundire militias. Of particular relevance is the analysis of the emergence, role, contribution and challenges posed by the pro-government Arrow Boys and Amulca (Rhino) militias, established to fight against Joseph Kony's Lord's Resistance Army (LRA) rebel group in northern Uganda.

Macharia Munene's chapter on 'Mayi Mayi and Interahamwe Militias: Threats to Peace and Security in the Great Lakes Region' examines how decades of war and protracted socio-political conflict in the Congo and Rwanda have produced a variety of civil militias, and posed a perpetual threat to the peace and stability of their nine neighbouring states. Munene explores how colonial and post-colonial history and political economy created the breeding ground for the emergence, proliferation and exportation of civil militias in the region. The political history explored in this chapter also highlights the international involvement in Congo's different wars, by both states and non-state or sub national groups such as the Interahamwe militias responsible for the genocide in neighbouring Rwanda.

Jeremy Ginifer and Hooman Peimani's chapter on 'Civil Defence Forces and Challenges to Post-Conflict Security: International Experiences and Implications for Africa' assesses the specific context of and challenges posed by civil militias in war-torn and transition societies. Of particular importance is the focus on the challenges posed to conflict and development interveners engaged in post-conflict reconstruction and development. Drawing from comparative case studies of the war-torn and post-conflict countries of Peru, Guatemala, Sri Lanka and Sierra Leone, the chapter examines the lessons learned in relation to challenges and implications for DDR, security sector reform, post-war peace and democratic consolidation. The comparative approach of Ginifer and Peimani identifies the key issues in terms of international responses to war-torn and transition societies, and the imperative for regulation of civil militias.

We have decided not to attempt to draw overall conclusions in this book because the contributions have highlighted the controversies, critical debates and emerging research issues and policy challenges. The next stage of this project is to explore in specific detail two country case studies and two additional regional analyses of the phenomenon of civil militiarism, as an attempt to build on what this volume has started.

Notes

[1]   www.pbs.org/williamsburg/calltoarms/glossary.html

[2]   N. Obasi, *Ethnic Militias, Vigilantes & Separatist Groups in Nigeria* Abuja: Third Millennium Ltd., 2002. See also; R. T. Akinyele, 'Ethnic Militancy and National Stability in Nigeria: A Case Study of the Oodua People's Congress' *African Affairs* Vol. 100, No. 402, 2001, pp.623-640 J. Harnischfeger, 'The Bakassi Boys: fighting crime in Nigeria' *Journal of Modern African Studies* Vol. 41, No. 1, 2003, pp. 23-49.

[3]   I. Mclean *Oxford Concise Dictionary of Politics* Oxford: Oxford University Press, 1996, p. 472. This section draws extensively from chapters 2 and 3 of D. Francis, *Uniting Africa: Building Regional Peace and Security Systems*, Ashgate: Aldershot, 2005, forthcoming.

[4]   For a comprehensive conceptualisation of the security risks faced by small states in contemporary world politics see the Commonwealth Report on *A Future for Small States: Overcoming Vulnerability* London: Commonwealth Secretariat, 1997.

[5]   State building according to Keith Jagger is defined as the 'state's ability to accumulate power. State building is the process by which the state not only grows in economic productivity and government coercion but, in political and institutional power' Keith Jagger, 'War and the three faces of power: War making and state making in Europe and the Americas' *Comparative Political Studies* 25, 11, 1992.

[6]   Martin Doornbos describes state formation as a set of ongoing processes which 'include the establishment, growth and differentiation of state structures, and the redefinition of the position of various social and political groups, and organisational networks within the wider context, These processes lie at the heart of the dynamics of state-society relationships' M. Doornbos, *Dynamics of State Fomation: India and Europe Compared*, London: Sage, 1997 p.181.

[7]   For a discussion of the international history of Africa see: John Darwin, 'Africa and World Politics since 1945: Theories of Decolonization' in Ngaire Woods (ed.) *Explaining International Relations Since 1945* Oxford: Oxford University Press, 1996; and John Harberson & Donald Rothchild (ed.) *Africa in World Politics: Post-Cold War Challenges* San Francisco: Westview Press, 1995.

[8]   Joshua Forrest defines 'state inversion' as the process wherein government institutions become increasingly dysfunctional and end up turning inwards toward themselves,

rather than outwards toward society' in Villalón, L. and Huxtable, P. (eds.) (1998), *The African State at a Critical Juncture: Between Disintegration and Reconfiguration* Lynne Rienner, London, pp. 46-7.

[9] See D. Fade (ed.) *Development in States of War* Oxford: Oxfam, 1996, p. 5; Jenny Pearce, 'Peacebuilding in the periphery': lessons from Central America' *Third World Quarterly* Vol. 20, No. 1, 1999.

[10] For further reading on CPEs see the following: Karl Joakim Gundel, *Humanitarian Assistance: Breaking the Waves of Complex Political Emergencies - A Literature Survey*, CDR Working Papers 99.5, Copenhagen August 1999; Lionel Cliffe & Robin Luckham (eds.) 'Complex Political Emergencies and the State: Failure and the Fate of the State' *Third World Quarterly* (Special Issue on CPEs) Vol. 20, No. 1, 1999, pp. 27-50; David Hume & Jonathan Goodhand, 'Peacebuilding and Complex Political Emergency' Working Paper Series No. 12, IDPM, University of Manchester, March 2002.

[11] The definition and conceptualisation of security draws largely from chapter 3 of Francis, *'Uniting Africa'*, 2005. Forthcoming.

[12] There is a vast literature on this subject, sometimes described as Critical Security Studies' including: Thomas, C. and Synder, C. (1999) *Contemporary Security and Strategy*, Macmillan, London, T. Homer-Dixon 'Environmental Scar Cities and Violent Conflict: Evidence from Cases' *International Security,* Vol.19, No.1, 1994, pp. 5-40. The redefinition of security has led to ten different conceptions of security: security dilemma, national security, international security, collective security, security community, security regime, common security, societal security, human security and global security/ environmental security. The militaristic focus of security led to the development of Strategic Studies with primary focus on the military aspects of the Cold War, such as nucear strategy and deterrence, proliferation of weapons of mass destruction, the nature of war, revolution in military affairs, the use and threat of force to achieve political objectives, and the strategic balance between the superpowers.

[13] See also, J. Harnischfeger, 'The Bakassi Boys' *Journal of Modern African Studies* Vol. 41, 2003; J. Comaroff & J. Comaroff (eds.) *Modernity and its malcontents: ritual and power in postcolonial Africa* Chicago, IL: University of Chicago, 1993, Stephen Ellis, *The Mask of Anarchy: The Destruction of Liberia and the Peligious Dimension of an African Civil War*, London: Hurst and Company, 1999.

[14] The Scotland Yard criminal investigation into the discovery of the torso of a boy in the Thames river in London. Association with *Muti* practice, and the Channel 4 documentary on 'Torso in the Thames: the Search for Adam's Killers', 23 September 2004, 22:00 GMT have gone a long way in raising public awareness of a sceptical British society that Spiritism and African Juju is a real life occurrence and is happening in Africa and now in 21st Century London.

[15] A recent personal experience in Bradford forced me into an unexpected 3 month research project (July-September 2004) through interviews, to ascertain the belief in and prevalence of occult practice and the spirit world amongst Africans in Britain. A total number of 150 Africans (84 men and 66 women) were interviewed through e-mail, telephone and personal contacts, from Bradford, London, Southampton, Manchester, Leeds and Glasgow. They included 31 academics and aspiring intellectuals (PhD. students), and the rest were ordinary Africans in different walks of life. The 3 month research produced an interesting and surprising result. 100 % of those interviewed acknowledged that occult practice is a common phenomenon in Africa and that they believe in its powers. When asked whether they had been involved in it themselves, 80 % denied that they had been involved, but 20 %, though confirming that they had been involved, were quick to affirm that their involvement was only for benevolent purposes,

such as good luck, success in business and studies, in particular scholarship opportunities. The distinction was made between charms and occult practices that are for good purposes and those that are malevolent, i.e. to harm and cast 'evil' spells on perceived enemies, to control people in positions of strategic influence or to exert controlling influence on rivals or people they disliked. All occult practices with malignant effect they described as *African Juju*. On whether civilised and exposed (widely travelled and westernised) Africans in the west or in the UK could be involved in such a practice, 75 % agreed, but 25% were either sceptical or just could not tell. Some of those involved keep it secret. The refusal to acknowledge involvement is based on the notion of 'shame', i.e. it is widely accepted as shameful and primitive for an educated and westernised African to be involved it *Juju* or *Voodoo*. 80 % of the women interviewed confirmed that the practice was common since it was perceived as a means to 'assist' their progress and success in life. The valid conclusion is that this is a phenomenon practiced by some Africans despite their level of education or exposure to western 'civilisation', norms and expectations. This research further reinforces the popular belief in the efficacy of the spirit world and occult practice.

References

African Leadership Forum (1992), *The Kampala Document: Towards a Conference on Security, Stability, Development and Co-operation.*

Akinyele, R. T. (2001), 'Ethnic Militancy and National Stability in Nigeria: A Case Study of the Oodua People's Congress' *African Affairs* Vol. 100, No. 402 www3.oup.co.uk/afrafj/

Ayoob M. (1995), *The Third World Security Predicament: State Making, Regional Conflict, and the International System,* Lynne Rienner, Boulder.

Bayart, J., Ellis, S. and Hibou, B. (1999), *The Criminalization of the State in Africa,* James Currey, Oxford.

Bristol, T. (1998), 'America's Militia Heritage – The Volunteer Militia', *Command Issue,* No. 48, April.

Buzan, B. (1998), *People State and Fear,* 2nd ed, Longman, London.

Buzan, B. (1983), *People, States and Fear: The National Security Problem in International Relations,* Wheafsheaf, Brighton.

Clapham, C. (1996), *Africa and the International System: The Politics of Survival,* Cambridge University Press, Cambridge.

Clapham, C. (1996), *Africa in the International System,* Cambridge University Press, Cambridge.

Clapham, C. (1998), 'Degrees of Statehood', *Review of International Studies,* 24, 22.

Cliffe, L. and Luckham, R. (eds.) (1999), 'Complex Political Emergencies and the State: Failure and the Fate of the State', *Third World Quarterly* (Special Issue on CPEs), Vol. 20, No. 1, pp. 27-50.

Comaroff, J. and Comaroff, J. (eds.) (1993), *Modernity and its malcontents: ritual and power in postcolonial Africa,* University of Chicago, Chicago.

Darwin, J. (1996), 'Africa and World Politics since 1945: Theories of Decolonization', in Woods, N. (ed.) *Explaining International Relations Since 1945,* Oxford University Press, Oxford.

Davidson, B. (1969), 'Introduction', in Chaliand, G. (ed.) *Armed Struggle in Africa,* Monthly Press Review, New York.

Doornbos, M. (1997), *Dynamics of State Fomation: India and Europe Compared*, Sage, London.

Duverger, M. (1967), *Political Parties*, Methuen, London.

Ellis, S. (1999), *The Mask of Anarchy: The Destruction of Liberia and the Religious Dimension of an African Civil War*, Hurst and Company, London.

Fade, D. (ed.) (1996), *Development in States of War*, Oxfam, Oxford.

Fatton Jr, R. (1995), 'Africa in the Age of Democratisation: The Civic Limitations of Civil Society', *African Studies Review*, Vol. 38, No. 2.

Francis, D. (2005, forthcoming) *Uniting Africa: Building Regional Peace and Security Systems*, Ashgate, Aldershot.

Gundel, K. J. (1999), *Humanitarian Assistance: Breaking the Waves of Complex Political Emergencies - A Literature Survey*, CDR Working Papers 99.5, August, Copenhagen.

Harberson, J. and Rothchild, D. (eds.) (1995), *Africa in World Politics: Post-Cold War Challenges*, Westview Press, San Francisco.

Harmon, J. (2003), *A Ten-Year Strategy for Increasing Capital Flows to Africa*, Commission on Capital Flows to Africa, NY: June.

Harnischfeger, J. (2003), 'The Bakassi Boys', *Journal of Modern African Studies*, Vol. 41, No.1, pp.23-49.

Harnischfeger, J. (2003), 'The Bakassi Boys: fighting crime in Nigeria' *Journal of Modern African Studies*, Vol. 41, No. 1, pp. 23-49.

Hartman, J. (1991), 'State, Civil Society and Ethnicity', Trok, B. (ed.) *Debt and Democracy*, Institute for African Alternatives, London.

Haynes, J. (1997), *Democracy and Civil Society in the Third World*, Polity Press, Oxford.

Homer-Dixon (1994), 'Environmental Scar Cities and Violent Conflict: Evidence from Cases', *International Security*, Vol. 19, No. 1, pp. 5-40.

Hume, D. and Goodhand, J. (2002), 'Peacebuilding and Complex Political Emergency', *Working Paper Series*, No. 12, March, IDPM, University of Manchester, Manchester.

Jackson, R. (1986), 'Sovereignty and Underdevelopment: Juridical Statehood in the African Crisis', *Journal of Modern African Studies*, Vol. 24, No. 1, pp. 1-31.

Jackson, R. (1990), *Quasi-States: Sovereignty, International Relations and the Third World*, Cambridge University Press, Cambridge.

Jackson, R. and Rosberg, C. (1982), *Personal Rule in Black Africa: Prince, Autocrat, Prophet Tyrant*, California University Press, Berkeley.

Jagger, K. (1992), 'War and the three faces of power: War making and state making in Europe and the Americas', *Comparative Political Studies*, 25, 11.

MacFarlean, N. (1984), 'Africa's Decaying Security System and the Rise of Intervention', *International Security*, Vol. 8, No. 4.

Mamdani, M. (1998), 'Why Foreign Invaders Can't Help Congo: Understanding the Democratic Republic of Congo', Africa Studies Centre, University of Cape Town, unpublished paper.

Mclean, I. (1996), *Oxford Concise Dictionary of Politics*, Oxford University Press, Oxford.

Obasi, N. (2002), *Ethnic Militias, Vigilantes & Separatist Groups in Nigeria*, Third Millennium Ltd., Abuja.

Pearce, J. (1999), '"Peacebuilding in the periphery": lessons from Central America', *Third World Quarterly*, Vol. 20, No. 1.

Reno, W. (1995), *Corruption and State Politics in Sierra Leone*, CUP.

Sorensen (2001), 'War and State-Making: Why Doesn't It Work in the Third World?', *Security Dialogue*, Vol. 32, No. 3, pp. 341-354.

Synder, C. (ed.) (1999), *Contemporary Security and Strategy*, Macmillan, Basingstoke.

Terriff, T., Croft, S., James L. and P. Morgan (1999), *Security Studies Today*, Polity, Cambridge.

Thomson, A. (2004), *An Introdroduction to African Politics*, Routledge, Oxford.

Tilly, C. (1975), *Formation of National States in Western Europe*, Princeton University Press, Princeton.

Ullman, R. (1983), 'Redefining Security', *International Security*, Vol. 8, No. 1.

UNDP (1997), *World Development Report 1997: The State in a Changing World*, UN Publications, New York.

UNDP (2003), *Human Development Report*, UN Publications, New York.

Villalón, L. and Huxtable, P. (eds.) (1998), *The African State at a Critical Juncture: Between Disintegration and Reconfiguration*, Lynne Rienner, London.

Wolfers A. (1962), *Discord and Collaboration*, Johns Hopkins University Press, Baltimore.

Zartman, I. W. (ed.) (1995), *Collapsed States: The Disintegration and Restoration of Legitimate Authority*, Lynne Rienner, Boulder.

Chapter 2

Militias as a Social Phenomenon: Towards a Theoretical Construction

Gani Joses Yoroms

Introduction

The threats arising from the emergence of civil militias in Africa are not only alarming but are becoming frightening like the holocaust of the Second World War. What this chapter intends to do to conceptualise the term militia within the context of the theory of social contract using some determinant variables in the literature. These variables would be validated by empirical analysis based on historical development of civil militias in Africa. The emphasis is to understand the menace and implications of civil militias for national and human as well as community securities in Africa. It is argued here that the rise of Militia is an indication of the failure of the state to address the fundamental issues of human and community securities,[1] which *ab initio* the state was established to tackle.

Revisiting the Theory of Social Contract

Conceptually, the historiography of militia could be placed within the framework of the theory of social contract and the formation of state system. The peopling of society into organised beings was intended to avoid the nasty and brutish life in the Hobbesian society, which was replete with insecurity. In Hobbesian society individuals were living by themselves but were incomplete as social beings. Therefore, there was need for a social contract between the state and the individuals who had found a peopled society warmer than the loneliness in Hobbesian society. In doing so, a standing army was constructed by the state as the guardian to protect the society against threats. Thomas Hobbes and Hugo Giotius believed that insecurity in the state of nature compelled man to seek security in social organisation where individuals give up their 'partial freedom'[2] for 'secured freedom'[3] provided by the state. This was further rationalised by Immanuel Kant who said that the desire of man for social fellowship of people or organisation was for individuals to exercise their will in a secured socio-political environment unhindered.

Accordingly, the theory of social contract emerged at the background of the society being under threats. As Jean-Jacques Rousseau noted 'man is born free, and everywhere he is in chains. He who believes himself the master of others does not escape being more of a slave than they' (Rousseau: 1987, p.141) Thus, those who claim to be free and masters found out that they are equally in chains as their freedom is constrained by the disorder in the society. It was only realised that social order becomes a sacred right, which serves as a foundation for all other rights. It becomes necessary for the society to enter into collective general will as social compact with the state. In the words of Rousseau, 'each of us places his person and all his power in common under the supreme direction of the general will, and as one we receive each member as an indivisible part of the whole' (Rousseau, 1987, p.147).

The theory of social contract, therefore, is taken as a security contract. Hence the sovereign state is empowered to defend, protect and provide for the citizens. It is in the light of this that, from the Weberian theory, the state is endowed with the legitimate monopoly of coercion, to police the society, impartially. The state is autonomous and independent of social classes and must be seen to be objective, the influences of hegemonic social classes notwithstanding. However, despite efforts at constructing human society, threats to security are increasing tremendously, and have remained embedded in human-society. Because of this, and capitalising on its mandate on security contract, the state has strengthened its security capacity by raising paramilitary forces to meet the challenges of governance. In doing so, the state manages to monopolise the use of force for the purpose of diffusing rather than intending to cause, violence. But at the end violence is inevitable (Jonowitz, 1975, pp.10-11). Meanwhile, pressures and demands from various sectors of the society, which the state found increasingly difficult to cope with, makes it possible for her to sponsor militias as reserve or part time military forces to tackle the encircled security threats that do not require the overkill features of the regular forces.

Indeed, in spite of this sound theoretical exposition, the state has, especially the postcolonial African State, become too partial, exclusivist, and is extremely weak in the pursuit of the cardinal rules of its existence, such as social justice, the rule of law and democratic governance. Therefore, it is impossible for the state to mediate impartially in social conflicts. Thus, the autonomy of the state and its legitimate power is called to question by the social forces in the society. The character of the state makes it difficult for a government that emerges from sharp and contradictory society to be equally endowed with any veneer of legitimacy (Ake, 1992, p.46). The state, therefore, exist at the level of primitive accumulation, creating the basis for conflicts, and the struggle by the social forces to control the state becomes warfare.

The behaviour of the state has implications for human security, which has been conceptualised from various perspectives (Naidoo, 2001, pp.7-15 and Macrae, 2001, pp.14-27). Thus the failure of the state calls to question its sovereignty-rights and its primary concerns of security, which no longer benefits the partners that brought her to existence. Because of this, the national security of the state is no longer at the service of the people but the sovereign alone. Life for the people is threatened and can no longer be lived. Therefore, a new trend is shifting the focus of security to human security. The emphasis on human security is that non-state actors are equally relevant as the state, and without them the state cannot exist. As such, maintaining human security is as well as ensuring the stability of the state. In this context, Claude Ake (1992) in his analysis of the African state noted the damage done to the structure of the social contract because of the overdeveloped nature of the state security. According to him:

> Power is over-valued and security lies only in getting more and more power. There is hardly any restraint on the means of acquiring power, holding it or using it. Might is coexistence with right ... Politics is endemic because of the normlessness and extremist pattern of political competition. The political class operates in a state of siege ... one of the paradoxes of the African social formation is that despite the monopoly of power by the state and its concentration within the state, a political order does not appear to have emerged. Rather violence is endemic, anarchy lurks just below the surface and the political system is disarticulated as the economy and as fragmented as the culture. (Ake, 1992, 46)

Following from above, Howe (2001) among others, has argued that the African State, in spite of its monopoly of the use of force, creates the military that by itself threatens the existence of the state. This is because politics and public policy do not conform to the institutional mechanics of the practices of the global state system. And where the state institutions are criminalized, the legitimacy of the state is held in suspect. Given this understanding, the African militaries lack the capabilities to strengthen the African State. Because the military has become unprofessional, being divided by the plural nature of the society, it is possible for the emergence of group and fluid militias to challenge the legitimacy of the state to monopolise the use of force. Because they are not as strong as the state military forces and other security organs, they engage in the act of terrorism. They blend into terrorist act and guerrilla tactics to express their frustration.

Understanding the Phenomenon of Civil Militias

Before we properly grasp the dynamics of the theoretical construct, there is the need to understand the evolution and concept of civil militia. The term militia is Latin in its origin conception meaning military. Its meaning in the English context 'military' conveys similar meaning from its Latin origin. However, in the course of time, the original Latin meaning became corrupted in the English usage. This was a result of the development of military science;. The term militia was integrated into English vocabulary and began to acquire a different meaning. While the concept of the military is taken to mean standing armed forces established to defend a given territorial sovereignty, militias gradually faded and took on subsidiary form in military history. The military is now seen in a more structured form under legal and permanent regulatory measures as a security organ of the state, the militia is seen either as a state subsidiary force or a private organisation. As a state organ it functions as either a reserve or part-time or paramilitary force, set up by the state to combat 'background threats' in time of emergencies. But in most cases it carries the meaning of a private outfit that threatens the state. This is probably because it is only those in the opposition that make use of militias as a defence mechanism against the oppressive state security system. Maurice Duverger captures a clearer definition of militia in this context:

> Militia is a kind of private army whose members are enrolled on military lines, are subjected to the same discipline and the same training as soldiers, like them wearing uniforms and badges, ready like them to meet the enemy with weapons in physical combat. But these members remain civilians, in general, they are not permanently mobilised non-maintained by the organisation they are simply obliged to meet and drill frequently. They must always be ready to hold themselves at the disposal of their leaders. (Maurice Duverger 1967, pp.36-37)

Because they arise from the civil populace with militant behaviour they are identified as civil militias. Given their historical antecedents they exhibit all sorts of characteristic traits and mindset, with the intension to draw attention to their plights. Civil militias are not irredentists but in turn emerge to become one once their agitations are not met by the internal logic of the state they found themselves. When this happens they turn revolutionary using guerrilla fighting tactics either as irredentists or separatists. Nevertheless the overall purpose of militias is merely to draw attention to their plight and to change the status quo when they are not attended to. It is from this perspective that we can appreciate the variant types of militias emerging from different historical environment.

In this respect, Bristow (1998) classified militias as being public as well as private organisations. He noted that legitimate militia units are essentially public in character, well-regulated under state discipline. As a public force, it is also seen broadly as military force consisting of citizens available for service in emergencies or a citizen force kept in reserve to combat any threat or used in time of emergency. Some analysts have looked at it as locally raised, part time forces to supplement or to replace the regular force in an emergency situation. In view of this, it is important to contextualise, within some specific theoretical variables, the theory of social contract in order to appreciate the nature of systemic failures that create multiple challenges to the legitimacy of the state. In this regard, there are three theoretical construct of what constitute militia. These are state-centric theory of militia, Non-state Actor Theory and the Fluid Theory of Militia. The failure of the state–centric militia leads to the emergence of the other two, which are positioned as second generation civil militias in Africa.

State-Centric Theory of Militias

There are two levels of understanding the state-centric theory of militias. These are the First Generation and Second Generation concepts of civil militias. The First Generation militias operate in strong and viable states. The second concept operates as a challenge to the state failure to meet the expectation that led the struggle against colonial rule. In this instance, the Second Generation militias operate at the level of Non State Actors (NSA). They could manifest some guerrilla and terrorist or as mercenarian-militias attributes.

Indeed the character of the state as a legitimate authority specifically determines the state-centric theory of militias over a given territorial entity. The centrality of this theoretical variable posits that militias emerge either as a result of increasing inability of regular professional military forces to cope with the ebbing social problems in the society. It could also be an attempt to complement the effort of the state military forces in time of wars, disasters, emergencies and related civil police actions among other contending social phenomena. The use of the military in less-combatant conflicts gives the impression of a war scenario. Therefore, to address the non- war driven scenario, militias become relevant in establishing the moral antecedent of the state, from its legitimate use of force, which has become repugnant in the society.

The state, expresses its moral force by establishing militias, which are referred to as reserve force, national auxiliary force or citizen soldiers. Whatever name it has acquired, militias are intended to serve as a state legitimate vigilante group, kept among the people. They are equally organised, trained and equipped to serve as active component of professional military. The militias are, therefore, a strategic reserve force and could be called upon to join the regular force within a short notice, in warfare as well as in peacetime. It is a quasi-military organisation intended to support military professionalism in any given critical situation. As an auxiliary force, Militias are not just non-regular or non-conventional forces, they are also involved in some kind of military discipline, organisation and tactics. Their activities complement rather than usurp the power and authority of regular force.

However, a thin line separates the state centric-theory from the governmentarian concept of militia. A government, other than the state, can create a militia outfit to defend the interest and stability of her regime, beyond the interest of the state. Sometimes, it is assumed that state militia could be taken as governmentarian militias. The two are however, distinct but sometimes overlapping, given the symbolic nature of their symbiosis. At times, the state may not require a militia but the government under threat may create one for the purpose of regime stability. This is a more prevalent military and dictatorial regime that find it difficult to deploy regular force or do not trust it with the defence of the regime. In some countries some forms of governmentarian militias are known as Presidential Guards, National Guards or Palace Guards. Such militias are disbanded once there is a change of government. Governmentarian militias are not most of the time constitutionally constructed by the state. They disappear with the exit of a particular government in power, but the state centric militia continued to exist and may only be restructure with time, constitutionally.

There are also the community militias. Community militias are citizen-soldiers. They are recruited, trained and located within the communities. They are made up of members of the communities where they are recruited and stationed. They are bound to their communities as part of the mandate and legacy which citizens' soldiers are known for. And as community soldiers, they are mostly made up of volunteer citizens, who willingly offer themselves for military training. Citizens from villages and communities are encouraged to take short-term military training in such a way that their normal vocational activities may not be affected during the period their services were required. Based on the foregoing, militias are defined as citizens primarily, soldiers only on occasion. Community militias should not be confused with the vigilante groups, which have been defined accordingly in this chapter. Community militias tend have the strong support of the state as it helps to decentralise the cumbersome processes of security watch.

This becomes necessary when the state security apparatus are insufficient to do so. In this case civil society militias, especially the community militias act as supplement to the state military power. However, with the growth of the society, following the pressure for self-determination, separation of powers between the structures of government, the quest for liberty and the right of individuals to freedom, the state is waned in its legitimate use of force. It is placed in a precarious position to cope with the best approach to exercise its legitimate use of force. This is because of the fear that it may trigger human rights abuses. Increasingly the state becomes culpable in the exercise of the use of force.

This is the fundamental basis for the rise of non-state militias with some objectives of challenging the existence of the state. While the state may be raising its armed forces to defend the general will of the people, it may also be confronting other social components not willing to concede to the general will that establishes the state. As the state increases the standard of its forces in terms of weaponries and establishment of militias of reserve forces, the rebellious groups may also be raising civil militia forces for their own defence and to contend with the state. The collapsed of the state is as a result of some social and economic disconnects, which create basis for revolutionary pressures from within the society (Ake, 1978). The state becomes weak as its basic functions can longer meet the security requirement of the population. In this case it cannot survive by coercion as much as it can no longer earn the confidence of the people (Dawisha and Zartman, 1988). This is because

    i.   the decision-making processes of the government are no longer effective,
    ii. the rule of law is no longer relevant because they cannot be preserved in the absence of social cohesion in the society,
    iii. territorially, the state cannot assure the population of its security even as the political institutions lost the legitimacy to command and conduct public security,
    iv. The state is no longer the target of demand as the supply of security from the state has become ineffective.

It is on the basis of this that the rise of Second Generation civil militias becomes prominent in Africa. Before we go into the understanding of the emergencies of this second Generation Militias it is important for us to clarify what constitute Non- state Militia Actors.

Non-State Theory

The Non-state Militia Actors or Group theory can be categorised into two. First we have those that are socially guaranteed by the state to perform some functions as defined by the existence of the state. These include Party militias and other volunteer groups. Apart from community militias, which has relationship with the state in maintaining the status quo there, exist also political party militias and private security militias, which exist as socially, guaranteed civil militias. These are Party militias and Private militias.

Party militias are the armed wings of political parties set up as militant propaganda machineries and protective organ of the party in its various meetings. They are distinct because of their features as armed wing of political parties, which are power-seeking organisations. Political parties raise militias to strengthen and defence their struggle for political power. They do have regular exercise like training and political education. Party militias help to maintain orderliness within the party. They play fundamental, sometime secondary and unobtrusive roles. The militias can be used to over throw a government.

Civil society militias may not be socially guaranteed by the state but are in some countries tolerated for some obvious reasons that they sometime covertly defend the either help the state are militias that emerge from various components of the civil societies. They could be ethnic, religious, labour, and ideological or some form of interface. They could be differentiated from community militias because they cut across boundaries and barriers. Unlike community militias that are territorially defined civil societies militias recruit their membership on the basis of interest, multiple identities and Ideologies. They could be private security outfits or groups recruited and trained to defend the interest of their sponsors or the course of the group once their interest are undermined. The second category is the type of first generation concept of civil militias that emerged as a reaction to the failure of the state to meet the rising expectation. It is this second-generation civil militias that disturb the balance of the state.

It is the reactive militias that concern us in this section. The state's militias are intended to maintain the status quo while the private militias response to the status quo by reacting positively or negatively.

The Non-state theory is defined by the fact that it is a private force. Therefore, following the theory of social contract, it is an illegitimate force established by groups to withstand the legitimate exercise of the use of force by the state. The militias in this category are organised into armed men for the purpose of challenging the status quo, or with the purpose of achieving their goals and objectives within the larger environment where they are marginalized, denied their rights and/or alienated. The Group militias see violence as a means of de-monopolising the instrument of power by intending to cause violence. The vogue is that the oppressor understands only the language of violence than non-violence.

As Davidson pointed out, their aim is not only to defeat an aggressive enemy-whether external or internal, but also with the aim of overthrowing a tyrannical leadership, arbitrariness or oppression. (Davidson, 1981) They engage mostly in irregular or non-conventional fight with the state, as their fighting strength cannot withstand the firing powers and the assaults of the regular force. Thus the militias are not just groups of armed bandits having political intention to defend their interests but in most cases also seek to deconstruct the state. Accordingly it is one kind of social organisation which relies to a greater extent on force to advance its goals than another... this will affect not only the psychic state of those subjected to the exercise of power but also the pattern of the relevant social structure and most social relations within it (Etzioni, 1968):

Similarly, Davidson (1969) on his part further added that Nothing is more remarkable than the portrayal of the awakening consciousness of ordinary men and women of their understanding of the need to accept any and every personal sacrifice in order to change not only their own lives but the lives of their whole people. The consciousness, which triggers social mobilisation, could also provide the constant measures for raising ethnic soldiers or ethnic militias for the purpose of defending a collective cause of struggle. They may hardly have the idea of how to handle weapons, and often ignorant of rudimentary rules of warfare. However, consciousness is the first basis for mobilisation and training. They engage gradually in political education alongside military training for the actualisation of their objectives and goals.

Non-state militias start with establishing cells for political education. The essence of this is to indoctrinate members about the objectives of the struggle and debrief them on certain policies of the state that are disadvantageous to them. It is believed the solution lies on turning their disaffection and frustrations into threats by making the country ungovernable. By this means, it draws attention to their collective plight. In the course of doing this, the group may become a guerrilla force when government decides to react by confronting them with her regular military force. This can drive them underground which they can begin to fight invincible war against government forces. In the process, they may draw strength from local and/or international sympathy that will enable them to expand their scope of operations to destabilise the state. In most cases not all the Non-State Militia Actors are registered. In most case only the moderate ones are given the rights of registration to operate. The most radical ones are not allowed to operate Because of the fundamental course they pursue; they operate outside the state purview. They maintain consistency in their attack of government policies and are prepared to retaliate once the state security organs physically assault them. They are however, known by their actions, territorial staging posts, demands and symbolic identities. They are much more organised than the fluid militias.

Fluid Theory

From both the state and Non-state Actor theories of militias, we can draw up the constituents of fluid theory of militia. Militia of this nature cannot be categorically identified and defined in terms of the characteristic traits of their membership. Often, they are not organised and articulate. They emerge as a result of social and economic conflagration in the state. And always, they have no formal identity as they feign registration as legal entities, because of their nocturnal operations. As such, it is difficult to apprehend them at any slightest confrontation. They function in the way they are called such as the mercenarian-militias, vigilante-militias and criminal-militias. They may not have clear objectives, but they are significant or potential recruits for destabilising the state. Unlike the non-state Actor militias the fluid militias use the crudest means of terror to express their demands. They don't have tangible objectives but create self-fulfilment scenarios by inflicting injuries on the innocent populace. This can be seen in the case of the Revolutionary force (RUF) in Sierra Leone where the rebels had no focus but caused a lot of mayhem to the general public. A lot of people's legs and arms were amputated.

Mercenary is a group of well-trained bandits specialised for fighting someone's war in order to make money. Both governments and groups may hire mercenaries to fight for their cause. However, in the light of the rise of militias, a new meaning is emerging on how mercenaries are constituted in Africa. They could be used as militias and integrated into the cause of their employers. They are identified here as mercenarian-militias. Mercenarian-militias therefore, are groups of armed men whose purpose could be both for war-profit making adventurism as well as fighting a cause, which may befit them in the long run. Most of the communal conflicts in Nigeria have been sustained by mercenerian-militias. The distinguishing character of mercenerian-militias is the art of camouflaging in military uniforms. This is intended to create a false impression of the presence of legitimate military force that is sympathetic to the resolution of the pending conflict. At the end, their unsuspecting victims are killed en mass, when they are not capable of withstanding the onslaught of the mercenerian-militias. Most of the time, the mercenarian-militias are defeated because they are not properly schooled of the topography of the theatre of the conflict they found themselves. From indications most of the mercenerian-militias are recruited from criminal-militias.

Criminal-militias are mostly juvenile delinquents who have been affected by social ills, either as a result of parental breakage, economic crisis, urban decay, failing moral values, lack of economic engagement and other social vices. Sometimes, these criminal behaviours are learnt in the process of interaction and association with those possessed by criminal attitudes.

This could be contacted in cinemas, peer group meetings and other illegitimate vices. In the process of identifying with pro-criminals, an individual acquires law-violating life styles. Subsequently, they engage themselves in activities that are criminalities like stealing, drudgery, raping, arson and fightings among others. They also acquire dangerous instruments and weapons, and undergo training of their own by their leaders. When trained they become rapid defender of a cause they may not be totally believe in. Thereafter, they easily become recruits for religious, political, ethnic and ideological conflicts on the continent. In Nigeria they are the Area Boys, *Yan Daba* and *Yan Banga*. In Rwanda they emerge as *Interahamwe and Maimai*. In Congo-Brazzaville we have Bernard Kolelas' *Ninja and* Lissouba's *Mambas*. There are many pockets of these mercenerian-militias and criminal militias all over Africa.

An important phenomenon in determining the fluid theory of militias is how to position the vigilante group. It is supposed to be a sort of militia established by the community to keep vigil overnight against armed robbers or miscreants. Unfortunately, most of the time, they turn criminals, besides the mandate given to them by the community to keep vigil in the neighbourhood. Also, rather than serve the community the vigilantes most of the time get out of control and become lawless. They illegally administer jungle justice to their victims whom they fear might not be adequately punished by the operational machineries of the state criminal justice (Obasi, 2002). However, it is clear that though vigilante groups may be unauthorised and most of the time they are officially encouraged groups of armed men who patrol an area to maintain internal security. Unfortunately they are often ready to take law into their own hands. They are more reactive than proactive, often with the aim of provoking or intimidating a particular individuals and social group in the society. One major features of it is that it operates in the night. Therefore, they may be taken for criminal and mercenarian-militias.

Thus, some armed groups within the fluid theory may be a state-created or sponsored against political opponents of the state. Those sponsored by the state remain the most important instruments of the state legitimising power.

Historical Development of the Militias

The history of militias has not been properly documented. Most of what is left of militias in the literature can only be collated by browsing through war records, memoirs and scattered histories of national militaries. It is therefore, a fact of history that nations found militias to be relevant for maintaining national stability and for attaining victory in external wars. But basically the rise of militias either from the public or private realm has to do with the failure of the state and its inability to cope with pressures and demands from the society. From the perspectives of the state, public militias are intended to establish stability and strengthen the capacity of the state security. But when this effort fails, the state is faced with the challenges either from internal or external threats. Historically, in most of the literature the focus has been on the First Generation Civil Militias which had the purpose of meeting the challenges of security, the expansion of their territorial frontiers and also winning wars. Thus militias are seen as a reinforcing mechanism to achieve the objectives of the state as well as the private organisations, which have been conditioned by the social circumstances to establish them.

According to Poirier and Conner (1983), arguing from the viewpoint of the defunct Soviet Union, 'victory in war is achieved by the side which mobilises the largest forces and... concentrates them at a critical point in time, and seizes the initiative in the initial period of war'. The reserve force helps to reduce the focus and the problem arising from conscripting fresh hands and reorganising or training them for war at a short time. The United States also maintains the same position, as almost half of its conventional forces are made up of two-thirds of reserve support forces. The objective of the overwhelming mobilisation of militias in support of conventional forces is to intimidate the enemy to submission to submission.

It is believed that this is the first stage of creating a psychological threat and subsequently a defeat of the enemy in a normal conventional warfare situation. The militias serve as camouflage and most of the times cover up the strengths and weaknesses of the military might of the country. This reinforces the position that in supporting the regular force the United State reserve forces have the capability to deter its adversaries (Stanford-Smith, 1981).

Thus George Washington, in the course of fighting for US independence, noted (Standford-Smith, 1981, p.2) that:

> The only probable means of preventing hostility for any length of time from being exempted from the consequent calamities of war is to put the National militia (Reserve Force) in such a condition that they may appear respectable in the eyes of our friends and formidable to those who would otherwise become our enemies.

Given this relevance therefore, there are three categories of state-sponsored militias, namely, the Ready Reserve Force, the Standby Force and the Retired Reserves. The Ready Reserve Force (RFR) is the most active of the reserve. They receive pay for attending training sessions and are kept ready for immediate call up service, to reinforce the regular armed forces in time of emergency. They can be called up for active service, for a period of up to two years. The RFR constitutes two thirds of the US Armed Force. They include the Army National Guard, Coast Guard and Air National Guard.

The second type of reserve is the Standby Reserve Force (SRF). They provide the reservoir of reservists who may be called up for active service in time of emergencies. They undergo training, after which they can go back to their normal activities that are essential to the economy and society. They are mobilised for both national service and national emergencies. The Stand-by Reserve may decide voluntarily for training without pay. The third category is the Retired Reserve, which is mainly made up of retired military men and officers who may also be called up for service in time of emergencies. Most of them, because of their age, serve as home guards; provide services and kitchenry during war. Some of them that are still active are deployed to the standby Force during emergency period or in war situation. The active militias, in conjunction with the regular armed forces, could be used in foreign campaigns, and/or against internal insurrection or insurgencies.

In Switzerland, the military component remains largely reserve. Young and able-bodied men are trained regularly in armed tactics. As often as they can return to their civil lives, they can be called upon at any time of emergencies. In peacetime, their services are utilised for development projects and other engaging programmes to keep the military in them at alert. What distinguishes the regular force from the militias is that the former has a longer period of training as well as regular exercises in the art of regular warfare. The militias are not quite often used to regular war despite the sophistication of weaponry at their disposal and which they use, for the purpose of intermittent training and manoeuvring. They may or may not be well grounded in the art of handling some of the sophisticated weaponries, but their relevance lies in the fact that with generally fair level of training, they are licensed to arm. In times of emergencies, they are fused into the regular force for the purpose of organisation, retraining and common or combined operations. At the initial state of the US independence, this was not only problematic but also controversial. (Malion, 1983)

The history of militias in the US started as from late 1500s with the English emigrants raising armed men to protect themselves from the hostile natives. The militias, who were kept in the wooden forts, formed militia companies to maintain order by patrolling the borders with the Native American Indians. Some served in time of severe crisis, especially in Spanish Armada in 1588, while others were bands that voluntarily had periodic training. And during the US civil war, both the federalists and the confederalists depended on militias to man military operations, as they were not prepared to arm and equip the borders of young men. Between 1757 and 1792, the US Congress legislated an Act by which able-bodied men of 18-45 years of age were conscripted into national militia and ready to be called upon to reinforce the operation of the regular forces. Some of the states in the US wanted militia, not only because they wanted their independence from the regular force but also to protect and secure their democracy.

In Britain the civil war between the royal authority and the Parliament resulted in both arms of government raising private armies. The circumstance in which they mobilised indicated that they were not regular professional armies but militias raised by the British monarch and the Parliament respectively, to defend each other's cause. The execution of King Charles I brought the country under a militia-dictator Oliver Cromwell. By 1600, when the monarchy was reactivated, the bands of militia that emerged from the civil war were phased out and replaced with a standing army. The British monarchy found it difficult to live with the horror of a standing army, as it was very expensive to maintain. It preferred the military being transformed to a police force. However, the Parliament exerted its influence in maintaining democratic control over the monarchical militias. This gradually brought about parliamentary democracy and the legislation for a standing military force.

Likewise during the Iberian Peninsular War of 1809-1812, the Duke of Wellington raised some Spanish and Portuguese irregulars, to fights against the French forces. (Browne and Temime, 1970). The guerrilla tactics employed by those irregulars included constant shifting attack operations, the use of sabotage and terrorism. It was during the Peninsular War that the word guerrilla was used to explain the tactic of the militias. At the Spanish civil war, the anti-fascist-militias were established in the absence of a regular public force, as there was no standing force in Barcelona to fight back. In the case of East Timor, the Indonesian government set up an army of militia that frustrated, intimidated and threatened the stability of the country after the UN plebiscite for the independence of the territory was conducted and put in place. The success of the Vietnamese at the end of the imperialist war perpetrated by the US in support of French imperialism over Vietnam is a test case of guerrilla war, where the people's militia defeated the enemies. In his explanation and analysis of the war, General VO Nguyem Giap (Stetler: 98) said:

The Vietnamese people's war of liberation won this great victory because we had a revolutionary armed force of the people, the heroic Vietnam people's army. Built in accordance with the political line of the party, this army was animated by an unflinching combative spirit, and accustomed to a style of persevering political work. It adopted the tactics and strategy of a people's war. It developed from nothing by combining the best elements among workers, peasants and revolutionary students and intellectuals stemming from the patriotic organisations of the popular masses. Born of the people, it fought for the people. It is an army led by the party of the working class.

Meanwhile, the most known known-state militia actors in history were political party and civil society militias. The introductory chapter of this work has captured some of the essence of the militias as social phenomena. Here, we shall focus on party militias. Though political parties are not exclusively formed on the basis of militias, such militias however played tremendous roles in building Parties in Germany and Italy. Hitler's Nazi party depended on Storm Troopers who were most active in Nazi propaganda. The Storm Troopers was organised in cells, battalions, and regiments and in Brigades; made of three to five thousand men. The German Communist Party, in reaction, set up stronger militias to defend the interest of the dominant elite. The fascist militias were brutal in their exercise of violence. The Storm Troopers facilitated the confusion that brought Hitler to power in Germany. Similarly Mussolini rose to power in Italy by the virtue of militias influence.

The phenomenon of civil militias is not new in Africa. The pre-colonial Africa is replete with the history of civil militias. In general terms Africa is characterised by both centralized and decentralized states. In any of theses, there were found frequent warfare, which necessitated the maintenance of internal security as well as to fight external aggressors. The Zulu kingdom in South Africa under Shaka had a strong standing militias with six brigades located round the kingdom. Similarly, in Borno Empire in West Africa, strong and well-trained militias were set up as standing force. They were constituted from foreign mercenaries and household slaves. They were used for fighting wars of expansion and were also utilized for farming once the wars were over. The Borno militias were so notorious that they could protest over the denial of their rights. In an instance reported by Barth they launched a protest before their officers for not being compensated after a successful war campaign (see Onwumechili, 1998). Like the Borno Militias, the Azande people of Northern Congo maintain a standing militia force. These were youth who volunteered to render their services to the state. During peacetime they had no military duty but utilized their services in working in the King's farm estates.

In the case of the Asante Kingdom, there were standing militias who were captured from the vassal states to fight wars for the Kingdom. There were two standing battalion of strong men. Each battalion had a name, such as Akonsan and Hiawo. Ordinarily they were to be disbanded after the war. However, some were later retained as palace regiment and others as community police during peacetime, to keep the security of community. This became possible when the Kingdom had experienced some forms of coup where the militias were implicated. For instance, in 1801 the militias were used to dethrone the Asantehene Osei Kwame. His successor decided to establish a palace regiment of foreigners to guard against the danger of coup phenomena. Even with this, Osie Yaw Akoto in 1823 solicited the support of the militias to install himself as the Asantehene as against Kwaku Dua Panin who was already preferred by the reigning Asantehene Osei Tutu Kwame.

In another development one of the African pre-colonial states that had fought several internal wars was the Yoruba. The Yoruba wars were fought by civil militias and mercenaries known as Omo Ogun (War boys). Some were raised as palace guards. As for most of the decentralized states in Africa like the Igbo society militias were raised only when there is war. Everyone felts the impact and volunteers to serve in defending the society.

It is on this gamut that we should understand the nature of struggle for decolonisation by most African countries during the colonial rule. During the colonial rule civil militias became part of the processes for self-determination. In fact, the African Liberation Committee of the Organisation of African Unity supported the intitutionalisation of revolutionary warfare against colonialism. Prior to this Almical Cabral among others had began to confront the repressive Portuguese colonial rule in Guinea Bissau. This was later followed by the rise of the Mau movement in Kenya. The Mau movement was noted as the first contemporary dramatization of civil militias in sub-Saharan Africa to confront the myth of the invincibility of the colonial military machinery (Otubanjo, 1993). As Otubanjo noted, the struggle for liberation in Africa brought about four different types of civil militias during the colonial rule.

First was the war against colonial powers, which took place in Angola, Mozambique, and Guinea Bissau. The second was the war against white dominated minority rule in Rhodesia and South Africa. Thirdly, the war of self-determination was fought in Eritrea, the civil war in Nigeria and Sudan. Lastly, we have the war to over throw indigenous national governments, which have become repressive, authoritarian and corrupt. This last war has led to several protests, agitation and riots in most of Africa countries. It is more or less a war of frustration-aggressions. It is a war against the African leaders for their failure to deliver the promises made at independence. The post independence failed to meet the rising expectation and created basis for underlying conflict, which Claude Ake warned of the eminence of the revolutionary pressures in Africa (Ake, 1978). It is this collapsing state structure that has necessitated the rise of second generation of civil militias in Africa.

Emergence of Second Generation Civil Militias in Africa

In view of the foregoing, the rise of civil militias in Africa is not a contemporary phenomenon. From the conceptual analyses we can make a general deduction that civil militias can emerge in any society for various reasons. Obasi (2002) among others have given multidimensional causal factors for the rise of militias. In the Africa context, the rise of militias had to do with fighting wars both internal and external. The periods between the pre-colonial and postcolonial era in Africa witness gradual rise of militias in Africa. Wars were intermittently fought during the pr-colonial period using these militias for the purpose of either to maintain their internal security or for expansion. It is in this instance that we can understand the reasons for the rise of civil militias in Africa. They often start as dissatisfied groups in the society and gradually snowballed into rebel groups or guerrilla fighters, and at times turning into terrorists.

Some of the bases for the emergence of the militias are rooted in the political economy of the society. These include first, defending the social and cultural values of the group. Secondly, demanding a share in the economic resources of the country by violence when regular procedures have failed. Thirdly, they also engaged in fighting to liberate themselves from political repression or marginalization. This involves making demand for greater autonomy of political participation or by changing the political structure of governance to their favour. In this case, sometimes, the militia becomes revolutionary by being irredentist or separatist in approach. Fourthly, where government fails to provide security some groups or individuals may organize vigilantes or personal security to protect themselves and their property without recourse to due process of the law. Fifthly, sometimes too, militias are formed for the purpose of protecting the environment from degradation as well as using it as a means to take ownership of resources, which they have, suffered denial.

Indeed, most of the revolutionary pressures in Eastern Europe and Africa were organised on the basis of militias, which later blossomed in to the regular army. Most of these militias are not necessarily registered but their memberships are motivated by ethnic, religious, primordial and ideological consciousness as well as personal motivations. In Africa, they occurred as a result of the struggle of the ethnic groups, classes and people against the colonial state. These groups and classes saw the formation of militias, commonly known as guerrilla forces as a means toward actualising their self-determination. This was common in Southern African counties like Zimbabwe, Angola, Namibia and South Africa. The Africa National Congress of South Africa was a unique case of multiple ethnic associations struggling for self-determination. They raised armed liberation militias known as Umkhoto We Sezwe. Along strikes and lockouts the militia groups began sporadic violence along with other armed groups that were fighting to liberate South Africa from Apartheid rule. Of recent, the hunter group in Sierra Leone, the Kamajors turned militias and fought on the side of government against the rebel Revolutionary United (RUF). Similarly, the Hutu extremist militias, the Interahamwe, were foremost in the Rwanda conflict.

France, Belgium and the late President Mobutu of Zaire (now Democratic Republic of Congo, DRC,) intervened to stop the Tutsi led Rwanda Patriotic Front (that helped Yoweri Museveni to power in Uganda) from infiltrating Rwanda to launch a military offensive in October 1990) to overthrow the Hutu government of Habyriamana. Effort towards peace were truncated by Habyriamana The suspected plane crashed which led to the death of Habyriamana opened the floodgate for the Tutsi extremists to unleashed terror on the Hutus, defeating the remnants of Habyriamana army, the Force Armies Rwandaises (FAR) extremist Hutu militias

Interahamwe and *Maimai*. The outcome was the genocide, which led to 800,000 deaths. This led the mass population of Hutu refugees, the remnant of FAR soldiers and the extremist Hutu *Interahamwe* militias to escape, with sophisticated weapons into DRC. They later joined Laurent Desire Kabila alliance force; Alliance des forces Democratique pour la liberation du Congo (AFDL) (Nzongola, 2002) to perpetuate the war in DRC.

While Kabila was using the militias to overthrow Mobutu's government, the Interahamwe militias were also using the occasion to establish their base from the DRC to fight their way back to power in Rwanda. In the process the Kagama led Tutsi government decided that the easiest way to exterminate the Hutus was to pursue them inside DRC. This brought Uganda to support them. Angola, Zimbabwe, Namibia and Chad began to show interest in the DRC for economic, political and off course geo-regional strategist interest. When Kabila overthrows Mobutu he became a problem to the peace process as the Hutus also tried to maintain their influence as having been the force that kept him in power. His death though changed the course of the peace process; DRC is yet to experience peace. The meeting of the South African Vice President, Zuma with the factions in the conflict yielded some temporary results.

Meanwhile the installation of Kabila's son, Joseph only provided a window of peace, which did not unfortunately last. At the other side of DRC, the Marxist – Leninist President Sassou-Ngueso, has engrossed the Republic of Congo in civil war from 1993 to 1999. The case of the Republic of Congo captures the general scenarios for the rise of militias in Africa. The 1992 elections led to the rise of private militias, formed by the political contenders. The election, which brought Pascal Lissouba to power, pitched him against his rival, Bernard Kolelas. The two rivals raised the Kolelas' Ninja and Lissouba's Mambas militias, which led to violent confrontation in the summer of 1993. And by December 1995 when peace accord was concluded, about 2,000 deaths had been recorded and 100,000 people displaced.

Even when Kolelas, by the peace accord, became the mayor of Brazzaville by submitting all his forces in support of the President, the 'militias were not disbanded and the weapons that remained in the possession of 'soldiers' could immediately be remobilised, leasing the distrust between the war leaders and balance of terror intact' (The Courier, 2002, pp.66-69). The outcome of this war the upsurge of the second phase of the civil war in 1997 when the former president with the backing of France raised a well-trained and armed militias, the Cobras, to fight his way back to power. While Kolela teamed up with President Lissouba to become the Prime Minister to enhance their chance of fighting Sassou-Ngueso.

They were able to surmount the military support of other neighbouring countries in the region like Mobutu's FAZ, Rwandan *Interahamrawes* and Israeli advisers who encircled Sassou-Ngueso's residence. Meanwhile Sassou-Ngueso got his support from Gabon and Angola. Already in the streets he had distributed weapons freely as children were recruited to swell the rank of militias. At the end Sassou-Ngueso was able to topple Lissouba, which brought about 10,000 deaths. Sassou-Ngueso presided over a police state, as he became ruthless in destroying towns and cities where opponent militias and supporters were based.

Several people were displaced in process. However, the president has not been able to satisfy various interests because ethnic, regional and personal interests are not balanced to meet the challenges of growing oppositions from within. And as it is 'the President ...has limited room for manoeuvring since each of the counsellors, like the majority of ministers, can at any moment call on his militias and cause blood to be split. The prospect of further fighting is also forcing the president to contemplate a fallback in a form of a withdrawal to his northern stronghold' (The *Courier*, 2002; p.69). The rise and spread of second Generation civil militias would continue in Africa if the African state fails to meet the expectation of the people. This has several implications for African security, social formation and development.

Implications for National and Human Securities

The rise of civil militias, in whatever form and shape it takes, has implications not only for Africa but also for the trend towards globalisation. Subsequent chapters in this work have addressed key empirical security implications of the rise of civil militias for national and human securities. However, it is important to highlight some key issues, which may run through their discussions.

First, it will, if not properly checked, gradually take the world to a stage of difficult-living. This will subsequently deconstruct humanity and community spirit of the Africans from their physical realm as fear and insecurity would pre-dominate the social and economic as well as political arena of the environment.

Secondly, its persistence can lead to the rise of multiple authoritarian leaderships across the continent on the ground that democracy has failed in Africa. The only solution to African political problem, it would be argued by the apologies is the return to single party or authoritarian rule to safeguard the society from the spectre of militias.

Thirdly, the menace of militias can as well create 'economy of affections' (Hyden, 1983). In this case the state becomes completely incompetent and lack of bureaucratic rationality for economic development.

Fourthly, however, it is important to point out that because the rise of civil militias has to do with politics of exclusion the menace helps the state and society to reassess the social contract and renegotiate the basis of the state. Some countries have decided early enough for sovereign National Conference to avert tempestuous crisis that t would break up the state. Those that have failed to come to term with realities would continue to suffer the implications from both national and human dimension of it.

Lastly, the continuous failure of the African states to address the internal logic of conflicts in their frontiers could make possible for the civil militias to become recruits for both national and international terrorism.

Conclusion

The attempt in this chapter is to provide theoretical background for the empirical validation by the other authors works in this project. The main issue in the discourse is that the rise of civil militias cannot be separated from the basic material conditions that brought peoples of different background together. These include security, social relations of production and political power. Thus, like conflict the menace of militias could be both functional and dysfunctional. The state cannot feign ignorance of its existence. And unless the state refocuses its energy towards expanding the political and economic space it will be difficult invoking and enforcing a law against the existence of ethnic militias. Unfortunately while the state and the militias tango it is the lager population that are at the receiving end, when the national security is precarious. The way out is for the state to pursue subsistence democracy, which is the crust of good governance for community security in Africa.

Notes

[1]   The concept of human security mean different thing to the Africans. In this context could be taken in the Western values to mean the security of the individual. Whereas, in Africa an individual cannot claim to be secured if the community is not . Therefore, what is invoked is Africa is community security. In Africa you move from the whole to the particular and not the other way round. In most African society the noun 'human' is singular and connotes an individual. When it is put in context of collectivity it becomes a community. Therefore, the security of the individual as a human being is incomplete without that of the society. Community security therefore, means the safety of the people and their environment. So that an individual, wherever he is, he is not alone. He is a moving community. In short, if an individual has his security without that of the people he will be like an oasis in the desert that has no impart on the desert.

[2]   Partial freedom in the state of nature means man's freedom to express himself to be limited by insecurity, fear and threats. He had freedom that couldn't be exercised without meeting the apparent threats. He does not seem to have rights or privileges, which were supposedly given, at the state of nature.

[3]   Secured freedom means man's move from partial freedom to secured freedom under a sovereign state. Here, though he gives up his partial freedom but it was secured enough for him to exercise his rights and privileges given by the sovereign state.

References

Ake, C. (1992), in Julius Ihonvbere, (ed.) *The Political Economy of Crisis and Underdevelopment in Africa: Selected works of Claude Ake*, Jad Publishers, Lagos.
Ake, C. (1978), *Revolutionary Pressure in Africa*, Zed, London.
Bangura, Y. (1992), 'Authoritarian rule and Democracy in Africa: A theoretical Discourse', in Peter Gibbon et al. (eds.), *Authoritarianism Democracy and Adjustment: The politics of Economic Reforms in Africa*, The Scandinavian Institute of African Studies, Uppsala.

Bristow, A. P. (1998), 'America's Militia Heritage – The Volunteer Militia', *Command Issue*, 48, April.

Browne, P. and Temime, E. (1970), *The Revolution and the Civil War in Spain*, Faber and Faber, London, p. 143.

Chilcote, R. H. (1991), *Amilcar Cabral's Revolutionary Theory and Practice :A Critical Guide*, Lynne Rienner, Boulder/London.

Davidson, B. (1981), *The People's Cause: A History of Guerrillas in Africa*, Longman, London.

Davidson, B. (1969), 'Introduction', in Gerard Chaliand (ed.), *Armed Struggle in Africa*, Monthly Review Press, N.Y., London.

Dawisha, A. and Zartman, I. W. (eds.) (1988), *Beyond Coercion: The Duality of the Arab State*, Croom Helm, London.

Duverger, M. (1967), *Political Parties*, Methuen & Co, England pp. 36-37.

Etzioni, A. (1968), *The Active Society: A Theory of Societal and Political Processes*, The Free Press, N.Y.

Graham, E. and Newnham, J. (1992), *The Dictionary of World Politcs*, Herdfordshires, U.K

Isiechei, E. (1985), *History of West Africa Since 1800*, Macmillan Publishers, London.

Jean-Francois, et al. (1999), *The Criminalisation of the African State*, Bloomington: India University Press.

Janowitz, M. (1975), *Military Conflict: Essays in the Institutional Analysis of War and Peace*, Sage Publications, Beverly Hills, London.

Hyden, G. (1988), 'The Post Colonial State: Crisis and Reconstruction', *IDS Bulletin*, vol. 19.4.

Howe, H. M. (2001), *Ambiguous Order: Military Forces in African States*, Lynne Rienner, London.

Macrae, R. (2002), 'Human Security in Globalised World', in Macrae, R. and Hurbert, D., (eds.), *Human Security and the New Diplomacy: Protecting People*, Promoting Peace McGill Queen's University Press, Montreal, Kingston.

Malion, J. K. (1983), *History of the Militia and the National Guard*, Macmillan, N.Y.

Martinez, Luis (1998), 'The Civil War in Algeria: Gaining from a State of Anarchy?' *CODESRIA Bulletin*, nos 3 and 4.

Naidoo, S. (2001), 'A Theoretical Conceptualisation of Human Security', in Goucha, M. and Jackie, C. (eds.), *Peace Human Security and Conflict Prevention in Africa*, ISS Pretoria.

Nzongola-Ntalaja, G. (1987), 'The Second Independence Movement in Congo-Kinshasa', in Peter Anyong Nyong'o (eds.), *Popular Struggle for Democracy in Africa*, United Nations University, Zed Books, London.

Nzongola-Ntalaja, G. (2002), 'Regional Security in the Great Lakes and the Crisis in the Democratic Republic of Congo: Implications for Security and Development', Paper Presented at a One Day International Seminar Organized by the Centre for Advanced Security Studies in Africa, CASSIA, Abuja 26th April (forthcoming as CASSIA Seminar paper Series).

Poirier, P. G., and Conner, A. Z. (1983), 'Soviet Strategic Reserves: The Forgotten Dimension', *Military Review*.

Obasi, N. K. (2002), *Ethnic Militias, Vigilantes and Separatist Groups in Nigeria*, Third Millennium, Abuja.

Osita, A. (2001), 'Ethnic Militias and the Threats to Democracy in Post Transition Nigeria', Research Project: Nordic Africa Institute, Uppsala.

Onwumechili, C. (1998), *African Democratization and Military Coups*, Praeger, USA.

Otubanjo, F. (1980), 'African Guerilla and Indigenous Governments', in Martha Crenshaw (ed.), *Terrorism in Africa*, Dartmouth, Aldershot, pp. 115-124.

Rousseau, Jean-Jacques (1712-1778), *The Political Writings translated by Donald A. Cress*, 1987, Hacket Publishing, Indianapolis/Cambridge, p.141.

Shaw, T. M. (1993), 'Unconventional Conflicts in Africa: Nuclear, Class and Guerrilla Struggles', in Martha Crenshaw (ed.) *Terrorism in Africa*, Dartmouth, USA. See also as published in the Jerusalem Journal of International Relations No. 7, pp. 63-78, 1984.

Shearer, 'The Civilian Militias and the Mythology of the Religious Rights' htt//www.isrp.org/articles4/militia.html.

Smith, R. (1976), *Warfare and Diplomacy in Pre-colonial West Africa*, The University of Wisconsin Press, Madison, 2nd edition.

Stanford-Smith, M. (1981), 'Reserve Readiness in a Changing Environment', *Defence Management Journal Third Quarter*.

Stetler, R. (ed.) *The Military Art of People's war: Selected writings of General V.O. Nguyen Giap.*, N.Y. Lond. p 98.

The *Courier*, ACP-EU, January-February 2002, pp. 66-62.

Yoroms, J.G. (1999), 'Transition to Democratic Rule in Africa: The Case of Nigeria and South Africa in Comparative Perspectives Scandinavian', *Journal for Development Alternatives and Area Studies*.

Yoroms, G. (2003), *Terrorism and Security in Africa: Implications for Global Security*, Research Proposal, NWC, Abuja.

Welch, C. (1970), *Soldier and State in Africa*, Northwestern University Press, Evastons Ill.

Zartman I. W. (ed.) (1995), *Collapsed States: The Disintegration and Restoration of Legitimate Authority*, Lynne Publishers, Boulder, Colorado.

Chapter 3

The Kamajor Militia in Sierra Leone: Liberators or Nihilists?

Joe Alie

Introduction

The last decade of the 20th century was a particularly trying period for Sierra Leone as the country was engulfed in a horrible civil conflict, which became one of the nastiest wars the world has witnessed since the end of the Second World War. This conflict was characterised by unspeakable brutality, and international war crimes of the worst type were routinely and systematically committed against Sierra Leoneans of all ages. The conflict, unlike many intra-state wars in contemporary Africa, was not ethnically or religiously motivated nor was it a communal one. It was not even a guerrilla war, nor was it caused by a crisis of modernity occasioned by the failed patrimonial systems of post-colonial governments. There is no doubt that there was widespread public disenchantment with the failing state, with corruption and with a lack of opportunities at the start of the conflict.[1] But Sierra Leone was not the only country in independent Africa that had faced similar problems. There were many examples, yet these did not lead to years of brutality by forces devoid of ideology, political support and ethnic identity, as was the case in Sierra Leone. What occurred in the country was an atrocious civil chaos championed by a group of rebellious Sierra Leoneans with vast external support, determined to capture political power through the barrel of the gun with a view to controlling the state's resources for their own ends.

The war brought into sharp focus the serious political problems that had plagued Sierra Leone since independence in 1961. For example, it dangerously exposed the weaknesses of the inefficient and highly politicised security apparatus, particularly the army. Large segments of the army not only failed to defend the citizens from the ravages of the rebel fighters, but unpatriotically and disloyally they sided with the enemy to inflict mayhem on the very people they were paid to protect. It was in the face of this 'Macbethian treachery' that civil militia groups emerged with the primary objective of defending their lands from the marauders, whether they were rebels or regular soldiers.

These groups conceptually belonged to what David Francis refers to in his Introduction as the Second Generation of civil militias, who are now a common feature in the political landscape of severely weak, war-torn or conflict-prone societies in Africa. Unlike the First Generation of civil militias, they are not trained as soldiers nor are they a reserve corps that the government can call upon in periods of crisis or emergency. Although they may be sponsored by government (national, regional or state), they have no legal basis for their existence. Often this Second Generation of civil militias operates outside the law and can challenge the authority of the state with impunity.

The civil militia forces that emerged in Sierra Leone in the wake of the civil conflict were not products of rigorous conventional military training and were in the main ordinary people, mostly farmers, of gun-bearing age who had little or no knowledge of the rules governing modern warfare. This ignorance was, however, not peculiar to the militia groups: it was true also of the rebel fighters and their cohorts who also did not observe the rules of engagement. For the vast majority of the militiamen, it was also their first experience in handling sophisticated weapons. The point being made is that nearly all the civil militia combatants were not professional fighters in the western sense of the word and most had no ambition of becoming one. But they were a highly motivated group.

It is important to note that the formation of civil militias to defend their territories is not new in modern Sierra Leone. During the 1790s and early 1800s, for instance, the administrators of the Sierra Leone Colony had formed militia groups to defend the Colony from external attacks.

Politically powerful groups in the Colony, particularly the Nova Scotians, also mobilised an effective militia force against the Sierra Leone Company government in 1800. This force almost overwhelmed the Company's forces, but for the timely arrival in Sierra Leone of a new group of immigrants, the Maroons, and a detachment of the Royal African Corps. Their arrival turned the scales in favour of the company against the Nova Scotian insurgents (Alie, 1990). Civil militias have also, in the past, protected their areas from the caprices of robbers. Thus, the emergence of civil militias is not a new phenomenon in Sierra Leone; it has its roots in the historical development of the country.

However, the civil militia organisations that surfaced during the civil conflict, and the methods they employed to confront their enemies, were a novelty in Sierra Leone. The Kamajor militia especially used some unorthodox methods that set them apart from their counterparts. They became the fiercest and most formidable group among the civil militia forces.

Start of a Macabre Civil Conflict

On 23 March 1991 Sierra Leone imploded into violence unparalleled in the country's recent history. A disparate group of Sierra Leonean, Liberian and Burkinabe rebels numbering less than 100 men and armed with light weapons (AK 47s) crossed into Sierra Leone from Liberia and attacked the border town of Bomaru (Kailahun District) in the eastern part of the country. The group, which called itself Revolutionary United Front (RUF), was led by ex-Corporal Foday Sankoh who had been dismissed from the Sierra Leone Army (SLA) and jailed twenty years earlier for being implicated in a coup plot. He and other dissident Sierra Leoneans who formed the leadership of the RUF, had undergone insurgency training in Libya. The group initially fought alongside Charles Taylor's National Patriotic Front of Liberia (NPFL) but later requested help from Taylor to start a rebellion in Sierra Leone.[2]

The RUF captured the local police station in Bomaru and soon overran the town. In less than a month the RUF and their allies had occupied many towns in Kailahun and Pujehun districts. In the latter district, for instance, the RUF took control of Zimmi, a town close to the Liberian border, which had been a safe haven for many Liberian refugees; it was also a diamond-mining centre.

The rebels aimed to overthrow the one-party All People's Congress (APC) government in Sierra Leone, which the rebel leadership described as corrupt, tribalistic and lacking popular mandate. The RUF espoused an 'Animal Farm'-like egalitarian principle characteristic of communist ideology.[3] The movement promised the total involvement of the masses in all decision-making processes as well as rapid socio-economic improvements in Sierra Leone when they took over the reins of government. This liberationist ideology of egalitarian development and popular democracy and rural transformation, appealed greatly to many marginalised youth and the rural poor, including teachers. However, this millenarian appeal soon dissipated when the RUF, with their NPFL allies, resorted to banditry, murder, torture, mutilation and rape, using terror tactics to cow the populace into submission. Very quickly, the RUF 'war of liberation' became a battle of annihilation.

It is instructive that the rebel onslaught began in Kailahun and Pujehun districts. These are the only districts in Sierra Leone that share borders with Liberia, where the NPFL and RUF were hatched. Moreover, there was little government presence in these districts, following years of an inept, over-centralised and corrupt administrative system in the country. In addition, Kailahun and Pujehun had been hotbeds of opposition to APC rule, as many residents in these districts had belonged to the then defunct Sierra Leone People's Party (SLPP).[4] It is reported that the RUF gave the districts' residents palm fronds as a symbol of their 'revolution'. The palm frond has both military and political significance in Sierra Leone. It was used by Mende freedom fighters during the House Tax War of 1898 to secretly spread their war message.[5] The palm tree is also the emblem of the SLPP. The RUF had probably hoped that, by displaying palm fronds in a traditionally SLPP stronghold, many people would be attracted to their cause.

The RUF offensive was deeply rooted in the political and socio-economic history of the country. With independence, the democratic traditions inherited from Britain functioned for a while, but were later transformed into a heavily centralised and incompetent single-party dictatorship that led to the social and political exclusion of many Sierra Leoneans (Foray, 1988). Corruption, nepotism, mismanagement, ineffective macro-economic policy reform measures and lavish displays of unearned wealth by the political class had resulted in economic stagnation, injustice and underdevelopment. There was widespread poverty, joblessness, especially among the youth, poor education and a dilapidated socio-economic structure. Other attendant ills were general frustration, anger and apathy among the citizenry.

The government's initial reaction to the RUF onslaught was criminally indifferent. Top government officials and APC functionaries argued arduously, if unconvincingly, that the Bomaru incident was nothing more than a minor clash over trading interests by border guards. Others felt that the skirmish was a ploy by some underground opposition elements to derail the democratic process that was unfolding in Sierra Leone.[6] Thus, rather than grapple with the problem headlong, the political leadership sought simplistic interpretations and conspiracy theories to address what turned out to be one of modern Africa's deadliest conflicts. Within four years the conflict had engulfed the entire country with the rebels making several desperate attempts to take over the capital city, Freetown.

The SLA response was treacherously ridiculous, to say the least. Called upon, for the first time, to defend their motherland in the face of the rebel aggression, the army officers responded with massive and indiscriminate recruitment of men to make up for what the force lacked in morale, training and equipment. The result was an influx of recruits who lacked the requisite qualification and discipline and some of whom were drug addicts, convicted criminals, fortune seekers and early school leavers. This group of misfits and criminal elements were to dominate the army, with disastrous consequences.[7]

It was in the midst of this confusion that some junior officers from the eastern warfront stormed Freetown in the early hours of 29 April 1992 to protest against poor conditions in the battlefield. However, by midday, what had started as a mutiny developed into a full-blown coup. President Joseph Momoh and his APC were swept out of power and he took refuge in Conakry, Guinea. The army officers then set up the National Provisional Ruling Council (NPRC) with Captain Valentine Strasser as Chairman (Zack-Williams and Riley, 1993).

The NPRC vowed to end the war quickly and return the country to constitutional rule. Initially, the regime was enormously popular, especially among the youth. The NPRC also achieved some military successes. During 1992 and 1993, for instance, the fortunes of the RUF fluctuated. On occasion, they took over the diamond areas, were pushed back, and took over the areas again. Civilians accused by the SLA of collaboration were arrested and some executed. But the penalty for not collaborating with the RUF was as severe or worse. The RUF had two major calling cards: dead civilians and scores of living civilians with their hands, feet, ears or genitals crudely amputated. The latter served as living and constant warnings to anyone in their path, and rumours of an impending RUF attack became enough to clear entire towns and villages.

Advent of Civil Defence Forces

Until the NPRC coup of April 1992, civil defence forces (CDF) were not a major factor in the conflict. The main fighting forces in Sierra Leone then were the RUF and their allies on the one hand, and the SLA and their allies, principally ULIMO forces, on the other. The appearance of CDFs on the battlefront was the brainchild of the NPRC. With increased RUF hit-and-run tactics, the SLA found it difficult to pursue them as the SLA seemed to have little experience in jungle warfare.

Consequently, the NPRC leadership sought the services of traditional hunters to help them fight the war, since the latter knew their terrain better.

Earlier, local leaders in the Southern and Eastern provinces had responded to the rebel menace by encouraging the formation of civil defence units (CDUs) or territorial defence units in their areas. One such leader was Dr Alpha Lavalie, a History Lecturer at Fourah Bay College who, out of sheer patriotism, left his position in the University soon after the start of the conflict, to train young men in Kenema District who could protect their settlements. He was killed in February 1994 after his vehicle hit a roadside bomb close to an SLA regiment near Kenema.[8]

The CDUs consisted of youths and other able-bodied men, mostly traditional hunters, who were given rudimentary military training and deployed alongside the SLA. Young men in the bigger towns also constituted themselves into vigilante groups; they manned checkpoints and carried out patrols. In Bo town, for instance (Sierra Leone's second largest city), vigilante groups successfully repelled the rebels and their collaborators throughout the period of the conflict.

Towards the end of 1993 at least three traditional hunting guilds assisted the SLA in prosecuting the war. They were the Tamaboros in Koinadugu District (northern Sierra Leone), Donsos (Kono District, eastern Sierra Leone) and the Kamajors (southern and eastern regions). Over time the Gbetis and Kapras from Temne-dominated areas in the northern region became an integral part of the CDF. The Kamajor militia, which was the largest and the most effective during the civil conflict, is the subject of this essay although references will be made to the CDF in general.

The Kamajor Movement

As the war intensified, the NPRC committed more soldiers to the battlefield, but they were lightly supported. The soldiers then began to live off the civilians they were meant to protect. Civilians became confused as they couldn't distinguish between a rebel and a soldier since both committed the same atrocities. It was also widely rumoured, but strenuously denied by the government, that there was an unholy alliance between some soldiers and rebels. It is reported, for instance, that during an attack on Njala town (Komboya Chiefdom, Bo District), the commander of the SLA forces was killed by one of his subordinates, apparently because he was a loyal soldier. After his death, SLA soldiers systematically looted the town. They came with a truck, opened fire as they entered and loaded their truck with food and valuables (Smith, Gambette and Longley, 2004). Civilians began to call these soldier-cum-rebels 'sobels'.

By 1994 many civilians in the southeast of the country had lost confidence in the SLA who, they alleged, carried out many of the road ambushes. These civilians further claimed, with justification, that whenever SLA forces were sent to protect a settlement, that town would be attacked shortly after their arrival. Some communities, like those in Moyamba town, stoutly resisted the deployment of SLA troops in their towns.

The situation in the army was also becoming critical with the defection of hundreds of soldiers. Many of those who remained in the army did so for personal gain. The disloyalty and unprofessionalism of the SLA soured the apparent good relations between the Kamajors and the SLA. The end result was that the Kamajors transformed themselves into a charismatic, liberatory, resistance movement that was intensely anti-SLA, anti-RUF and pro-government.

Who are the Kamajors? The term is derived from the Mende words, *Kama joi* (or *Kamasoi*); plural *Kamajoisia* (or *Kamasoisia*). In simple terms both words jointly mean an experienced hunter with mystical powers. In the true sense of the word, therefore, not every hunter in Mendeland could be called a Kamajoi, but only those who were brave and had extraordinary or magical powers. These hunters used mainly single-barrelled shotguns or home-made guns to hunt wild game and their magical powers often helped them in times of trouble: for instance, if the game turned on them in retaliation. It was therefore not uncommon for a Kamajoi to vanish into thin air, if he faced imminent danger. The word Kamajor, which is now in current use, is an anglicised form of the original term (Muana, 1997).

In the context of the Sierra Leone conflict, a Kamajor was a militiaman who had been initiated into the Kamajor society where he was schooled in modern weapons handling and invested with certain powers that made him impervious to enemy bullets (See also Kenneth Omeje's Chapter on 'The Egbesu and Bakassi Boys . . .', where the twin concepts of African spiritism and the use of magic in warfare are explored more fully).

Initiation Rites

In precolonial Sierra Leone, one of the most important functions of women was procreation. This life-giving role forbade them from engaging in activities that involved the shedding of blood or loss of life, such as hunting and warfare. Women were also considered the 'weaker sex' and therefore unsuitable for hunting or militaristic activities, both of which had an organic connection with the spirit world.

Although traditional Sierra Leone society never had a standing army, some communities like the Kpaa Mende (a sub-group of the Mende), had institutions such as the Wonde, which trained boys in the art of warfare and sanctioned their transition from boys to men. These male social institutions became dysfunctional during the war and the *Kamajor* initiator emerged to fill this void. Thus, the initiator became a critical guarantor of the *Kamajor's* physical safety as well as his social standing as a man and a militia member. Kamajors symbolised the traditional role of men as protectors of the community.

The initiation ceremonies began about 1995 in a small town on the Bonthe mainland (southern Sierra Leone). That they started in Bonthe District is probably not accidental. Bonthe District is strategic in the sense that it shares borders with the three other districts in the Southern Province, namely Bo, Pujehun and Moyamba districts. Bonthe, like Pujehun, had tasted the bitter experience of the civil conflict as early as April 1991, when the insurgents invaded some of the district's mainland settlements and committed mayhem on the inhabitants. For example, in the town of Tihun (Sogbini Chiefdom) the RUF had slaughtered over 300 members of the Bio family and others.[9] Earlier, a prominent Paramount Chief of Kwamebai Krim, Farma Mahulor III, had been killed by RUF rebels and his body left to decompose. In another instance, some fifteen under-age girls were ruthlessly gang-raped in Gbap Chiefdom (Sandi, 2002). In other places the RUF rounded up hundreds of civilians and killed many in cold blood. These and many other dastardly acts by the RUF further strengthened the resolve of the citizens of Bonthe District to resist the rebels.

There was a lot of secrecy surrounding the initiation rites, which revolved around an assortment of mystical beliefs and charms, performed by the High Priest, one Aliu Kundorwai (called 'Dr' by his adherents) and assisted by a council. The purpose of the ceremony was to render initiates fit to serve at the war front, through the granting of special powers such as the ability to be 'bullet-proof' and being able to smell enemies. An initiate was bound to observe all the rules of the Kamajor society to the letter, and infractions of these rules could deprive the culprit of his magical powers and thereby make him vulnerable to enemy bullets. These rules were necessary, perhaps to prevent the movement from degenerating into banditry and lawlessness, which were characteristic of the rebels and SLA.[10]

The choice of Aliu Kundorwai as the High Priest was perhaps not fortuitous. Kundorwai claimed to have had an encounter with his dead brother Kposowai (killed by the RUF in Jong Chiefdom) who showed him some herbs and instructed that a stringent initiation process should precede the 'washing' of the warriors with the herbs. This concoction 'would make them invincible in battle, impervious to bullets, and endow them with powers of clairvoyance if all taboos were kept' (Sandi, 2002). It is significant that although other initiators had magical powers, Kundorwai's was unparalleled. In fact, he did more initiations than all the other high priests put together.

To ensure that misfits did not join the movement, youths were nominated for initiation by their chiefdom authorities, and after initiation went back to serve in their domains. This arrangement was nothing new. During the 1960s, for example, under the Chiefdom Council Act, firearms permits were issued by police authorities on the recommendation of village headmen and the local chief. It meant in practice that local notables were vouching for the good character of hunters; they were the guarantors for the proper use of firearms in the community (Alie 2000).

Men joined the *Kamajor* society for a variety of reasons. For many, it was out of sheer patriotism – the desire to defend their homelands and protect their property. For some, it was a necessity as joining the movement assured them of security. For many more, it was the desire to avenge the death of loved ones or for adventure.[11] As Kamajor initiation rites became commonplace in the south and east of the country, subunits emerged, with different names and peculiar behaviour. There were, for example, the *A V□nd□r*, Born Naked, and *Yaa M□□t□* groups. The Born Naked group, as their name indicates, went to battle without clothes; the *Yaa M□ □t□* were like the Sumba warriors in the Mane armies of old; it was widely believed that the *Yaa M□□t□* ate some of their dead enemies.[12]

Period of Expansion and Friction

The number of initiates into the Kamajor society increased dramatically between 1995 and 1997 as other high priests emerged in many parts of the southern and eastern regions. Significantly, there was one woman high priest, Mama Munda, who operated in Bo District. The proliferation of Kamajor societies brought new challenges. For example, many young men of doubtful character became members, there was a loss of discipline and some initiates brought the name of the movement into disrepute.

In late February and early March 1996, Sierra Leoneans went to the polls, to elect a legitimate government. The SLPP and its leader, Ahmad Tejan Kabbah, emerged victorious. The ascendancy of the SLPP raised the profile of the militia forces and especially that of the Kamajor militia. But it also heightened the already strained relationship between the Kamajors and the SLA. President Kabbah appointed the Kamajor National Coordinator, Chief Sam Hinga Norman, Deputy Defence Minister. Later in August, the CDF officially came into being from a union of the various local militias operating in the country. The government then began to provide various forms of assistance to the CDF, including food and ammunition (Kabbah, 2003). The appointment of Chief Sam Hinga Norman as Deputy Defence Minister did not, however, go down well with the disloyal elements in the army (the 'sobels'). They feared that Chief Norman, though himself a retired military officer, would pay more attention to the CDF than to the SLA.

The CDF subsequently developed a command hierarchy at the national level analogous to that of the SLA. The battalions were divided into companies, platoons and sections of varying numbers. In the absence of civil authority in chiefdoms under their control, the CDF established administrative structures to help them govern. In some places they created welfare officers to liaise between them and the civilians (Smith, Gambette and Longley, 2004).

These military-cum-civilian arrangements implied that there was a semblance of command and control in the militia and that incidents of lawlessness would be drastically dealt with. But this was not always the case. Groups of militia owed allegiance to various local leaders, and not to a national body. There were many cases of open conflict among the Kamajor groups.

In spite of their internal problems, the Kamajor militia continued to score major successes against the RUF. For instance, they overran the main RUF base – Camp Zogoda – in Kenema District in mid 1996. By early November of that same year, the Kamajors had liberated all the chiefdoms in Pujehun District, which made it possible for most of the district's residents to return to their towns (Alie and Gaima, 2001). These Kamajor accomplishments may have forced the RUF to the negotiating table in 1996, which culminated in the signing of the Abidjan Peace Accord in November 1996.[13]

By this time, however, relations between the SLA and the Kamajors had almost reached breaking point. The Kamajors progressively distanced themselves from their former allies, accusing them of betrayal. The SLA, on the other hand, objected to the high profile role of the Kamajors, accusing the government of paying more attention to the CDF than to them, they being the constitutional army. Firefights between them were now more frequent. In July 1996 they fiercely fought each other in and around Matttu Jong (Bonthe District), resulting in many casualties on both sides. It was therefore only a matter of time before the two groups would completely fall apart.

The Military Coup of 25 May 1997

Relations between the Kamajors and the SLA came to a head after 25 May 1997 when junior army officers again staged a coup and ousted the government. The junta leaders formed the Armed Forces Revolutionary Council (AFRC), released hundreds of prisoners from Pademba Road Prison in Freetown, including Major Johnny Paul Koroma, then awaiting trial for an alleged coup plot a few months earlier, and installed him as the AFRC Chairman.[14] Johnny Paul Koroma immediately invited the RUF (whose leader Foday Sankoh was in custody in Nigeria for firearms offences) to join them in forming the government. Sankoh was even made deputy chairman of the AFRC. Johnny Paul also announced that the civil conflict was over and that the SLA and the RUF would now form a 'People's Army' (Gberie, 1997). This action, and the rapidity with which the RUF positively responded to the AFRC invitation, confirmed the fears of many Sierra Leoneans who had all along believed that the army were working hand in glove with the RUF to inflict suffering on the poor and defenceless people. In a broadcast statement to his RUF fighters over the Sierra Leone Broadcasting Service, Foday Sankoh said, among other things, that:

> You will always get instructions from me through Johnny Paul Koroma. They are our brothers. Let no one fool you. You have to work with them to put the situation under control, especially in the Western Area. As you [sic] field commander, instruct your other commander . . . to stand by for any reinforcement needed by Johnny Paul Koroma for any eventualities. We have to defend our sovereignty. You are to act on these orders immediately. (Smith, Gambette and Longley, 2004)

Chairman Johnny Paul Koroma officially disbanded the CDF and asked its leaders to surrender to the Police, an order the Kamajor leadership ignored. Instead they intensified their attacks on AFRC/RUF positions.

·   Meanwhile, President Kabbah and some members of his government, together with many United Nations (UN) agencies and other international organisations, had taken refuge in Conakry, Guinea where they operated a government in exile. The international community and most Sierra Leoneans rebuffed the AFRC. The period from 25 May 1997 to February 1998 was characterised by anarchy, brutality and massive looting by junta supporters (military and civilian) across the country.[15] The AFRC/RUF gangs employed crude methods to dispossess civilians of their property. One such method was dubbed 'Operation from your hand to my hand, from your pocket to my pocket'. The period was also marked by unprecedented civil disobedience as patriotic Sierra

Leoneans refused to cooperate with the junta. During the period of junta rule ECOWAS made several attempts to reason with the coup plotters and their RUF allies to return the country to constitutional rule. But the AFRC/RUF seemed bent on holding on to power even though they lacked the skills and means to govern.[16]

The Kamajors and their New Allies – ECOMOG

The coup of May 1997 further aggravated tensions between the AFRC/RUF and ECOMOG, with the latter making determined efforts to reverse the coup and reinstall the constitutionally elected government of President Kabbah.[17] Bloody clashes between them were now regular. The first major incident occurred on 2 June, a week after the coup, at Cape Sierra Hotel in Freetown. Many people were killed and ECOMOG temporarily withdrew from the hotel, but continued to control strategic places such as Lungi International Airport. In the meantime ECOMOG strength in the country progressively increased to about 5000.

ECOMOG cooperated with the Kamajors during the junta period although there was occasional friction, due in part to the excesses of the latter. ECOMOG trained CDF fighters and assisted them in other ways. With considerable logistical support from ECOMOG, the Kamajors intensified their attacks on the People's Army positions across the country, particularly in the south and in the east. They, for instance, prevented the RUF Field Commander Sam Bockarie (alias 'Maskita') from moving some 300 rebel fighters from Kenema to Freetown in early June 1997 as Kamajor militia units controlled the road between Kenema and Bo. Over 5000 Kamajors had also blocked the route between Freetown and the northeastern towns. In the meantime, several thousand Kamajors from Kenema were threatening to march on Freetown, but ousted President Kabbah successfully appealed to them not to march.

The Kamajors also gave direct support to ECOMOG at critical times. A major ECOMOG base at Gondama, seven miles from Bo and home to thousands of displaced persons from Bonthe and Pujehun districts, was the target of repeated AFRC attacks in the months following the coup. On one occasion, the AFRC troops almost took over the camp and ECOMOG soldiers were forced to retreat. The soldiers took refuge in a nearby settlement where they stayed for almost eleven days. The situation of the ECOMOG troops was becoming desperate because they were running out of food. It was then that the local Kamajor commander decided to rescue them using a helicopter. The mission was successfully accomplished (Smith, Gambette and Longley, 2004).

While in exile President Kabbah made contact with a British security firm, Sandline International, for them to oust the AFRC and liberate the diamond areas. In early February 1998, twenty-eight tons of small arms arrived in Sierra Leone as part of this deal but were impounded by ECOMOG as a contravention of a UN arms embargo (Legg and Ibbs, 1998). Later that month, ECOMOG and the Kamajors drove the AFRC/RUF out of Freetown and other centres in the south of the country in a fierce battle that took the lives of many civilians. By then, estimates of the number of dead in the rebel war ranged upward from 50,000. At different times in the previous six years, estimates of the number of displaced people were as high as 2.5 million – more than half of the entire population.

Remnants of the AFRC/RUF regrouped in northeastern Sierra Leone where they conducted a violent rampage throughout the rest of the year. They, with their allies, again appeared at the gates to Freetown on 6 January 1999, catching both the government and ECOMOG off guard. Using women and children as human shields, some RUF and AFRC fighters were able to bypass ECOMOG troops and join comrades who had already infiltrated the city. The invading force consisted of several nationalities including Liberians, Ukrainians, Burkinabes, South Africans, Libyans and Israelis. The expedition had been planned, financed and executed by President Charles Taylor of Liberia (London Times, 11 February 1999).

In the fighting that ensued, an estimated 5000 people died including cabinet ministers, journalists and lawyers who were specifically targeted. Before the rebels were ejected from Freetown, large parts of the city were burned and about 3000 children abducted as the rebels retreated (Pratt and Nepean-Carleton, 1999). While many of the convicted AFRC/RUF collaborators were freed, Foday Sankoh remained in government custody. RUF commander Sam Bockarie is reported to have said at the end of January: 'No government can succeed in this country if it doesn't include Foday Sankoh.' Unless the RUF was given a share of power, he said, 'No government can rule. We'll make the country ungovernable.'

Despite the atrocities and wide-scale destruction, or because of them, the Government, with the support of civil society groups, agreed to hold peace talks with the rebels in Togo.[18] Foday Sankoh was allowed to go to Lomé to meet with his commanders and to begin negotiations. A cease-fire was agreed and with the assistance of the UN, ECOWAS and other leaders, a new peace agreement was signed on 7 July 1999.

Kamajor-Civilian Relations

A study of Kamajor-civilian relations raises some interesting questions. The movement began as a liberating force, whose raison d'etre was to protect civilians from the predatory activities of the SLA and RUF. Many of the taboos they observed to maintain their bullet-proof status such as treachery, disloyalty, cowardice and greed, which were acts characteristic of the SLA, marked the Kamajors out as a loyal people's army or a grassroots organisation. They initially won the affection of the general populace because of their good work in defending their territories. Many civilians actually supported them with food and non-food items. However, as their numbers increased and as many young men joined with different motives, certain Sierra Leoneans began to question the image of the Kamajors as a liberating movement.

Moreover, some of the tactics the Kamajors employed to control their areas, including their deliberately fierce appearance, for example, going into the battlefield naked or draped in charms and amulets, and displaying the severed heads of dead enemies, suggest the use of violence on a grand scale. Until 1996 when the government gave official recognition to the CDF and began assisting them financially and otherwise, the Kamajors and indeed all the civil militia in Sierra Leone lived off the land, often demanding mandatory contributions from citizens within their jurisdiction.

In many places in the south and east, there was a total absence of civil order, as many of the local authorities, who became targets of the RUF, had run away to bigger towns for safety. In these circumstances, the local Kamajor leaders filled that void soon after liberating a certain town. They constituted themselves into a government. Their functions were largely extractive: collecting taxes, imposing fines and extorting money and other items from the people. Often the Kamajor hierarchy behaved very much like the colonial Frontier Police in late 19th century Sierra Leone, who deposed chiefs and maltreated them and their subjects in many ways.[19] Reports of atrocities such as rape, looting and even ritual murder became routine. All these acts contributed to a general feeling that the Kamajors were both a volatile blessing and a curse, preying on as well as protecting civilians and the official state institutions. Thus, the Kamajor movement paradoxically became a force that used violence against the state and the citizenry in order to simultaneously protect both. Occasionally, the Kamajor leadership made some attempts to punish violators. The excessive use of violence and weird appearance of the Kamajors was perhaps meant to instil fear in their opponents. For instance, the RUF in particular feared the Kamajors more than they did the regular soldiers.

Kamajor and civilian relationships were even tenser during the AFRC junta rule and its immediate aftermath. Civilians accused of collaborating with the AFRC regime were rounded up and often killed, sometimes in a very gruesome manner. It must be noted, however, that the Kamajors were operating in a very difficult and sometimes hostile environment; they were fighting an unconventional war where it was not always easy to distinguish between friend and foe. The Kamajors were a people on the move who, for instance, did not have the resources to keep prisoners of war. This is not to suggest that their excesses could be condoned. Indeed many of them over-reacted and took the law into their own hands.

It must also be borne in mind that other warring parties committed serious acts of cruelty against Sierra Leoneans. Human Rights Watch put it this way:

> Sierra Leone's . . . conflict was characterized by unspeakable brutality. International war crimes of the worst type were routinely and systematically committed against Sierra Leoneans of all ages. The suffering inflicted upon the civilian population has been profound. While all sides committed human rights violations, rebel forces were responsible for the overwhelming majority.[20]

It is also significant to note that most of the misdeeds of the Kamajor militia were committed during the period of military rule in Sierra Leone – from 1992 to March 1996 when the NPRC was in power, and from May 1997 to February 1998 when the AFRC masqueraded as a government. These different administrations were powerless in bringing the Kamajor militia in line, as they too had their own domestic problems. The NPRC or AFRC could not even control their own fighters, let alone the Kamajors. Despite their serious shortcomings, there were many

Kamajors who were true liberators and many people appreciated their invaluable role in defending their communities (Cole, 1998).

The Kamajors and the State

The relationship between the Kamajor movement and the state is very revealing. The movement emerged at a very critical period, when the state apparatus was very weak, almost at the point of total collapse. The advent of the Kamajor force literally revived the state; they provided a modicum of security and civil authority where these were lacking. Their activities challenged the western-centric view about wars in postcolonial Africa. Contrary to certain opinions, the Kamajors were not a tribal army. It is true that the bulk of the fighting force consisted of Mende, but they were not fighting a tribal war. They vented their spleen on disloyal elements, regardless of their ethnic or social background.[21]

Unfortunately, the Kamajor movement became embroiled in the ongoing political struggle between the two main political parties in the country. Some critics of the Kabbah government charged that the Kamajors were a tribal movement, whose loyalty lay with the SLPP and not the state, and consequently called for their disbandment. Given the circumstances, it would have been suicidal for the government to disband the Kamajors. Also, the government's apparent inability to curb Kamajor excesses fuelled the debate on the alliance between the ruling elite and the Kamajors, even though the political role of the latter throughout the conflict had been rather limited.

The Kamajors did not practise the 'warlord' politics that characterised the RUF and their collaborators and largely refused official incorporation into the armed forces of the state. Their goal was not to overthrow or reform the state, but to protect it against enemies, whoever they were. During the period of junta rule (1997-98) the Kamajors were the strongest local paramilitary force that relentlessly fought for the restoration of the democratically elected government and in the process incurred the wrath of many opposition elements and a cross-section of the army.

The civil conflict officially came to an end in January 2002 and all parties – RUF, CDF, SLA and others – pledged to uphold the peace process. The Kamajors participated in the disarmament process and many returned to their settlements to continue their prewar activities. But there is a lingering suspicion that many of the Kamajors did not disarm; they secretly hid their weapons and this may pose a serious security threat in the future. There is little hard evidence for this view. However, in the early stages of the disarmament, many Kamajors did not meet the eligibility criteria for entry into the disarmament, demobilisation and reintegration programme. One such requirement was that a combatant had to produce a conventional weapon, not home-made guns which many Kamajors used (Kai-Kai, 2000). Some Kamajors, it is rumoured, may have crossed over to Liberia with their weapons to act as mercenaries, thereby compounding the security situation in the subregion.

Informed by the recent experience of the terrible conflict, the government has, since the year 2000, attempted to overhaul the country's security complex. This was also borne from the realisation that there could be no sustainable development without security. The restructuring must of necessity take into account the internal political, social and economic dynamics of the country.

The security sector, as envisioned by the Sierra Leone Government, consists primarily of the following institutions:

- Republic of Sierra Leone Armed Forces (RSLAF)
- Police Force
- Office of National Security
- Central Intelligence and Security Unit
- Prisons
- Fire Force
- Immigration.

Indeed there is no mention of the CDF. The exclusion of the CDF from the new security apparatus is largely political. Even members of the Security Sector Working Group were divided over the issue of the inclusion of the CDF into the overall security framework, largely because of the Kamajor factor in the CDF. Two arguments in favour of CDF inclusion were:

With the war over and the 'right-sizing' of the army now a reality, coupled with the engagement of the army in development-related programmes all over the country, there was a need for the CDF who would ably complement the efforts of the military.

Given the right type of training, the CDFs could effectively patrol Sierra Leone's porous borders, thereby reducing the burden on the military. They could also collect critical security information and pass this over to the relevant authorities.

But the counter arguments seemed overwhelming and they have come mostly from two important constituencies – the army and politicians. The old rivalry and suspicion between the soldiers and especially the Kamajors have not gone away. The soldiers, for instance, argued that the CDF would constitute a parallel army and they would be difficult to control. Moreover, some units within the CDF were better organised and more powerful than the others (an indirect reference to the Kamajors) and these would have undue advantage over their counterparts. Opposition politicians believed that the CDFs would become regional or tribal armies that would threaten the stability of the state. Then there were the financial implications. The upkeep of the army and the CDF would impose a severe burden on the limited resources of the state.[22] Given this scenario, the government advised itself to exclude the CDF from the new security complex.

A Sierra Leone Ministry of Defence White Paper cleverly summed up the position of the CDF in the new security plans this way:

The population at large will not forget the role of the Civil Defence Force (CDF) during the war. They provided active and vital support to the then Sierra

Leone Army (SLA). With this in mind many people acknowledge and recognise the need for civilians to give support to the RSLAF in the defence of our country. However, in keeping with the spirit of reconciliation and particularly the Lomé Peace Agreement this Government no longer recognises the CDF, but does acknowledge that there may be a need in the future for some form of part-time reserve force fully integrated into the command structure of the RSLAF. Such a part-time force would need to be representative of all sectors of society and totally non-political in the same way as their full-time colleagues in the RSLAF.

Conclusion

Are the Kamajor militia a threat to national security in Sierra Leone? The answer is 'yes' and 'no'. From the onset certain Sierra Leoneans, for various reasons, did not welcome the Kamajor militia; they felt the Kamajors could be a potential source of instability in the country. The militia's close alliance with the SLPP-led government, coupled with the charlatan and ruthless behaviour of overzealous Kamajors only underlined the fears of these critics. During the conflict many Kamajor leaders became petty tyrants and little judges who systematically practised jungle justice with criminal precision. Many openly boasted that they had rescued the state and were therefore beyond its control. They even flouted state authority with impunity. For example, those Kamajors who remained in Freetown in the wake of the January 1999 RUF/AFRC attack on the city, repeatedly refused to vacate some public buildings they had occupied, despite several pleas. In the end, however, common sense prevailed.

The rather abrupt manner in which the Kamajors returned to their settlements and disappeared from public view (without a formal ceremony recognising their contribution in ending the war), angered the rank and file of the movement. It was also a source of worry, for it recalls the recent behaviour of Saddam Hussein's Republican Guards, who quietly disappeared in the face of superior coalition firepower. But they simply ran away to fight another day.

The Kamajors are therefore very bitter and frustrated. Many feel that they were not adequately rewarded and their role in ending the civil conflict was unappreciated. This belief is reinforced by the incarceration of their erstwhile leader, Chief Sam Hinga Norman, their high priest Aliu Kundorwai and former Director of War Moinina Fofana, by the Special Court. The Chief, who at the time of his arrest in March 2003 was Minister of Internal Affairs, together with the other two Kamajor leaders, faces an eight-count charge for crimes against humanity, violations of Article 3 common to the Geneva Conventions and of Additional Protocol II, and other serious violations of International Humanitarian Law.[23] These arrests have become a serious political issue, with the Kamajors intermittently threatening to sabotage the whole judicial process.

The situation has not been helped by the legal tussles between the Truth and Reconciliation Commission (TRC)[24] and the Special Court, in a series of exchanges between them from September to November 2003. The TRC had made a submission to the Special Court, requesting it to conduct a public hearing with

Chief Sam Hinga Norman. The Chief was not averse to the request, because he felt it would give him an opportunity to recount his role in the conflict. The Special Court Prosecutor, however, felt differently. The Court was of the view that Chief Norman might abuse the privilege and incite his former followers, and so disallowed a public hearing.[25]

On 21 January 2004 the Special Court issued a Press Release, part of which read as follows:

> The Registrar of the Special Court for Sierra Leone has ordered that all communication involving Sam Hinga Norman – except for those with his legal representation – be restricted for a period of 14 days after a telephone intercept recorded late Monday. The content of the intercepted conversation indicated his involvement in coordinating activities calculated to cause civil unrest in Sierra Leone. Effective immediately, Norman will no longer be able to make or receive telephone calls, except to his legal representatives. Visits, except from his lawyers, are also prohibited. The order will be reviewed by the Registrar after 14 days.[26]

The Special Court's rebuff of the TRC request and the subsequent press release would indicate that the Kamajors are a potential threat and a source of instability in Sierra Leone.

It must be noted, however, that during the civil conflict, the Kamajors were perceived as and did become the embodiment of the collective will and determination of the people of Sierra Leone to resist the combined forces of the RUF, AFRC and all other forces opposed to democratic order. They were more cohesive and enjoyed wider support locally and internationally, particularly from Sierra Leoneans in the diaspora, than the other civil defence groups.

Although they are angry and frustrated, the Kamajors have remained largely peaceful and law-abiding. They have refrained from molesting the citizens or seriously challenging the authority of the state in the post-conflict period. The Kamajors, like the RUF and their allies, had occupied vast tracts of territory at the height of the conflict, but unlike the RUF, they never aimed to overthrow the government and seize power. Their goal was to maintain the territorial integrity of Sierra Leone at a time when the Sierra Leone Army was in total disarray. In conclusion, whether the Kamajors are a threat or not to national security may probably become evident if their arrested leaders are found guilty by the Special Court. Thus, only time will tell.

Notes

[1]   See Paul Richards, *Fighting for the Rain Forest: War, Youth and Resources in Sierra Leone.* Oxford: James Curry, 1995; and Yusuf Bangura, 'Understanding the Political and Cultural Dynamics of the Sierra Leone War: A Critique of Paul Richards', *Fighting for the Rain Forest . . .* , *Africa Development*, Vol. XXII, Nos. 3/4, 1997, pp. 117-148.

[2]   The NPFL was formed in Burkina Faso with support from Libya, to oppose the Samuel Doe regime in Liberia (See Richards, *Fighting for the Rain Forest . . .*).

[3] See *Footpaths to Democracy – Toward a New Sierra Leone* (Basic Document of RUF/SL) in http://sierra-leone.org/footpaths.html. For a brief history of the RUF, see Ibrahim Abdullah, 'Bush Path to Destruction: The Origin and Character of the Revolutionary United Front/Sierra Leone', *The Journal of Modern African Studies*, 36 (2), 1998.

[4] In Pujehun District, for instance, some residents in Soro Gbema Chiefdom, organised a guerrilla movement, the Ndorgbowusi, in the aftermath of the 1982 general elections to protest against election manipulations and the high-handedness of the APC regime. The conflict subsided when the insurgents surrendered in the face of superior military firepower. When the RUF rebels invaded the chiefdom at the start of the conflict, many youths joined the rebels at the behest of their parents who saw the rebellion as an opportunity to revenge on the APC.

[5] The Hut (House) Tax War began in 1898 following the British declaration of a protectorate over the Sierra Leone hinterland in 1896. The war was a protest against British administration in the Protectorate (see Alie, *A New History of Sierra Leone*, Chapter 7).

[6] In June 1978 the APC government under President Siaka Stevens declared Sierra Leone a one-party state, thereby effectively blocking all constitutional channels of opposition. However, following the 'wind of change' that blew across Eastern Europe and saw the crumbling of despotic regimes in that region and elsewhere, and domestic pressures for political reform, Stevens's handpicked successor, Major General Joseph Saidu Momoh, initiated moves in late 1990 to dismantle the one-party system.

[7] Another army strategy was to recruit some Liberian fighters, principally United Liberation Movement for Democracy (ULIMO) forces to fight alongside the Sierra Leone Army. The ULIMO fighters were recruited mainly from Krahn and Mandingo refugees fleeing the fighting in Liberia. These groups had been targeted by Charles Taylor's NPFL for various reasons. ULIMO, which later split into ULIMO K led by Alhaji Kroma (a Mandingo) and ULIMO J under Roosevelt Johnson (a Krahn), became a law onto themselves in Sierra Leone.

[8] Dr Alpha Lavalie was killed near Kenema town in the eastern region and it was widely rumoured that the SLA had planted the bomb that shattered his vehicle. After Lavalie's death, administrative leadership of the CDU passed to Chief Sam Hinga Norman. Chief Hinga Norman was a retired military officer and Regent Chief in Jaiama-Bongor Chiefdom, Bo District.

[9] A prominent member of the Bio Family was Julius Maada Bio, then Deputy Chairman and Secretary of State, Defence in the NPRC government. The RUF killed his relatives perhaps in revenge against the reverses the RUF were facing in the battlefield.

[10] Belief in the invincibility of traditional herbs in battle is common in Africa. There are many examples; such was the case among local warriors during the Maji Maji rebellion against the Germans in Tanganyika in 1905-07, and among the Kikuyu during the Mau Mau rebellion against British rule in Kenya in the 1950s.

[11] Interview with a former local Kamajor commander in Moyamba town, southern Sierra Leone (2 March 2004).

[12] The Mane warriors were ferocious fighters who hailed from the medieval empire of Mali in the 16th century. They were led by a woman named Masarico. Among their ranks were the Sumba, a notorious group that ate their enemies. The Mane invaded parts of present-day Sierra Leone in the 16th century, and these invasions radically altered the country's socio-cultural distribution (see Walter Rodney, *History of the Upper Guinea Coast, 1545-1800*. Oxford: Oxford University Press, 1970).

[13] On 30 November 1996, President Konan Bedié of Côte d'Ivoire, together with other ECOWAS leaders, the Organisation of African Unity and Commonwealth, brokered the

Abidjan Peace Accord between the Government of President Ahmad Tejan Kabbah and the RUF leadership. The accord received wide support from Sierra Leoneans who hoped that the agreement would end the conflict. But it did not. The agreement had major flaws, for example, it had no implementation, monitoring or dispute resolution mechanism.

14   It is believed in many circles that Johnny Paul Koroma was a 'sobel' and he led the attack on SIEROMCO Bauxite mines in Mokanji and Sierra Rutile mines in Mobimbi (both in Moyamba District) in 1995.

15   See, for example, Amnesty International, *Sierra Leone – A Disastrous Setback for Human Rights* (20 October 1997); and *Sierra Leone 1998 – A Year of Atrocities Against Civilians*, AFR51/22/98 (November 1998), International Secretariat, 1 Easton Street, London.

16   One such effort was the Conakry Peace Plan brokered by ECOWAS and the AFRC on 23 October 1997. The key provisions were: An end to all hostilities, resumption of humanitarian aid and reinstallation of the ousted government by 22 April 1998. Kabbah Government representatives were only observers at the talks. Despite the peace plan, fighting continued, with the CDF making life difficult for the junta in the provinces.

17   The Economic Community of West African States (ECOWAS) Monitoring Group (ECOMOG) is a non-standing military force consisting of land, sea and air components. It was set up in 1990 by member states of the ECOWAS to deal with the security problem that followed the collapse of the formal state structure in Liberia. Freetown became the base of ECOMOG operations in Liberia. The force restored an atmosphere that permitted the reinstatement of a functional state structure in that country. ECOMOG was also engaged in the process of re-establishing democratic order and ending the eleven-year civil carnage in Sierra Leone. (For an analysis of the ECOMOG intervention in West Africa, see, for example, David Francis, *The Politics of Economic Regionalism: Sierra Leone in ECOWAS*. Aldershot: Ashgate, 2001; David Francis, 'ECOMOG: A New Security Agenda in World Politics', in Bakut and Dutt (eds), *Africa at the Millennium: An Agenda for Mature Development*, Basingstoke: Palgrave, 2000; Mitikishe M Khobe, 'The Evolution and Conduct of ECOMOG Operations in West Africa'; Published in Monograph No 44: *Boundaries of Peace Support Operations, February* 2000; West Africa, 'ECOMOG as you never knew it', No. 4218, 20-26 March 2000.

18   This was necessary for many reasons. Firstly, the government could not rely on its army to prosecute the war. Secondly, the political situation in Nigeria had changed drastically, with serious implications for the war in Sierra Leone. Nigeria's military ruler Sani Abacha, whose support for President Kabbah had been very strong, died in June 1998. His successor General Abdulsalami Abubakar, pledged to return Nigeria to civilian rule and to gradually withdraw Nigerian soldiers from Sierra Leone where an estimated 800-1200 Nigerian soldiers had been killed during the war. Nigeria was also spending about $1 million a day to maintain the troops in Sierra Leone. Thirdly, continued fighting would have meant more suffering for civilians, destruction of infrastructure and increased government expenditure on the war. The money could be better used to provide much needed services for the people.

19   For more information on the Frontier Police Force, see Christopher Fyfe, *Sierra Leone Inheritance*, Oxford: Oxford University Press, 1964.

20   Human Rights Watch, 'Letter to Mr Modibo Sidibe, Minister of Foreign Affairs of the Republic of Mali and Chairperson of the Joint Implementation Committee (of the Lomé Peace Agreement)', Africa Division (23 January 2000).

21   For example, whereas the leadership of the RUF comprised Temne and other groups, the majority of their fighters were Mende, initially conscripted from Kailahun and Pujehun

Districts. There were also many Mende in the SLA, but that did not prevent the Kamajors from fighting them.

[22] In 2000 alone, for instance, the government spent nearly 2.5 billion leones (about $1 million) on the CDF. This figure excludes the cost of arms and ammunition (Kabbah 2003).

[23] The Special Court for Sierra Leone was established in January 2002 by the UN Security Council, at the request of the Sierra Leone Government, to bring to justice persons who 'bear the greatest responsibility' for serious violations of international humanitarian law and Sierra Leone Law committed during the civil conflict. To date, the Court has indicted, among others, Sam Hinga Norman (former pro-government Kamajor militia leader and until his arrest, Internal Affairs Minister). Former junta leader Johnny Paul Koroma and ex-Liberian President Charles Taylor have also been indicted, but only Sam Hinga Norman is in custody. Sierra Leoneans are divided over the ability of the Special Court to deliver. Already, the indictments it has made have been surrounded by controversies. Some opponents of the court think that the huge resources used by the Court could be better utilised to improve the lives of war victims.

[24] Another body with specific mandate to address the complex issues of justice and reconciliation in post-conflict Sierra Leone is the Truth and Reconciliation Commission (TRC), which seeks to provide restorative justice. Unlike the Special Court, the TRC does not promote reconciliation by punishing offenders. The TRC facilitates healing between victims and perpetrators by asking all people to tell the truth and then reconcile with each other. There appears to be considerable support for the TRC and many Sierra Leoneans are hopeful that it will act as a catalyst for social engineering in the country. (For a discussion on the objects of the TRC, see, for example, Joe A. D. Alie, 'A Price for Peace? Justice and Reconciliation in Post-War Sierra Leone', in Ayissi and Poulton (Eds), *Bound to Cooperate: Conflict, Peace and People in Sierra Leone*.

[25] For a discussion of the submissions of both parties, see Special Court for Sierra Leone – The Prosecutor Against: Sam Hinga Norman (Case No. SCSL-2003-08-PT), 28 November 2003.

[26] http:://scsl-server/sc-sl/new/pressrelease-012104.html.

References

Abdullah, I. (1998), 'Bush Path to Destruction: The Origin and Character of the Revolutionary United Front/Sierra Leone', *The Journal of Modern African Studies*, 36 (2), pp.203-35.

Alie, J. A. D. (1990), *A New History of Sierra Leone*, Macmillan, London.

Alie, J. A. D. (2000), 'Background to the Conflict (1961-1991): What Went Wrong and Why?', in Ayissi, Anatole and Robin-Edward Poulton (Eds), *Bound to Cooperate: Conflict, Peace and People in Sierra Leone*, Geneva: UNIDIR, pp.15-35.

Alie, J. A. D. and Gaima, E. A. (2001), *Conflict in Sierra Leone: Rising from the Ashes*, UNDP, New York.

Amnesty International (1997/98), *Sierra Leone – A Disastrous Setback for Human Rights* (20 October 1997); and *Sierra Leone 1998 – A Year of Atrocities Against Civilians*, AFR51/22/98 (November 1998), International Secretariat, 1 Easton Street, London.

Bangura, Y. (1997) 'Understanding the Political and Cultural Dynamics of the Sierra Leone War: A Critique of Paul Richards *Fighting for the Rain Forest ...*, *Africa Development*, Vol. XXII, Nos. 3/4, pp. 117-148.

Cole, B. (1998), 'The Role of the Civil Defence Force in Internal Security', *WANPOT*, Newsletter of the United Nations System in Sierra Leone, III (1), pp.20-22.

Ero, Comfort (2000), 'Sierra Leone Security Complex', *Working Paper (Executive Summary), The Conflict, Security and Development Group*, Centre for Defence Studies, King's College, University of London.

Foray, C. P. (1988), 'The Road to One-Party State: The Sierra Leone Experience', Africanus Horton Memorial Lecture delivered at the Centre of African Studies, University of Edinburgh, UK, on 9 September 1988.

Francis, D. (2001), *The Politics of Economic Regionalism: Sierra Leone in ECOWAS*, Ashgate, Aldershot.

Francis, D. (2000), 'ECOMOG: A New Security Agenda in World Politics', in Bakut and Dutt (Ed), *Africa at the Millennium: An Agenda for Mature Development*. Basingstoke: Palgrave.

Gberie, L. (1997), 'The May 25 Coup d'Etat in Sierra Leone: A Militariat Revolt?', *Africa Development*, XXII (3/4), pp.149-70.

Kai-Kai, F. (2000), 'Disarmament, Demobilization and Reintegration in Post-War Sierra Leone', in Ayissi, Anatole and Robin-Edward Poulton (Eds), *Bound to Cooperate: Conflict, Peace and People in Sierra Leone*, UNIDIR, Geneva, pp.113-28.

Kabbah, Alhaji Dr. Ahmad Tejan (2003), 'A Statement by His Excellency the President, Alhaji Dr. Ahmad Tejan Kabbah, Made Before the Truth and Reconciliation Commission on Tuesday, 5th August 2003', Freetown: Sierra Leone (Typescript).

Khobe, M.she M. (2000), 'The Evolution and Conduct of ECOMOG Operations in West Africa', Published in Monograph No 44: *Boundaries of Peace Support Operations*, February.

Legg, Sir Thomas and Sir Robin Ibbs (1998), *Report of the Sierra Leone Arms Investigations*. http://www.fco.gov.uk/Files/kfile/complete.zip.

London Times, 11 February 1999.

Muana, P. (1997), 'The Kamajor Militia: Violence, Internal Displacement and the Politics of Counter-Insurgency', *Africa Development*, XXII (3/4), pp.77-100.

Pratt, D. and Nepan-Carleton (1999), 'Sierra Leone: The Forgotten Crisis – Report to the (Canadian) Minister of Foreign Affairs the Hon. Llyod Axworthy', 23 April 1999. www.sierra-leone.org/pratt042399.html. (See also, Sorious Samura's 'Cry Freetown'. This is a documentary which portrays the brutal events in Freetown in January 1999. http://www.cryfreetown.org.)

Richards, P. (1995), *Fighting for the Rain Forest: War, Youth and Resources in Sierra Leone*, James Curry, Oxford.

RUF/SL, *Footpaths to Democracy – Toward a New Sierra Leone* (Basic Document of RUF/SL) in http://sierra-leone.org/footpaths.html.

Sandi, P. (2002), 'Charismatic Movements and Resistance to Degeneracy: A Sociology Study of the Kamajors of Bonthe District' (Long Essay – Department of Sociology, Fourah Bay College).

Sierra Leone Ministry of Defence, *Defence White Paper: Informing the People*, Freetown: MOD, n.d.

Smith, L. A., Gambette, C. and Longley, T. (2004), *Conflict Mapping in Sierra Leone: Violations of International Humanitarian Law from 1991 to 2002*, Freetown: NPWJ.

West Africa, 'ECOMOG as you never knew it', No. 4218, 20-26 March 2000.

Zack-Williams, A. and Riley, S. (1993), 'Sierra Leone: The Coup and its Consequences', *Review of Political Economy*, pp.91-98.

Chapter 4

The Egbesu and Bakassi Boys: African Spiritism and the Mystical Re-traditionalisation of Security

Kenneth Omeje

Introduction

In September 2004, on the eve of Nigeria's 44th independence anniversary, the state was faced with the threat of a major para-military assault from a civil militia, the Niger Delta Volunteer Force (NDVF) led by a famous Ijaw militant Asari Dokubo. The NDVF threats were so substantially disruptive that they quickly raised the international oil price to an historic mark of US$50 per barrel for the first time. The NDVF and a host of other Ijaw-dominated anti-oil militias operating in Nigeria's Niger Delta region are widely believed to be extraordinarily emboldened in their resistance against the state and oil industry because of their collective resort to spiritism and magical paraphernalia of warfare. This study analyses the interface of African spiritism with the security sector, a nexus that results in the mystical re-traditionalisation of security. The operations of two Nigerian ethnic militias, the Egbesu and Bakassi Boys, which articulate and represent the rhetoric of popular responses to the failure of the state to provide public order and socio-economic development, are used to advance the thesis that state failure has necessitated a collective retreat to security re-traditionalisation. There are hardly any prospects that the unfolding pattern of security re-traditionalisation, via the upsurge of diverse local militias that re-invent and embrace African spiritism as an organising instrument of security, will lead to a more dynamic and functional security sector as some uncritical optimists and media documentaries have proposed. Indeed, nearly all practice indications suggest a rather gloomier picture. The supposedly best practical scenarios of cooptation of the re-traditionalised security systems by the state have chiefly resulted in a legalisation of jungle justice, lawlessness and the most horrendous forms of human rights violations. Discredited politicians and state officials have also used cooptation of the re-traditionalised militias as a weapon for the persecution and victimisation of political opponents and rival groups.

In the worst practice scenarios, the state has been compelled to define the rather confrontational, re-traditionalised, voluntary security systems, such as the Egbesu Boys, as security threats. This definitional stigmatisation is a disingenuous securitisation strategy that enables the state to carry out considerable military reprisals in the operational homelands of the stigmatised militia groups, leading to indiscriminate extra-judicial killings and devastation of defenceless local communities. The middle ground of non-state interference with the operations of the re-traditionalised security systems is tantamount to a legitimisation of the rule of the jungle and bewitchment of large communities of people, where penal justice is at best administered without the benefit of a proper trial and the sentences awarded to convicted culprits hardly have any proportionality to the alleged crimes. At worst, justice is miscarried with impunity. Clearly, despite any merits credited to it, the mystical re-traditionalisation of security in the context of the complexities of 21st century civilisation is scarcely a reliable solution to the failure of the state to meet its obligations of providing internal order, protection of lives and property and provision of basic developmental facilities.

This study adopts the Second Generation conceptualisation of civil militias in the context of conflict-prone societies. From this conceptual framework, well articulated by David Francis in chapter one of this volume, civil militias are armed ensembles within prebendal states, organised by diverse interest groups and stakeholders, including governments or regimes in power, non-states and sub-national groups, mostly with no constitutional provision or legislation legalising their existence. As actors within the security sector, civil militias, depending on their origin, motives and goals, may aim to complement or substitute for the security provision and law enforcement functions of the states or, conversely, may aim to combat and subvert the state and its conventional forces. An extreme case scenario of the operation and pervasiveness of civil militias would be a failed state marked by societal regression into what Robert Kaplan (1994) calls 'criminal anarchy'.

The Historical and Sociological Context of Security Re-traditionalisation

African ontology, dating from pre-colonial antiquity, subsumes a ubiquity and, in some cultures or communities, a hierarchy of deities, deified objects and spiritual forces that in various ways connect the people to the conceivably more decisive supernatural realm. In the people's pristine cosmology, the supernatural realm is the repository of the spiritual powers necessary for individual and collective protection and security, material prosperity and therapeutic healing, as well as for the explanation of the unknown and the control of any present or impending adversities. In short, in the way it is constructed and propagated, African spiritism is credited with encompassing powers and influence. By the nature of supernatural powers and functions attributed to the system, African spiritism presupposes a potent ensemble of deities and supernatural intermediaries (albeit not mutually exclusive in many cultures) associated with both benevolent and malevolent powers. Whilst the former are powers that could be ritualistically harnessed for the positive material benefits of adherents and clients, the latter are usually tapped to reverse any evil occurrences plaguing the clients or to strengthen the clients' defensive and offensive capabilities against perceived human or spiritual adversaries. Some of these spiritual forces and gods are believed to inhabit the cosmic system or some natural forces and creatures, including the sun, the moon, virgin forests, mountains, rivers, lakes, caves, and totems (Ellis, 1999). For a vast number of deities, believed to possess malevolent powers, there is usually a closed cult of initiated adherents, worshippers, custodians and priests who regulate access to the deity and in some cases claim exclusive right to the incantation and use of the deity's supernatural powers. The tendency to monopolise the malevolent powers (real or perceived) of a traditional deity by an initiated few invariably positions the latter as a dreaded and powerful group within a community, a rhetoric which many cult members often exploit to gain privileges in the society. Although the tendency to control the malevolent powers of oracular deities is predominantly male-dominated or masculinity-biased, female secret societies exist in many African communities and have used or tended to monopolise the malignant powers of the spirit world.

In many pre-colonial African communities, where they existed, malevolent cults played a crucial role in the maintenance of social order, public authority and the security of the entire political community. The instrumental deities, among other things, formed the basis for the construction of social norms, moral justice, law enforcement and sanctions and also the rallying point for the conduct of external warfare, usually prosecuted through a nexus of military and magical means. The imperatives of maintaining internal social order and external defence necessitated, in some local communities, the mobilisation of youths and young men into secret cults and vigilante groups that often performed traditional law enforcement and collective security functions. Some of the typical pre-colonial secret cults and vigilante groups in Nigeria included the Hisba in the Islamic cultures of the Hausa-Fulani dominated northern Nigeria, as well as the Ekpo, Ekpe, Ekong and some of the age grade societies in different parts of southern Nigeria. In most cases, members of these largely closed cults and the larger communities they served professed substantial allegiance or deference to a common awesome deity or a plurality of related spirit beings whose supernatural authority was believed to underpin a number of key moral codes, legal norms and socio-political traditions. In this way, there prevailed a functional interface of the traditional religious system with the political and socio-legal systems, including for that matter, the entire concept and practice of security. From the perspective of most local people, local agricultural production, which was the main-stay of most pre-colonial economies, was conceivably vitalised through the invocation of the benevolent powers of the respective traditional deities.

European colonialism, and the concomitant occidental civilization it tried to universalise, constructed and imposed a diametrically opposed system that, to a considerable extent, disarticulated and supplanted the observed African pre-colonial social order. First, a modern state institution that, inter alia claims a monopoly of the legitimate use of violence was arbitrarily created. As opposed to polytheism and some closely-knitted primordial social structures, underpinned by the unity of the material and the supernatural, a personalisable sovereign God was introduced amid a secularised institutional framework. Security was systematically detached from society and its interrelated social structures, vested in the modern bureaucratic state and, consequently, the phenomenon become overly professionalised, secularised and militarised.

But the pre-colonial social order was by no means completely obliterated or displaced by the antithetical colonial system. In many respects, the two systems were operated *pari passu* under colonial rule but not without some obvious points of structural intersection, cooperation and conflict. The post-colonial state inherited, and has perpetuated, the structural dualism and implicit contradictions between the 'traditional' and the 'modern', which have largely characterised the cultural, social, economic, legal and political frameworks of society.

For a greater part of post-independence history, there has been a tendency on the part of the state in both Nigeria and much of the developing world, to continue the unfinished business of colonialism by deepening and accelerating the conquest of the traditional systems. To a large extent, the politics and economics of modernisation, which have found expression in many development policies and programmes of the post-colonial state, are substantially premised on finishing the conquest of the traditional order by the modern. For most African countries, the result has been mixed. Progress has been generally slow and the expectation that economic and political modernisation will translate into more developmental dividends and improved living conditions for the vast majority of the people has been rather illusory. Correspondingly, disillusionment with the performance of the modernisation project has increasingly generated a nostalgic re-invention of and fallback on traditionalism. The proliferation of the incidents of state failure and state collapse in Africa from the 1980s onwards leading to a deplorable weakening, in some cases an outright erosion, of the capacity of most states to fulfil their minimum obligations of maintaining internal order and providing security to their citizens, has markedly accelerated the re-invention and comeback of traditionalism in all sectors of society. The revival, upsurge and spread of civil militias and other local insurgencies, that in various practical contexts have, among other things, tended to substitute for or to violently challenge the security provision failings of many African states (Nigeria included), are some of the emerging grassroots responses to the institutional incapacity and non-performance of the state.

In Nigeria, as in many African countries, the phenomenon of state failure has in recent years provoked two relatively distinct forms of grassroots reaction: the subsitutionary and the adversarial. In the substitutionary category, various communities and organisations are prompted by the ineptitude, corruption and inactivity of state criminal justice and law enforcement institutions to create armed vigilante groups that substitute for the law enforcement functions of the state, especially in the area of fighting crime. The Bakassi Boys, an ethnic militia of the largely commerce-oriented Ibo nation of southeastern Nigeria, are perhaps the best known contemporary example of the substitutionary element.

The adversarial, on the other hand, is an emerging popular form of grassroots reaction to the politics of neopatrimonial plunder, prebendalism, elite aggrandisement and most of all, social exclusion, in the Nigerian federation, which has witnessed growing bands of armed youth militias that are often resistant to the state and predatory of big businesses and the rich. Two constructions of social exclusion tend to be more incidental to the adversarial reaction. The first is the generational construction and the second is the ethno-national. There are widespread intersections of the two. The generational construction thrives on the huge army of unemployed, impoverished and hopeless young people of various ethnic nationalities who in many urban and local communities organise themselves into an assertive vanguard inclined to negotiate their identity and survivability by desperate measures, including the use of violence. The infamous Lagos Area Boys, the Yanbanga and Yantauri groups of Kano and the Gbege Boys of Warri and the environs, who employ violent methods to advance their claims of ownership of their homelands in the face of the migrant populations (often perceived as more prosperous) and to, at any rate, extort money from the latter, are most typical of the generational fallout. The university undergraduate secret cult practices, where adversarial violence is interspersed with ritual killings and fetishism, are perhaps an even more horrendous aspect of the generational exclusion. In addition to their disposition to identity-related types of violence, the hopelessness of the youth populations caught in the generational web of social exclusion also makes them vulnerable pawns in the hands of the wealthy political elites who quite easily rent them (the Area Boys and the like) for political thuggery and similar violent malpractices.

In the ethno-national strand of social exclusion, popular pressure, protests and resistance are employed by a range of armed militias who challenge the perceived exclusion of their ethnic or sub-ethnic communities in the distribution of resources by the state and other powerful social forces, such as the transnational oil companies (TNOCs) that reproduce the ethno-national imbalances – in terms of control of strategic positions and resources and the derivative power relations – characteristic of the state. Armed militia groups representing several minority ethnic populations of the oil-rich Niger Delta region have, since the early 1990s, waged this type of resource-based struggle against the Nigerian state and the various TNOCs carrying out oil operations in their region. The Egbesu Boys, who cut across various militant groups but largely represent the Ijaw nationality, the largest of the minority ethnic groups in the Nigerian Niger Delta, have been one of the most vociferous and defiant in the campaign against the perceived politics of exclusion against the Nigerian oil-bearing region. The observed politics of exclusion is indeed a national irony (given that oil produced in the Delta region is the main-stay of Nigeria's economy), which the bulk of Niger Delta populations define as 'marginalisation'.

Broadly, both the Egbesu and Bakassi Boys, depicted in the preceding analysis, are particularly intriguing in the sense that they not only represent alternative constructions of the contemporary grassroots response to the failure of the state, but more importantly, the operations of these militia groups exemplify the emerging paradox of security re-traditionalisation in Nigeria.

The Bakassi Boys: Substitutionary Security and Patterns of Re-traditionalisation

The Bakassi Boys emerged in late 1997 in the Ibo commercial city of Aba in Abia State as a desperate societal response to the inability of the relevant state institutions, namely the police and the judicial system, to solve the pervasive problem of violent crime. Corruption, inefficiency and double-standards were seen as the bane of state institutions and armed robbers had no difficulties in using their stolen riches to bribe their way through the system. At this point, the police and the judiciary had lost all their moral authority and were generally distrusted not only in Aba but also in other big commercial cities of the country where armed bandits reigned unchallenged in an evolving dispensation of 'criminal anarchy' (Kaplan, 1994). It literally made no sense reporting crime suspects or incidents to the police or pursuing related litigations in court because justice would hardly be done. People withdrew from the state and resorted to self-help in fighting crime. Local vigilantism and mob action against suspected criminals became rampant.

The Bakassi Boys were organised by the shoemakers' association of Ariaria market, Aba, to defend themselves against the onslaught of the armed hoodlums. They were just one among the numerous vigilante groups that inundated many towns and villages of southeastern Nigeria. But unlike the typical local vigilantes that are usually composed of individuals from the local community or neighbourhood, the Bakassi Boys were an amorphous group of obscure young men drawn from different local communities. The major defining characteristic of the group, which also largely distinguished it from many other local vigilante groups, was its possession of a peculiar type of occult power that, supposedly, made members impervious to bullets. Using a combination of the occult power and gun violence, the Bakassi Boys hunted down and exterminated members of the Aba criminal gangs and, thus, were able to rid the commercial city of violent crime in a matter of days. Their campaign was unprecedentedly brutal but at the same time efficient. The 'success' of this debut operation led to the employment of the militiamen as a more permanent security outfit in Aba, with initial funding and infrastructure provided by the market traders' association.

The militiamen also established a Bakassi training camp on the outskirts of Aba, where young recruits were provided with some paramilitary training but not until they had gone through a rigorous occult initiation and talismanic empowerment in some undisclosed shrine locations, believed to be somewhere in Ogoniland in Rivers State.[1] The 'bullet-proof' brand of occult power, credited to the Bakassi Boys, does not seem to be quintessentially of Ibo provenance. It is a type of magical power that has been more historically associated with a number of ethnic Yoruba clans, notably the Ijebu; the Edo of the old Mid-West; and the Ogoni and Ijaw minority groups of the Niger Delta. Since pre-colonial history, however, bullet-proof occult power has been less famously credited to a number of powerful medicinemen and cults in such Ibo communities as Arochukwu, Ohafia, Umuleri, Ogbaru, and Enugu-Ezike. It is debateable whether the power has developed autochthonously in Iboland or has rather diffused from other ethnic groups it has been more customarily and famously associated with.

Meanwhile, worried by the fetishism and arbitrary killings promoted by the Bakassi Boys, some sections of the public, including different Christian groups, called for the disbanding of the vigilante group. The local Police Command, who had been considerably displaced and humiliated by the emergence of the self-help vigilante team, remained hostile to the militia group and was building up a dossier of the unlawful killings of the Bakassi Boys, as a means to instituting criminal proceedings against them at the earliest opportunity. These controversies prompted the Abia State government, who were impressed by the traders' self-help security initiative and the performance of the vigilante group, to step in quickly with supportive legislation that officially endorsed the operation of the Bakassi Boys and regularised their appointment as the Abia Vigilante Services. Other major south-eastern towns and State governments that had hitherto watched the developments in Aba with enthusiasm eventually followed this example. Hence, within a few months, Bakassi operations were extended to the commercial towns of Onitsha and Owerri with the backing of their State governments, who formalised their operations as the Anambra Vigilante Services, and the Imo Vigilante Services, respectively.

The method employed by the Bakassi Boys in fighting crime provokes a combination of awe and deference from the general public, including their arch rivals, the local Police Command. The method is based on their presumed ability to use occult powers skilfully to detect violent criminals from a crowd, to confirm in the course of their secret trials if any accused person under their custody is guilty of violent crime, and above all, to come out unhurt when sprayed with gunfire. It is the latter, more than any other factor, which has made the numerically insignificant militia group such an enigmatic and dreaded force. In every town where they have been commissioned, there are hardly more than 20-30 members of the Bakassi team, and it is this small group that is able to effectively fight crime in and beyond the town, sometimes extending their operations to a greater part of the State, albeit not without the cooperation of other private vigilante groups and local syndicates (*Tell*, 2000; Harnischfeger, 2003, p.31).

The militiamen do not have any illusions about the public esteem and awe their magical powers and presumed invincibility inspire. Every Bakassi member wears visible amulets across his neck, hips, upper arm or ankles and it is reported that the militiamen have, occasionally, displayed their invincibility by using submachine guns to indiscriminately spray bullets at one another at close range. The bullets fell off their clothes to the admiration of an entertained pool of bystanders and onlookers (Harnischfeger, 2003, p.29). It is public displays of this nature, and the popular sentiments they evoke, that were said to have often intimated and scared both armed robbers and members of local Police Command and prevented them from engaging the Bakassi Boys in a face-to-face combat. The Nigerian police seem to have been cautiously guided by the bitter lesson of their abortive attempt to flush out the ethnic Yoruba militias, the Oodua People's Congress (OPC), in 1999 and thus deployed their officers into street fighting in Lagos against the militias. About two hundred police officers lost their lives in this violent confrontation (Akinyele, 2001). Hundreds of civilians also died in the crossfire but it is not known how many members of the OPC, believed to be inoculated to gunfire with bullet-proof charms, died in the violent clashes. The OPC has, since that fateful encounter, not only thrived unabated but has also carried out a range of large-scale violent campaigns against the Ijaw and the Hausa-Fulani in different parts of Lagos, in spite of federal government's proscription of the organisation in 1999. This act of defiance has reinforced the belief, held among significant sections of the public, about the intractability and invincibility of the OPC Boys.

The Bakassi Boys encourage members of the public to report or to deliver crime suspects to them. Often too, the militiamen have stormed criminal gang hideouts or mounted roadblocks across streets and highways to flush out criminals from ransacked vehicles. Diverse charms are used to identify a criminal suspect from a crowd, the most well-known being the 'magic machete test.' In this test, the Bakassi Boys wave their magical instrument across the faces of all the surrendered suspects and, it is said, the metallic machete usually turns red when positioned across the face of a practising armed robber. The latter is usually whisked off to the Bakassi headquarters for detention and interrogation. If, upon his arrest the suspect is searched and, for instance, found to be in possession of an unlawful firearm, the militiamen do not require any further evidence to confirm their suspect is an armed criminal. Instant justice usually follows in such a case, and the suspected criminal is decapitated with the magic machete and/or set alight in the full glare of bystanders. The dismembered corpse is abandoned on the roadside and it might take some days for it to be removed by the municipal council authority or perhaps the family of the deceased. For the cases that are ultimately taken to the conspicuously juju-adorned Bakassi headquarters for trial, the interrogation of suspects is often interspersed with torture. In this method the Bakassi Boys were not different from the Nigerian police who are notorious for inflicting severe torture on crime suspects and detainees in a bid to extract confessions from them.[2] The militiamen often extend their investigations to their detainees' homes, which they ransack for firearms and stolen items. If a detainee has not been directly apprehended by the militiamen but has been reported or delivered up by a third party, confidential evidence is usually taken from the 'reporter', to guide the militiamen in their investigation. Detainees could be released if they were found to be innocent, have limbs amputated or be beaten up and cautioned if they are adjudged to be petty offenders, and lastly, executed in one of the several Bakassi execution sites if they were found guilty of armed robbery.

There have also been a number of instances where the militiamen have executed some people not directly convicted of armed robbery but believed to have abetted the phenomenon by wilfully accommodating and encouraging alleged robbers or by equipping suspects with the necessary munitions and charms to strengthen their operational capacities, in return for some gratuitous reward. Most of the alleged accomplices executed in this category include the girl friends of suspected criminals, some controversial local politicians and businessmen and some famous occult priests, such as Prophet Eddie Okeke, popularly known as Eddie Nawgu. The arrest, trial and execution of the latter was remarkably controversial because the local spiritist Church he operated at the Nawgu community of Anambra State was a Mecca to many influential politicians and businessmen who allegedly visited the Prophet for protective charms and talismanic empowerment. These dignitaries were said to have mobilised strong pressure to have their benefactor released. The Nawgu Prophet's arrest and execution was only made possible by the popular demand and supportive protests of the Onitsha traders and members of the public who perceived the Prophet as a satanic high priest who used the Church as a cover for fetishism, ritual murder and making juju for evil persons intent on unscrupulous riches.

It is noteworthy that there are several syncretic religious groups similar to the Eddie Nawgu variant in Nigeria and many parts of sub-Saharan Africa, who specialise in the conflation of some fetish practices attendant on African traditional religion and aspects of the Christian faith (Omeje, 2001). Indeed, the Bakassi Boys, who are mostly self-confessed Christians, are themselves not far from promoting a comparable variant of syncretism and many of the militiamen are seen wearing necklaces of the Christian crucifix alongside their amulets and they also occasionally join Christian prayer meetings in the various sections of the Onitsha and Aba markets. Some of their prayer partners and members of the public are quick to exonerate the militiamen from the pernicious types of syncretism ascribed to people like the late Eddie Nawgu, arguing that the militiamen are genuine Christians who only tap into 'the powers of darkness' as a means to fight satanic forces. 'A kingdom divided against itself cannot stand and, therefore, you need the power of Satan to fight satanic forces', many would argue defensively from a rather distorted view of the bible.

Generally, the vast majority of the public tend to be fascinated with the operations of the Bakassi Boys and the measure of order their intervention has brought about, especially in the big Ibo commercial towns of Onitsha and Aba. Some previous threats and news reports that the federal government (known to be highly apprehensive about the potential security threats posed by the charismatic Ibo vigilantes) intends to proscribe the Bakassi group provoked massive grassroots demonstrations in Anambra and Abia States. There is an implicit faith in the judgement and incorruptibility of the Bakassi Boys and in the efficacity of their spiritual power among most supporters of the group. 'You don't have any reason to fear the Bakassi Boys if you are not a criminal', most protagonists would argue. Even many top politicians, government officials and intellectuals in the south-eastern States, including the Abia State Governor Orji Uzo Kalu, and the ex-Governor of Anambra State Dr Chinwoke Mbadinuju, are among those who have publicly expressed such uncritically supportive sentiments (HRW/CLEEN, 2002). A significant section of the media also lends enthusiastic support to the Bakassi Boys. It is this broad range of favourable perception and support for the Ibo militias that have made them the preferred substitute for the largely corrupt, inefficient and discredited State's Police Command. In fact, there has been persistent pressure from diverse social groups and sections of the public in the other Ibo States of Ebonyi and Enugu, for an extension of the vigilante services of the Bakassi Boys to their States.

It is pertinent to observe that given the tremendous public approval of the Bakassi Boys, a number of local vigilante groups have counterfeited the team to falsely present themselves as the highly revered Ibo militiamen. In doing so, these counterfeit and largely extortionist groups have usually tried to imitate the regalia and dress codes, slang, sign language and abracadabra of the Bakassi Boys, but not the latter's collective discipline, particularly in respect of sexual continence and perhaps bribery and corruption. Probably, the most well-known episodes of the 'fake' Bakassi are the activities of the team employed by the Imo State government in response to popular agitations. Lacking the distinguishing magical power of the authentic Abia and Anambra Bakassi Boys, the Imo Bakassi operated more like a quasi-intelligence bureau by building up dossiers on crime suspects based entirely on their shabby investigations, and information supplied by members of the public. Corruption and miscarriage of justice became rampant and the public felt outraged that a team of Bakassi Boys, devoid of the dreaded magical features and tainted with corruption, should claim the moral authority to replace the police.

The Imo Bakassi evaded repeated pressures from the public to allow loaded automatic rifles to be fired at them and sharpened daggers thrust into their bowels to prove their invincibility as the authentic Bakassi have had done on some occasions. As a matter of fact, this customary invincibility show, especially the comparatively 'lighter' aspect of thrusting a sharpened dagger into one's bowel, is occasionally performed in magical concerts staged at public motor parks by magicians employed to promote the sale of indigenous herbal medicine in different Nigerian towns. For the Imo Bakassi Boys, the last straw occurred when at their public presentation at the Owerri township stadium, the militiamen once again evaded the pressure of the public to perform the customary invincibility show. The Imo public became restive and staged a violent demonstration at Owerri, the State capital, against what they saw as the 'fake' Bakassi their State government had deceptively arranged (Harnischfeger, 2003,p.35). The Imo State Bakassi group have hardly functioned, following this authenticity crisis, even after they had been reconstituted by the State government. However, the Imo State government has occasionally hired the services of the genuine Bakassi Boys from the neighbouring States of Abia and Anambra and this has considerably placated the discontent of the people.

Beyond the façade of a strong, disciplined, incorruptible, and efficient Bakassi lays a horrendous catalogue of human rights violations, extra-judicial killings, and manipulations of the vigilante group by some State government politicians for the persecution and elimination of political opponents. Since their inception, thousands of people have been arbitrarily abducted, tortured, mutilated and executed by the Bakassi Boys each year. Being a secret society, many of the activities of the vigilante group, including abductions, trials, torture, amputation and execution are conducted in secret. There are allegations that the militiamen use the blood and sensitive body parts of some of their victims for ritual purposes, and that they also eat the flesh and drink the blood for spiritual empowerment. These allegations may not be entirely far-fetched because previous researchers on African militant secret societies in both colonial and contemporary histories have revealed that many war medicines were made from human body parts, and warriors become 'brave' by eating parts of the enemy's body, by drinking his blood or by using his skull as a drinking bowl (Harley, 1970; Ellis, 1999). Writing in this volume, Joe

Alie reports that the *Yaa M□ □t□*, a refractory unit of the Kamajor militias was widely believed to eat some of their dead enemies.

The enormous scale of secret abductions, killings and disappearance of crime suspects, promoted by these ethnic militias, translates into a reign of terror over an overly mesmerised, helpless and subdued population. The Bakassi Boys operate overcrowded detention camps and deplorable cells in different inaccessible and sometimes secret locations. Most victims of the vigilante group are anonymous and defenceless people who once they are arrested or abducted for whatever reasons, are shackled and kept in detention centres with hardly any visitation rights, medical care or hope of fair trial. Detainees are extremely brutalised and starved. There is hardly any right of appeal against the incarceration, mistreatment and sentencing of the vigilante group. With the exception of the hegemonic cabals in the State governments, whose political interest in imposing a mesmerising paradigm of order in which the masses are hoodwinked and political opponents are blackmailed and systematically liquidated, there is scarcely any other group that exercises meaningful control and oversight over the Bakassi Boys. The voice of the public is only heard after repeated violent demonstrations, but the use of this 'weapon' is limited to some perceptibly reprehensible obvert actions and inactions of the ethnic militias. A large number of the secret atrocities of the militiamen, which have been investigated and documented by a number of human rights organisations, such as the Civil Liberty Organisation, Human Rights Watch, and the Centre for Law Enforcement Education of Nigeria (HRW/CLEEN, 2001) are hardly visible to the general public or understood by them in a human rights context.

The Egbesu Boys: Adversarial Security and Mystical Re-traditionalisation

The term Egbesu Boys is loosely used to refer to the various Ijaw militants engaged in a long-drawn-out resistance against the Nigerian state and the oil industry; two collaborative powerful forces that, from the perspective of the local Niger Delta people, are responsible for their collective exploitation, socio-economic marginalisation and the devastation of their environment through the negative externalities of oil extraction. Contrary to some of the dominant conceptions, the Egbesu Boys do not belong to a common resistance movement but rather cut across a mosaic of ethnic Ijaw-dominated anti-oil movements. The vast majority of these movements are engaged in armed struggles and this brings them into persistent clashes with the state's security forces. These organisations include the Niger Delta Volunteer Force (NDVF), Pan Niger Delta Revolutionary Militia (PNDRM), Ijaw Youth Council (IYC), Federated Niger Delta Ijaw Communities (FNDIC), Movement for the Survival of Ijaw Ethnic Nationality (MOSIEN), and the Niger Delta Oil Producing Communities (NDOPC) (Ikelegbe, 2001, pp.434-459). Outmatched by the military power of their adversaries, these Ijaw groups reinvent and tap into the spiritual power of the ancient Egbesu deity in their homeland, a magical device that complements their limited firepower. Most Ijaw youth fighters are generally believed to be members of the Egbesu cult, and it is widely held that the Egbesu offers magical protection against gunfire to these young militias.

The Egbesu is an indigenous god behind a precolonial religious institution usually invoked to enforce public morality, discipline and accountability in the community and also to provide protection and security to its adherents and faithfuls (Gore and Pratten, 2003, pp.223-224). In both precolonial and colonial histories, the various Ijaw communities and clans complemented the conventional military capabilities of their armies with the spiritual power of the Egbesu to prosecute wars against their adversaries; these included wars with some neighbouring tribal communities, and the Dutch and British conquistadors. The early conquest of the entire region of southern Nigeria in the late 19th century by the British colonial authorities, the consequent imposition of colonial rule, the impact of urbanisation on traditional social structures and the spread of Christianity in the region since the colonial period, have progressively and significantly diminished the influence, credibility, and authority of the Egbesu cult throughout Ijawland. Until recently, most Ijaws only became acquainted with the legendary Egbesu cult through the peoples' traditional folklore and war songs.

The imperatives of the contemporary struggles of the people for environmental and economic justice have, however, necessitated a revival of the Egbesu cult, a spiritual renaissance that has immensely excited and enticed a great number of young people and activists in the anti-oil campaign. The latter undergo secret initiations into the Egbesu cult, performed by some of the most powerful Ijaw witchdoctors who are believed to impart the supernatural powers of the Egbesu. Initiation into the Egbesu cult carries with it some strict moral codes that have to do with forthrightness and propriety, and members also learn some incantatory language and signs applicable to different threats and occasions. The real essence of the initiation is the acquisition of an invisible 'bullet-proof charm,' supposedly represented by some cicatrices etched on some hidden part of a person's body by the witchdoctor and which covenants the individual cult member to the Egbesu deity.[3] In chapter three of this volume, Joe Alie has reported a comparable pattern of initiation rites undergone by the Kamajor militias in Sierra Leone and which were primarily meant 'to render initiates fit to serve at the war front, through the granting of special powers such as the ability to be bullet-proof and be able to smell enemies.'

The Egbesu secret cults exist in a number of Ijaw towns and each local chapter handles its own cult initiation, although the procedures are believed to be similar. Some cult members wear amulets in addition to the cicatrices on their bodies and this may have to do with some nuances in the existing patterns of initiation and the fact that there are also people who go beyond the cult to source extra talismanic power. The workings of the presumed bulletproof charm can only be explained *ex-post-facto*. But, by and large, the efficacy of the charm to protect against gunfire and other dangerous weapons is apparently dependent on a bearer's observance of its applicable ethical codes and abracadabra.

Armed with the presumably invincible power of the Egbesu, the Ijaw Boys have become greatly emboldened and defiant in their resistance in spite of the state's intensified military crackdown in recent years. It is noteworthy that in a few isolated incidents, especially in non-combatant situations, the Ijaw militant groups have gained temporal advantages over the state's security forces. Examples include the storming at the Yenogua Government House in July 1998 by thousands of Ijaw youths who overpowered the state's security forces to release the detained MOSIEN president Timi Ogoriba. Also there was the successful abduction and killing of seven policemen on a peaceful fact-finding mission to the Ijaw town of Odi by a lawless youth gang in November 1999. Moreover, there was the mass destruction of Shell's oil pipelines and facilities in targeted parts of the Delta and Bayelsa States in April 2004 by some defiant members of an Ijaw anti-oil coalition known as the Delta-Bayelsa Freedom Fighters. The latter had no difficulty in overrunning the regular police guards and patrol teams on duty, forcing the government to make a major military deployment and crackdown to combat the threats. But in almost all cases, such temporal advantages, which invariably add credence to the presumed magical power and invincibility of the Ijaw militants, have ultimately resulted in a more severe state reprisal and the laying of a military siege to Ijawland.

The case of Odi, in which a band of lawless Ijaw youths believed to be Egbesu Boys abducted and killed a team of policemen on an intelligence-gathering mission, is particularly striking because the violence was not strictly speaking oil-related. Yet the incident provoked the single largest state genocidal action in the Niger Delta since the escalation of grassroots petro-violence in the oil-rich region in the early 1990s. The policemen had gone to Odi to investigate rumours that some Ijaw youths were mobilising to storm the city of Lagos in reprisal for attacks carried out a month earlier on Ijaw residents in the ethnic Yoruba metropolis of Lagos by the hardline Yoruba organization, the Oodua People's Congress (OPC) (Ibeanu, 2002, p.165). President Obasanjo responded to the murder incident by ordering the Bayelsa State Governor Diepreye Alamieyeseigha, in a letter dated 4 November 1999, to produce the culprits within fourteen days for prosecution. When, at the expiration of the President's ultimatum, the lawless Odi gang could not be traced or produced, the presidency ordered over 2,000 troops to invade Odi in a swift two day operation that almost completely destroyed the town's building infrastructure and left 2,483 civilians killed (Vanguard, 2002; ERA, 2002). The federal government eventually rationalised the destruction of Odi by arguing that the action was taken to protect oil operations and facilities because the lawless Odi Youths in question were a threat to the oil industry (Vanguard, 2002).

In another major act of defiance, the Egbesu Boys convened a grand conference of over 5,000 Ijaw youths, in the relatively remote Ijaw town of Kaiama, in December 1998, at which they adopted the famous Kaiama Declaration, a radical communiqué issued to both the federal government and TNOCs. The Declaration, which was an extraordinarily bold attempt at self-determination, stated that 'all land and natural resources, including mineral resources, within Ijaw territory belong to Ijaw communities and are the basis of their survival', and further demanded 'self-government and control of the resources for Ijaw people within a federation of ethnic minorities' (Frynas, 2000, p.47).

In accordance with its self-determination preambles, the Declaration specifically called for a more local control of oil revenues and gave the government until 31 December 1998 to respond positively to the demands of the youths or risk having all the oil companies ejected from Ijawland. As expected, the federal government responded negatively through pre-emptive militarisation, hunting, arrests and incarceration of the youth leaders, a crackdown on protests, and the brutal conquest of Kaiama and Yenogua, the two largest towns in the Ijaw-dominated oil State of Bayelsa. Scores of Ijaw youths and innocent citizens were killed and several properties destroyed in this violent military campaign.

Evidently, the state's use of military violence has scarcely succeeded in curbing the Ijaw resistance. There is no doubt that the profile of Ijaw resistance is extraordinarily enhanced by the belief of the general public, including members of the armed forces, that most Ijaw militants complement their armed protests with a special occult power sourced from the people's formidable Egbesu deity that also makes them impervious to bullets[4] (Ibeanu, 2000, p.28). Two Ijaw youth leaders, as well as members of Shell's security team interviewed at Port Harcourt corroborated the myth of the Egbesu charm purportedly used by the Ijaw militants in fighting the state's security forces. Responding to a rather curious question on why government forces were able to accomplish an 'extensive massacre' at Odi, an Ijaw community famous for the Egbesu cult, one of the police officers among Shell's security team answered as follows:

> The Ijaw did not originate bulletproof charms. It is a supernatural power widely distributed among various tribes in Nigeria and Africa. Even in India and other parts of the world, people are known to have such spiritual power. People don't acquire such power because they are members of a particular tribe; you acquire it because you belong to a cult that provides it. So there are also officers of the security forces that operate such powers even though officially the armed forces do not acknowledge the existence of occult power. What happened in the Odi operation was a case of cult power versus cult power but government forces ultimately won because of their superior firepower. The *impervious* (my emphasis) Egbesu youths were not killed in that encounter, they fled. It was the uninitiated and vulnerable persons, including women and children, who, in any case, comprise the majority of the local population that were killed in Odi.[5]

Occult Belief Systems and Politics in Africa

Occult belief systems, it must be emphasized, have substantial impact on current power relations, politics and development in Africa. In contemporary history, there have been different instances from countries like Côte d'Ivoire, Kenya, Tanzania, Togo, the Benin Republic and South Africa of occult systems permeating the public realm over a broad range of issues, such as mesmerisation and persecution of people using witchcraft; divination and oath-taking to affirm political loyalty or to establish official wrongdoing; talismanic empowerment for personal protection, undertaken by some public office holders; regime security; and offensive defence and combating of threats (Omeje, 2001; Kohnert, 2003; Kelsall, 2003).

The case of South Africa is particularly instructive. Grassroots stakeholders in the battle against the apartheid regime in the country's most impoverished provinces of Limpopo and Eastern Cape were, from the middle of the 1980s, reported to be increasingly menaced by witchcraft attacks – in most cases sudden and mysterious deaths. Traditional social structures such as age grades, peer groups, women's guilds, and village or local community-based political authorities, became sharply split on the basis of witchcraft, and real or imaginary adversaries of society were increasingly confronted with witchcraft accusations, which in post-apartheid dispensation have overshadowed race and class as the major line of conflict. In the past few years, reports Kohnert (2003, p.218), witchcraft-related violence has increased dramatically; the death toll running into thousands, especially in the former homelands of Lebowa, Gazankulu and, Venda, as well as in the districts of Tsolo and Qumbu (Transkei). The state's security forces (police and army) and civic institutions (Church and NGOs) have repeatedly intervened to stop the violence but apparently with limited success. Kohnert (2003, p.218) remarks that apart from the immeasurable harm that witchcraft violence has inflicted on individuals and families, the phenomenon has destabilised the social, economic and political setting of a whole region, seriously endangering the state's monopoly of force, and undermining the legitimacy of the new post-apartheid government in the eyes of the local population. Clearly, the question of causality in respect of the use of occult power and its presumed outcome can hardly be consistently explained to the satisfaction of a researcher's 'scientific mind', and thus remains in that sense, mystical and mysterious (Kelsall, 2003, p.197).

A more stunning example is the case of the Ogwugwu shrines in the remote Ibo village of Okija, a mini-Mecca to many top Nigerian politicians and business tycoons, which was raided on $3^{rd}/4^{th}$ August 2004 by a team of about 500 policemen. More than 20 human skulls and 50 corpses at different stages of decomposition, supposedly slaughtered for ritual purposes, were discovered during the raid, in which some 31 priests of the deity were also arrested (*This Day*, 19/08/04). Further revelation since the discovery of the Ogwugwu 'ritual killings' have shown that among regular visitors to the shrines were many federal and State government legislators, as well as State governors who frequented the oracular deity for personal talismanic protection, good faith and loyalty-related oath-taking and for settlement of disputes (*This Day*, 15/08/04). The federal government has directed the police to carry out a detailed investigation of the Ogwugwu cult with a view to prosecuting the culprits. There are, however, fears that the powerful politicians implicated in the infamous occult saga will use their influence to stifle the investigation and any possible judicial proceedings.

Given the prebendal nature of politics in many African countries, the instrumental use of power for corrupt enrichment and victimisation of opponents, the restiveness of large sections of the impoverished and disaffected populace, threats to regime survival are inextricably interfaced with threats to the personal safety of political office holders. Too often, the threats to the personal safety and lives of office holders are continued well after they have vacated office, usually because of the level of atrocities they might have committed while in office. This factor, coupled with the prospect of a possible prosecution for diverse wrongdoings and the fear of slipping into the miasma of poverty, makes the prospect of leaving political office a dreadful option for many. Desperate measures, including creation of pro-government militias, hijacking and cooption of some civil society based militias, systematic repression and liquidation of opposition, and application of occult methods are, therefore, adopted by different political office holders as strategies of governance to perpetuate their hegemony and survivability. For many analysts, the concomitance of occultism in governance is perceived as a retreat from modernity.

Conclusion

This article is by no means an apology for African spiritism nor a vindication of its potency. Far from it! It is simply an attempt to analyse one of the most profound but under-researched ways the phenomenon of state failure in Africa has affected the conduct of security and the invidious problems spawned by the emerging paradigm shift represented by the mystical re-traditionalisation of security. While the appalling performances of the state's security establishment are appreciated and by no means excused, this article has no illusions about the inherent disaster in trying to reconstruct or reform the African security sector by integrating voluntary vigilante systems and secret cults whose methods and structures are clearly founded on traditional patterns of spiritism. In a nutshell, such methods of security re-traditionalisation amount to a regressive endorsement and importation of the atavistic relics, rituals, abuses and impunity of 19th century African societies into the cosmopolitan social structures and institutions of the 21st century. It is in a wider sense substitution within the security sector of the abuses and violations perpetrated by the modern state system with the abuses and violations of the re-invented 19th century traditional African systems. Presented with the two grim choices, the general public tends to prefer the latter, a choice that coincidentally serves the political interest of some powerful government functionaries and proponents of occult security at the subnational level. But the public deserves to be presented with better and more functional choices than the preceding grim realities and this should be the essence of any future security sector reforms.

Whilst this article does not intend to enunciate a detailed proposal for security sector reform in Nigeria and Africa, it suffices to highlight that there are a multiplicity of informal and indigenous vigilante groups that perform functional and transparent security functions in various communities and residential neighbourhoods. These groups derive their moral authority and credibility from the communities they serve as night guards and they often complement the police in identifying and handing over criminal suspects to the appropriate judicial authorities for prosecution (HRW/CLEEN, 2002, p.7). The imperatives of reforming the African security sector should of necessity go beyond the familiar proposal of reorganisation and capacitation of the formal state institutions to explore more constructive ways of engaging with and capacitating the non-occult and non-secret informal vigilante groups. In addition, there is an urgent need for a substantial demilitarisation of security and a more inclusive securitisation of development (including youth skill acquisition training and employment) across the domestic political landscape. These measures, when effectively implemented, will help to mitigate the proclivity of the highly alienated youth populations towards adversarial forms of security and their occult dimensions.

Notes

[1] The Bakassi Boys apparently have a strong association with Ogoniland and there are a few prominent members of the group known to be Ogoni indigenes.

[2] HRW/CLEEN (2002) and Harnischfeger (2003) have made a detailed analysis of this point. But it suffices to add that the analysis of the operational methods and dynamics of the Bakassi Boys are mostly based on my personal observations of events in the various States concerned and my conversations with diverse members of the public since the emergence of the militiamen.

[3] All the information about initiation into the Egbesu cult has been generated through my conversations with various Ijaw indigenes and Egbesu Boys in the course of my doctoral fieldwork in the Niger Delta during the first quarter of 2003. Note that the bulletproof charm is believed to offer spiritual protection not only against bullets but also against other dangerous weapons and instruments, such as spears, arrows and machetes.

[4] Verbal confessions of some of the soldiers that took part in the Odi operation, as well as a significant amount of the graffiti they left on the walls of the destroyed buildings in the town, reveal that the soldiers were inspired to genocidal action by their curious resolve to test and possibly demystify the highly publicised invincibility of the Egbesu cult. When ultimately the devastation of Odi proved a cakewalk, the soldiers celebrated their victory by taunting the Egbesu both verbally and through their graffiti (ERA, 2002; *Vanguard*, 2002).

[5] Interview was held at the Shell premises, Port Harcourt on 14/02/03.

References

Akinyele, R. T. (2001), 'Ethnic Militancy and National Stability in Nigeria: A Case Study of the Oodua People's Congress', *African Affairs*, No. 100, pp.623-640.

Ellis, S. (1999), *The Mask of Anarchy: The Destruction of Liberia and the Religious Dimension of an African Civil War*, Hurst & Company, London.

ERA (2002), *A Blanket of Silence: Images of the Odi Genocide*, Special report Environmental Rights Action/Friends of the Earth, Nigeria.

Frynas, J. G. (2000), *Oil in Nigeria: Conflicts and Litigations Between Oil Companies and Village Communities*, Lit Verlag Munster, Hamburg.

Gore, C. and Pratten, D. (2003), 'The Politics of Plunder: The Rhetorics of Order and Disorder in Southern Nigeria', *African Affairs*, No. 102, pp.211-240.

Harley, G. W. (1970), *Native African Medicine, with Special Reference to Its Practice in the Mano Tribe of Liberia*, Frank Cass, London.

Harnischfeger, J. (2003), 'The Bakassi Boys: Fighting Crime in Nigeria', *Journal of Modern African Studies*. Vol.41/1, pp.23-49.

HRW/CLEEN (2002), *The Bakassi Boys: The Legitimisation of Murder and Torture*. Special Report, Human Rights Watch, New York and the Lagos based Centre for Law Enforcement Education of Nigeria.

Ibeanu, O. (2000), 'Oiling the Friction: Environmental Conflict Management in the Niger Delta, Nigeria', *Environmental Change and Security Project Report*, No. 6, The Woodrow Wilson Centre, Washington D. C., Summer.

Ibeanu, O. (2002), 'Janus Unbounded: Petrobusiness and Petropolitics in the Niger Delta', *Review of African Political Economy*, No. 91, pp.163-167.

Ikelegbe, A. (2001), 'Civil Society, Oil and Conflict in the Niger Delta Region of Nigeria: Ramifications of Civil Society for a Regional Resource Struggle', *Journal of Modern African Studies*, vol. 39, No. 3, pp.437-469.

Kaplan, R. D. (1994), 'The Coming Anarchy', *The Atlantic Monthly*, Vol. 273, No. 2, pp.44-76.

Kelsall, T. (2003), 'Rituals of Verification: Indigenous and Imported Accountability in Northern Tanzania', *Africa*, Vol. 73, No. 2, pp.174-201.

Kohnert, D. (2003), 'Witchcraft and Transnational Social Space: Witchcraft Violence, Reconciliation and Development in South Africa's Transition Process', *Journal of Modern African Studies*, Vol. 41, No. 2, pp.217-245.

Omeje, K. (2001), 'Sexual Exploitation of Cult Women: The Challenges of Problematising Harmful Traditional Practices in Africa from a Doctrinalist Approach', *Social & Legal Studies*. Vol. 10/1, pp.45-61.

Tell (2001), *The Bakassi Boys, Tell* – A Nigerian Weekly News Magazine. March 26.

This Day (2004), 'The Earthquake in Okija', 15 August;
     http://www.thisdayonline.com/archive/2004/08/15/20040815com01.html.

This Day (2004), 'Okija Priests to be Prosecuted', 19 August;
     http://www.thisdayonline.com.

Vanguard (2002), '2,483 Lives Lost in Odi Armed Invasion'. 20/11/02. http://allafrica.com/Nigeria/newswire/.

Chapter 5

Civil Militias: Indonesia and Nigeria in Comparative Perspective

Ruben Thorning

Introduction

What seems to be a growing number of African states are harrowed by internal security problems related to civil militias.[1] Nevertheless, the problem of increasing militiarism is not exclusive to Africa. Strikingly similar dynamics of organised civilian groups challenging state authority can be observed across the globe, from former Yugoslavia and Chechnya, to Colombia, Peru, Tajikistan and Indonesia. These developments are most common in *weak states* with poor domestic security capabilities. Such states suffer from a domestic *security vacuum*, which means that, because the official police force is corrupt, poorly trained or inefficient in other ways, they enjoy no legitimacy or authority in the eyes of the population. This naturally leads to a crisis in the relationship between civil society and the state that has failed to fulfill its most important obligation, namely to provide security for its citizens. In such a situation, where the state is unable to provide security for its citizens, security as a basic human need will be sought by other means and this is where the militiarisation of society often takes place. When observing the dynamics in a significant number of conflict-prone transition societies, it appears that while governments and institutions are debating approaches to internal or local security, alternative 'solutions', find their way to insecure societies devastated by destructive conflicts. Often the ineffective formal security structures are replaced by informal structures set up, primarily, by civil society. In practice these new security structures emerge as civilian groupings that take on the duty to provide security for the population in a local area or region, they are most often called civil militias or vigilante groups.

By comparing the cases of local security organised by civil society in Indonesia and Nigeria, the aim of this essay is to show how civil security is established/maintained in weak states by informal security structures such as militias, neighbourhood-watch groups and vigilante groups. The question this essay will seek to answer is: are these civil militias and informal security structures a viable alternative to the state as a provider of security? The findings will be illustrated by describing cases of militiarism and alternative informal security structures in Indonesia and Nigeria. This comparison is chosen because Indonesia and Nigeria represent two cases with similar dynamics, but in different contexts, and therefore suggest that this phenomenon is not exclusive to Africa. Rather it indicates that militiarism is a social phenomenon with a possible global reach.

The importance of examining the developments of militiarism lies not only in the fact that groups which have turned their violent organisation into an often lucrative business, are widespread and seem to be on the rise. More pertinently this development represents a significant challenge to the authority of the State.[2] And secondly, as this essay will argue later, because of the internal dynamics and several important external factors, these militias imply potential dangers towards civil society itself.

The cases of Indonesia and Nigeria are chosen because both countries suffer from very similar problems related to civil militias. Additionally, security in relation to civil society in weak states is frustratingly under researched. The only cases in which academe has dealt with these issues, has been in relation to failed or collapsed states, that is, in states where the disaster has already happened. Indonesia and Nigeria have not failed yet. They are merely transition societies in a weak state structure on the treacherous path from decades of authoritarianism and rampant corruption to pluralistic democracy. In directing the analytical apparatus towards two states that have not yet failed, it is the ambition of this essay to shed light on dynamics which might lead to failure, or which, if sanctioned properly, could be diverted towards an alternative, less destructive ending.

The Human Rights Commission's report of 2003 states that, 'Human Security helps identify structures in the infrastructure of protection as well as to strengthen and improve it' (Ogata and Sen, 2003). Finding this both sympathetic, and necessary, a final ambition of this essay is to assist in identifying such structures and finally contribute with suggestions on how these developments should be tackled in order to lessen violence related to civil militias and civil security groups in weak states.

Conceptualising Civil Security in Weak States

Many adjectives have been applied in academic literature, to describe states that in different ways lack authority, capability or legitimacy. State weakness, naturally, must be measured along a continuum and these adjectives or labels generally signify various levels of state weakness. From being merely a weak state some states move to face total state failure and become Collapsed States (Zartman 1995).[3] Within the weak state discourse, terms like Shadow States (Reno 1998), Quasi-States (Jackson 1996), Inverted States (Forrest), and Felonious States (Bayart 1999) have also been used. Many of these concepts were initially applied to African states, but developments in former Yugoslavia, Russia and several Central Asian states as well as Indonesia and Colombia, make the terminology very applicable to non-African states too.

These entities have a number of characteristics in common. Generally they signify lack of legitimacy, poor judicial and legislative capabilities. They suffer from corruption and high levels of internal instability in forms of insurgencies and violent political or religious opposition. For two main reasons this chapter will use

Barry Buzan's definition of a weak state, as a state with relatively 'low socio-political cohesion' (Buzan 1991, p.97). The first reason is that the weak state discourse offers no clear analytical borders between the various concepts, and the level of statelessness or disintegration, neither does it provide an effective conceptual border between the different terms. Many such states are being 'criminalised' and are governed by 'warlord politics'. Most of them have traits of collapse, inversion and failure. The truth is that the degree of overlapping characteristics and flux that these concepts are subjected to makes it, for this study, analytically futile to consider their specificities apart from one-another. A second reason is that Nigeria and Indonesia, who are the subjects of analysis here, are not yet failed, or collapsed, states. They possess many of the characteristics of several of the above mentioned concepts and a further disintegration of the state is very likely. But as yet it has not happened, and the trend might be reversed towards state consolidation and greater stability. In other words, this chapter will not bind itself to the small differences of the particularistic concepts, but adopt Buzan's more general and flexible term.

In recent years the field of security studies has broadened from focusing exclusively on the security of the nation state (strategic studies) to become more inclusive and consider other forms of security (Snyder and Malik 1999; Tickner, 1996). One important development is that security studies has directed its focus towards the security of human beings. On a broad level the concept of human security indicates a wish to change focus from an: 'exclusive concern with the security of the state to a concern with the security of people' (Ogata and Sen, 2003). Although the concept of human security has a lot of valuable suggestions and observations it is still an underdeveloped section of the new security paradigm and as such the concept is too broad as an analytical tool when approaching the security of human beings in their societal context. Perhaps the most comprehensive analytical approach to this section of security analysis has been suggested by the so-called Copenhagen School of security (Buzan et al, 1998). The Copenhagen School follows up on Buzan's (1991) initial suggestion of dividing security into sectors. With regard to level of analysis of security in weak states, Barry Buzan argued that:

> viewed from within they [weak states] are anarchic, with different armed self-governing groups controlling their own territories and contesting central government, with each other, by force...Because of this it can be more appropriate to view security within very weak states in terms of their contending groups, organisations and individuals (Buzan, 1991, p.101).

Thus, I shall here follow Buzan's suggestion to 'look to individuals and sub-state units for the most meaningful security referents' (Buzan, 1991, p.101). This method is just as applicable when looking at the impact on the security of the groups themselves. More recently he has written with Wæver and de Vilde that:

> Both militias and mafias can serve their members as referent objects for military security. And when the state fails...militias, mafias, clans and gangs come to the

fore. Some still speak in the name of the state, but others become self-seeking and self-referencing security entities. (Buzan et al. 1998, p.54)

The aim is to analyse how both the state and human security are affected by the militiarisation of society. Accepting that the section of security studies dealing with human beings as referent objects of security is still a field which needs to be developed, I allow myself to draw from different approaches to security related to civil society in weak states. I will use the framework for analysis suggested by the Copenhagen School, but also use many of the assumptions and suggestions from Ogata and Sen's (2003) work on human security.

Regarding the concept of security, focus here is on threats derived from the lack of state capacity to protect citizens because of weak formal security structures. Thus, insecurities of civil society in weak states will derive from relatively high levels of crime causing fear from robbery, assault, fraud and damage to property. The fact that many weak states are also harrowed by internal conflict will increase insecurities of the civilian population dramatically, forcing them to flee or counter-mobilise.

Thus, the primary concern here, at least initially, is more 'basic' threats to the lives and livelihoods of people.

Federico Varese, in his work on the Russian Mafia, underlines that demand for protection alone is not sufficient to explain the spread of mafia-like organisations. It also requires 'a ready supply of people willing and able to carry out violent and protective duties' (Varese 2001, pp.246-247). To understand the social dynamics within these sub-state units, and the motivation behind actions of individuals active in violent militias, this study will utilise two theories of individual motivation for violent action.

The first is Ted Robert Gurr's theory of relative deprivation, which seeks to explain the 'psychological and social sources of the potential for collective violence' (Gurr 1970, pp.7-8). According to this theory, violence cannot be explained with rational logic. Using the frustration/aggression theory[4] as a basis for his theory, Gurr (1970) concludes that violence erupts when people feel deprived. He defines relative deprivation as:

> a perceived discrepancy between men's value expectations and their value capabilities. Value expectations are the goods and conditions of life to which people believe they are rightfully entitled. Value capabilities are the goods and conditions they think they are capable of attaining or maintaining. (Gurr, 1970, p.139)

In short, this means that groups experiencing relative deprivation resort to grievance-motivated violence as an attempt to change an intolerable status quo.

Paul Collier and Anke Hoeffler's theory of 'opportunity based violence' has often been considered a rival explanation to Gurr's theory. Their main proposition is that greed, rather than grievance, causes people to engage in violent conflict. Individual motivation in this theory is driven, mainly by an expectation of economic gain, stimulated by what Collier and Hoeffler call: the availability of 'lootable goods' (Collier and Hoeffler, 2001).

For this analysis I will broaden the analytical context by not focusing exclusively on material gains or deprivation. This analysis will add psychological dimensions like identity building and status restoration/building[5]. The psychology of group dynamics is important in this respect because: '...one's self-concept, or individual identity becomes in part defined by the group membership' (Fisher, 1990), and as John Burton notes:

> Empirical evidence suggests that a paramount need being satisfied by the violent is the need for recognition as an individual or group. Individuals in society have always employed whatever means are currently available to them to attain recognition and identity. (Burton 1997)

It is the assumption of this dissertation that security can be seen as a commodity, subject to the rules of demand and supply. Quoting economic historian Frederic Lane, Charles Tilly (1985) writes:

> Governments are in the business of selling protection...whether people want it or not...the very activity of producing and controlling violence, favoured monopoly because competition, within that realm generally raised costs...The production of violence...enjoyed large economies of scale. (Tilly, 1985, p.175)

Within the logic of the modern state system the 'market of security' is controlled and monopolised by the state, just as it monopolises violence (Weber, 1970). However, weak states have, for various reasons, lost the ability to maintain security for their populations and thereby lost the monopoly over the market. This failure has resulted in a liberalisation of the market of security and people in weak states must seek competent provision of security elsewhere and, as already mentioned, the alternative suppliers often emerge from within civil society. Federico Varese (2001) referring to the early birth of the Sicilian Mafia says:

> Protection did not undergo the customary process of centralization to become the monopoly of the state, but was available through autonomous suppliers. Autonomous suppliers of private protection started to offer their services to the then numerous property owners. This complex historical process gave rise to the Sicilian Mafia. (Varese, 2001, p.10)

Groups or organisations that today mount up to fill the security vacuum have different specialties – some appeal to certain ethnic groups or religious affiliations while others have focused their services on supporters of a particular political party. Common to all of them is that they need to be compensated for their services, thus, at the end of the day such providers are only relevant to people who can pay.

The following will outline some of the conceptual considerations that must be employed with regard to civil security in weak states. The object of research here is a civil militia that takes over the traditional state function of providing security. Such militias will be termed Civil Security Forces (CSF). The label signifies any civil grouping with the declared task of creating or maintaining security for a 'client'[6] regardless of the group's affiliation, *modi operandi* or previous alignments and tasks. The concept does not refer to a static situation, but rather to a period in a continuum along which a militia group develops from being a militia set up on public demand to the defense of a given 'cause'. Over time, as the group advance to a higher level of organisation, increased power and authority corrupts the 'cause' because of the possibilities of material gain offered by both civil society and political or corporate elites. The militia is now a CSF (see Table 5.1). It is more flexible and independent in choosing 'jobs' and *modi operandi*. However, operating in the grey-zone between public and private spheres, the organisation is still dependent on some degree of public consent, meaning that they still have to honour the legitimising 'cause' which once established them. Thus, CSFs are not just hired thugs, who jump from one side of a conflict to the other for increased profit. To label such groups mafias would be a simplification.

Table 5.1   The Militia Continuum

Public_____Private

'Ideological' Militia ---Civil Security Forces---Private Security Companies

CSFs have much resemblance with PSCs (Private Security Companies),[7] but are different in a few important ways. Firstly, PSCs are always corporately affiliated and regulated by law. Although CSFs may have corporate traits, they are different because of their 'ideological heritage' which provides for public legitimacy and support due to their 'altruistic' background. Furthermore, while PSCs hve a wide area of operation, most CSFs are operated by locals or fellow nationals, which again enhance legitimacy and provide the group with inside knowledge of local/regional customs.[8]

This way of categorisation means that we will not follow the 'separatist', 'religious' or 'ethnic' militia labels. The fact that a group is paid or rewarded in one form or another for a security task qualifies for analysis here, regardless of the groups' or the clients' declared affiliation or label. Although it is tempting to label these groups mafias or gangsters, their often political affiliation and their societal duties as extra-legal cops and security-providers wearing uniforms gives them a semi-official status which traditional mafias do not enjoy. The Nigerian militia, The Area Boys, which Gani calls a 'Criminal militia' (Gani, 2002), contrary to the Bakassi Boys, is a case of pure gangsterism. Calling them a militia only confuses the terminology, they are but big city hoodlums with no case or declared ideological objective. They have no legitimacy and that is the big difference between gangsters and CSFs. However, despite its social function, ideology for a CSF is not the prime-driver. It is mainly concerned with income generation and status restoration. Narratives of ideology, ethnic history or crime busting, for CSFs, only serve as a legitimising gateway to controversial private entrepreneurship in the business of violence.

The broad conception of civil militias makes a conceptual refinement imperative. Gani's very helpful work on militiarism as a social phenomenon suggests that Nigeria has three types of militia (criminal, ethnic and mercenarian) (Gani, 2002). This chapter will categorise differently and not attempt to establish borders between such types. The proposition here is, firstly, that such categorisation ignores important internal group dynamics and, secondly, that such groups are 'fluid' and their affiliations, objectives and *modi operandi* overlap to an extent that eventually obscures the above categorisations. Thus, in this essay we shall work with one type only, the CSF. They might be any or all of mercenarian, ethnic or criminal following Gani's typology (2002). Often the term loosely signifies an armed group, which is not part of the official state security force. Civil militias, thus, have been given many different labels and names according to their performance or affiliations. This method of categorisation though, ignores the in-group complexity of many such violent militias by reducing their 'members' to mindless troops of whatever label given, i.e. religious fanatics, separatists or gangsters. However, civil militias are not just the sum of their parts and such categorisation fails to identify one of the core dynamics in violent groups, namely the motivation that drives individuals to action. These dynamics, both external and internal, need to be understood if we wish to analyse the viability of civil militias as an alternative provider of security in weak states.

In the Human Rights Commission's report 2003, Sadako Ogata writes 'while the leaders of conflicts often come from the more prosperous parts of society, poverty can provide rich recruiting grounds for the 'foot soldiers' of violent engagements' (Ogata and Sen, 2002, p.7). Professor Clement Adibe put it this way 'poor people die – rich people sponsor them'.[9] This remark touches on a crucial fact that has to be treated carefully when analysing the organisation of civil militias, namely, the presence of, and distinction between, 'leaders' and 'foot soldiers'. This means that one cannot ascribe one ethnic, religious or economic agenda to a group. The truth is that a multitude of motivations and agendas co-exist in CSFs (and any other group subjected to simplistic external ascription and labeling). To assess this conceptual problem and explain the dynamics affecting the *modi operandi* of CSFs, I propose to label the individual violent actors according to their motivation. The outcome is three different types of motivated actors, defined by combinations of two variables, namely 'Personal capability to mobilise human and material resources.' and 'Inclination to follow perceived opportunities for personal gain in status or material wealth, despite normative controversy'. The two first motivations: *entrepreneurial* and *opportunistic* are opportunity based,[10] while the last: *deprived*, is grievance based.

- The *entrepreneurial* actor essentially figures in a power position in which he has control of both human and material resources with which he is able to greater or lesser extent to manipulate conflicts in a direction serving his personal benefits.
- Contrary to this the *deprived* actor has very little control. The agency distribution to this category will, thus, often derive from the lowest

echelons of a social hierarchy. A deprived actor will often be unemployed or for other reasons lack economic and social status. He joins the fight mainly due to frustration with the status quo (his personal position). This frustration may also stem from fear and insecurity.

- The *opportunist* differs from the deprived by being somehow more resourceful and ideologically flexible. He has the moral inclination to benefit personally from violent action, and grabs the possibility to earn a little extra when provided with the opportunity. His social status will often be low or middle. It might in fact be his social status he wants to improve.[11]

The Emergence of Militiarism in Nigeria and Indonesia: Background

Since the fall of Suharto and Abacha in 1998, collective violence has spread across the territories of Indonesia and Nigeria. It has struck both at the centre and in the periphery, from Medan Merdeka in Jakarta across the tourist areas of West Lombok to the isolated Kei islands in the Moluccan archipelago. In Nigeria violence has erupted from downtown Lagos and Ibadan in the south, across the Ariaria market in Aba, to Abuja and Kano in the North. Few provinces or states have been spared and violence has taken many forms: separatist attacks on army posts have been followed by state retaliation. Rioting crowds have been on the rampage in large cities and lynch mobs have been executing suspected criminals. Accusations of killings and torture of political, ethnic or religious minorities, by militia members and alleged army personnel, flourish. Muslim militias have threatened Jihad against Christian minorities, who have responded by mobilising against the Muslims.

When examining a phenomenon like collective violence, several factors need to be studied. For this chapter the focus will largely be on the violent actors. However, to understand them we must first examine the context of their actions. Studying actors alone will not suffice, as Donald Horowitz has claimed: '*Who* needs to be aligned with *when*' (Horowitz, 2001, p.150). Accordingly, this section will describe the historical context underlying the increasing militia violence of contemporary Nigeria and Indonesia.

The regimes of Suharto and Abacha are often characterised with words like corruption, cronyism, impunity and militarism. Constitutionally secured strong executive powers vested in the presidency left Suharto and Abacha relatively unchallenged by the political establishment, and the banning of opposition parties and newspapers and the arrest of political and intellectual critics silenced the few who stood up against the political elite. Suharto is often portrayed as a *Dalang*, a 'puppet master' controlling all the threads in an Indonesian 'powerplay'. Similarly, as noted by Nigeria specialist Karl Maier, Abacha ran the country 'as his personal fiefdom' (Maier, 2000, p.3). Both leaders were military generals and depended heavily on the support of the armed forces.[12] The military bureaucracy and the leading capitalists developed what David Potter (1994) calls a 'Pact of

Domination', which nurtured their common interests and 'drove forward late capitalism' (Potter, 1994).

Violence during the rule of Suharto and Abacha, respectively, was characterised by a particular pattern: that of a powerful state monopolising violence and directing it against its subjects. The targets were often political, ethnic or religious groups who had voiced opposition to the regime. In Indonesia the worst single incidents were the Tandjung Priok Incident in which probably more than 100 Muslim demonstrators were killed by government troops. The infamous Santa Cruz massacre in Dili, the capital of former East Timor, allegedly claimed the lives of more than 200 East Timorese. The Indonesian armed forces have also carried through various lengthy violent campaigns more or less covertly. The *Petrus Killings* refer to a campaign against urban criminals launched in the early eighties, by the Suharto government. So called 'death squads' killed thousands of known criminals at nighttime and left their bodies exposed on public places.[13] Other violent campaigns have generally been applied to areas subject to separatist sentiments such as former East Timor, Aceh and the easternmost province of Papua (formerly Irian Jaya). However, strategic details and figures from these campaigns are difficult to come by, and each separatist movement has its own figures of casualties and accusations of violent strategies, which are dismissed as subverting exaggerations by the central government.

In Nigeria the pattern is similar, although the country has a more consistent history of civilian inter-ethnic clashes, relative to modern Indonesia. Ethnic strife has been a sad factor of political history for decades (Diamond, 1988, pp.33-92). Clashes between the Arogbo Ijaw and the Ugbo Ilaje in Ondo State, the Yoruba and Fulani in Oyo, and the Ife–Modakeke conflict have claimed thousands of civilian lives. Many conflicts, such as the one between the Yoruba farmers and the Fulani herdsmen, started out as a dispute over economic interests.

As in Indonesia, state violence was characterised by clampdowns on political dissidents and ethnic minorities, when talking about the prospects for wealth accumulation in the political bureaucracy, the 'brutality of political conflict' was triggered by the incentives to 'control state power' (Diamond, 1988, p.67).

However, the above sketched pattern of structural violence committed by the state apparatus, or on behalf of the state, and directed against the civilian population seems to have changed over the past years. The trend of growing antagonism and collective violence is broadly characterised by *civilian* groupings targeting each other (Dijk, 2000; Elaigwu, 2002). In fact the role of the security forces has been sidelined to the point where they have been widely criticised for their passivity towards violent incidents. As already mentioned, this civilian violence is often organised in militias that operate differently from the traditional neighbourhood watch groups of Nigeria and Indonesia. As noted in a report by Human Rights Watch and Cleen, a 'new type of civil militia or vigilante group' has evolved after the fall of President Sani Abacha (HRW/Cleen, 2002).

Violent conflicts in Nigeria and Indonesia have often been labeled Low Intensity Conflict (LIC). LICs are 'normally low-tech, manpower-intensive, low-frequency conflicts' (Snyder and Malik, 1999, p.199), involving paramilitary strategies with localised armed clashes and civilian targets. In fact the LICs have been the most bloody conflicts since 1945 and when Martin van Creveld foresaw a 'transformation of war' (Creveld, 1991) he noted the following:

> Truth to say, what we are dealing with here is neither low-intensity nor some bastard offspring of war. Rather it is WARRE in the elemental Hobbesian sense of the word, by far the most important form of armed conflict in our time (Creveld, 1991)

Creveld's warning of Hobbesian anarchy has since been echoed in much scholarly work on contemporary conflict and much focus has been on the role of the state in those conflicts. Mary Kaldor (2002), realising that the 'transformation' was already taking place, wrote about the 'new wars' that they:

> arise in the context of the erosion of the autonomy of the state, and in some extreme cases, the disintegration of the state. In particular, they occur in the context of the erosion of the monopoly of legitimate organized violence (Kaldor, 2001, p.4).

Such erosion of the monopoly of legitimate organised violence is the centre of focus of this thesis. A trend that is, as the following chapters will show, very recogniseable in Nigeria, which has been said to be 'on the brink of failure' while Indonesia was recently called 'a failing state on a slippery slope towards disintegration' (Bostock 2002).

Like LICs, the new wars are fought by various small-armed groups such as 'paramilitary units, local warlords, criminal gangs, police forces, mercenary groups and also regular armies including breakaway units of regular armies' (Kaldor, 2002, p.8). However, the new wars primarily differ from 'earlier wars' because they are driven rather by 'identity politics' than ideological or 'geo-political goals'. Identity politics, as coined by Mary Kaldor (2002), means a 'claim to power on the basis of a political identity – be it national, clan, religious or linguistic (Kaldor, 2002, p.6). Furthermore, the financing of the new wars differs from old wars because many new wars have their own 'war economy', which, as has been suggested by several scholars, seem to sustain instability by giving combatants incentives to fight (Keen, 2000; Duffield, 2001). This brings us to the greed and grievance debate, which, as mentioned in the theoretical framework, is concerned with the question of whether greed or grievance is the primary motivating factor in violent conflicts. It should be noted that while Paul Collier, who initially started the 'greed school' argued that greed was the main motive-related driver in violent conflict, others like Berdal and Malone (2000) and Kivimäki and Thorning (2002) have suggested that both greed and grievance are at play in conflicts. It is not greed or grievance but greed *and* grievance.[14] It becomes obvious from reading news from Indonesia and Nigeria that economic incentives play an at least significant role in their domestic conflicts, and several scholars have also touched upon the subject (Chabal and Daloz, 1999; Elaigwu, 2002; Kristiansen, 2001; Lintner, 2003; Moore, 2001).

Accordingly, the following will focus primarily on the two factors of *economy* and *identity* in relation to the organisation, establishment and maintenance of civil security in weak states.[15] The conflicts in Nigeria and Indonesia are not necessarily new wars. Most incidents happen as isolated incidents and, as mentioned, one of the focal points of this essay is to expose a particular period in a continuum of violent conflict that might lead to the emergence of new wars in Nigeria and Indonesia. The term 'conflict', when applied to political violence, is generally used to describe a series of violent incidents involving two or more opposing groups that engage in violent activity. The Correlates of War project based at Uppsala University in Sweden defines 'intra-state war' as: 'Sustained combat between two armed forces within the territorial boundaries of a state that meets the violence threshold (1,000 battle-related fatalities per year, counting civilian as well as military deaths)'.[16] Thus, following this definition, regional conflicts in Indonesia like the Maluku conflict at its peak in 1999, the West Kalimantan conflict in 1996-97 and the current Aceh campaign, are wars. The important point here is that within the national boundaries of both Nigeria and Indonesia, the level of communal violence in periods rises to levels that, in terms of the intensity of violence that the population experience, resemble regular war situations.

The classic Hobbesian prophecy about society turning into violent anarchy if the state is not in control[17] is in many respects applicable to Indonesia and Nigeria. According to the observation of several scholars, the fall of Suharto and Abacha has created a power vacuum and much contemporary violence is thought to be related to the competition within society's elite to fill this vacuum (Elaigwu, 2002; Gani, 2002; Kristiansen, 2001; Lindsey, 2001). Additionally, this competition, in which the security forces take active part, combined with poor political performance, mean that a general distrust in the state institutions prevails (Aragon, 2001; Munir, 2001; Wessel, 2001). Having given a background to the elusive security of contemporary Indonesia and Nigeria, we shall now examine factors stimulating the escalation of violence in those countries.

A Free Market of Security: The Emergence of Informal Security Structures

Civil Society: Security in the Hands of the Public

Civil militias in the form of neighbourhood watch groups and local vigilante units are no strangers to either Nigerian or Indonesian society. Local security organisations have been widely used throughout the country as a supplement to official police forces since pre-colonial times. However, as mentioned, such organisations have changed their nature lately, and this section will look at some examples of modern militias in Nigeria and Indonesia.

One form of collective civil violence, which has not been given much attention by international media, and seems to be on the increase, is the lynching of suspected criminals (see: Bourchier, 1994, p.199; Dijk, 2001; Djalal, 2000; Lindsey, 2001, pp.292-295). Often when a burglar or suspected thief is spotted, the witness will shout 'thief' and start pursuing the alleged criminal. Very soon passers-by and residents will enter the scene and join the chase, and once the suspected thief is caught he will be punished on the spot, often with, collective beatings. A commonly used method of punishment is to pour petrol over the perpetrator and set him on fire. Kees van Dijk (2001) notes with regard to the widespread mob violence in Indonesia: 'judging from what is happening nowadays. Mob revenge is still very ugly. Whether such acts have not become even more gruesome is open to debate' (Dijk, 2001). An article from the Jakarta Post gives examples of six separate incidents of mob violence, in Jakarta, which in a week's time cost the lives of six alleged criminals:

> As in similar previous cases, the angry mobs, mostly made up of local residents who spotted the victims committing a crime, firstly severely beat the alleged criminals before one of them poured gasoline on the bodies of the dying men and set them on fire. Police were alerted only after the victims were already dead. (JP, 2001, p.3)

Lynching does not always target criminals, it often victimises people who have been wrongly suspected of criminal activity. This is exemplified in another article explaining how two men in the city of Bogor (Java) had a verbal fight on a public street. The fight turned physical and one started chasing the other: 'As they were running a man saw them and thought someone was chasing a thief, so he screamed 'Thief', residents then hunted the two disputants down and started beating them, ultimately killing them both' (JP, 2000, p.3). As can be concluded from Joshua Barker's (1999) research on local security in Bandung some of these extra-legal incidents of collective violence take place within the institutional framework of local security organisations in the *Siskamling* system (Sistem Keamanan Lingkungan – Neighbourhood Security System) (Barker, 1999). The Siskamling system has three components, firstly, the SATPAM and the HANSIP guards, who are respectively taking care of security at commercial buildings and in residential neighbourhoods. Whereas the two aforementioned civil forces are uniformed and low-waged workers, the Siskamling additionally incorporate the *Ronda*, a traditional system of neighbourhood security, which is a voluntary unpaid force, considered as a sort of community service. In practice the Ronda is a group of men patrolling and guarding their neighbourhood at nighttime, making sure that no suspicious individuals or strangers to the community are jeopardising communal safety (for elaborations see Barker, 1999). The police set up this system in 1980 because 'existing anti-crime strategies had failed and drastic measures should be taken to fight it' (Bourchier, 1994, p.183).

The lynchers often react within their own neighborhoods and their behaviour suggests that these extralegal killings are the results of frustration and grievance based violence. Lynchers do not rob the alleged criminals or attempt to make them pay fines or in other ways compensate for eventual property damage. Lynching should be considered primarily an act of self-protection carried out by a local community. The beatings and killings are a message to other criminals that they should not target this particular village. According to Ronald J. Fisher, individuals join groups to satisfy physical, psychological and social needs.

Furthermore, groups are chosen particularly due to 'similarity of opinions and attitudes with the "applicant"' (Fisher, 1990, p.60) and thus, groups are formed on the basis of shared identities. However, some of the violent incidents examined here indicate that shared history is not a must for mobilisation. Contrary to violence related to local community protection on a relatively organised level, the lynching also provides an example of collective violence where individuals with no prior common affiliations constitute the targeting group. This suggests that security work in the form of pacification of criminals is not only linked to territoriality as it is in the Siskamling system. It also works on a more general level, with targeter-group formation materialising spontaneously. This points to the possibility of a moral consensus in the society that vigilante justice is acceptable (this has also been argued by David Bourchier with regard to the general public acceptance of the Indonesian Petrus campaign, as already mentioned). The construction of an ad-hoc identity of the lynchers seems to be based on in-group perceptions of 'conformers to the law' vs. 'non-conformers' and 'locals' vs. 'strangers'. Santikarma (2003) writes with regard to lynching of thieves in Bali, that locals view 'outsiders' (meaning transmigrants from outside Bali) as an indirect threat to their livelihoods because they harm the Balinese culture. The 'outsiders' bring crime, violence and insecurity to Bali, which is economically dependent on its reputation in the tourism industry for being peaceful and harmonious. The Balinese culture is seen as a 'precious object that can be marked with a price tag and sold to tourists' (Santikarma, 2003, p.11). Therefore Balinese rally around cultural identities when organising to establish peace in their local communities. In that respect lynching, although seemingly unorganised, is organised in the sense that the act refers to an organised moral consensus, which triggers violence in particular situations.

Other incidents of militia violence suggest that some individuals join groups, which, on important accounts, do not match their social identities. For example, why do Papuans or East Timorese join much-hated pro-integration militias like Satgas Merah/Putih (SMP)? One interpretation is that the applicants are true Indonesian nationalists. Another is that they do it because the membership of a particular group represents an opportunity for personal gain. The example of SMP is interesting because the membership chosen is contrary to what one would expect. Let us take the case of Papua.[18] There is no doubt that antipathy towards the central government is widespread and strong,[19] so why would the Papuan SMP members join this nationalistic Indonesian force? There can be no doubt that the general public opinion would be against them. For the ones on the list, they were peasants and the rural areas outside transmigration settlements are populated exclusively by Papuans, likely to sanction such a membership. This suggests that group membership is not motivated by shared identity alone, but that individuals also join groups which are contrary to their social identity. There are several indications that controversial group membership is chosen because the particular group facilitates the practise of private enterprise drawing on the power and respect provided by powerful affiliations or symbols. Thus, much opportunistic violence is conducted by men motivated by the prospect of getting paid for their violent performance. They are usually termed *preman*[20] and have been used by political parties, the military, and other interest groups for decades (Bresnan, 1993; Eklöf, 1999; Ryter, 2001). The picture emerging from the compilation of recent literature mentioning the *provocateur* is that being a provocateur is a job like many others. He is paid or tributed in some way for urging fellow citizens, ethnics, and comrades to go on the rampage. The employer provides cash, or perhaps food, and sometimes the tools needed by the 'employee' to perform well in the given task:

> The man…who had received 20.000 rp, to take part in a demonstration, was ordered by a man in military uniform to throw stones, which the uniformed man also provided for him. Vehicles arrived providing bottles for petrol as well as alcoholic drinks to the rioters (Eklöf, 1999, p.199).

Stein Kristiansen's (2001) fieldwork from Lombok also reveals that economic incentives play a role in violent security groups. His study of a local group – Amphibi[21] reveals that the security business in West Lombok (as elsewhere) is big business. On the question of why a member joined the group he answers: 'because it makes me stronger. I feel safe, I have insurance for my motorbike and I can earn some money on security.'

In Nigeria the most prominent and well-documented example is The Bakassi Boys. This militia group was set up in late 1999 as a response to organised crime haunting the large Ariaria market in the town of Aba in Abia State. The Shoemakers Association in Ariaria established the first militia with the purpose of ridding the market of its high level of crime. After having hunted down and killed a large number of alleged criminals the group was established as a permanent institution with waged members. The Bakassi Boys' effectiveness in combating crime in Abia caused other states suffering from high levels of crime to inquire for their services (Harnischfeger, 2003; Ogwuda, 2001). Thus, the uniformed and often heavily armed Bakassi Boys were now patrolling the streets in several states. Their effectiveness in lowering the crime level in their areas of operation initially provided them with widespread public support. However, human rights groups and some public figures have been critical of their operations. They have been accused of summary executions, arbitrary arrests and detentions and torturing their detainees. Many reports suggest that the Bakassi Boys often punish their suspects themselves instead of handing them over to the police authority, which was the initial agreement when the militia was legally inaugurated in Anambra State in August 2000 (HRW/Cleen, 2001). Furthermore, the Bakassi Boys are 'taking up all kinds of civil cases landlord/tenant rifts and default in contractual obligation' (Nwanguma, 1999). They are also accused of being tools of local political elites as a sort of 'private army' for governors and other high-ranking officials, who in return for the militia's allegiance protect members from prosecution by police forces. Several cases documented by HRW and Cleen (2002) suggest that the Bakassi Boys have been used to target political opponents, but also that they function as privately hired thugs for businesses and ordinary citizens (Harnischfeger, 2003; HRW/Cleen, 2002; Nwabuisi, 2002). It is a fact that this CSF enjoys widespread support among the public in areas with much violent crime because the official police forces have proven themselves unable to maintain security for the civil population (Ekeh, 2002; Faris, 2002; Isaacs, 2002). However, it has become increasingly clear that the Bakassi Boys are not just a local vigilante group. The extent of their organisation is difficult to measure but it seems that the group has become more a 'brand' of a militia service, which will provide extralegal and often violent services to individuals or organisations that are willing to pay an appropriate compensation either in terms of cash, material goods or political protection.

The State: Orchestrating Violence

Although the main actors in contemporary conflicts seem to come from civil society, the state often plays a very significant part in the dynamics of violence. Often, state institutions or high-ranking employees have been responsible for instrumentalising conflicts for personal benefit. This has been done covertly through death-squads and secret operations, and publicly through propaganda pointing out scapegoats, and creating what Horowitz (2001) calls a social approval of violence',[22] legitimising violent civil sanctions against the group targeted.

Referring to the ethnic violence in Nigeria, Larry Diamond (1988) confirms how the elite has used ethnic identities to mobilise political forces for their own benefit. The politicians, he writes: '...as they appealed relentlessly to ethnic consciousness...inflamed group suspicion and fear to the point where ethnic mobilisation assumed an explosive momentum of its own' (Diamond 1988, p.64). Richard Carver (1997) supports this in saying that: '...successive governments have also exploited ethnic rivalries for political and repressive purposes, as well as actively instigating ethnic or religious violence on occasions' (Carver 1997).

The Bakassi Boys were called upon by the governor in Anambra state to re-establish security for the traders of the largest market in Nigeria in the town of Onitsha. However, many have indicated that it is the security of the governor, rather than the traders, that the groups are meant to cater for. When the militia was banned by the central government the governor changed the name of the Bakassi Boys to Anambra State Vigilante Services, making them official. And when traders who wanted to finance the Bakassi Boys as an independent group complained about the 'official' take-over the governor arrested several of the traders and detained them for a week (Harnischfeger, 2003).

Nils Bubandt's (2001) work on the Maluku conflict in Indonesia supports these claims (Bubandt, 2001). Bubandt argues that the substantial benefits for the regents within the *Regional Autonomy Plan*[23] increased local political competition prompting politicians to 're-invent' local traditions and culture within the context of violence, to further their own political ends. He describes how the two traditional sultanates of, respectively, Tidore[24] and Ternate were recently 'reconstructed' by the local political elite, when the 48th Sultan of Ternate, Muddafar Syah, revived his traditional palace guard to keep public order, in a situation where 'military and police sanctioned order had virtually collapsed'. Syah's political rival, the Regent of Central Halmahera, on the island of Tidore,

Bahar Andili, responded by inaugurating a new sultan of Tidore and a decision to rebuild the sultanate palace in Tidore, with a newly recruited palace guard:

> the Sultan of Tidore provided a convenient 'traditional' rallying point against Ternate within the context of the conflict and the political struggle for the spoils of decentralization, because the title appealed to communal sentiments and notions of identity in a way that a political elected figure could never do. (Bubandt 2001, p.8)

Making crucial distinction easy the Tidore guards wore white headbands, as opposed to the yellow colours of the Ternate followers. Thus two easily recognisable antagonistic groups were mobilised for the protection of traditional culture: Andili and Syah used cultural models and shared history from the traditions of respective sultanates, to facilitate and legitimise violence, which in turn was intended to strengthen their personal political positions. A statement by Muddafar Syah indicates very clearly the connection between instrumentalised culture and the failing state system:

> The Sultan preserves local tradition. He protects our original culture. We still don't know what our national values are. [The state philosophy of] Pancasila is equally unclear and therefore does not perform a function. Therefore it is my principle to uphold the traditional values of the local region (Bubandt, 2001, p.9).

As for the security forces, it seems to become increasingly clear that they have found their own place in the instability of Nigeria and Indonesia. The earlier mentioned passivity or partiality is often subjected to a selective process; if it is beneficial for the troops to interfere, they will. If not, their role is often similar to that of bystanders to violent incidents.

Numerous stories testify to police or military personnel providing armed support to one group in a conflict if not directly arming or employing this side (Aditjondro, 2001; Bourchier, 1994; Eklöf, 1999; Moore, 2001). The Indonesian weekly *Tempo* writes about the Special Forces, *Kopassus*:

> Kopassus lost its way when...the red berets changed from being a tool of the state to being a tool of power...the elite unit's expertise...was no longer used against enemies of the state but against rivals for power. (Tempo, 2002)

The article on Kopassus goes further by stating that this lack of morale is not confined to Kopassus alone, but 'nearly all institutions in this republic', and the troops should not be blamed exclusively, because it is 'the result of a collective failing of the nation' (Tempo, 2002).

The situation appearing from these dynamics is that of a failed state and a vulnerable public set against a massive patchwork of small locally or regionally powerful patrons, be they corporate CEOs, local politicians, police chiefs or army unit leaders. In this situation the public can rely on no one but their local community or private security collectives, such as militias, for security, and, even in these cases, many militias get corrupted, leaving the public where they started and ultimately enhancing the security vacuum.

The Organisation of Public Security: Identity Politics, Fear and Opportunity

Like most CSFs the Bakassi Boys emerged as a response to an intolerable situation. Such groups initially consist of mainly frustrated individuals willing to change the (their) situation. Gani writes: 'their memberships are motivated by ethnic, religious, primordial or ideological consciousness' (Gani, 2002, p.15). I dare to suggest that many young men also join these groups because they constitute not only a source of income generation, but also a possibility for identity change. Cash or material benefits are not the only possibilities for personal gain; an interview with a member of the out-lawed Papuan militia, Satgas Papua, revealed the following profile: The young man was 24 years old. He had dropped out of school because he had to work as a fisherman to assist his father in providing for the household costs (he was a bachelor living with his parents). However, lately there had not been enough work, so he considered himself unemployed. He had joined the Satgas Papua because there was not much else to do, and he felt that he was doing something good in his work for the militia. He had received basic training in martial arts and weapon-use in a secret OPM camp.[25] A procedure every member had to go through. When asked how he benefited from his engagement with the militia, he replied that the work was unpaid, but that the members were given tips, sometimes cash, sometimes food, by residents and shops in the area where they upheld security (SP1, 2001).

In July 2001 I passed a small shelter on a main street in a commercial area on Batam.[26] The shelter was covered with flags displaying a red-eyed bull, the logo of the *PDI-P*.[27] A sign read *Pos Barisan Banteng*[28] and around the shelter 10-15 boys were loitering about, some wearing the red bull t-shirts of the party. From inside loud rock music was playing and a marihuana-butt was circulating among the youngsters. When I asked them what their task was, one said proudly: 'we are taking care of *Keamanan*' (peace/security). The Barisan Banteng boys were as teenagers in most groups are: playing it tough, mocking and hitting each other and challenging passers by with minor insults. This was more than a youth club for them. Besides a place to hang out, the shelter provided a symbol for them, uniting them against everybody outside their collective. They were cool. They were 'taking care of security'.

My point with these two anecdotes is to introduce another possibility for gain from membership of a violent group, which is not material. The identity of these boys was very much associated with their status as 'members', 'taking care of security'. This identity is probably an alternative to an 'unemployed-identity' or a 'bus-ticket-collector-identity'. No wonder that being in a security group is more appealing for many young men. This relation is very much in accord with the theoretical statements on identity and group-membership by Burton (1997) and Fisher (1990) in which they emphasise the importance of an identity, which is recognised and feels a sense of belonging to a group. These views are substantiated by Stein Kristiansen's (2001) research in Lombok and Yogjakarta, he writes: 'members use their organisation's uniforms and symbols for individual identity strengthening...and creating respect and fear in other milieus' (Kristiansen,

2001, p.15). Joshua Barker (1999) also notes the pride of group belonging when referring to his visit to the house of a SATPAM guard:

> his certificate of graduation from the one-month SATPAM course was prominently displayed on the wall. When I pointed it out he took it down and proudly showed me the picture of himself on it and the signature of the supervising police official. (Barker, 1999, p.124)

Also Laskar Jihad Fighters who join the militia to get a respected identity as defenders of Islam will be categorised as opportunists. Many are said to give up material goods to join the honourable fight against Christians.[29]

As has been noted here, many members of violent groups are able to sustain themselves with the tributes they get from their 'work' as 'peacekeepers' or 'watchmen' and a significant factor motivating applicants to violent groups is the potential income from a particular affiliation.

However, the strong identity a member gets from being in a violent group, also has significance in motivating both the initial membership and subsequent acts of violence. As Fisher (1990) and Klapp (1972) note, the members are likely to compete with *out groups*, and from this competition aggression is likely to grow. On top of that, groups also serve as a filter against moral constraints, stimulating *groupthink* and ultimately legitimising violent acts.

As mentioned the escalating violence and the continued failure of the security apparatus to provide security forces civil society to mobilise in order to provide security for themselves. In fact they have on several occasions even been encouraged to do so by the state admitting its incapability of maintaining security. The security forces lost grip on their duties and: '[widespread] corruption and dishonesty...[was] endangering the already low public confidence' (Akosah-Sarpong, 2001). Thus, the 'militiarism' of post-Suharto Indonesia and the 'militianisation of Africa's war' (Ero, 2000) stems from the failure of the state to provide security. Y.J. Gani claims that the rise of militias, either from the public or private realm, has to do with the failure of the state 'to cope with pressures and demands from the society' (Gani, 2002, p.10) and such vigilantism 'was filling a [security] vacuum' (Ekeh, 2002). In the same line Comfort Ero writes that the response of frustrated populations:

> is to search for security from outside the formal security structures of the state. For the ordinary citizen, creating a defence mechanism against insecurity has become a necessity and not an option. Often, the answer has been to create private self-defence units. (Ero, 2002)

The 'Hobbesian treaty' with the state[30] promising to provide security has been breached, and security is now in the hands of the public. The emergence of a security vacuum has caused what Robert Cribb has called social panic (Cribb, 2000). The effect is clear; the Indonesian Muslim militia Laskar Jihad, for instance, repeatedly referred to its task as being to provide security for the Muslims, as long as the state did not manage to do so (Fealy, 2001, pp.28-29;

Noorhadi, 2002). The answer to the lack of security is clear: simultaneously, neighbourhoods from Sumatra to Papua see the emergence of watch-groups, and private security groups have mushroomed in the wake of the New Order collapse while in Nigeria the Bakassi Boys have emerged as a response to an intolerable situation.

The Privatisation of Security and the Consequences for National and Human Security

Dynamics of Contemporary Militiarism

It has so far been indicated that CSFs initially consist of mainly frustrated individuals willing to change the (their) situation. They furthermore enjoy widespread public support (at this stage) and seem in many cases to be more effective in combating crime than official security forces. However, the establishment of many such groups has a dangerous side effect, which is stimulated by the failure of the state to provide economic security and development. Militias tend to transform, over time, into security businesses, where 'security jobs' are paid in cash or material goods. The above mentioned examples of politicians taking CSFs in as their own private army is a clear indication that when militias reach a certain level of organisation, even though they started out with 'pure' intentions, they are prone to corruption and political/economic instrumentalism. This process of *polluting* of the cause seems to be a common development at the CSF-stage of a criminalisation process. The HRW/Cleen report (2002) mentions 'authentic Bakassi' who still honour their 'cause', without a wide scope of extra-legal activities on the side, and 'fake Bakassi' who have been involved in many violent incidents not related to their initial 'cause' (HRW/Cleen, 2002). Following the logic of the militia continuum, the 'authentic Bakassi' is simply positioned closer to the public/ideological end than the 'fake Bakassi'.

The case of the Bakassi Boys, which has been treated in this chapter, provides a good example of this development. Initially they 'were hailed as heroes' as they fought the crime of Aba market. Eventually, as their organisation grew, their operations spread to other states, and they started doing various jobs for various clients. The Bakassi Boys reached a level of strength where they would fight official police forces. Their popularity in the eyes of the public has faded a bit, but most people still think they should be there, because they manage to maintain security, where the police have failed.

As mentioned earlier membership of CSFs or militias in general might be partly motivated by personal opportunity beyond material desires. Opponents of the greed interpretation of violent mobilisation often claim that 'greed' or opportunity based violence is essentially founded in frustration; 'Groups may out of frustration take violent route to demand appropriate share of the scarce...resources...' (Elaigwu, 2002, p.11). This might be true when the interpretation is applied to rebel groups.[31] However this argument is only applicable to foot soldiers of violent groups. The argument disregards the fact that many very resourceful individuals also instigate violence, if not directly then indirectly through orders. Both local and national politicians, high ranking military officers and corporate leaders have significant influence on the dynamics in many low-intensity conflicts involving civil militias in general, and CSFs in particular, in weak states. In many civil militias frustration has been replaced by opportunism as ideology and loyalty to the cause perish in the face of market capitalist priorities.[32]

The *referent object* of this kind of militia is first and foremost the survival of its organization.[33] Although the security of the traders in the Abia market is a high priority for the Bakassi Boys, it is only so because it is crucial to continued public support, and thus indirectly crucial to the survival of the Bakassi Boys as a business. Another important factor influencing the dynamics of militia violence is that of inter-group rivalry. Perceived threats towards established CSFs may come from rival groups, who wish to compete over clients in a given area. This might trigger a dangerous escalatory spiral of inter-group violence. As an interviewed APC militia member said: 'Because there is OPC there must be APC...If there is only OPC, who will defend us?' (Singer, 2001). These dynamics are described by the concept of *auto-defence*:

> Wherein individuals and groups, given easy access to light weapons and the absence of security provided by the government, have taken law into their own hands. This often escalates beyond 'defense' and takes on militias with their own agenda. (Kivimäki et al., 1998)

Threats to such militias may also be perceived to come from official police forces. In the case of an effective police reform in Nigeria, the legitimacy of the Bakassi Boys will be challenged, and they would thus have an interest in discrediting the police forces. In areas where these militias are firmly consolidated the official forces might find getting the 'market back' difficult.[34]

The increased power of the militias also has a dangerous residual effect: as civil militias' legitimacy grows, the legitimacy of state forces declines, paving the way for further dilution of state authority.

In conclusion, civil society is a great risk of being hijacked by the dynamics of the security vacuum, meaning that civilians in organised militias are vulnerable to instrumentalist exploitation from the political, corporate or military elite .[35] For the general public this means that state authority is further diluted and security will only be provided to those who, in one way or another, contribute to the continued power position of the militias.

The Paradox of the Security Business

A pertinent question still needs answering: how does the emergence of CSFs affect the state? To answer that question we should take note of Barry Buzan's question on whether different forms of domestic threats to weak states in fact are threats to the state or merely threats to the government or ruling elite (Buzan, 1991). When we analyse the nature of CSFs it becomes clear that this type of civil militia indeed does pose a threat to the state, and not only the sitting government. Because rebel groups, military coups and ethnic militias often are driven by demands for policy, leadership or ideological change, they are more threatening to the leaders, governance structures and values of the government. Perhaps with the exception of separatist movements, they do not pose a direct threat to the idea of the state. The case of CSFs is a different matter. They have no ideological goal fitting into the framework of state governance. CSFs are in essence entrepreneurial entities with semi-official traits and capitalist objectives, which in reality feed on not only weakening governance but also the weakness of the very state structure. By usurping a key state function such as providing security for citizens, they lay claim to the bulk of state legitimacy. Parasitically CSFs feed on the weak state, and as they suck the strength out of the state they themselves gain in influence and authority. Their function is not different from PSCs, but they might still be able to gain some level of popular support. They are the materialisation of what Bayart (1999) called. 'a noxious cocktail of commerce and violence' (Bayart 1999, p.xiv). CSFs do not offer an alternative to weak governance. They offer an alternative to the state structure – an increasing privatisation of civil security. At the extreme end of this development, where general security is in the hands of CSFs, there will be no legitimate state and thus no citizens, only clients.

Conclusion

The popularity of the Bakassi Boys among the broad public speaks for itself, and advocates for civil militias will say that CSFs actually are successful in providing security in areas where the police have failed. A centralised government is no guarantee against criminalisation and corruption and, yes, state forces are also corrupt and unprofessional in most weak states. However, these arguments ignore the factors of legitimacy and accountability, which are imperatives in any force maintaining law and order. In fact the Bakassi Boys do not maintain law and order, they maintain security for their clients. They satisfy the demand of the market as simple service-providers. The situation for citizens in the privatised areas of the CSFs is similar to those of Reno's warlord state '...the inhabitants do not enjoy security by right of membership in a state. Security is coincidental; it is reliant on the venture's profitability...' (Reno 1998).

Privatisation of security and violence is not a new thing, but the corporate PMCs and PSCs that we know are products of corporate speculation in market demand. The worrying thing about CSFs is that they originate from civil society itself, and thus have an unlimited source of manpower available. Another problem is that in many weak states there is easy access to light arms, and as CSFs accumulate power vis-à-vis a weakening state, they will increasingly be able to physically threaten the state by challenging official forces. Territories ruled by militias and paramilitary groups might prove extremely difficult to regain for a weak state; the Colombian rebel organisation FARC started out as a protection militia and now controls large regions in Colombia.

The perhaps biggest problem of CSFs is that while it is their main duty to provide and maintain security, this task at the same time is directly in contradiction to their own survival. Since security, or rather insecurity, is their livelihood, they have a clear interest in maintaining instability to justify their continued employment. This paradox, in its most extreme consequence, will lead to a free market of violence, where different 'businesses' of violence, rather than security, will compete over the markets of insecure citizens: 'As small scale violence multiplies…state armies will continue to shrink, being gradually replaced by a booming private security business as in west Africa' (Kaplan, 1994, p.74).

This chapter has proposed a new way of labeling civil militias and suggests that militias engaged in security tasks in weak states are likely to mutate from their original task and become a serious threat to the civilian population *and* the state. Nevertheless, the idea of civil militias should not be discarded. It has often been said that to get weak states back on their feet, development should be focused on building civilian institutions. The despotism of the past has proved that the state cannot go it alone. However, the dynamics we are seeing now are showing us that civil society cannot go it alone either. The conclusion is that both parties should work together to maintain or establish a secure environment for the populace in a given nation. An effective security sector reform might very well incorporate large sections of civil society, but civilian law-enforcers need to be accountable to someone other than themselves or a local strongman.

Notes

[1]   Weak states may use civil militias overtly to support or substitute police forces in areas of instability, while covertly civil forces may be used as death squads or as defenders of the government (rather than the state). Non-statutory forces are commonly termed civil militias. They can have various agendas and affiliations and may be linked to separatist groups, political parties, religious organisations, military factions or multinational corporations. They might be neighbourhood watch groups or vigilante groups, and some might perform several of these tasks and adhere to several affiliations.

[2]   This chapter will look at the possible implications of civil militias on state security as defined by Buzan (1991).

[3]   I should note here that Zartman's concept of collapsed state is very applicable to and will be considered in, this analysis. Zartman emphasises the dilution of domestic security control by the state: 'It [state collapse] refers to a situation where the structure, authority (legitimate power), law and political order have fallen apart and must be reconstituted in some form, old or new…it is not necessarily anarchy…it is the collapse of old orders, notably the state, that brings about the retreat to ethnic nationalism as the residual, viable identity' (Zartman, 1999, p.1). I have not used Zartman's term in general because I find Buzan's 'weak state' definition less exclusive, and more applicable for this analysis. I also recognise that many traits signifying the other state concepts (shadow, inverted, quasi) may be included in the weak state term.

[4]   The basic proposition of this theory, developed by Dollard and Doob in 1939, is that frustration always leads to aggression, and that aggression is always the result of frustration.

5   This analytical broadening is inspired by Stein Kristiansen's fieldwork from Lombok and Yogjakarta (in Indonesia), in which he concludes that membership of violent security groups is motivated by economic gains together with personal psychological gains in the shape of 'identity creation'. The argument is that many unemployed youngsters find a reward in the identity attached to membership of a violent group. (Kristiansen, 2001).

6   It may be an ethnic group, a mining company, the population of a given area or followers of a religious observation or political party.

7   For a brief introduction to PSCs see: Vines, A. (2000) 'Mercenaries, Human Rights and Legality', *Mercenaries: An African Security Dilemma*, Abdel-Fatau Musah and J. 'Kayode Fayemi. (Eds.) London: Pluto Press, pp. 183-97.

8   *Local* should be seen as opposed to *foreign*, which is often the case with PSC personnel. It is not local in the strict sense. Quite on the contrary the mobility of CSFs is what separates them from vigilante forces (see Stephen Akiga's comment in HRW/Cleen, 2001, p.39). It may be argued though, that a CSF might eventually become a PSC, when its power-base gets consolidated and its organisation reaches a recognised level of professionalism.

9   Professor Adibe's comments were delivered at his speech at a Danish Foreign Ministry conference on terrorism and development aid in Copenhagen in September 2003.

10 The distinction between opportunist and entrepreneur is relevant in relation to peace-building, because the two actors, although both essentially motivated by opportunity, have to be approached differently. They have different resources and therefore follow different opportunity structures. In short, whereas the unemployed plantation worker (opportunist) might be discouraged from acts of violence by being provided with a minimum waged job, the business tycoon (entrepreneur) would hardly be satisfied with the same offer. In reality their relationship will often be that the entrepreneur hires the opportunist for a 'job' which, if successfully carried out, will result in some sort of gain to the entrepreneur. This also means that the entrepreneur, most often, commits violent acts indirectly, by arranging the incidents and having an opportunist commit the act.

11 The typology is simple in construction and should not demand further explanation except, perhaps, for the fact that there is no type describing the combination of High – 'Personal capability to mobilise human and material resources', and Low – 'Inclination to follow perceived opportunities for personal gain in status or material wealth, despite normative controversy'. My exclusion of this category is not to suggest that an individual featuring this combination is an empirical impossibility, but merely because this combination is problematic in several ways. A combination of personal power and low inclination for following opportunities for increase of personal gains could be called 'idealist'. The problem with this construction is that true 'idealists' are difficult to locate, because almost all violent actors would label themselves as 'idealists'. People tend to depict their own engagement in a conflict as an altruistic reaction to injustice, rather than admitting that they kill and loot because they are paid for it. I will in this regard lean towards Collier and Hoeffler's (1999) claim that idealists don't exist. Whether idealism or altruism is an empirical fact is not so much the cause of exclusion, as the fact that it is too problematic to rely on such a construction.

12 Although Suharto, towards the end of his rule, started to meet political demands of the increasingly strengthened Islamic community (Cribb, R. and C. Brown. *Modern Indonesia – a History since 1945*. London: Longman, 1995). However, today, in both Nigeria and Indonesia, the military is still very influential in politics. Thus, Obasanjo's civilian rule was seen by many as 'old wine in new bottles' (Momoh, A. and P-S. Thovoethin (2001) 'An Overview of the 1998-1999 Democratisation Process in Nigeria', *Development Policy Management Network Bulletin* XIII.No. 3, pp. 4-9). In

Indonesia former President Megawati passed on increased powers to the military after the terrrorist attack in Bali in 2002. How new President Susilo Bambang Yudhoyono will perform remains to be seen.

¹³ Petrus is short for Penembakan Misterius (mysterious killers). This particular campaign has been treated by Justus v Kroef (1985), 'Petrus: Patterns of prophylactic murder in Indonesia', *Asian Survey*, vol. 25 no.7. And by Robert Cribb (2000), and David Bourchier (1994).

¹⁴ It should be noted that while Paul Collier, who initially started the 'greed school', argued that greed was the main motive-related driver in violent conflict, others like Keen (2001), Kivimäki (1998) and Duffield (2001) have suggested that both greed and grievance are at play in conflicts. It is not greed or grievance but greed *and* grievance.

¹⁵ Mary Kaldor also mentions globalisation as an important factor shaping the new wars. But, as mentioned in the delimitations, this thesis is primarily concerned with a period in a continuum where insecurity and conflict are still localised and less transnational. Thus, although globalisation is also an influential factor at this level, it will, for the sake of brevity be left for others to explore.

¹⁶ COW. Dataset for the Correlates of War Project. Dataset. Uppsala Univsersitet/ Department of Peace and Conflict Research. Available:
http://www.pcr.uu.se/research/UCDP/conflict_dataset_catalog/COW.htm#intra.

¹⁷ Hobbes argued that the legitimacy of the state lies in its ability, as the highest authority, to maintain stability and prevent anarchy in society (Curley, 1994, pp.viii-xlvii)...during the time men live without a common power to keep them All in awe, they are in that condition which is called war, and such a war is of every man against every man' Curley, 1994, p.74.) Thus, if the state fails in maintaining its authority, violent anarchy will take over.

¹⁸ The human rights Institute of Papua (ELSHAM) sent out a press release claiming that a suspected list of SMP members enrolled by the armed forces was in their possession (see Timberlake, 2002).

¹⁹ I have visited the province three times and spent, altogether, three months there, conducting dozens of interviews, and I never met one single Papuan who was positive towards the Indonesian regime. Quite on the contrary I have had Papuans approaching me on the street and expressing their frustration, even though I was a stranger. On one occasion a man asked me to deliver his testimony to Amnesty International. On another, a middle-aged man quickly approached me saying; 'I hope you enjoy your stay in West Papua and that when you return to your home country you will support our independence', these incidents happened in 1996 and 1999 respectively.

²⁰ Often a provocateur is also used. In reality the provocateur is a preman with the special task of inciting riots or fuelling the fire in a tense situation, because his 'master' (the entrepreneur) has an interest in sustaining or escalating a particular conflict situation. Both terms will be used when appropriate.

²¹ The largest 'self security group' (Pam Swakarsa) in Lombok, est. 1998 by Haji Sibawahi. 'The organisation claims more than 700,000 registered members ... The ideological basis is twofold: Pancasila (Indonesia's national slogan) and Islam' (Kristiansen, 2001, p.9).

²² 'Social approval of violence means that superiors agree with the rioters that the target group has committed something like a collective offence. Justification then attaches easily' (Horowitz, 2001, p.530).

²³ 'District governments are thereby given the authority to negotiate and grant business contracts within areas such as mining, logging and fishing – a very lucrative prospect for the leaders of resource-rich districts in Outer Indonesia. In addition... 80 per cent of mining, timber and fishery revenue; 15 per cent of oil revenues; 90 per cent of real

estate taxes and 30 per cent of revenues from natural gas should remain in the hands of the regional government' (Bubandt 2001, p.7)

[24] 'Unlike the Sultanate of Ternate, the Tidore Sultanate had been all but defunct since...1967' (Bubandt 2001, p.7).

[25] OPM (Operasi Papua Merdeka) is the armed wing of the independence movement in Papua.

[26] Small Indonesian island off the cost of Singapore, in the province of Riau.

[27] Partai Demokrasi Indonesia Perjuangan (The Indonesian Democratic Party of Struggle) the party of president Megawati Sukarnoputri.

[28] Bulls Front Post – referring to the party's logo, a red bull.

[29] LJ1. Interview with Laskar Jihad Fighter, by Timo Kivimäki. Conducted within the framework of *Indonesian Conflict Studies Network*, 2000.

[30] According to Hobbes, the state and the public have a contract relationship in which the state promises to provide security in return for taxes and compliance to the law (Curley 1994).

[31] As done by both Gurr (1970) and Collier and Hoefller (2001).

[32] This is not to say that all ideology can be traded for material or identity improvements. It suggest that individuals still dedicated to the cause are likely to leave the sprouting militia (perhaps to join genuinely ideological militia), but indeed also that some individuals will be satisfied with the gains won from membership of a militia.

[33] The ousting of OTA by the Bakassi Boys provide a good example of one group taking over the market of another that has lost legitimacy in the eyes of the public.

[34] The Bakassi Boys have defied or directly clashed with police on several occasions (Faris, 2002; HRW/Cleen, 2002, p.37).

[35] It should be noted that the Bakassi Boys came to prominence just when 'the balance of power between federal and state governments shifted'. In reality 'increased revenue has been distributed to state and local government levels. Political posts, with the opportunities of self-enrichments and patronage that they represent, became more highly prized and vigourously defended' (HRW/Cleen, 2002, p.8). The report further notes that the Bakassi Boys have acted with badges portraying the Anambra state governor and referring to 'government orders' when arresting people (HRW/Cleen, 2002, p.11).

References

Aditjondro, G. (2001), 'Guns, Pamphlets and Handie-talkies', I. Wessel and G. Wimhöfer (eds), *Violence in Indonesia*, Hamburg, Abera Verlag, pp. 100-128.

Akosah-Sarpong, K. (2002), *Law, Order and Vigilantes in Nigeria*, Federations 2, No. 4 June/July.

Aragon, L. (2001), 'Communal Violence in Poso, Central Sulawesi', *Indonesia* (72), pp. 45-79.

Barker, J. (1999), 'Surveillance and Territoriality in Bandung', V. L. Rafael (ed), *Figures of Criminality in Indonesia, the Philippines, and Colonial Vietnam*, Ithaca, NY, Cornell Southeast Asia Program Publications. No. 25, pp. 95-127.

Bayart, J. F. ed. (1999), *The Criminalisation of the State in Africa*, London: James Currey Publications.

Berdal, M. and Malone, D. (eds) (2000), *Greed and Grievance: Economic Agendas in Civil Wars*, London: Lynne Rienner.

Bostock, I. (2002), 'Indonesia: Getting it right', *The Age*, Melbourne.

Bourchier, D. (1994), 'Crime, Law and State authority in Indonesia', *State and Civil Society in Indonesia*, A. Budiman. Clayton, Victoria, Monash University, Centre of Southeast Asian Studies: pp.177-212.

Bresnan, J. (1993), *Managing Indonesia: The Modern Political Economy*, New York: Columbia University Press.

Bubandt, N. (2001), 'Decentralisation, Conflict and the New politics of Tradition in North Maluku', Conference on Governance Identity and Conflict in Indonesia, Nordic Institute of Asian Studies, Copenhagen.

Burton, J. W. (1997), *Violence Explained: The Sources of Conflict, Violence and Crime and their Prevention*, University Press, New York: Manchester

Buzan, B. (1991), *People, States and Fear: An Agenda for International Security Studies in the Post-Cold War Era*, Hertfordshire: Simon and Schuster International Group.

Buzan, B., O. Wæver, et al. (1998), *Security: A New Framework for Analysis*, Boulder, Colorado: Lynne Rienner Publishers Inc.

Carver, R. (1997), 'Deadly Marionettes: State sponsored violence in Africa', *Article 19*: October: http://www.article19.org/docimages/477.htm.

Chabal, P. and J-P. Daloz (1999), *Africa Works: Disorder as Political Instrument*, Indiana University Press.

Collier, P. and A. Hoeffler (1999), 'Justice-Seeking and Loot-Seeking in Civil Wars', Washington DC: Worldbank paper, Worldbank, 1999.

Collier, P. and A. Hoeffler (2001), 'Greed and Grievance in Civil War', Washington DC: Worldbank paper, Available at:
http://www.worldbank.org /research/conflict/papers/greedgrievance_23oct.pdf.

Creveld, M. van. (1991), *The Transformation of War*, The Free Press, New York.

Cribb, R. (2000), 'From Petrus to Ninja: death squads in Indonesia', *Death Squads in Global Perspective: Murder with Deniability*, B. B. Campbell and A. D. Brenner, St Martin's Press: pp. 181-202, New York

Curley, E. (1994), 'Introduction to Hobbes's Leviathan', E. Curley, ed., *Leviathan* (with selected variants from the latin edition of 1668), Indianapolis, Hackett Publishing Company Inc.

Diamond, L. (1988), 'Nigeria: Pluralism, Statism, and the Struggle for Democracy', *Democracy in Developing Countries: Africa*, L. E. A. Diamond, Boulder, US: Lynne Rienner Publishers Inc. (Vol. 2): pp. 33-92.

Dijk, K. v. (2000), *The Good, the Bad and the Ugly: Explaining the Unexplainable. Workshop on Violence in Indonesia*, Leiden University, Leiden NL.

Dijk, K. V. (2001), *A Country in Despair*, KITLV Press, Leiden.

Duffield, M. (2001), *Global Governance and the New Wars: The Merging of Development and Security*, Zed Books Ltd., London.

Ekeh, P. P. (2002), 'The Bakassi Boys: The Legitimization of Murder and Torture', A Review of HRW's and CLEEN's Report on state sponsored vigilante groups in Nigeria: http://www.waado.org/NigerDelta/Documents/ConstitutionalMatters/PoliceVigilante/ReviewBakassiBoys-Ekeh.html.

Eklöf, S. (1999), *Indonesian Politics in Crisis, The Long fall of Suharto, 1996-98*, NIAS Publishing, Copenhagen, Denmark.

Elaigwu, J. I. (2002), 'Ethnic Militias and Democracy in Nigeria', paper presented at the National Workshop on Ethnic Militias, Democracy and National Security in Nigeria, National War College, Abuja.

Ero, C. (2000), 'Vigilantes, Civil Defence Forces and Militia Groups: The Other Side of the Privatisation of Security in Africa', *Conflict Trends* (1).

Faris, S. (2002), 'Nigeria's Vigilante Justice': http://www.motherjones.com/ news/ feature/2002/04/bakassi.html

Fealy, G. (2001), 'Inside the Laskar Jihad', *Inside Indonesia*, pp. 28-29.

Fisher, R. J. (1990), *The Social Psychology of Intergroup and International Conflict Resolution*, Springer Verlag, New York.

Gani, Y. J. (2002), 'Militia as a Social Phenomenon: Towards a Theoretical Construct', National Workshop on Ethnic Militias, Democracy and National Security in Nigeria, National War College, Abuja.

Gurr, T. R. (1970), *Why Men Rebel*, Princeton, Princeton University Press, New Jersey.

Harnischfeger, J. (2003), 'The Bakassi Boys: Fighting Crime in Nigeria', *Journal of Modern African Studies* 41(1), 23-49.

Hasan, N. (2002), 'Faith and Politics: The Rise of Laskar Jihad in the Era of Transition in Indonesia', *Indonesia* (73), pp. 145-169.

Horowitz, D. (2001), *The Deadly Ethnic Riot*, University of California Press, Berkeley and Los Angeles.

HRW/Cleen (2002), 'Nigeria: The Bakassi Boys: The Legitimisation of Murder and Torture', Human Rights Watch report.

Isaacs, D. (2002). 'Crackdown on Nigerian vigilantes', *BBC World News* (Online).

JP (2000), 'Two killed in misunderstanding', *Jakarta Post*, Jakarta, July 21: p. 3.

Kaldor, M. (2002), *New and Old Wars: Organized Violence in a Global Era*. Cambridge, U.K: Polity Press.

Keen, D. (2000), 'Incentives and Disincentives for Violence', M. Berdal and D. Malone eds. *Greed and Grievance: Economic Agendas in Civil Wars*, Boulder, Lynne Rienner Publishers Inc.

Kivimäki, T. and Thorning, R. (2002), 'Democratisations and Regional Power Sharing in Papua/Irian Jaya: increased opportunities and decreased motivations for violence', *Asian Survey*, No. 4, Vol. 42, pp.651-672.

Kivimäki, T., T. Lehtinen, et al. (1998), *Arms Management and Conflict Transformation in Mali: A reinterpretation*, Helsinki: Department of Political Science, University of Helsinki.

Kristiansen, S. (2001), 'Unemployment, Identity and Business: Violent Youth Groups in Yogjakarta and Nusa Tenggara Barat', Conference on Governance Identity and Conflict in Indonesia, Nordic Institute of Asian Studies, Copenhagen.

Lindsey, T. (2001), 'The Criminal State: Premanisme and the New Indonesia', G. L. S. Smith, ed., *Indonesia Today, Challenges of History*, Singapore: Institute of Southeast Asian Studies.

Lintner, B. (2003), *Blood Brothers*, Palgrave Macmillan, New York.

LJ1 (2000), Interview with Laskar Jihad fighter by the author, Conducted within the Framework of Indonesian Conflict Studies Network.

Maier, K. (2000), *This House has Fallen: Nigeria in Crisis*, Penguin Books Ltd., London: UK.

Moore, S. (2001), 'The Indonesian Military's Last Years in East Timor: An Analysis of its Secret Documents', *Indonesia* (72): pp. 9-44.

Munir (2001), 'Indonesia, Violence and the Integration Problem', I. Wessel and G. Wimhöfer, eds., *Violence in Indonesia*, Hamburg, Abera Verlag: pp.17-24.

Nwabuisi, S. O. (2002), 'Stopping Bakassi Boys in Abia State', *This Day*, Lagos.

Nwanguma, O. (2000), 'Human rights Abuses by Vigilantes', *Law Enforcement Review*, July-September, Lagos: CLEEN.

Ogata, S. and A. Sen (2003), *Human Security Now*, Human Rights Commission Report: New York.

Ogwuda, A. (2001), 'Traders Protest Rising Crime Wave in Asaba, Ask for Bakassi Boys', *Vanguard*, Lagos.

Potter, D. (1994), 'Democratization in Asia', D. Held (ed.) *Prospects for Democracy*, Polity Press, Cambridge, UK.

Reno, W. (1998), *Warlords Politics and African States*, Lynne Rienner Publishers, Inc., London.

Ryter, L. (2001), 'Pemuda Pancasila: The Last Loyalist Freemen of Suharto's New Order?', B. R. O. G. Anderson (ed.) *Violence and the State in Suharto's New Order*, Ithaca, NY: Cornell Southeast Asia Program Publications, 30: pp. 125-155.

Singer, R. (2001), 'Militias Fracture Nigerian Society', *The Christian Science Monitor*.

Snyder, C. A. and M. J. Malik (1999), 'Developments in Modern Warfare', C. A. Snyder (ed.) *Contemporary Security and Strategy*, Macmillan Press Ltd., London.

SP1 (2001), Interview with Satgas Papua militia-member by the author, Conducted within the framework of Indonesian Conflict Studies Network. Abepura.

Tempo (2002). 'Why Has Kopassus Lost its Way?' Tempo Interaktif: http://www.tempo.co.id/majalah/free/edl-list-e.html.

Tickner, J. A. (1996), 'Re-Visioning Security', K. Booth and S. Smith (eds.) *International Relations Theory Today*, Polity Press, Cambridge, UK.

Tilly, C. (1985), 'War Making and State Making as Organized Crime', P. Evans, B, D. Rueschmeyer and T. Skocpol (eds.) *Bringing the State Back in*, Cambridge University Press, Cambridge.

Varese, F. (2001), *The Russian Mafia: Private Protection in a New Market Economy*, Oxford University Press Inc., New York.

Weber, M. (1970), 'Politics as a Vocation', from *Max Weber: Essays in Sociology*, H. H. Gerth and C. W. Mills, Routledge and Kegan Paul Ltd., London.

Wessel, I. (2001), 'The Politics of Violence in New Order Indonesia in the Last Decade of the 20th Century', I. Wessel and G. Wimhöfer (eds.) *Violence in Indonesia*, Hamburg: Abera Verlag: 64-81.

Zartman, W. (1995), *Collapsed States, the Disintegration and Restoration of Legitimate Authority*, Lynne Rienner Publishers, Inc. , London

Chapter 6

Civil Militias: Threats to National and Human Security in West Africa

Istifanus Zabadi

Introduction

The end of the Cold War at the beginning of the 1990s did not result in peace dividends for Africa. Instead, it took the lid off grievances and frustrations which had been bottled up during this period, resulting in the eruption of violent conflicts in most countries in Africa. As the last decade of the 20th century wore out, even some of the countries which were seen as immune to violent conflicts were overrun by this new virus. Africa took on the identity of a continent bedevilled by violence, human misery and the collapse of the state as an institution. This in turn generated the phenomenon of privatised security, as armed non-state forces emerged to fill in the space left by the armed forces constituted by the state. These irregular forces include mercenaries, private security companies[1] and civil militias also known as ethnic militias or Non–State Armed Groups. The involvement of these irregular forces in the conflicts which have taken place in Africa has made peace and security the most sought-after 'commodities'.

West Africa has been plagued by the menace of civil militias since 1989 with the outbreak of the Liberian conflict. Since the irregular forces of the National Patriotic Front of Liberia (NPFL) and the United Liberation Movement for Democracy (ULIMO) took on the Armed Forces of Liberia (AFL) in a war to remove President Samuel Doe from power, they started an action whose domino effects have left West Africa unstable and insecure. Other countries in the region, such as Côte d'Ivoire, Guinea, Guinea-Bissau, Mali, Niger, Nigeria, Senegal and Sierra Leone,[2] have become afflicted by violence perpetuated by the several militias operating within them. They have put in grave danger the security of both humans (who are refugees elsewhere or internally displaced) and the countries in which they operate. The gravity of the situation is easily seen in the number of peace operations, both ECOWAS and UN, which West Africa has been hosting. Furthermore, the violent conflicts generated and sustained by these militia groups transcend national borders and are now impacting on the region as a whole. These conflicts have become intractable as a result. Furthermore, the West Africa-wide approach adopted here provides the opportunity to engage critically with both contexts of civil militias that is: (i) conflict-prone societies such as in Nigeria, and (ii) war-torn or post conflict countries like Sierra Leone and Liberia.

Therefore, this chapter seeks to understand this phenomenon of persisting instability and insecurity resulting from the activities of civil militias. Their impact on national and human security is also brought out by using examples from some of the countries listed above. The persistence of the militias and their violent activities in defiance of the solutions applied is explained and we argue that the transnational character of this problem recommends a regional rather than a national solution. We also look at the challenges which civil militias pose to returning conflict-torn societies to peace and at what ECOWAS is doing to address the problems arising from these groups.

Civil Militias, National and Human Security: A Conceptual Understanding

There are so many armed groups which have sprung up since the early 1990s in the countries experiencing conflicts in West Africa that it is necessary to clearly define and isolate civil militias. These groups, whether they are referred to as Non-State Armed Groups (NSAs), ethnic militias (as in Nigeria), or rebels, all have in common the use of armed violence to achieve their aims. They also contend against the formal armed forces constituted by the state but their goals may differ markedly and they may not all be categorised as militias.

Therefore, the term militia should refer to an irregular force of civilians who have been trained to use arms the same way the military forces of the state have been. Members of these militias may have even been in the military forces of the state or received military training and be armed with the same small arms and light weapons to carry out military duties. However, when this is understood, within the Weberian conception of the state as the only institution vested with the monopoly of the legitimate use of force, militias are irregular forces. Thus, some characteristics which distinguish civil militias from others have been given as:

- A paramilitary group whose members must have received training similar to the military, and so can actually function like the military in some regards;
- Neither part of nor are they individually members of a regular professional military force;
- They are perhaps legally permitted to carry arms and light weapons, usually for defensive purposes;
- Not being regular soldiers, they may not necessarily subscribe to the same rigid organisational command and control structures and discipline which are hallmarks of the professional military;
- They are usually established for particular purposes: maybe, to protect or defend the civilian populace during emergencies, either in the absence of a regular army or as a complement to them.[3]

The conceptual framework adopted for civil militias in this chapter is the Second Generation understanding of the militia suggested in the introductory chapter of this volume.[4] However, within the context of West Africa, civil militias are understood to include non-state armed groups, a generic categorisation which covers insurgency groups, rebel armies and vigilantes. This may appear to some as contradictory to the conceptual framework already adopted. A closer look will show that in the context of the countries in which such groups exist and operate, vigilantes, rebel armies and insurgency groups tend to share a common characteristic of being ethnic or religious in origin. In some instances, there is the coincidence of both ethnicity and religion determining the origin and activities of such vigilantes, insurgency groups and rebel armies. This is the case, for example, with the Bakassi Boys and the movement for the Actualisation of the Sovereign State of Biafra (MASSOB), both being of the Ibo ethnic group in Nigeria. In war-torn or post-conflict countries such as Côte d'Ivoire and Liberia, the insurgency groups which have tried to take over central governments have been defined by their ethnic and religious rather than national character. More often, they have emerged in response to what they see as the exclusion of their ethnic or religious groups from sharing political power and other resources of the state. Invariably, the interests being defended through the use of armed violence by these groups are essentially sectional. Therefore, the lack of distinction between these and civil militias in the discourse here is merely to serve the purpose of being specific about their uniqueness.

In line with the above, a large number and diversity of non-state armed groups or civil militias are in existence in West Africa. These include rebel and insurgency movements, pro-state militias, vigilantes and ethnic and religious organisations. There are some 25 such civil militias actively operating in the 9 ECOWAS member countries already listed.[5] The increasing use of civil militias including mercenaries, child soldiers and the proliferation of small arms is responsible for much of the instability in West Africa. As a result, national and human security has been put in grave danger in each country where these civil militias operate and it has become a major concern for ECOWAS and the United Nations.[6]

National security entails the extent of safety of the territory, populace, resources, values, culture and institutions from attack and destruction by hostile forces, both external and internal. Therefore, national security is a broad concept which covers both the military and non military aspects of the safety of the sovereign state. To that extent, human security is also seen as the safety of the citizen of a country from the threat of attack on his person, property, family, community, livelihood and environment and is covered by national security. Since human security is better guaranteed within the national context, when civil militias threaten or attack national security they put the former at risk also.

The emergence and activities of militia groups in a given context, ethnic or religious, seems to have domino effects, encouraging the formation of similar organisations in other contexts. These groups are prone to involvement in inter-ethnic, inter-religious and even interpersonal disputes and conflicts that disrupt public order and undermine individual safety. Within the economic context of national security, the atmosphere of insecurity engendered by these groups can disrupt normal productive activities and discourage both local and foreign investors. The environment of insecurity created by the activities of these groups provides very fertile ground for external interests who may wish to encourage local dissidents in a bid to destabilise the country in question.

Table 6.1 Ethnic Militias/Non-State Armed Groups in West Africa by Country

Country	Ethnic Militia	Origins	Area of Activity	Strength
1. Côte d' Ivoire	A) Patriotic Movement of Ivory Coast (MPCI).	The movement is made up of northerners, Boule soldiers, as well as some western groups.	Northern and central regions of the country.	MPCI has increased from 800 in 2002 to approximately 5,000 combatants as of March 2003.
	B) Ivorian Popular Movement for the Great West (MPIGO).	The group is mainly composed of English-speaking Yacouba, as well as Sierra Leoneans and Liberians.	The west of the country.	The total strength of both MPIGO and MJP is estimated to be around 2,000.
	C) Movement for Justice and Peace (MJP).	MJP is composed of many Sierra Leoneans and Liberians, as well as traditional hunters.	The western part of the country.	The total strength of both MPIGO and MJP is estimated to be around 2,000.
	D) Lima.	They emerged in March 2003 as a group of Liberian mercenaries based in Côte d'Ivoire.	Lima operated in the west of the country.	Lima is thought to be 1,000 strong.
	E) Convention of Patriots for Peace (CPP).	The group is a pro-government movement composed of young activists drawn from student networks and political parties, including the ruling Ivorian Popular Front.	CPP militias are active in Abidjan, as well as in the west and southwest of the country.	No precise figure of their total size is available, although membership is said to number several thousand.
2. Guinea	A) Movement of the Democratic Forces of Guinea (RFDG).	RFDG was composed of Guinean dissidents as well as Sierra Leonean and Liberian fighters.	They are located along Guinea's southern border with Sierra Leone and Liberia, including Macenta, Guéckédou, Kissidougou, Pamalap, N'Zérékoré, and Madina Woula.	It was estimated to be 1,800-strong.
	B) Young Volunteers Militia.	A group of young volunteers mobilized to counter the 2000–01 attacks by RFDG.	The volunteers were recruited in the areas threatened by the rebel attacks (Guéckédou, Kissidougou, Faranah).	Approximately 9,000 young volunteers.

3. **Liberia**	A) Liberians United for Reconciliation and Democracy (LURD).	It is primarily composed of ethnic Mandingos and Krahns.	LURD's stronghold is Lofa County, in the northwest of the country.	The estimated size of LURD is 8,000 combatants, not including child soldiers.
	B) Movement for Democracy in Liberia (MODEL).	MODEL is mainly composed of Krahn supporters who split from LURD in March 2003.	MODEL was active in the eastern and south-eastern parts of Liberia, which border Côte d'Ivoire.	The estimated size of MODEL is 5,000 combatants, not including child soldiers.
	C) Government of Liberia Militias and Paramilitaries.	These armed groups included fighters of the pre-1997 civil war.	Monrovia, Bong, and Nimba Counties.	About 15,000 strong.
4. **Mali**	A) Movements and United Fronts of Azawad (MFUA).	MFUA is an umbrella organization comprised of the four groups most active in the Tuareg/Arab rebellion	The groups comprising MFUA are active within the northern half of eastern Mali.	It is estimated to contain between 3,000 and 10,000 potential combatants.
	B) Patriotic Movement of Ganda Koy (MPGK).	MPGK was formed in reaction to the Tuareg/Arab rebellion.	They operate in areas of predominantly Songhay ethnicity.	NA.
5. **Niger**	A) Tuareg and Toubou rebel groups.	Tuareg and Toubou ethnic groups.	The rebellion was active in the regions of Aïr, Azawak & Manga.	Estimates of the total number of ex-combatants vary between 5,000 and 7,000.
	B) Arab and Peulh self-defence militias.	Arab and Peulh communities.	The Peulh and Arab militias operated in the Manga region.	NA.
6. **Nigeria**	A) Bakassi Boys.	They arose from a number of disparate vigilante groups active in 1997–98 in Abia State.	Large Cities in the South East, such as Aba, Onitsha.	NA.
	Anambra State Vigilante Service (AVS).		Anambra State of especially Onitsha, Akwa.	
	B) O'odua People's Congress (OPC).	Yoruba Ethnic group, that emerged in 1994.	South-Western Nigeria.	There are (at least) 20 OPC 'zonal commanders' each claiming to lead 200 armed men.

	C) Arewa People's Congress (APC).	It is a northern group created to safe guard northern interests.	Located in Northern Nigeria	NA.
	D) Egbesu Boys of Africa (EBA).	Was formed in 1998 as an umbrella organization of Ijaw civil and youth groups.	Active throughout Nigeria's six south-eastern states that comprise the Niger Delta.	5,000 youths from 25 Ijaw associations.
	E) Niger Delta Volunteer Force (NDVF).	Closely associated with the Egbesu.	Niger Delta, in particular, the Rivers state and its capital, Port Harcourt.	NA.
	F) Movement for the Actualization of the Sovereign State of Biafra (MASSOB).	The group was formed by Ibo elements in late 1999 to revive the secessionist state of Biafra, which had led to the Nigerian civil war in 1967–70.	South-Eastern Nigeria.	NA.
	G) Federated Niger Delta Ijaw Communities (FNDIC).	Mainly composed of Ijaw groups.	Warri South-South.	NA.
	H) Al-Sunna Wal Jamma (Followers of the Prophet) (also known as 'Taleban').	A Taleban style group. Its adherents are believed to be predominantly university students from the northeast region.	Borno & Yobe States, North-Eastern Nigeria.	About 200 members of the group apparently took up arms for the first time in December 2003.
	I) Zamfara State Vigilante Service (ZSVS).	A 'ragtag volunteer army'.	Zamfara State.	NA.
7. Senegal	A) Movement of the Democratic Forces of Casamance (MFDC).	Predominantly composed of the Diola ethnic group.	Basse-Cassamance region.	MFDC was estimated to be 2,000–3,000 strong in 2002.
8. Sierra-Leone	A) Revolutionary United Front (RUF).	Main Sierra-Leonean Rebel group.	Northern and Eastern provinces.	At its height, the RUF may have numbered around 20,000.

	B) Civil Defence Force (CDF).	CDF constituted a loose-knit collection of tribally based hunting societies.	The Koinadugu, Kono,Tonkol and Port Loko and Tonkolili districts.	NA.
	C) Armed Forces Revolutionary Council (AFRC).	Disgruntled members of the armed forces established the group at the time of the coup d'état.	Freetown.	NA.
	D) West Side Boys (WSB).	The nucleus of WSB included former SLA members.	Largely limited to the Rokel Creek area near Occra Hills in Port Loko district.	Their strength was believed to number in the hundreds.

Source: Mapping of Non-state Armed Groups in the ECOWAS Region Preliminary report presented at the 6th Ministerial Meeting of the Human Security Network Bamako, Mali, 27–29 May 2004 and The Daily Sun Newspaper, Friday, September 17, 2004.

Militia groups have accounted for numerous deaths, the destruction of key government installations and public utilities, and disruption of peace and order. They have limited the capacity of governments to ensure meaningful and sustainable development as scarce resources have to be diverted into measures to curb their excesses. Added to this is their capacity to scare away investors thereby frustrating government efforts towards a sound and rapid socio-economic development of the country in question.

The activities of civil militias also constitute a usurpation of the role of government law enforcement agents. While the government is constitutionally given the monopoly of the legitimate use of force, the use of arms by militias delegitimises the rule of law and thus undermines peace and internal security. They encourage violence and increase militancy. Their activities, through reprisals and revenge killings, often based on rumours, spark off new rounds of savagery and brutality between warring groups. They create insecurity rather than their purported objective of providing security and they erode public confidence in government and its institutions. The conduct and activities of civil militias encourage debasement of values and the derogation of constituted authority. Criminal elements hide under the guise of militias to perpetuate crimes. This link between the activities of civil militias and national and human insecurity in West Africa requires that we look at how these irregular forces emerged.

Why Civil Militias Emerge

The emergence and proliferation of Civil Militias in West Africa can be located within the context of several factors, including each country's history, economy and political and administrative arrangements of government. Other factors include bad governance, the exclusion of some groups from political power sharing, weak state institutions, poverty and abuse of human rights. The countries of West Africa are still afflicted by these problems as well as the profound distrust by the populace of the ability of law enforcement agencies to ensure security, public order and individual safety.

Civil militias emerge as a consequence of the failure of the post-colonial state in West Africa to provide formal and positive value orientation for the growing population of the youth. The absence, failure or ineffectiveness of the state to secure the lives and property of citizens has given room for self-help initiatives by citizens both within and beyond the scope of the law. Perceived marginalisation and persecution of ethnic elements has accentuated the feeling of deprivation among various groups, creating the grounds for incessant conflicts. Increasing socio-economic inequality, demographic pressures and diminishing resources have led to intensification of struggles between geo-ethnic groups. The West African sub region parades many of the poorest countries in the world which have in turn provided the conducive environment for conflicts and civil militias to thrive.

The proliferation of small arms and light weapons has made them easily accessible for use in conflicts and other violent forms of crime across West Africa. Inadequate border controls and policing have meant that unscrupulous elements move in and out of these countries easily, perpetrate crimes as hired mercenaries by warring groups, and escape unpunished. The poor arrangements for reintegration of ex-servicemen into civilian life, whereby they are allowed back into the society without much institutional or systemic support, has led them to find relevance by 'helping' their communities any way they can.

All these factors represent the crisis of the state, or indeed the failure of the state to deliver to the people the public goods of security, liberty and development in West Africa. The result has been the creation of a dangerous vacuum in each country, which was filled by civil militias. West Africa became home to a large and diverse number of civil militias, or non-state armed groups, as they are also known. One study estimates that there are about 25 civil militias, which are very active in a majority of the countries in West Africa. These include rebel movements, pro-government militias, community based vigilante groups, and religious movements.[7] They have stepped into the void to contest for their own space against the state and other militias, with chilling consequences for human security and stability in the sub region.

In Côte d'Ivoire, for instance, at least five militia groups with ethnic and regional backgrounds have emerged since the failed coup against President Laurent Gbagbo on 19 September 2002. This action was the work of about 800 combatants known as the Patriot Movement of Ivory Coast (MPCI). The MPCI emerged to protect the interests of Northerners, a majority of whom are Muslims, accusing President Gbagbo of discriminating against them. Another group, the Ivorian Popular Movement for the Great West (MPIGO) emerged in November 2002 with the aim of avenging the death of former President General Robert Guei and defending the rights of the Yacouba ethnic group. The Movement for Justice and Peace (MJP) appeared with MPIGO in the western part of Côte d'Ivoire with the same objective. MJP has in its ranks Sierra Leoneans, Liberians and traditional hunters. On the other hand, the Convention of Patriots for Peace (CPP) is a pro-government group of young activists among students and the ruling Ivorian Popular Front, most of them from the Bete ethnic group as is President Gbagbo. Together, these militia groups have divided the country and kept it unstable and insecure, with a serious threat of secession.

The Mano River Union countries continue to be plagued by the activities of militias. Guinea was attacked by militias of the Movement of the Democratic Forces of Guinea (RFDG), a group made up of Guinean dissidents and Sierra Leonean and Liberian fighters. In response to this, in neighbouring Liberia, armed conflict resumed in 1999 as two rebel groups challenged President Charles Taylor's grip on the country. These were: the Liberians United for Reconciliation and Democracy (LURD) and the Movement for Democracy in Liberia (MODEL). LURD was formed in 2000 by Liberians who felt excluded from the implementation of the Abuja Peace Accords on Liberia. The ethnic base of LURD remained the same as that of the former United Liberation Movement of Liberia for Democracy (ULIMO), the Krahns and Mandingos. The Mandingos have ties in Guinea which explains why LURD could operate freely from Guinea and in Lofa county. Sierra Leonean militia groups such as the Revolutionary United Front (RUF) and the West Side Boys fought on the side of LURD. MODEL shares the same Krahn ethnic base with LURD, having split from the latter in 2003. MODEL also operated in the region bordering Côte d'Ivoire, taking advantage of the ethnic affinity between the Krahn and the We of Côte d'Ivoire. The government of Liberia under Charles Taylor raised several militia groups on its own to confront its enemies. The result was that Liberia relapsed into violence on the scale witnessed during the civil war, until ECOWAS and the international community intervened and got Charles Taylor out of power in 2003.

Sierra Leone was used by the RUF and other militias to inflict a reign of terror on the people, after the RUF attacked their country from Liberia in March 1991. The RUF initially enjoyed popular support among the people of the hinterland who were disgruntled with the central government in Freetown. However, it was their brutality against the people when they joined with the Armed Forces Revolutionary Council (AFRC) which had overthrown the government of President Tejan Kabbah in May 1997 that turned the people against them. The violence and brutality of the RUF/AFRC resulted in the emergence of the Civil Defence Force (CDF), a collection of tribally based hunting societies, also known as the kamajors. The kamajors operated as a government militia with the national Coordinator being a Deputy Minister of Defence in the government of President Kabbah. The West Side Boys were another militia group, which contributed to the horrible crimes against the people of Sierra Leone. As in the case of Liberia, it took the concerted efforts of ECOWAS and the international community to bring the situation to an end.

Nigeria has been afflicted by many ethnic and religious militia groups, which have killed many people in politically motivated violence since the return to democratic rule in 1999. The most prominent among these militias is the O'odua Peoples Congress (OPC), which fought to defend the interests of the Yoruba ethnic group, after the annulment of the Presidential election of 12 June 1993 presumably won by Chief MKO Abiola, their kinsman. The activities of OPC encouraged the emergence of other ethnic based militias such as the Egbesu Boys of Africa among the Ijaw of the Niger Delta; the Movement for the Actualisation of the Sovereign States of Biafra (MASSOB) among the Igbo; the Yan Daba and other militant groups in the core Northern states of Nigeria. There are also many ethnically based vigilante groups such as the Bakassi Boys, which sprang up among communities in Nigeria. These have been involved in the violent conflicts, which took place in Nigeria over the period. The consequence for Nigeria and all the other West African countries where the militias have been active is that national and human security remains imperilled. This can be seen from how they have impacted on their societies.

The Impact of Civil Militias on National and Human Security

The activities of the civil militias have impacted negatively and profoundly on the security of the countries in which they operate, and on human security. This is far out of proportion to the small size of these militias in relation to the rest of the population. They have been able to make the West African sub-region insecure and unstable and the human security situation dire. By their activities, the militias have made the phenomenon of the failed state a possibility in countries such as Liberia, Sierra Leone, Guinea Bissau, and Côte d'Ivoire. These states remain in a state of fragile stability with the ever-present danger of state collapse. There is persistent insecurity in other countries such as Guinea Conakry, Nigeria, Niger and Senegal due to the activities of militia groups. At the level of human security, the ordinary people have suffered most at the hands of the militias. They have committed numerous atrocities against civilian populations, including killings, torture rape, amputations, mutilations, abductions, assaults, looting, forced labour and forced recruitment, especially of children.

The extent to which West Africa has become conflict prone, insecure and unstable can be seen from the fact that it has hosted more peace operations than any region in Africa since the end of the Liberian Civil War in 1997. These peace operations have included the ECOWAS Monitoring Group (ECOMOG) in Sierra Leone from 1998 to 1999 when the United Nations Mission in Sierra Leone (UNAMSIL) took off. As UNAMSIL was returning Sierra Leone to stability, the situation in Liberia relapsed into one of near anarchy. The urgency of the development forced ECOWAS to launch a peace operation, the ECOWAS Mission in Liberia (ECOMIL), as a holding operation before that of the UN took over. ECOMIL, which was launched in July 2003, was succeeded by the UN Mission in Liberia (UNMIL) in October 2003. Since the failed coup of 19 September 2002 by the Patriotic Movement of Ivory Coast (MPCI) against President Laurent Gbagbo, the international community has been trying to keep Côte d'Ivoire from disintegrating. These efforts resulted in the ECOWAS Mission in Côte d'Ivoire (ECOMICI) and the UN Mission in Côte d'Ivoire (MINUCI) which replaced the UN operation in Côte d'Ivoire (UNOCI) on 5 April 2004.

Despite the number of peace operations going on in West Africa, the goal of security is yet to be realised. There is fear that a relapse into anarchy remains a high probability, especially in countries of the Mano River Union (Liberia, Sierra Leone and Guinea) and the neighbouring Côte d'Ivoire. This concern that the conflicts have defied the measures taken to tackle them is clearly seen in the attention, which the UN has given to the sub-region. The UN has not only directed its agencies in the area to coordinate their activities, which are aimed at bringing peace. It has, through the UN office for West Africa (UNOWA), coordinated with ECOWAS to find lasting solutions to the conflicts and the factors, which cause them. Meanwhile these efforts have to contend with the fact that some of these militias operate at transnational levels as is the case in the Mano River Union countries and Côte d'Ivoire, whereas solutions have remained at national levels. This has been compounded by the fact that there is a lack of political will on the part of some governments to tackle these militias. The main reason for this is that some of these governments have supported militia groups operating in neighbouring countries. It is clear, for example, that the conflict in Côte d'Ivoire can be resolved only with the active support of countries such as Burkina Faso. As long as such situations persist, of governments using militia groups as instruments of foreign policy the security environment in West Africa, both national and human, will continue to be a desperate one.

The condition of ordinary people in the countries where militias remain active in West Africa is a very desperate one indeed. The first human security problem, which is usually created by militia violence, is that of refugees and internally displaced persons (IDPs). All the violent conflicts, which have taken place in West Africa have created both refugees and IDPs. The first Liberian conflict sent many Liberians across West Africa and even beyond, and by August 2003 there were aproximately 300,000 still scattered across the sub-region.[8] The other conflicts also generated a large number of refugees with Guinea hosting about 1 million over a period of 10 years and, as at September 2003, more than 280,000 remained. The conflict in Côte d'Ivoire led to the return of more than 300,000 people to Burkina Faso in 2003 alone. On the issue of IDPs, the same picture is evident: there were at least 600,000 as at August 2003, Guinea had approximately 100,000 in May 2003 and Côte d'Ivoire had 500,000 to 800,000 as at October 2003. These are just a few cases of a big regional problem.

The humanitarian situation has remained in what Jan Egeland described as a 'crisis of protection', in many communities in the sub region.[9] There is often general disruption of normal life for refugees and IDPs such that it is not possible to engage in productive activities such as agriculture. There is also no access to education for children, no healthcare or social services, thereby exacerbating poverty and further insecurity. This was confirmed in the case of the conflict in Côte d'Ivoire, by the Chairperson of the Commission of the African Union when he reported that:

> The humanitarian situation continues to be of serious concern. It should be recalled that, during his visit to Korogho... my Special Representative for Côte d'Ivoire signalled the rapid decline in the education and health systems. In the education

sector, the priority is to reopen the Universities in the Northern part of the country, rehabilitate the schools, provide the means of transport and recruit 4000 teachers...At the medical and health level, the Ministry of Health has estimated the total cost of the rehabilitation of the health infrastructure and the normal resumption of all activities at 75 billion CFA francs.[10]

The civil militias or non-state armed groups, which still operate in many countries in West Africa remain a major threat to human, and therefore national security. Removing this threat will greatly enhance the prospects of restoring security to the sub-region, and create the environment for development to take place.

ECOWAS and the Challenge of Civil Militias

Although the activities of civil militias have seriously challenged and severely limited the capacity of ECOWAS to bring peace to war-torn countries in the sub-region, the organisation is yet to specifically address them as an issue. At most, the menace of the civil militias has been taken as part of the conflicts, which have been waged by various non-state armed groups against member states. To that extent, they have been handled within the framework put in place for security in the sub-region. These include, for example, the Moratorium on Manufacture, Import and Export of Light Weapons adopted in 1998, a Code of Conduct (1999) and Programme for the Coordination of Assistance on Security and Development (PCASED, 1999) whose implementation has been largely disappointing. The other is the ECOWAS Protocol Relating to Mechanism for Conflict Prevention, Management, Resolution, Peacekeeping and Security (1999). The Mechanism covers areas such as the prevention, management and resolution of internal conflicts; peacekeeping; humanitarian assistance; peace building measures; and sub-regional security. The inability to use these existing arrangements to bring peace and security to West Africa has meant that the civil militias remain a major challenge to ECOWAS. It is a challenge, which has to be addressed under the leadership of ECOWAS as an institution.

However, owing to the domino effects of the insecurity, which militia groups have generated within West Africa, the phenomenon has become transnational. Many of these militias have operated across national boundaries as was seen in the conflicts in the Mano River Union countries and Côte d'Ivoire. Even in Nigeria, there have been persistent allegations that foreign armed groups have taken part in many of the ethno-religious conflicts which occurred since the return to democratic rule in 1999. It has become necessary, therefore, to address the menace of civil militias and resultant insecurity at the level of the West African sub-region in addition to on-going national efforts. The United Nations, the African Union and ECOWAS have already reached such a conclusion: a regional approach is required to address these security problems.

The decision to adopt a regional approach has already shifted action in the direction of encouraging cooperation and coordination between the UN, the international community and ECOWAS. The regional organisation ECOWAS as well as its various programmes designed to restore peace and security to the area are to be strengthened by external support being directed to these. This consensus was reflected in the recommendation by the Executive Secretary of ECOWAS, Ibn Chambas that:

> The suggestion that the DDRR Programmes in Mano River Union countries, including Côte d'Ivoire, should be tackled and coordinated regionally ought to be given great consideration. Collaboration and coordination between the United Nations Mission in Sierra Leone (UNAMSIL), the United Nations Mission in Liberia (UNMIL), the United Nations Mission in Côte d'Ivoire (MINUCI), the UNOWA and ECOWAS could be a great asset to the endeavour to rid the Mano River basin of illicit arms, mercenaries and transnational drug and diamond traffickers and armed marauders.[11]

Conclusion

National security and human security are not mutually exclusive, rather they are mutually reinforcing in their interrelatedness. From a conception of security, which is holistic and integrated to include the safety of the territory of the state and that of the people within it, national security is inconceivable without human security. When the people cannot be guaranteed their physical safety and the basic necessities of life, they can be said to be insecure. When they are insecure, the state is made insecure as people take to desperate and dangerous measures to change their situations. Some of these desperate actions have also created and sustained militias within national territories, rendering the states concerned very insecure as in the Hobbesean state of nature. The state of insecurity in West Africa has been addressed within the context of the countries in which the militias operate, without much success.

There is no doubt that a regional approach to this and other problems afflicting West Africa is the most viable option available. However, a high level of political will is required from leaders in the sub-region for there to be a chance of success. As already indicated, some governments have sustained militias by using them to cause trouble and insecurity in neighbouring countries. This way, conflicts such as those in Liberia, Sierra Leone and Côte d'Ivoire have lasted longer than would have been the case if the militia groups had not received support from governments in the neighbourhood. For the moment, this lack of political will seems to be the most serious obstacle to re-building peace and security in West Africa, because where there is a will, there is a way.

Notes

[1] Most of the discussion in this section benefited from Human Security Network, *Ibid.*, which survey non-state armed groups in the ECOWAS Region.

[2]   *Region Report Presented at the 6th Ministerial Meeting of the Human Security Network*, Bamako, Mali, 26–28 May, 2004.

[3]   Amadu Sesay, Charles Ukeje, Olabisi Aina and Adetonwa Odebiyi (eds) *Ethnic Militias and the Future of Democracy in Nigeria* (Ile Ife: Obafemi Awolowo University Press) 2003, p.24.

[4]   See David J. Francis, 'Introduction'.

[5]   *Op cit.*

[6]   See for example, *Report of the Secretary General on Ways to Combat Subregional and Cross-border Problems in West Africa, S/2004/200.* UN Security Council, 12 Mar 2004; and *Security Council calls for regional approach in West Africa to address such cross border issues as child soldiers, mercenaries, small arms sc/8038*, UN Security Council, 25 Mar 2004.

[7]   Human Security Network, *Op cit.*, p.26.

[8]   *Ibid.*, p.12.

[9]   Jan Egeland, Under Secretary General for Humanitarian Affairs and Emergency Relief Coordination in UN Security Council meeting on West Africa. *SC/8037*, 26 Mar 2004.

[10] African Union Report of the Chairperson of the Commission on the Situation in Côte d'Ivoire PSC/PR/3(V), 13 April 2004. http://www.reliefweb.int/

[11] See 'Security Council Calls for Regional Approach…' *Op cit.*

Chapter 7

Counter-Insurgents or Ethnic Vanguards? Civil Militia and State Violence in Darfur Region, Western Sudan

Usman Tar

Introduction

Sudan's protracted instability and the rise of the civil militia known as Janjaweed in the western part of the country represent a particular complex dimension of war-torn society. For a number of years, Darfur region in western Sudan has been a scene of violent clashes between mainly sedentary farming communities of the three 'African' ethnic groups (Fur, Masalit and Zaghawa) and 'Arab' nomads. For all these years, successive Sudanese governments have claimed that these clashes were caused by competition over resources.[1] In the last couple of years, however, what used to be constructed as resource conflict dramatically turned into a complex humanitarian crisis and ethnic genocide, affecting about two million western Sudanese in Darfur region. The crisis erupted when, in February 2003, two rebel movements – the Sudanese Liberation Army/Movement (SLA/M) and Justice and Equality Movement (JEM) – emerged and 'demanded an end to chronic marginalisation[,]…sought power-sharing within the Arab ruled Sudanese state…[and] government action to end the abuses of their rivals, Arab pastoralists who were driven onto African farmlands by drought and desertification – and who had a nomadic tradition of armed militias' (Human Rights Watch, 2004a, p.1). It eventually developed into a sustained armed conflict between, on the one hand, the armed forces of Sudan and its allied proxy militia drawn from Arab ethnicity and, on the other, the two rebel groups comprising mainly of non-Arab African ethnic groups.

Instead of resolving the armed conflict through dialogue, the government of Sudan responded by targeting civilian populations suspected of providing fighting forces for rebel groups. To achieve its strategic objective of containing the rebellion, the state allegedly entered into a working alliance with Arab nomads whom it organised into militia outfits, trained, armed and provided with the necessary legal protection to carry out atrocities in the name of counter-insurgency. Having been allowed what Amnesty International (2004c) calls 'free rein', the militias became an important irregular arm of the Sudanese Army and were often deployed in tandem with the armed forces (both infantry and air force) in attacking communities suspected of supporting rebel movements; killing, and abducting men, women, minors and the elderly raping women, as well as destroying their domiciles and property.

The Western rebellion and the humanitarian crisis it generated in Darfur region is analytically important not least because it opens a new chapter in the history of insurgency in the Republic of Sudan.[2] For the past four decades or so, the country has been bedevilled by a continuity of civil wars, and governmental instability. One common cause of all armed rebellion in Sudan, irrespective of regions and time – Anya-Nya (1955-72); SPLA/M (1983-2004) and SLA/SLM/JEM (2003-date) – is that in terms of development, representation and justice, successive northern (mainly Arab) civilian and military oligarchies in Khartoum have conducted the business of government with little or no regard to the wishes and aspirations of the majority of non-Arab citizens especially those domiciled in the South and West.[3]

The crisis in Darfur, which followed the western rebellion, is an unfolding complex emergency with disastrous implications not only for Sudan's wider national crisis but also for peace and security in the African sub-region. In a BBC interview on March 19, 2004 the then UN Humanitarian Coordinator in Sudan, Mukesh Kapila, captured the enormity of the crisis, comparing it to the Rwandan genocide of the 1990s: 'the world's greatest humanitarian crisis...the only difference between Rwanda and Darfur now is the numbers [of casualties] involved' (Hentoff, 2004, p.2). One factor that further exacerbated the crisis in Darfur was that it erupted at the same time as the negotiations to end the southern rebellion were taking place in Naivasha Kenya.[4] This single development contributed in no small measure to whittling down the urgency of the situation in Darfur, allowing the crisis to escalate. Initially, both the government of Sudan and the international community viewed the western rebellion as insignificant and diversionary in the context of the southern peace process. The rebel groups, on the other hand, became further agitated by the sarcastic posture of an ever-defiant government in Khartoum exploiting the southern peace process to continue its domination in the west. They eventually intensified their attacks with the initial help of the SPLA[5] and attacked important regional centres of power and commerce such as Al-Fasher, Geneina, Nyala, Kapkabiya, Murnei, and Wadi Saleh destroying both military and civilian infrastructure. By the time the attention of the government and the international community had shifted to Darfur towards the end of 2003 and early 2004, the crisis had plummeted deeply with breath-taking effects.

One of the most disturbing and complex issues associated with the western conflict is the government's decision to recruit its proxy civil militia, known as Janjaweed,[6] in confronting SLA/M/JEM insurgencies. Several allegations and debates have emerged regarding government's arming, training and involvement of Janjaweed militia as an instrument of 'ethnic cleansing' and counter-insurgency. In addition to torture and execution of thousands of innocent civilians of the Fur, Masalit and Zaghawa ethnic groups, other forms of atrocities alleged to have been committed by the Sudanese army/militia alliance include raping of women, often in front of their relatives, hostage-taking, abduction, setting villages and towns on fire, stealing the wealth and property of targeted civil communities and so on.[7]

This chapter examines issues around civil militia and state violence in the Darfur region of Western Sudan. The chapter assesses the mysteries surrounding the emergence and violent activities of the Janjaweed militia, an outfit believed to be armed by the Sudanese government in its effort to fight rebellion in the region. The key question is whether the Janjaweed militia members are counter-insurgents, since they are always seen together with the regular Sudanese army in counter-insurgency operations; or they are trigger-happy, violent 'Arab' militia that have been unleashing ethnically and racially-motivated acts of violence in the region? To capture this theme in proper perspective, the second part of the chapter examines the materialist and power relation dimensions of heterogeneity, civil war and instability in Sudan. The third part traces the phenomenon of civil militias as one of several manifestations of Sudan's instability. Subsequent parts of the chapter dwell on the origin of conflict in Darfur, the main theatre of the conflict under review; the western rebellion and its aftermaths, the main causal epicentre of the rise of the Janjaweed militia in its present form; state complicity in the arming of and provision of legal impunity to the Janjaweed to commit ethnically-motivated violence against non-Arabs; and the structure, composition and operations of Janjaweed to determine whether the they are a counterinsurgency unit of the Sudanese army or an ethnic militia.

Background: Heterogeneity, Civil Wars and Instability in Sudan

Sudan's diversity and instability could perhaps be situated in the context of power relations and domestic political analysis. In their struggles for power and resources, the country's governing elites and other interest groups are on record as manipulating and mobilising divisive tendencies among the population to instigate conflict. This explains why most conflicts are not only highly contested and protracted but are also motivated by a combination of regional, ethnic, racial and religious differences.

In terms of landmass, Sudan is the largest nation-state in Africa sharing borders with several states in the region – Chad, Egypt, Congo, Central African Republic, Eritrea, Ethiopia, Kenya, Libya and Uganda. It is also one of the most ethnically and religiously diverse countries with a population estimated at close to 28 million drawn from about 20 linguistic groups and half a dozen hundred sub-dialects (van de Veen, 1999, p.168). Precisely, Sudan's '597 tribes speak more than 400 languages and dialects and practice a variety of religious traditions with each of the three major groupings: Islam, indigenous African beliefs and Christianity in that quantitative order' (Bechtold, 1991, p.1). Ethnically, the Arabs constitute 39 percent while Africans make up 61 percent. Religiously, Muslims make up 70 percent while the rest are Christians and traditional believers (Human Rights Watch, 2004c). Sudan's diversity 'has resulted in one of the world's most heterogeneous societies that is almost a microcosm of Africa' – a unique characteristic that poses 'extraordinary challenge to any government' (Bechtold, ibid). Because of their sheer majority, Arab Muslims have been dominant in Sudan's central government since independence in 1956.

A strong culture of domination, the imposition of Islamic law as national legal instrument, especially after government's breach, in 1983, of the Addis Ababa Treaty, together with unequal regional development combined to provide the impetus for rebellion and secessionist struggles from marginalised southern Sudanese. Domestic conflict has therefore been one of the key features of Sudan since independence.[8] With the probable exception of the period 1972-83, Sudan's history as a sovereign political system has been fraught with armed insurrection mainly from southern dissident groups – the Anya-Nya and latterly the Sudan Peoples Liberation Movement/Army (SPLM/A) – demanding greater autonomy to end what they perceive as inequality perpetrated by the traditional northern Muslim dominated oligarchy.[9] Even then, the so-called decade of relative stability attained in the seventies has been refuted as an interval that 'fanned the embers of one war to ignite another' (Daly, 1993, p. 1). Other manifestations of Sudan's instability include, among others, governmental crisis arising from incessant conflict among political actors – resulting on the one hand in collapse of shaky coalitions and on the other in the oscillation of power between those coalitions and repressive military regimes; the domination of national power by the northern, Arab dominated, section of the country and their introduction of repressive and unacceptable laws in the southern, mostly marginalized, sections of the country. The resort to armed struggles by aggrieved southern Sudanese is essentially aimed at overcoming domination, underdevelopment and attaining some level of autonomy, somewhat similar to that obtainable in a confederation, within a pluralist Sudan.

Over the past four decades, Sudan has featured prominently as a scene of protracted civil wars. In 1955, the first rebellion started when the Anya-Nya Movement took arms against successive governments in Khartoum. It ended in 1972 when the movement negotiated limited autonomy for Southern Sudan, albeit within a united state. The Addis Ababa Agreement of 1972 which ended the war was designed as a grand master plan for resolving related national problems – 'political instability; lack of socio-economic development; and the disunity created by conflicting aspirations based on the political, cultural, racial and, most important, religious heterogeneity of Sudan' (Wakoson, 1993, p. 27).

The violation of the Addis Ababa Agreement by the former military ruler, General Numayri and his imposition of Islamic Law sparked a second rebellion in March 1983. Subsequently, Southern troops based in Bor, Janglei Province, disobeyed orders to transfer to the north as part of unification. Attempts by the government to disarm them failed and they withdrew to the bush and formed the Southern Sudan Peoples Army (SPLA), which became an armed unit of the Southern Sudan Revolutionary Movement (SPLM) led by John Garang le Maboir (Lual, 2001, pp.2-3).

In early 2003, while negotiations were underway for resolving the SPLM/SPLA rebellion, another wave of conflict erupted, this time in the Western region of Darfur, considered for decades as a traditional northern 'sphere of influence'. Initially, the crisis in Darfur was played down by both by Khartoum and the international community, lest it might jeopardise the Naivasha (Kenya) peace process being brokered by the United States and EU nations. The crisis in Darfur exposes the multifaceted natures of both domination and anti-domination struggles in Sudan. In the past, the South has been depicted as the centrepiece of struggles against northern domination. Since the eruption of crisis in Darfur, however, a new reality has emerged in the politics of unequal development and the response to it in Sudan: unlike the southern rebellion which was normally stereotypically constructed by the government as one coming from the 'disbelievers' or 'southerners', the western rebellion came from the mainly Muslim west. Perhaps for the first time, religion is losing relevance as a divisive factor in the current spectre of Sudan's civil war.

Civil Militias in Contemporary Sudan: Trends, Factors and Perverse Manifestations

The phenomenon of civil militias is not limited to the current crisis in Darfur; it is deeply rooted in the country's civil war and instability.[10] Indeed, Alex de Waal (1993a) is of the opinion that for a long time, there has been alarming growth in the number of armed militia groups in Sudan mostly in the south and in the Kordofan and Darfur regions of the west, with serious implications for the 'integrity and governability of the country'. According to him:

> Militia activity has resulted in the complete breakdown of law ...[They] have in places become even more powerful than the armed forces, with the result that the power of central government can no longer extend to these areas. Fear of growing power of militia with narrow political or sectarian loyalties was an important stimulus for the Armed Forces' Memorandum to the government of Sadiq Al-Mahdi in February 1989. (de Waal, 1993a, p.142)

As early as the eighties, reports by human rights groups such as Amnesty International have revealed that militias constituted part and parcel of human rights violations in Sudan – mass killing of civilians, looting, destruction of property, and kidnapping. For instance, AI's 1989 report on Sudan indicted not only the main warring factions (the government and SPLA/SPLM) but also their allied/rival militias for committing human rights atrocities (Amnesty International, 1990). By 1990, the Human Rights Watch described Sudan as 'a human rights disaster' partly because of the atrocities committed by militia in what it calls 'denying the honour of living' (Human Rights Watch, 1990a). These allegations were to be repeated in several recent reports of major international human rights organisations in the light of recent development, especially the unfolding crisis in Darfur.[11]

Several militia organisations have emerged in contemporary Sudan. Three kinds are noticeable in the country's long history of instability, which ranges from one region to another. The first category of militia organisations was found among rebel groups rival to the SPLA in southern Sudan. They included among others Anya-Nya II force, Mundiri, Murle and Fertit. An important factor that ignited and sustained rivalries among these groups, often manifesting in violent rebel-militias or intra and inter-militia confrontations, was that the government of Sudan often utilised the rivalries prevailing among them in planning and executing its counter-insurgency strategies against the SPLA/SPLM rebels. Several Sudanese governments were known to have sided with and armed militia groups rival to the SPLA/SPLM in order to undermine its insurgency. The second category of militia, found mainly in urban centres of power, was often associated with political parties and power brokers. An example is the militia wing of the National Islamic Front. This kind of militia outfit is common in many unstable states and fragile democracies where the struggle for power often takes a zero-sum dimension.[12]

The third category of militia was found mainly in western Sudan. This category, commonly known as the Muraheleen, emerged in Darfur and southern Kordofan mainly among Bagara Arabs (notably Riqayqat and Misiriya). The Murahaleen militia emerged during the regime of Sadiq al-Mahdi (1986-89) when the state adopted a policy of arming Arab Baggara militias as counter-insurgency forces against the SPLA/SPLM.[13] Successive governments continued to use the Muraheleen, whose activities focused primarily on looting, raiding, enslaving and punishing the Dinka and Nuer civilians living in SPLA territories from which rebel recruits were drawn (Human Rights Watch 2004a, p.8).

After taking power in a coup in 1989, the National Islamic Front ruling party absorbed many militia forces into the Popular Defence Forces (PDFs), a new organ established to take care of civil matters such as crime and community protection. However, as they were used to committing violence with state impunity, there were reports that PDF paramilitaries have committed a lot of human rights abuses as documented by many organisations (Human Rights Watch, 2004a). Following the 2003 rebellion in the west, the current government in Sudan followed the precedent set by its predecessors by forging an alliance with an outgrowth of Muraheleen militia known as Janjaweed to perform a similar counter-insurgency function. However, as revealed by unfolding realities, the Janjaweed militia seems to have gone beyond its strategic bounds of counter-insurgency to that of committing systematic violence against non-Arab, mainly black, Africans. As a patron and an ally of the Janjaweed, the government of Sudan is seriously implicated in committing violence against its own citizens.

Several factors are responsible for the emergence and growth of militia in contemporary Sudan. Alex de Waal identified four but his typology is drawn mainly from past experience, which needs to be critically reviewed in the light of recent trends, especially the current crisis in Darfur. The first factor is *local disputes* involving two or more groups especially 'when established systems of conflict-resolution have broken down and increased access to guns through black market facilitates violent escalation of disputes' (de Waal, 1993a, p.142). In the light of the current crisis in western Sudan, while the breakdown of conflict resolution between nomadic Arabs and sedentary African communities is a causal factor, a more volatile one is the conspiracy by Arab dominated states in fuelling the embers of ethnic tension by allying with the Arabs and their militia in carrying out violence against non-Arab western Sudanese.

De Waal considers state violence and state conspiracy with friendly militia as a factor in its own right (as will be seen), but seems to overlook the ethnic and racial dimensions of it. In addition, while de Waal's emphasis on black markets as a source of small arms cannot be ruled out, it has been suggested in the context of the current crisis in western Sudan that governmental and military sources are often responsible for the leakage of those arms to militia forces.[14] The second factor is *economic deprivation*, which involves the raiding activities of militia and other criminal elements for material gain. Most militia raids were associated with theft and pillage of the hard-earned wealth of victims: livestock, jewellery, food and so on. The third factor is what de Waal calls 'deliberate military strategy' by government using militia as weapons of counter-insurgency – and therefore the phenomenon of militia is deeply-rooted in the prevalence of insurgency in Sudan:

> The Sudan armed forces have been active in fighting insurgents in the Southern Sudan since 1980s and the SPLA since 1983. The armed forces do not have sufficient manpower to mount the extensive counter-insurgency operations required by the nature of guerrilla war. Instead of resorting to mass conscription in the northern provinces, which has been politically unacceptable, the government and army have instead used local militia as a deliberate strategy for containing [rebellion] (de Waal, 1993a, p.143).

While de Waal sees government strategy in the context of war between Khartoum and the SPLA, limiting it to north-south political dynamics, such strategy has taken a new form in the context of the current crisis in the western part of the country. The past precedent in which successive governments of Sudan mobilised and deployed civil militia in their fights against southern rebellion have assumed a new dimension in the current crisis in Darfur. While past militia outfits such as Muraheleen were founded and mobilised to fight southern unbelievers' in the name of 'Jihad', the current Janjaweed outfits have taken more of an ethnic than religious colouration.[15] They are composed mainly of Arabs and their loyalty to an Arab government in Sudan cannot be compromised. Some sources have suggested that the government of Sudan is using Janjaweed as a weapon of SLA/JEM counter-insurgency because the government fears that its standing army, whose rank and file are drawn mostly from the insurgent communities it is fighting against, is too risky to be trusted lest they prove disloyal or change sides while conducting counter-insurgency operations – a bitter lesson it learnt a long time ago in its fight against Anya-Nya (1955-72). In this case, the government seems to have more confidence in the loyalty of its proxy militia than its standing army (Human Rights Watch, 2004a, 2004b).

The final factors behind the emergence of civil militias are the local and national political aspirations of those associated with it. This particular factor, according to de Waal, is 'shadowy and politically controversial' in the sense that it is often associated with militia groups set up by rival politicians and their parties as paraphernalia for political competition and power struggles.[16] However, it is possible to illuminate this factor in the current situation in western Sudan: civil militia is used by Sudan's ruling oligarchy as an agent for achieving the strategic and, by extension, political aspirations of confronting and containing western rebellion.

Old Conflict, New Complex Emergency: Darfur[17] as a Theatre of Conflict

Greater Darfur, a territory roughly the size of France or Texas[18] and with an estimated population of about four to five million people, is Sudan's largest region in terms of landmass and population. Yet it is one of the least developed regions in the country with a long history of ethnic and racial strife. Located in the northwestern region of the country, Darfur shares Sudan's international borders with the Republic of Chad to the west, Libya to the northwest and Central Africa Republic to the southwest.[19] In the context of the on-going insurgency and its drastic aftermaths, however, the border region between Chad and Sudan provides the flashpoint of the crisis.[20] There is a long history of migration and commerce across the border and today people traverse both sides of the political divide for economic activities. Indeed, during the colonial era, Darfur served as one of the two main axes of Sudan's international trade (Woodward, 1990, p.23).

The ecology of the area, ranging from desert in the north, fertile belt in the Jabel Marra region to mixed vegetation of the southern zone, provides a massive resource base for agriculture resulting in conflict between sedentary farmers and nomads.[21] In the past, such clashes have occurred between mainly Fur, Masalit and other 'African' farming communities and pastoralist 'Arab' tribes, particularly those from Beni Hussein, from Kabkabiya region (North Darfur) and Beni Halba (South Darfur).[22] Following administrative divisions in 1994, Darfur has been divided into three provinces: North, South and West. These provinces comprise mainly of the Fur and Masalit, albeit with a panoramic mixture of other ethnic groups.[23] The pattern of farmers-pastoralists clashes cut across the three administrative divisions of Darfur but intensified as a result of annual migration by pastoralists seeking greener pasture for their livestock.

In the past, clashes between cattle and camel rearing Arab tribes and sedentary African farming communities were often resolved through age-hallowed means of conflict resolution reinforced by Anglo-Egyptian legal heritages.[24] Acting as third party mediators, community leaders and tribal chiefs – *Sheikh Kabilah* – often serve as veritable tools for conflict management. These traditional mediation mechanisms often prove fruitful, resulting in compensations for lost crops, establishing the time and pattern of seasonal migration, as well as setting buffer zones for grazing. Nevertheless, they may also fail to resolve the conflict or even degenerate into further strife. For instance in January 1999, Arab and Masalit tribal heads gathered to restore normalcy following a standoff between farmers and pastoralists over the latter's grazing on the former's cultivated farmland. The arbitration collapsed when angry Masalit farmers shot at the tribal heads killing an Arab chief. Political interference, undue influence and biased top-level conspiracies did nothing more than to further add insult to the injury:

The Sudanese government claimed that the Masalit were fifth column of the Sudan's People Liberation Army... and sealed off Dar Masalit. Reportedly the Arab militias then killed more than 1,000 Masalit. The government set up special courts to try leaders of the clashes, sentencing fourteen people to death, and sponsored a tribal reconciliation conference [which] concluded that 292 Masalit and seven Arabs were dead; 2,673 houses burned down; and large numbers of livestock looted, with Masalit suffering most. The Arabs refused to pay compensation. About 29,500 fearful Masalit refugees remained in Chad, where the Arab militia reportedly came to kill eighty Masalit refugees in mid-1999. (Human Rights Watch, 2004b, p. 9, fn 7)

From the foregoing statement, evidence abounds for the partisan role of the state in its indictment of the Masalit which sent a clear signal of the state's tacit approval for Arab militia to vent their anger, before setting up judicial process to try offenders perhaps in terms convenient to the government. Thus, even though the conflict over resources in Darfur is age-long, over the past two decades or so it has been intensified by several political, security and socio-economic factors:

... a combination of extended periods of drought; competition for dwindling resources; lack of good governance and democracy; and easy availability of guns have made local clashes increasingly bloody and politicised. (Human Rights Watch, 2004b:7)

Among the factors mentioned above, two of them – one natural, the other man-made – devastatingly changed the course of the conflict in the late 1980s. The first was the drought and famine that struck Darfur in 1984-1985 and left many Arab pastoralists with heavy loss of their livestock. As a result, they resorted to raiding the stock of others who were less affected by the catastrophe. Victims who resisted or tracked back the footprint of raiders had to face battle with the raiding gangs leading to loss of human lives and wealth. In addition to raiding, the drought also led pastoralists, who were left with few malnourished herds, to find solace by grazing on the farmlands of settled African farmers provoking their anger in the process. The farmers' retaliation to such acts often resulted in violent clashes between them and frustrated pastoralists.

The second factor, which emerged almost at the same period as the drought of the late 1980s, was the introduction of small arms into farming and pastoral communities. While in the distant past the kinds of arms available to farmers and pastoralists were traditional dane guns, swords, machetes and bows and arrows, the introduction of small arms tragically transformed the violent means of fighting available to rival communities and tribes. By January 1988 it was reported that 'there were at least 50, 000 automatic weapons in Darfur – one for every sixteen adult men.'[25] The proliferation of small arms became worse after the government of Sadiq Al-Mahdi (1986-89) introduced a policy of arming Muraheleen militia in Darfur and Kordofan regions. The proliferation of automatic weapons, fuelled by governmental influence in such an 'unstable state' as Sudan (Woodward, 1990), fits into what Stohl and Smith (1999) term 'a deadly combination' by which they mean the lethal configuration of state instability and unfettered proliferation of small arms coupled up with all their associated security risks. Successive regimes in Sudan have continued to abuse the volatile situation by allowing 'loyal' and favoured groups to possess arms as a means of 'defending themselves'.

Allegations of biased and counter-productive interference by successive Sudanese governments not only fomented the conflict in Darfur, but also further politicised ethnic and racial tension among Darfurians of African and Arab identities, especially on such sensitive macro-political issues as representation and local government. For a long time, Arabs have shown resentment over their insufficient representation in local governments, which, they complain, were dominated mainly by Fur and Masalit. They agitated for a fairer representation by forging pan-Arabic political platforms and interest groups. In 1986, they formed the Arab Alliance, a movement aimed at regaining control of Darfur and stamping Arab influence in the region. This development culminated in allegations by African Darfurians of government's favouring of Arabs in policy-making and execution, even if such policies are detrimental to the fragile peace and security of the region.[26] Instances of policy biases include appointment of 'Arabs' into sensitive and high-powered posts; the arming of Muraheleen militia, giving them legal protection to commit violence, as well as favouritism towards Arabs in the dispensation of justice, especially over land matters and communal crises. This resulted in feelings of domination and distrust from Fur, Masalit and Zaghawa political leaders, fears that were later proved grounded in 1994 following President Omar El-Bashir's administrative reforms in Darfur which gave Arab leaders more positions of power. This policy shift was seen as a deliberate and systematic strategy aimed at reversing power imbalances in favour of Arabs and simultaneously undermining the power of 'Africans'.

It was against the backdrop of the foregoing factors and incidences that, by 1998/99, the pattern of clashes in Darfur took a tangible shape, in a manner that was not necessarily so in the past: protracted clashes between 'African' Fur, Masalit and Zaghawa on the one hand and 'Arabs' on the other. The deliberate but hidden 'strategic' and 'ethnic' agenda of the government of Sudan has also come to play an increasing role in fuelling the conflict. Rather than taking concrete steps to ease ethnic tension and/or resolve the resource conflict, the government of President El-Bashir, as did its predecessors, is largely seen to have been taking enraging steps by arming Arabs and their militia (Janjaweed) to the detriment of defenceless farming communities. Certainly, the key antidote to the conflict in Darfur region lies in structural reform of the state's centre of power in its dealings with the peripheries: provision of social justice and security, equal development, non-partisan policy formulation and implementation as well as the use of dialogue, rather than state violence, in resolving dissent and rebellion.

The Western Rebellion and its Aftermaths

The current crisis in Darfur, which began following the SLA/JEM rebellion against the government in early 2003, can neither be configured as a phenomenon that is isolated from the past conflicts described above nor one that is exclusively caused by the western rebellion. To effectively comprehend it, reference has to be made to the previous conflicts, but there are pressing urgencies that make the current conflict both unique and fatal. In its recent report on the crisis in Darfur, the Human Rights Watch offers a more balanced view of the urgency of the current crisis in Darfur and its correlation with recent western rebellion and previous conflicts in the region:

> The current conflict in Darfur has deep roots. It is but the latest culmination of a protracted problem, yet there are key differences between the 2003-2004 conflict and prior bouts of fighting. The current conflict has developed serious racial and ethnic overtones and clearly risks shattering historic if fragile pattern of co-existence. A number of ethnic groups previously neutral are now positioning themselves along the Arab/African divide, aligning and co-operating with either the rebel movements or the government and its allied militia. Remaining neutral and outside the conflict is becoming impossible, though some groups have tried to do so. (Human Rights Watch, 2004a, p.8)

The causal epicentre of the current crisis in Darfur is, of course, the eruption of the western rebellion. In February 2003, the Darfur Liberation Front (DLF) emerged and captured the town of Gulu and, thereafter, transformed itself into the Sudan Liberation Army/Movement (SLA/M). The key political motivations behind the rebellion were 'that Khartoum authorities address the marginalisation and underdevelopment to which the region was reportedly subjected' (UNCHR, 2004, p.3); and bring 'an end to tribal militias, and [adopt] a power share [of the peripheral west] with the central government' (Human Rights Watch, 2004a, p.9). Initially, the Sudanese government refused to heed the demands of SLA/M, neither did it seek to negotiate with the group. The seriousness of the rebellion became clear when the rebels attacked El-Fashir, the capital of North Darfur, in April 2003 in which they destroyed a number of Sudanese military aircrafts and helicopters, looted fuel and munition facilities and captured a Sudanese Air Force officer who was forced to give an interview to the 'Arab' international Television Channel, Al-Jazeera. They subsequently attacked other important garrison towns in north Darfur, looting food and arms depots. The situation worsened following the emergence of a similar, albeit initially factional, rebel group known as the Justice and Equality Movement (JEM). The JEM eventually merged, even if temporarily, with the SLA/M in carrying out intensive, more disastrous attacks on key military and civil targets. In May 2003, the Sudanese authorities responded by making key political and appointive changes and establishing a heavy military presence in the Darfur region.

Several factors escalated the rebellion. The first was the refusal of the Sudanese government either to recognise the rebel groups or honour their demands. Well known to the government, the rebellion, as recently reported by the United Nations High Commission for Refugees, was 'rooted in the structural imbalance in the Sudan in terms of governance and economic development between the centre and the rest of the country' (UNCHR, 2004, p.21, Para 85). The most effective solution to this structural imbalance ought to have been taking concrete short and long term measures to address the 'imbalances'. In the short term, the rebellion could have been reined in, or at least tamed, had the government invited the rebel groups to the negotiating table and agreed on what was to be done. In the long run, the path for lasting peace could have been built through concrete policy measures aimed at reversing the resource and power disequilibria which have been in favour of the Arabs since independence; these measures have to be followed by genuine political will in formulating and implementing egalitarian regional development programmes.

The second factor that has compounded the western rebellion is the prospect for complacency offered by progress made in the southern peace process since 2002. In late 2002, a ceasefire was signed between the government and the southern rebel group – the SPLA/M. Further progress has been made in 2003 and 2004 following the *Naivasha Peace Accord* brokered by the US and some members of the European Union. Instead of utilising these international goodwill and cutting-edge initiatives by brewing more peace, its seems conversely to have made the Sudanese government complacent, ready and willing to deploy its military might to nascent scenes of rebellion such as Darfur, seemingly constructed as 'insignificant' compared to the southern rebellion. The third factor, which exacerbated the western rebellion, is the macro-economic impact of the discovery of petroleum in commercial quantities in Sudan. Since the commencement of production and export of petroleum in 1999 the Sudanese government has experienced phenomenal improvement in its real term fortunes. Ironically, instead of using the benefits accruing from petroleum to fund development projects that could improve the lives of Sudanese people and reverse 'ages' of unequal internal development, the Sudanese government, it seemed, accorded greater priority to reinforcing its military capability – an institution fatigued by a long-haul civil war in its combat with the Anya-Nya and SPLA/M rebellion in the past forty years.

The fourth factor is the massive geopolitical terrain conducive for rebellion provided by Darfur region, especially the boundary between Chad and Sudan. For a long time, the region has been a launching pad for coups and rebellion in the neighbouring Republic of Chad. In addition the two rebel groups draw part of their fighting forces from the republic of Chad, especially from the politically ambitious Zaghawa ethnic groups, as a result of the porous nature of the border region. The final and perhaps most important factor is the Sudanese government's decision to employ the Janjaweed militia composed of 'Arabs' as part of its counter-insurgency forces in a highly balkanised region ridden with ethnic, racial and resources conflicts. The importance of this factor as well as the risks it generated have been underscored the Acting UN High Commissioner for Human Rights, Bertrand Ramcharan, in a Report submitted to the Sixty-first session of the United Nations High Commission for Human Rights and follow-up to the World Conference on Human Rights:

> It is the manner of the response to this rebellion by the Government of the Sudan which has led to the current crisis in Darfur. Following SLA victories in the first months of 2003, the Government of the Sudan appears to have sponsored a militia composed of a loose collection of fighters, apparently of Arab background, mainly from Darfur, known as the 'janjaweed'. In other words, and worryingly, what

appears to have been an ethnically based rebellion has been met with an ethnically based response, building in large part on long-standing, but hitherto contained tribal rivalries. (UNCHR, Report No E/CN.4/2005/3, 7th May 2004, p.6)

The most volatile consequence of the western rebellion, therefore, is the creation and intensification of one big ethnic cum racial divide among a plethora of conflicting Arab and African communities in Darfur. While mutual ethnic suspicion and racial hate have been obvious in past resource conflicts, they were essentially blurred and crosscutting: much as they were Arab/African clashes, there were few incidences of clashes between farmers and rearers of the same ethnic group. After the rebellion however, the hitherto blurred boundaries of identity and resource conflict gradually collapsed; in their place emerged a definite dualised, but explosive, divide. While the Arabs pitched tents with the government, other ethnic/racial groups joined forces with the two rebel movements, namely the Sudan liberation Army/Movement (SLA/M) and Justice and Equality Movement (JEM).

At the early phase of the rebellion, especially during the first year of the insurgency, the two rebel groups were mainly composed of the three 'African' ethnic groups: Fur, Masalit and Zaghawa.[27] Eventually however, other 'minority' African ethnic groups such as Dorok and Jebel who were previously not considering themselves as party to the conflict were left with no alternative other than to identify with their 'kinds' in the rebel groups, a choice impelled by the calculated nature of attacks by an alliance of government forces and Janjaweed militia on their communities.

Perhaps a more serious effect of the western rebellion is the complex emergency it created in Darfur region. Perhaps, one of the most perilous strategic blunders committed by the government of Sudan, in its handling of the rebellion, is its refusal to come to terms with the rebel group; and a far greater one is its decision to arm the Janjaweed militia. While the government seemingly involved the Janjaweed militia to serve as counter-insurgents, they eventually went out of control as they began to unleash their own ethnic hate in targeting rival ethnic communities. This reality vindicates a common Muslim belief, one held among parties to the conflict, most if not all of whom are Muslims, that: 'Crisis is a sleeping monster, do not wake or provoke it. Doing so risks disastrous consequence that can be hard to rein in'.[28] The provoked 'sleeping monster' here is 'ethnic tension and racial hate' while its 'provocation' can be seen as the Sudanese government's exploitation of ethnic/racial tension and hate by creating and supporting a militia force comprising of only one side of a long-standing tribal, resource etc conflict in a drive to contain another conflict (insurgency, rebellion). Even though the insurgency is related in a way to the long-standing resource conflict, the two are not significantly tangential. By this I mean if the Sudanese government had not resorted to mobilising ethnic/racial divisions by recruiting the Janjaweed militia, the conflict could have stood exclusively as one between a marginalised region struggling to regain some form of equal treatment and a marginalising regime.

In the context of the current crisis in Darfur, the 'sleeping monster' has no doubt been provoked, with unforeseen consequences that could perhaps take years to overcome. The humanitarian situation in Darfur is not easy to describe in few lines, neither can it be 'underestimated' (UNCHR, 2004, p.7). More worrisome is the fact that the crisis is deteriorating by the day with huge spill-over effects on neighbouring Republic of Chad. The UNCHR estimates that as at May 2004, there are over one million Internally Displaced Persons (IDPs) inside Darfur as compared to 250,000 in September 2003. Over half of the IDPs (570,000) are located in Western Darfur while the rest are spread across North and South Darfur (290,000 and 140,000 respectively). The rising spate of humanitarian disaster in Darfur is caused primarily by targeted attacks on civilian populations by government forces and the Janjaweed militia.

Several reports, media documentaries, researches and fact-finding missions have revealed an ugly picture of calculated attacks on civilian communities in Darfur committed by Janjaweed militia forces in liaison with the Sudan Armed forces (Darfur Monitoring Group 2004; UN High Mission to Darfur, 2004: Para 4-8; AI, 2004a, 2004b, Human Rights Watch, 2004a, 2004b). A representative sample of the orgy of revelations emerging from these exercises can be garnered from a paragraph of a recent report of the Human Rights Watch:

> The government and its Janjaweed allies have killed thousands of Fur, Masalit and Zaghawa – often in cold blood, raped women, and destroyed villages, food stocks and other supplies essential to the civilian population. They have driven more than one million civilians, mostly farmers, into camps and settlements in Darfur where they live on the very edge of survival, hostage to Janjaweed abuses. More than 110,000 others have fled to neighbouring Chad but the vast majority of war victims remain trapped in Darfur. (Human Rights Watch, 2004b, p.1)

All fingers of blame are therefore pointed at the government of Sudan as the key mastermind behind the complex emergency in Darfur, as well as the atrocities committed by its sponsored Janjaweed militia.

Counter-Insurgents or Ethnic Vanguards?

At the heart of the current crisis in Darfur are the mysteries surrounding the very existence of the Janjaweed militia and atrocities committed against non-Arab civil populations of the Fur, Masalit and Zaghawa ethnic groups. An important question arising from this dilemma is whether the Janjaweed militia are counter-insurgents, as official nuances and conspiracies may seem to suggest; or they are an armed ethnic militia who have existed in different guises and together with other elements in the past (Fursan, Pershmerga, outcasts, criminals, thieves, livestock raiders etc) but were mobilised by the government in the current crisis to contain and punish those perceived by the government as rebelling forces and their communities. A careful evaluation of the Janjaweed militia and their activities, as will be seen in subsequent sections, may suggest that it is inadequate, even misleading, to consider the Janjaweed militia either as exclusively 'counter-insurgents' or 'ethnic militia': in the context of the current crisis, the two elements come together as a composite descriptive feature of the Janjaweed. The binding force for these two descriptive elements is the role played by the government in supporting the militia group to commit all sorts of ethnically motivated human rights abuses in the name of counter-insurgency.

In the past, armed Arab militias have no doubt played key roles in the long-standing resource, ethnic and racial conflicts in western Sudan. They emerged out of looming clashes between Arab nomads and black farmers by providing the former with armed elements capable of fighting the latter (as well as going beyond boundaries by indulging in stealing and robbery). Since 2003, however, the western rebellion and the nature of government response to it has transformed the Janjaweed militia from a naïve and outlawed ethnic vanguard to an organised government-backed paramilitary armed with sophisticated arms, communication equipment such as satellite phones, logistical support and legal protection – they seem to have been 'strategically' reactivated and reinforced by the Sudanese government to serve as a counter-insurgency force. What is obvious now, though, is that the Janjaweed militia have seemingly cashed in on their strategic positions as agents of the Sudanese government, perhaps with the tacit approval of the latter, to vent their racial/ethnic anger and hatred on rival African communities with whom they have clashed for decades over economic resources and ethnic/racial differences.

The government of Sudan has consistently claimed that Arab militia have always been present in the region and that they are 'a few side-lined ostracised outlaws' using the current crisis to carry out criminal activities. Conversely, however, concerned international institutions have refuted this position based on their direct involvement in and assessment of the situation in Darfur: their common position is that the government is deliberately involving the Janjaweed militia as a state sponsored armed tribal militia for systematic and deliberate attacks on non-combatant non-Arab civil communities (Human Rights Watch 2004a, 2004b, 2004c, UNCHR, 2004, AI, 2004a, 2004b etc). This indictment was recently re-echoed by the UN Secretary General, Mr Kofi Annan and the US Secretary of State, Mr Colin Powell, in a Joint Press Conference.[29] The role of the government in supporting Janjaweed as well as the latter's structure and activities need to be critically examined with a view to appreciating its violent activities (committed in tandem with the army) as well as the extent to which the government is implicated.

Khartoum Conspiracy: The Government as a Patron and an Ally

There is a relative consensus both within Sudan and outside on the role of the government of Sudan in the recruitment, deployment and maintenance of the Janjaweed militia in its fight against the SLA/M/JEM rebellion in western Sudan. While the government continues to keep mute or at best give garbled official positions, confessions by several serving and past state officials, as well as evidence from intercepted classified official documents tend to reveal that that the Janjaweed militia is indeed an ad hoc unit of Sudan's army.[30] Outside Sudan, several concerned individuals, international statesmen and bodies such as the UN secretary-General, Mr Kofi Annan, US Secretary of State, Mr Colin Powell, and UK Secretary for International Development, Mr Hilary Benn; Amnesty International, Human Rights Watch, UNCHR and so on have critically blamed the government of Sudan for its complicity in arming the Janjaweed militia.[31] As aptly described by the Human Rights Watch in its recent report on Darfur, 'the government [of Sudan is] working hand in glove with Janjaweed' (2004b, p.42), a precedent that has ever been used by the state in its counter-insurgency strategies:

> The Arab militia group known as Janjaweed are but the latest incarnation in a longstanding strategy of militia use by successive governments. The militias in Darfur are clearly supported by the Sudanese government, which uses them as counterinsurgency proxy to attack civilians while somewhat hiding the government's hand. (Human Rights Watch, 2004a, p.22)

Within Sudan, experiential testimonies of threats and utterances screamed by Janjaweed militia at their victims as well as statements made by key state functionaries prove the concerns held by the international community: a deliberate and well planned decision by the government in involving and supporting the Janjaweed militia, both as a client and an ally, to carry out counter-insurgency and ethnic cleansing against Fur, Masalit and Zaghawa Sudanese in Darfur region. Some of the oft-repeated claims made by the Janjaweed in their encounters with victims suggest that they enjoy state patronage: 'we are the government', 'if you have problem don't go the police' [which are dominated by members of rebelling Masalit ethnic group]...'come to the Janajaweed...The Janjaweed is the government. The Janjaweed is Omar Al-Bashir' [Sudan's head of state].[32] Similarly, victims of Janjaweed attack have repeatedly submitted that while conducting operations government forces and Janjaweed militia were always seen together: 'they come together, they fight together and leave together'.[33]

On several occasions, and without knowing it, several agents of the government of Sudan have admitted Sudan's working relationship with the Janjaweed militia or supported its cause. A recent statement made by the Sudanese Minister of Foreign Affairs, reveals confessions of a common cause between government counter-insurgency drives and the Janjaweed militia, implying that the cause of the militia 'was a just one... Because those militia are targeting the rebellion'. The Minister further reiterated government's denial of Janjaweed as a gang of tribal militia involved in ethnic cleansing and grossly under-estimated the human cost of their atrocities: 'I would say not more than 600 people [have been killed] at most' (Cited in Human Rights Watch (2004b, p.43). Similarly, in an address to the people of Kulbus on December 31st 2003, the President of Sudan, Omar Al-Bashir, said that in pursuing the government priority of defeating rebellion in Western Sudan, 'the horsemen' [that is, Janjaweed] were used alongside the army (Human Rights Watch, ibid).

Why did the government conspire with Janjaweed militia? There are three possible closely-knit reasons. First, the government is suspicious that some Fur, Masalit and Zaghawa elements within the army might sabotage its counter-insurgency drive. By involving the Janjaweed militia, not only are the possibilities of sabotage overcome, but also a trustworthy 'ally' can work alongside the military. Secondly, by virtue of being nomads the Janjaweed militia are familiar with the terrain in Darfur and are able to provide better compass and direction to counter-insurgency operations. Perhaps a stronger reason is that as rival to the rebelling ethnic groups and one loyal to the government, the Janjaweed militia are better poised to face both rebel groups and their 'anti-establishment' civil communities.

The Composition, Structure and Operation of Janjaweed Militia

Over the past couple of years, the Janjaweed militia has emerged as a robust coercive outfit drawing its authority and source of impunity from the state. It has gradually developed into a structured paramilitary formation as well as an irregular auxiliary unit of the Sudanese army, even though the government keeps hiding its complicity with the Janjaweed. It is extremely difficult to confirm the precise number of members of the Janjaweed militia. However, latest reports reveal that the Sudanese government has recruited 20,000 Janjaweed militia members (Human Rights Watch, 2004a, p.22). What is certain, though, is that the ethnic composition of the Janjaweed militia is almost are hundred percent 'Arab'; the few, even negligible, non-Arab members are those intimidated into identifying with the Arab cause. The clans and tribes frequently mentioned by refugees, IDPs and human rights groups as the main sources of Janjaweed militia are the Irayqat and Ouled Zed subclans of the camel herding northern Rezeigat, the Mahariya and the Beni Hussein. In terms of nationality, Janjaweed militia members are drawn both from Sudanese and Chadian Arabs. This is because, within the Janjaweed, the key determinant of ethnic consciousness, identity pride and esprit de corps is advancing the Arab cause and getting rid of 'inferior' ethnic rivals, rather than advancing national causes. Indeed, there are claims that the majority of Janjaweed militia members are Chadian rather than Sudanese citizens, the key factors behind this being increasing ethnic polarisation in the region, the prospects for loot and pillage (Human Rights Watch, 2004a, p.23) as well as the porous nature of Chad-Sudan border.

The leadership of the organisation is drawn mainly from the leadership of the Arab clan system and those politically appointed: 'many or most of the Janjaweed leaders were emirs or *Omdas* from Arab tribe, and several were appointed by the government in the administrative reorganisation of the mid-1990s' (Human Rights Watch, 2004b, p.45). The Janjaweed have been structured into brigades or *Liwa,* each headed by a general. Rebel leaders claim that there are no less than six Janjaweed Liwas, while victims and IDPs identify two: the Buffalo Brigade – Liwa al-Jammous – formerly headed by Musa Hilal; and Victory Brigade – Liwa al-Nasr – formerly headed by Abdul Rahim Ahmad Mohammad alias 'Shukurtallah'. These brigades are structured along the rank and file tradition and esprit de corps of the Sudanese army. Their uniforms and ranking insignia are patterned in the same colour, quality and design as those of the regular army. However, there are features that distinguish Janjaweed from other sections of the

Sudan's army: the breast pockets of Janjaweed uniforms and fatigues have fixed badges showing an armed horseman or a red patch on the shoulder and their typical, and symbolic, means of transportation is either camel or horse. Apart from this, other military conditions of service and incentives apply both to Janjaweed and the army: Janjaweed 'officers' use the same four-wheeled drive Toyota Land Cruiser vehicles and are accompanied by bodyguards as are those in the army. In addition, they mount checkpointslike the army, impose tax on commuters and carry the same Thuraya satellite phones as senior army officers.[34]

Men and officers of Janjaweed are believed to receive an attractive wage from the state. Credible claims have it that new conscripts receive a starter wage of 100-400 US dollars per month, as well as other incentives such as a confirmation of continuing state support for their relatives should they die in combat. Long serving Janjaweed members are believed to receive salaries and incentives that outweigh those of regular army members. In addition to regular supplies of reinforcements and food items, they are also issued with state-endorsed identity cards confirming their rank and other personal details.[35] Since the eruption of the western rebellion, the Janjaweed militia have been armed with new weapons and communications facilities. The assault rifle and allied equipment carried by each Janjaweed militia – such as Kalashnikovs, 'Bazuka', Belgique and G-3s, long-range vision equipment – as well as communication gadgets – such as walkie-talkies and satellite phones – are commonly believed to be provided by the state, as they are either illegal or too expensive to carry under normal circumstances. Furthermore, in 'their' barracks (see next paragraph) and homes the leadership of Janjaweed have been provided with massive leisure equipment such as those enjoyed by state functionaries: satellite dishes for receiving international television channels (such as Al-Jazeera, Sudan TV, Kuwait TV, Nile TV and so on), landline telephones (to complement Thuraya), computers and so on.[36]

Though they are not stationed in the same barracks with the military, they are known to be using abandoned decommissioned military and para-military facilities owned by the government.[37] There are controversies surrounding the overall hierarchy of command in the Janjaweed.[38] However, there is consensus that the command headquarters and operational base of the Janjaweed is in Geneina, the headquarters of West Darfur. The Geneina barrack – a former Customs Yard known as Medina al-Hajja – is believed to have a training camp situated outside the town and to be equipped with modest training facilities and features, to serve the training and strategic needs of the Janjaweed. It is believed to have sufficient facilities to serve as the headquarters of Janjaweed Central Command (JCC) – a possible classified acronym for a mysterious organisation! – for coordinating remuneration, training and armament needs of Janjaweed militia members. Medina al-Hajjaj also serves as the main contact point for the Sudanese army, especially men of the military intelligence unit, who regularly visit the facility to distribute arms and reinforcements (for instance bullets, new uniforms, food supplies, communication equipment etc) and receive briefings from and relay government instructions to the Janjaweed leadership. It also serves as a payment unit for army paymasters who regularly come to hand out salaries and other incentives to Janjaweed members.

While there are mysteries surrounding its structure, there are few or no controversies surrounding the operations and activities of the Janjaweed militia. With the probable exception of manning sophisticated and heavy-duty military vehicles, and conducting aerial reconnaissance/attacks – all of which require highly specialised military skills – the Janjaweed are known to have conducted almost every bit of counter-insurgency operations together with the regular Sudanese army. Indeed, there are some functions for which the army relied heavily on the Janjaweed. First, the army depends on Janjaweed for forward air control capacity in which advance teams of Janjaweed penetrate and cordon off targeted communities with a view to facilitating smooth aerial and ground attacks (Human Rights Watch, 2004b, p.17). Secondly, as iterant nomadic people, the Janjaweed are very much familiar with the terrain in Darfur region: they know every nook and cranny of Darfur and have precise knowledge of communities and their leaders, especially those suspected of supporting the rebellion. They are believed to have first hand knowledge of where, how and when to strike on suspected communities, making operations easier and more effective. Thirdly, the Janjaweed are useful tools for making claims that may exonerate the Sudanese army in covering-up some of its violent acts, such as wholesale cleansing of communities in the name of counter-insurgency. Any military operations conducted by the army without the company of the Janjaweed can easily implicate the state if they result in clear ethnic cleansing, as they always appear so. The state has been claiming that the Janjaweed usually track and chance on non-violent security operations of the army by committing criminal activities on communities after the soldiers have left. This claim hardly holds water, as the Janjaweed are seen together with the army both in combats with SLA/M/JEM and attacks on non-combatant civil communities.

Most, if not all, attacks are ethnically and racially motivated, aimed at 'cleansing' of targeted adult Fur, Masalit and Zaghawa men, and are often preceded or followed by raping of women and young girls (usually in front of their relatives), pillage of stored food, livestock, jewellery, and setting the attacked settlements on fire. Other vulnerable members of the community are not spared: the infants, old and handicapped often get killed as a result of their incapacity to obey hostile and immediate orders during operations. Many also die of neglect, broken heart, or lack of care after attacks when able men or women are either killed, have escaped/been abducted or are too weak (for instance raped women) to tender for them.

The range and nature of violent, ethnically motivated, abuses carried out by the Janjaweed militia are wide, gruesome and horrific. In a recent report, the UNCHR classified Janjaweed/army violence into the following categories: indiscriminate attack against civilians; rape and other forms of sexual violence; destruction of property and pillage; forced displacement; disappearances; and persecution and discrimination. For all these violent acts, the report not only claimed that they are ethnically motivated, but indicted their perpetrators in clear terms: the Sudanese government and Janjaweed militia attacking defenceless civilians from Fur, Masalit and Zaghawa ethnic communities for suspected support of the western rebellion (UNCHR, 2004).

Similar reports by Amnesty International and Human Rights Watch, not only indicted the government and Janjaweed, but also documented detailed testimonies from victims of violence (IDPs within Sudan and refugees who have fled to neighbouring Chad Republic) of how these attacks were carried out (AI, 2004a, 2004b; Human Rights Watch, 2004a, 2004b, 2004c). According to many accounts from those reports, the pattern of attacks comes in phases, ascending in order of severity: initial, intermediate and chronic attacks. The initial phase involves visitation by well-armed Janjaweed militia often resulting in theft of livestock, verbal threats on the population and firing into the air. The intermediate and chronic phases, usually occurring in quick successions, and involving combined attacks by the militia and army, graduate into more violent attacks on communities. An account from a Masalit refugee from West Darfur is worth citing here:

> There have been three attacks [on my village] since October 2003, but the last attack [in January 2004] was the worst. The first time, the [Janjaweed] men came on camels and horses and frightened us, but in the third attack they came by car and killed a lot of people. All the inhabitants fled at once after the last attack. The military told us they would erase us. We asked why they wanted to hurt us and they answered that it was none of our business, that orders come from above.[39]

In the foregoing account the role of the state is clearly revealed in the form of threatening confession made by a member of the Sudanese army. The account also showed the stage(s) at which state means of coercions are heavily applied: the second and third degree attacks. At these stages, heavy military equipment and aircraft are brought to bear as revealed by a victim, a man from Fara Wiya town, a commercial town and administrative district in Darfur destroyed for suspected presence of SLA rebels:

> The government bombed us with Antonov, MiG, and helicopters. About 140 bombs dropped in Fara Wiya town in that month. The MiGs specifically hit the school – the hole was more than two metres deep. After that we were afraid and took own children away into the mountains. After the bombing in the morning, we saw about 2,000 soldiers come with tanks in the early afternoon. They surrounded the village on three sides and the Janjaweed came on the fourth side. The plane had already destroyed the health clinic. The Janjaweed and the soldiers broke onto the shops and looted, then they burnt the houses. The Janjaweed put a dead animal in the well.[40]

Other forms of violence such as rape, abduction, disappearances, deliberate destruction of water sources, and so on come together (before, during or after) with attacks.

Prospects for Demobilisation and Peace

One scholar of Darfur has rightly described the Janjaweed militia as 'wild cats' illustrating the huge challenge associated with 'taming' (demobilising) it.

According to him, while peace in the Darfur region is primarily dependent on reining in the Janjaweed, it is no mean task: the Janjaweed have become one of the richest groups in Sudan, perhaps a new entrant into the elite syndicate.[41] They have amassed cars, houses and money and, therefore, developed a huge stake in the current crisis. They have also come to wield significant degree of power by virtue of the convergence of interest they share with the state. If taming them could prove such a herculean task, the prospect of disarming them is an even harder challenge facing Sudan and others concerned in the crisis.

The prospects for demobilising the Janjaweed militia and restoring peace in western Sudan hang on a number of factors: the willingness of parties to the conflict (the government, SLA/M and JEM) to come to terms and end the conflict, the willingness by Khartoum to disarm the Janjaweed and by Janjaweed members/leaders to be disarmed. These factors have been brought to test, often with sordid results, in international and national responses to the conflict. Responses to the crisis have come from three main sources: the Sudanese authorities and rebel groups; member-nations and the main body of the African Union; and the international community. The response of the Sudanese state can be described, at best, as dismal or un-forthcoming. While the abuses committed by the Janjaweed militia have become undeniable, the government of Sudan continues to distance itself from the militia or its activities. It has become obvious, more than ever before, that the Sudanese government has to unconditionally disarm its 'wild cats' as a minimum step in curbing the current conflict and humanitarian crisis in Darfur. It also has to deal with the rebels in friendly and honest terms. Conversely, the authorities in Khartoum have been adamant, even sarcastic, towards the situation. While pillages and killing were going on, President Al-Bashir mockingly declared a victory against the rebels in February 2004. This action provoked the rebels and brought to naught the Abeche ceasefire agreement, brokered by the president, signed in August 2003.

Within Africa, the African Union has played a positive role in restoring peace in Darfur. The AU has been an observer and facilitator, to peace talks brokered by Chad in 2003 and 2004. However, it has never asserted a prevailing voice on the Sudanese government to disarm the Janjaweed. In April, the AU Peace and Security Council issued a communiqué expressing concern with the humanitarian situation in Darfur and calling on the government to bring to justice those responsible for violations of human rights. But the communiqué neither indicted the state nor urged it to disarm the Janjaweed. Other members of the African Union have even remained supportive to the government. At the UN, for instance, African countries have undermined a UNCHR proposed resolution seeking to appoint a special rapporteur to the Sudan and condemn the actions of the state in arming the Janjaweed. They also supported Sudan's candidature for membership of UNCHR in spite of the country's poor human rights records.

The republic of Chad has played a significant role not only in brokering a ceasefire, but also calling on Khartoum to disarm the Janjaweed.[42] Following the breach by the Sudanese government of the Abeche ceasefire agreement, and under increasing pressure from the international system, in March 2004 the government of Sudan and rebel forces began another series of talks under the auspices of the

Chadian government. Another agreement has been signed, albeit hastily, on April 8, 2004 in which both parties to the conflict, with the exception of JEM, agreed to down arms, including the disarmament of the Janjaweed by the Sudanese authorities. While ceasefires have been signed, the will by parties to implement them has been absent so far.

Within the international system, the UN has continued to exert pressure on Sudan to disarm the Janjaweed and restore peace in Darfur. The latest resolution announced on 31st July 2004 gave Sudan a one-month ultimatum to disarm the Janjaweed.[43] Other units within the UN system, such as UNCHR, have continued both to reveal the extent of the crisis and to exert pressure on Sudan but such pressure has been weak given the limitations of scope for international organisations to interfere in the internal affairs of member states. Other members of the international system – the EU and the United States – have played significant, albeit mixed, roles in calling on Sudan to disarm the Janjaweed. However disagreements within the EU and between the EU and the US on how to approach the issue have resulted in undermining of their initiatives, giving the Sudanese government an opportunity to remain adamant: while some countries such as the UK, Netherlands and France have supported piecemeal approaches and strong involvement of the AU, others such as Germany and the US have favoured stricter options possibly involving UN peace keeping forces.

Conclusion

The western rebellion in the Republic of Sudan, which began in early 2003, is the manifestation of a violent response by deprived Sudanese, those placed at the margins of state welfare and development. Being a highly heterogeneous state and one dominated by the Arab ruling class of the upper Nile region, rebellion by non-Arab Sudanese against an Arab controlled state has remained one of the descriptive features of the country, not least because the state has continued to adopt enraging steps that seek to fuel the embers of division. While past rebellion from southern Sudan has been constructed in religious (in addition to ethnic) terms, the current rebellion in the west has incapacitated the state preventing it from mobilising religious differences, as parties to the conflict and its victims are mainly Muslims. However, with the exception of religion, attempts by the state to mobilise ethnic, tribal and racial difference among western Sudanese, were revealed in its decision to recruit the Janjaweed militia both as counter-insurgents and as tools of ethnic cleansing.

The aftermath of arming the Janjaweed militia is the on-going humanitarian crisis in western Darfur affecting over one million western Sudanese. The state army and its Janjaweed allies have been indicted for a dynamic ethnic complicity to wipe out the entirety of non-Arab ethnic groups in Western Sudan. They have committed undeniable acts of violence against the Fur, Masalit and Zaghawa communities: bombing, execution, killings, abduction, rape, pillage, burning, intimidation, and extortion among others. While rebel groups have played roles both in inciting and compounding the conflict (for instance, by stationing themselves near civil communities) they have so far proved themselves a lesser evil compared to the state. The state lacks any justification for extinguishing its citizens in the name of ethnically motivated counter-insurgency.

Since 2003, the Darfur region has been used both as a base and target of salvation by the SEL/M and JEM rebel groups, a factor chiefly responsible for high-handedness by the government toward innocent civil communities. The state seems to have declared the Darfur region an outcast, one that has to be wiped out of its domiciled communities and replaced by more loyal settlers (Human Rights Watch, 2004a, 2004b). The decision by the state to arm and support the Janjaweed militia is a manifestation of the extent to which a ruling state oligarchy from one ethnic/racial extraction could mobilise divisive tendencies and use state means of violence in negotiating, by violent means, with millions of its citizens for suspected anti-statism (liberation?).

By virtue of the huge humanitarian dislocation and wanton destruction carried out in Darfur region, the Janjaweed militia and Sudanese army have proved themselves a combined force for ethnic cleansing wrapped in the cocoon of counter-insurgency. With the failure of Chadian-brokered peace initiatives and lesser efforts by the AU, the international community is duty-bound to bring a swift end to the ugly situation in Darfur. Sadly, however, the current approach adopted by the international system has fallen short of real emergency action. Beyond calling Darfur a region in humanitarian disaster, one requiring urgent international aid, there is an urgent need to declare Darfur a genocide region and Sudan a genocide-committing state, this would necessitate the immediate application of force through the UN system.

Notes

[1] This is one of the key excuses the current General Omar El-Bashirs's regime in Khartoum uses to justify 'Arab' militia atrocities, which it backs, against 'African' ethnic groups in the current crisis in Darfur.

[2] The rebellion is atypical of the pattern of political dissent and struggle for autonomy in Sudan which normally come from the south. Perhaps for the first time in Sudan's post-colonial history, a rebellion is emerging from the western region which has always been constructed as part of the dominant north and one that has perhaps remained loyal to its domination. With the exception of race (Arab versus Africans), people in western Sudan have shared common religious and cultural identities with those in the north. In the past, rebellions were therefore constructed as coming from 'southerners' or 'disbelievers'.

[3] It is estimated that, since 1983, over 1.5 million people have perished as a result of civil war between SPLA/SPLM and the Sudanese government. Added to this are recent casualties arising from the current crisis in Darfur. It is also estimated that in material terms civil strife costs the Republic of Sudan a staggering one million dollars daily. For estimate of the human cost of the SPLA war see Kaya (2004). For an emerging data on civil casualties and material destruction in Darfur, see Human Rights Watch (2004a, 2004b, 2004c and 2004d. (Specifically, 2004b Appendix 'D' contains graphic images of victims and places destroyed). See also Amnesty International (2003, 2004a 2004b and 2004c).

[4]   The Accord was aimed at ending the twenty-one year war between the government of Sudan and SPLA/SPLM rebels in the south.

[5]   The SPLA/SPLM was known to have contributed to the early stages of rebellion in western Sudan by offering training, arms and logistics support to the SLA, one of the warring factions. However it was reported to have eventually withdrawn such support following the successes made at the Naivasha Peace process. It seems that the SPLA/SPLM now relates the conflict in western Sudan with the wider instability in Sudan for which it is a contending party. In an article posted at the official website of the group, it is stated that 'the conflict in Darfur is running parallel to Sudan's wider war, in which southern rebels have been fighting Khartoum's forces for more than 20 years...' What cannot be ruled out, though, is the possibility that the SPLM may strategically exploit conflict in any other part of Sudan with the aim of negotiating a better deal in case the peace accord reaches a deadlock or is breached in the future. For details see Kaya (2004, p.2).

[6]   The word Janjaweed is a controversial one. Historically it refers to an outcast or one associated with crimes. In the context of the current crisis in Darfur however, it refers to 'people on horseback' meaning nomads who usually use horse as their means of transportation and raids but have now converted to irregular armed regiments of the Sudanese army in its fight against the western rebellion. As a controversial paramilitary outfit, it has other cross-reference terms such as 'Fursan' or 'Pershmerga'. See UNHCR, 2004: 15 Para. 54.

[7]   For recent first hand details of atrocities committed by the Janjaweed militia in alliance with government forces see Human Rights Watch (2004e; especially pp 2-8).

[8]   A number of published academic materials have documented both the history and politics of Sudan's instability. For further details see, for instance, Woodward (2003, in particular Chapter 2, pp. 36-64 which deals with Sudan); Woodward (1990 especially Part 2, Chapters 4, 5, and 6); Daly (1993, pp.1-26), and Bechtold (1991, especially Chapter 1, pp.1-23).

[9]   For details of southern rebellion see Beshir (1968, especially Chapters 8, 9, 10 and 11), and Wakoson (1993, pp.27-50). For an account of a southern activist in the conflict see Albino (1970).

[10]   However, even early indications showed that Darfur was one of the few regions that spotted the growth of militia in Sudan. Most of these regions, if not all of them, have deeply rooted histories of ethnic balkanisation between Sudanese of Arab and African descent.

[11]   Most of these recent reports and press releases contain horrible images of human rights abuses and destruction often based on factual ethnographic accounts from victims (and often perpetrators) of atrocities as well as pictorial evidence of destructions collected by researchers from the field. See Human Rights Watch (especially 2004a, 2004b) and Amnesty International (especially 2003, 2004a and 2004b).

[12]   For instance, in Nigeria, as in other unstable democracies, paramilitaries comprising mainly thugs and hooligans constitute an important instrument for power struggles. Every major political party and most politicians, especially the so-called 'power brokers' or 'money bag politicians', have to employ the services of regular militias as weapons for the protection of supporters and intimidation of rivals. This scenario is somewhat similar to urban militias in Sudan.

[13]   One common denominator of the two categories of civil militia (those within SPLA territory and the Muraheleen based in the West) is the influence of the state, at least at some points in time, in its drive to combat and defeat insurgency. Thus, while the southern-based militia groups were used to fight the SPLA/SPLM from 'within', the Muraheleen were used from outside the nucleus of the southern rebellion. The strategic

advantage of each choice was perhaps to contain the SPLA/SPLM rebellion both 'internally' and 'externally'.

[14] In the context of Janjaweed militia for instance, recruitment or access to guns comes not from the black market, as de Waal (1993) suggests, but from government sources. Indeed a recent human rights report suggests, 'the Sudanese government...have recruited [and armed] 20,000 Janjaweed militia members'. See Human Rights (2004a, p.22).

[15] The majority of the population in southern Sudan are either Christians or traditionalists. In addition, one of the key demands of the southern-based SPLA/M in its confrontation with the government is putting an end to the so-called 'September Laws', a series of Islamic legal instruments introduced by the government of Nimiery in September 1983, in contravention of the 1972 Addis Ababa Agreement which brought earlier the *Anya Nya* Rebellion to an end.

[16] See note number 12 for a comparative insight into the role of party paramilitaries in the struggle for power in Nigeria, which seems to tally with the situation in Sudan.

[17] The term Darfur is derived from two words: *Dar* means 'home' while *Fur* stands for the Fur 'tribe'. Literally it means the homeland, settlement or territory of the Fur people. Similar categories include *Darmasalit,* Masalit territory, and so on.

[18] This geopolitical comparison is highly symbolic not least because it seems to underpin the crisis bedevilling a massive territory with a huge population (4-5 million). If Darfur were France or Alaska, the international uproar that would have been created, and the solidarity assistance rushed to the region would have been far more than the international community is currently doing in the region. See Amnesty International (2004c, p.1), Human Rights Watch (2004b, p.6, fn 1).

[19] Most of these borders are porous and permeable. The one between Chad and Sudan, 1,000 Kilometres as claimed by the Human Rights Watch (2004a) or 800 Kilometres as contained in a Report of the UNCHR (2004), demonstrates literally that there is no physical divide between the two countries. Many of the demographic characteristics of the people living across those international boundaries, such as economic activities, racial, ethnic and religious division and so on are similar. Patterns of conflict over resources, especially clashes over grazing areas/farmland, as well as the mediation and resolution of conflict often cut across those international boundaries. In addition, communities across borders often engage in trade (both legal and illegal) intermarriages and mixing of religious congregations making it very difficult to distinguish citizenship and other identities in the borderlands.

[20] It is estimated that more than 110,000 people mainly Fur, Masalit and Zaghawa, have fled across the border to Chad to find refuge there; while at least 750,000 remained displaced in Sudan at the mercy of militia attacks (Human Rights Watch, 2004a, p.1).

[21] Settled agricultural communities in Darfur consist mainly of non-Arab or 'African' blacks (called Zurga) and include such ethnic groups as Bergit, Bertit, Fur, Masalit, Tama and Tunjur living and farming in the central zone. On the other hand, nomadic communities consist mainly of Arab herders of the northern belt who rear camels. They include Rizeigat, Mahariya, Irayqat and Bani Hussain as well as 'African' Zaghawa. Furthermore, there are cattle rearing Arab communities such as Rizeigat, Habbaniya and Bani Halba living and herding in the southern and eastern zones. Conflict often occurs when herding communities trample their animals into the lands of settled farming communities.

[22] The use of 'African' and 'Arab' are being re-invented as new forms of racial identity construction in the context of the current crisis in western Sudan. In the past people of African origin identified themselves as 'Darfurians' or 'Zurga'. However, following the eruption of the conflict and systematic attacks on them by the government supported

Janjaweed militia, they now identify themselves as 'Africans' or 'blacks' as an identity referent that contrasts with the 'Arabs'. Furthermore, in the context of conflict over resources, it is worthy of note that although conflicts are often constructed racially as between Arabs and Africans, they also occasionally occur within a single racial category: an insignificant per cent of the clashes occur between African farmers and rearers themselves (such as between Fur or Masalit farmers and Zaghawa cattle rearers or Masalit farmers and rearers).

[23]   West Darfur has a population of 1.7 million people and contains a plethora of ethnic groups. The Masalit comprise 60 per cent of the population in Geneina and Habila provinces followed by Arabs, Zaghawa, Erenga, Gimr, Dajo, Borgo and Fur. The Fur constitute the majority in Zalingei, Jebel Marra and Wadi Salih Provinces while Kulbus province comprises 50 per cent Gimr, 30 per cent Eranga, 15 per cent Zaghawa and 5 per cent Arab (Human Rights Watch, 2004b, p.5).

[24]   For details of Anglo-Egyptian legal and political legacies over Sudan see Peter Woodward's (1990) *Sudan 1898-1989: the Unstable State*. Part one of the book traces the establishment of the Anglo-Egyptian condominium (chapter one); the crisis that it faced (chapter two) and its formal end following the granting of independence to Sudan (chapter three). For an analysis of the interface between imperialism and nationalism in Sudan see also Woodward (1979).

[25]   As at now, the quantity of arms used in Darfur is incalculable. The figure cited was originally reported by the Sudanese *Al-Ayyam* newspaper and was re-echoed in a report released at that time by the Human Rights Watch (1990b, p.3).

[26]   These complaints seem to carry heavy political weight because they are constructed, in ethnic and racial terms, as a response by an Arab controlled central government in Sudan to cries of marginalisation coming from its Arab kith and kin in a region (west) where 'Arabs' perceive themselves as a minority. Since the country gained independence in 1956, the Arab political class mainly from the northern Nile Valley region, has dominated political power in Sudan. This political class is commonly described in the streets of marginalised regions, as an ethnic and racial oligarchy whose power has to be stripped if Sudan is to remain an egalitarian society. This is one of the causes of southern rebellion as well as of the one going on in the west.

[27]   There were divisions and tension among and within these ethnic groups over preference and loyalty to one of the two rebel groups. For instance, among the three sub-ethnic groups of the Zaghawa, the Bideyat and Kobe are commonly found in the JEM, while the Wagi constitute the majority of SLA/M rebels. Before they became united, at least partially for a shortwhile, the two rebel groups were not on good terms with each other, their bone of contention being the ideology and strategies of the rebellion.

[28]   As a politically motivated conflict, the crisis in Darfur, for all intents and purposes, cannot be seen as one between actors of different religious faiths whose leaders mobilise such differences to justify violence as was the case in the context of the southern rebellion. It seems that key parties to the conflict in Darfur who are mainly Muslims – the authorities in Khartoum, rebel groups, the Janjaweed militia etc – are not motivated by a religious cause as was the case when the Muslim controlled state was fighting the mainly Christian rebellion in the name of Jihad in the 1980s and 1990s.

[29]   Monitored on BBC World News, 23rd July 2004.

[30]   For instance, on 21st July 2004, a former governor of Darfur, Ahmed Diraige stated in a live chat with the BBC programme – *Breakfast* – that the Sudanese army and Janjaweed militia are operating as allied forces in carrying out attacks on Fur, Masalit and Zaghawa communities (Monitored on BBC News, 21/06/2004). Similarly, intercepted official documents collected by the Human Rights Watch reveal that the government has given

approval for the recruitment of more Janjaweeds as well as their remuneration (Human Rights Watch, 2004b, p.46).

[31] Having followed the crisis since it erupted and been part of a loose consortium of concerned groups seeking solutions to the problem, these individuals and groups have first hand knowledge of the extent of the government's complicity in the deployment of the Janjaweed. Their informed opinion is derived from direct contact both with state officials, rebels and victims of the rebellion.

[32] Interview conducted by Human Rights Watch with Adam, a victim of Janjaweed abuse, Chad April 2, 2004.

[33] Interview conducted by Human Rights Watch with Abdullah, a forty nine year old headman of Terbeba village, held in Chad March 24, 2004.

[34] Reports of the Human Rights Watch contain a number of cases of Janjaweed and the army imposing tax on IDPs and escaping refugees. An example is worth citing here: 'Displaced Fur civilians in Garsila, Deleig, Mugjir and other towns controlled by government forces and Janjaweed are regularly forced to pay bribes and subjected to violence by Janjaweed 'officials' when attempting to move outside the displaced settlements and camps around these towns...' (Human Rights Watch, 2004b, p.38).

[35] The evidence for this claim is revealed in a confidential army document captured by the rebels in one of their attacks on military facilities in December 2003 (see Human Rights Watch, 2004a, p.24 and fn 46).

[36] Many Janjaweed leaders combine their militia leadership with clan leadership and have homes in major centres of power across Sudan and Chad. They use those homes when they are off-duty, on holidays or come to consult with state officials (Sudan). Among the clan/Janjaweed leaders are Hamid Dawai, an Emir of the Bani Habila tribe and Janjaweed leader in the Terbeba-Arara-Bayda triangle where 460 civilians were killed in August 2003 and April 2004 – he has residences in Geneina and Bayda; Abdullah Abu Sheneibat, an emir of the Beni Halba tribe and Janjaweed leader in the Habila-Murnei region who has residences in Geneina and Habila; Omda Saef, a chief of the Awlad Zeid clan and leader of the Janjaweed between Geneina and Murnei – he has a residence in Geneina; Omar Babbush, a chief of the Misseriya tribe and Janjaweed leader from Habila to Fogranga with a residence in Forgranga and Ahmad Dekheir, a Malia chief who leads Janjaweed in Murnei (Human Rights Watch, 2004b:45).

[37] The Sudanese government is perhaps careful not to mix Janjaweed militia with its regular army in the same military facilities or to join their hierarchies of command. There are two possible reasons: first, the Sudanese government has consistently claimed that it has no hand in the recruitment of Janjaweed militia; hence mixing them in the same facilities could justify claims, especially those from the international community, accusing Khartoum of arming Janjaweed. Secondly, the Janjaweed is an all-Arab ethnic militia, while the mainstream Sudanese army, consists of a tribal mix of all Sudanese, even though this claim stands the risk of being falsified as the integrity of the army as a national institution continues to be tattered by its blind-folded involvement in the current and other insurgencies all of which are/were motivated by sectarian or ethnic, rather than national interest(s). While the Janjaweed is seen to possess a specific ethnic agenda, the army is constructed by the state as a national institution that is too risky to be openly politicised. While secretly mixing the two in counter-insurgency operations, the Sudanese government, it seems, has internalised the two units to serve as checks: Arab militias have a duty to defend the interests of the Arab controlled government ('we are the government' as they usually claim), the army, especially men and officers from Fur, Masalit and Zaghawa ethnic extraction are duty bound to apply the state's means of coercion, in any way and to any extent, in obedience to commands even if it is against their wishes.

[38] There is debate over who holds the position of the General Officer Commanding the Janjaweed militia. Some sources believe that the overall commander is 'General' Shukurtallah, the Commander of Victory Brigade (Liwa al-Nasr) and a former military officer convicted and imprisoned for killing civilians but later discharged and given amnesty by the Sudanese government to head the Janjaweed. He is believed to be a member of Mahariya clan from Arbukni village in the outskirts of Geneina. There are indications that he was killed while fighting in North Darfur in January 2004. Others believe that the overall Janjaweed commander is a Rezeigat tribal chief from Kutum who is believed to command a high degree of respect and obedience from the rank and file of the Janjaweed. Because of the mystery surrounding it and its relationship with state, however, the command structure of the Janjaweed continues to be closely guarded.

[39] Interview by Human Rights Watch, Chad, February 11, 2004 (Cited in Human Rights Watch 2004a, p.21).

[40] Interview by Human Rights Watch, Chad, February 23, 2004 (Cited in Human Rights Watch 2004a, p.20).

[41] Telephone interview by Human Rights Watch, March 10, 2004 (see Human Rights Watch 2004a, p.42).

[42] The president of Chad, Mr Idris Derby, and members of his cabinet are also aware of the nature of rebellion and how it could possibly degenerate into political instability in their country. In the mid-1990s Derby and his rebel group used Darfur as an insurgency base to fight and overthrow the government in N'Djamena. In addition, it is commonly believed that many Chadian citizens are serving in the rebel groups (Zaghawa) and Janjaweed (Arabs) while many Darfurian victims of Janjaweed attack have escaped to Chad and settled as refugees.

[43] Monitored on BBC World News, July 31, 2004.

References

Albino, Oliver (1970), *The Sudan: a Southern Viewpoint*, Institute of Race Relations/Oxford University Press, London.

Amnesty International (1989), *Human Rights Violation in the Context of Civil War*, Amnesty International, London.

Amnesty International (2000), *Sudan*, Annual Report 2000 available: http:web.amnesty.org/web/ar2000web.nsf/countries/afadc28d7852596802568f2005529 … (accessed on 22/06/2004).

Amnesty International (2001), *Sudan*, Report 2001 available: http:web.amnesty.org/web/ar2001.nsf/webafrcountries/SUDAN?OpesDocument (accessed on 22/06/2004)

Amnesty International (2003), *Sudan*, Annual Report Summary 2003 available: http://web.amnesty.org/report2003/sdn-summary-eng (accessed on 26/06/2004).

Amnesty International (2004a), *Sudan Report 2004*, available: http:web.amnesty.org/report2004/sdn-summary-eng (accessed on 22/06/2004)

Amnesty International (2004b), *Sudan: Government Responsible for Humanitarian Devastation but Still in Denial*, Press Release, Ref: AI Index: AFR 54/067/2004 (Public), News Service No: 155, 20 June 2004 available: http: web.amnesty.org/library/index/ENGAFR540672004 (accessed on 22/06/2004).

Amnesty International (2004c), *Sudan Crisis: In our Silence We are Complicit*, available http://web.amnesty.org/pages/sdn-index-eng (accessed on 18/06/2004).

Alier, A. (1990), *Southern Sudan: Too Many Agreements Dishonoured*, Ithaca Press, Exeter.

An-Na'im, A. and Kok, P. (1991), *Fundamentalism and Militarism: a Report on the Root Causes of Human Rights Violations in the Sudan*, The Fund for Peace, New York.

Bechtold, P. K. (1991), 'More turbulence in Sudan: a new politics this time?', in J. O. Voll (ed.), *Sudan: State and Society in Crisis*, Middle East Institute, Washington D.C.

Beshir, M O. (1968), *The Southern Sudan: Background to Conflict*, C. Hurst and Co, London.

Daly, M. W. (1993), 'Broken bridge and empty basket: the political and economic background of the Sudanese civil war', in M.W. Daly and Ahmad Alawad Sakainga (eds.), *Civil War in the Sudan*, British Academic Press, London.

Darfur Monitoring Group (2004), *Ethnic Cleansing in Darfur Region of Sudan* available: www.d-a.org.uk/pages/dmg1.htm (accessed on 22/06/2004).

Deng, F. M. (1995), *War of Visions: Conflict of Identities in Sudan*, The Brookings Institution, Washington D.C.

Deng, F. M. (1993), 'Hidden agendas in the peace process', in M.W. Daly and A. A. Sakainga (eds.), *Civil War in the Sudan*, British Academic Press, London.

Deng, F. M (1991), 'War of visions for the nation', in J. O. Voll (ed.), *Sudan: State and Society in Crisis*, Middle East Institute, Washington D.C.

de Waal, A. (1993a), 'Some comments on militia in the contemporary Sudan', in M.W. Daly and A. A. Sakainga (eds.), *Civil War in the Sudan*, British Academic Press, London.

de Waal, A. (1993b), 'Starving out the South, 1984-9', in M.W. Daly and A. A. Sakainga (eds.), *Civil War in the Sudan*, British Academic Press, London.

Hentoff, N. (2004), 'The Sudan Genocide: Arab Muslims are viciously killing and raping Black', available: http://www.fuckfrance.com/read.html?postid=665368&replies=0 (accessed on 10/06/2004).

Holt, P. and Daly, M. W. (1988), *A History of Sudan from the Coming of Islam to the Present Day*, Longman, London.

Human Rights Watch (1990a), *Denying the Honour of Living: Sudan, a Human Rights Disaster*, Human Rights Watch, Africa, Washington D.C.

Human Right Watch (1990b), *The Forgotten War in Darfur Flares Again*, A Human Rights Watch Report Volume 2 No 11 (A), April, Human Rights Watch, Africa, Washington D.C.

Human Rights Watch (1995), *Children of Sudan: Slaves, Street Children and Child Soldiers*, Human Rights Watch, Africa, Washington D.C.

Human Rights Watch (1994), *Abuse by all Parties in the Southern Sudan*, Human Rights Watch, Africa, Washington D.C.

Human Rights Watch (2004a), *Darfur in Flames: Atrocities in Western Sudan* Report of the Human Rights Watch, April Vol. 16 No 5 (A), available: http://www.hrw.org/reports/2004/sudan0404/ (accessed on 03/082004).

Human Rights Watch (2004b), *Darfur Destroyed: Ethnic cleansing by Government and Militia Forces in Western Sudan*, Report of the Human Rights Watch, April Vol. 16, No. 6 (A), available: http://hrw.org/reports/2004/sudan0504/ (accessed on 03/082004).

Human Rights Watch (2004c), 'Q & A: Crisis in Darfur' available: http://hrw.org/english/docs/2004/05/05/darfur8536.htm (accessed on 04/08/2004).

Human Rights Watch (2004d), *Darfur Documents Confirm Government Policy of Militia Support,* a Human Rights Watch Briefing Paper 20th July 2004 available: http://hrw.org/english/docs/2004/07/19/darfur9096.htm (accessed on 04/08/2004).

Human Rights Watch (2004e), 'Sudan: Peace, but at what price?' Testimony by Julie Flint before U.S Senate Foreign Relations Committee, June 15, 2004 available: http://hrw.org/english/docs/2004/06/15/darfur8850.htm. (accessed on 05/08/2004).

Kaya, A. A. (2004), 'Sudan accused of Darfur truce breach as militia attacks Chad town', available:

http://www.splmtoday.com/modules.php?name=News&file=article&sid=1331 (accessed on 10/09/2004).

Lual, M. A. (2001), 'The Sudan: prospects for a peaceful settlement of the civil war', *Peace and Environment News*, August; available: http://perc.ca/PEN/1992-03/achull.html; (accessed on 10/06/2004).

Nation, F. (1999), A Continent at War, and in Discourse', in Mekenkamp, M., P. van Tongeren and H. van de Veen (eds.), *Searching for Peace in Africa: an Overview of Conflict Prevention and Management Activities*, European Centre for Conflict Prevention and Transformation, Utrecht, the Netherlands (in association with the African Centre for the Constructive Resolution of Dispute).

Rone, Jemera (1996), *Behind the Red Line: Political Repression in Sudan*, Human Rights Watch, Africa, Washington D.C.

Pol, Mirjam (1998), *We Have to Sit Down: Women, War and Peace in Southern Sudan*, Pax Christi, Utrecht, the Netherlands.

Schirch, Lisa (1995), *Keeping the Peace: Exploring the Civilian Alternatives in Conflict Resolution*, Life and Peace Institute, Uppsala.

Stohl, R. and Smith, D. (1999), 'Small arms in failed states: a deadly combination', presentation for the Failed states and International Security Conference, Centre for Defence Information, USA, April 8-11 available:
http://www.cdi.org/issues/failedstates/march99.html (accessed on 10/06/2004).

UNCHR (2004), 'Situation of human rights in the Darfur region of Sudan', a Report of the United Nations High Commissioner for Human Rights and follow-up to the World Conference on Human Rights; Document No E/CN.4/2005/3.

UN High Mission to Darfur (2004), *Mission Report*, UN High Mission to Darfur, the Sudan 27 April-2 May 2004 Khartoum: United Nations Office available: www.unsudanig.org (accessed on 22/06/2004).

US State Department (2002), *Sudan Country Report on Human Rights Practices*, The US State Department, Washington D.C.

van de Veen, H. (1999), 'Sudan: Who has the will for peace?', in Mekenkamp, M., P. van Tongeren and H. van de Veen (eds.), *Searching for Peace in Africa: an Overview of Conflict Prevention and Management Activities*, European Centre for Conflict Prevention and Transformation, Utrecht, the Netherlands (in association with the African Centre for the Constructive Resolution of Dispute).

Wakoson, E. N. (1993), 'The politics of southern self government, 1972-83', in M.W. Daly and Sakainga, A. A. (eds.), *Civil War in the Sudan*, British Academic Press, London.

Woodward, P. (2003), *The Horn of Africa: Politics and International Relations*, I. B. Tauris and Company Ltd, London.

Woodward, P. (1990), *Sudan, 1898-1989: the Unstable State*, Lynne Rienner Publishers Inc, Boulder.

Woodward, P. (1979), *Condominium and Sudanese Nationalism*, Rex Collings, London.

Chapter 8

The 'Anti-Gang' Civil Militias in Cameroon and the Threat to National and Human Security

Cage Banseka

Introduction

In Cameroon, like everywhere else, the security of the people is often considered as the highest priority, and a lot of human effort is expended on the achievement of this goal. The legitimacy of state governments is often tied to the provision of reasoned freedom and the resources with which people can live their lives. However, the search for what constitutes security is not uniform, and there could hardly be a definition of security today that will encompass everyone, everywhere, and under all circumstances. Bread, water, militias, civil wars, Osama Bin Laden, Al Qaeda, enduring freedom, suicide bombing are all expressions that might feature prominently in definitions of security depending on who defines it, and where it is defined. For some people security is found on the fields, where they have to dig, cut and cultivate, for others it is found on institutions, and for many more in family ties and lineage. What is common to all of these is the fact that it is one of the highest goals to be attained and cherished in life. It stems from the human law of struggle for survival. This chapter, although set in one narrow context, is an attempt to portray these varying degrees of understanding about security that became entrenched in the Cameroonian society about two decades ago. We attempt to expose how a community-based civil militia, named the 'Anti-Gang Movement' (AGM), and the public security institutions could threaten and enfeeble human security, especially in the context of a conflict-prone transition society at a time of political adversity. We will provide an elaborate historical background and discuss the nature of domestic politics and state weakness that led to the upsurge of the substitutionary civil forces that emerged in nearly every small community in Cameroon.

The outset of multi-party politics in Cameroon in the 1980s brought about some monumental and forward-looking changes in the socio-political landscape of the country. However, the new and emerging phenomenon of democracy in Cameroon was to aggravate human security in ways that were not foreseen at the time. This was largely because democracy became seen at this stage to mean everything and anything, and everyone interpreted it in the way they saw fit or beneficial to themselves. It bore the footprints of the common understandings of what democracy constitutes in societies experiencing political transformation, and seeking to resist patriarchal forms of leadership. Democracy to the schoolboy was an assurance of more academic avenues or even scholarships abroad, to his parents, a chance for more food and more schools for their children, a provision of more health facilities, more development, more accessibility and more roads for traders, more assurances for quick gains and prosperity and a guarantee of pensions and security in old age. The young interpreted democracy as a chance of better qualifications and the opportunity for a promising profession, for those vying for power, more hope for a political career; the young unemployed saw more chances for conscription into the military or the police force and other security organs in the 'new and transformed' governmental network (Macpherson, 1973; Macpherson, 1992). Democracy was seen as that panacea that was to remedy all the existing economic and political ills, indeed 'a Daniel come to judgement'. It was an innovation that was to transform the face of the country in ways that the whole of the post-colonial history had not imagined. Joblessness, uncertainty and anxiety about the future were now seen to be a thing of the past. Democracy simply meant security of sorts. The subsequent birth of civil militias, and the security tension they were to cause in the country, was congruent with these views of democracy. The AGM phenomenon was widely greeted and welcomed, not only in urban centres, as is the case in some other African countries where they exist, but also in the remote areas of the country. In this chapter we shall be interested in finding out the reasons, which led to the failure in Cameroon to examine alternative scenarios of security, and the implications of the birth and life of the AGMs. The chapter analyses, not only the threats to human security that have been brought forth by these so-called AGMs, but also the national security role of the Cameroonian government at this time of political angst.

An Historical Perspective

The first opposition party formed in Cameroon in the mid-1980s, the Social Democratic Front (SDF), was more popular when its initials became transcribed into the Pidgin English version as 'Suffer Don Finish' meaning difficult times have come to an end. The country was at the dawn of a hopeful vision of national affairs that would forsake the pessimistic premise of endless insecurity, and cycles of struggles for survival that is normally taken to be the lot of the Third World. Democracy was ultimately taken to be a synonym of the famous Marshall Aid Plan, implemented after the Second World War to facilitate the economic recovery of the war shattered countries of Central Europe.

What brought about this sense of optimism could be anyone's guess, but it takes no science to realise that these are all legitimate human aspirations, but which in this case reflected typical promises that inexperienced politicians would make to potential voters in times of political euphoria. In the case of Cameroon, this sense of hope for a brighter future coincided with the introduction of multi-party politics, and was to become an unforeseeable source of insecurity. The common assertion that democratic countries are also liberal and economically more advanced, that their social welfare systems are better and thereby provide individuals with more opportunities for personal development became common parlance. A particular group of this hopeful generation is of special interest to us in this chapter, namely the unemployed youths that were either promised, or were awaiting, conscription into the police or armed forces and other security organs of the public sector at the dawn of democracy. We will step back into their history and attempt an analysis of the impact they have had on human security in Cameroon, and the implications of the vortex of conflicting loyalties their presence has engendered. However, their emergence at this time came to depict a certain weakness on the part of the government in the provision of security to the citizens. Although this group had been considered too weak to influence policy formulation they have made the definition and provision of security in Cameroon even more problematic.

The aforementioned enthusiastic young men, without waiting for further official statements from the newfound political groupings, decided to implement the noble principle of 'charity begins at home'. They grouped themselves into a self-made security apparatus, which later became commonly referred to as 'Anti-Gang Movements' (hereafter referred to as AGMs). These movements were, in their understanding, supposed to act as recruitment and preliminary training camps for potential members of the police and armed forces. They were to be the votaries for security in the communities in which they lived. This new army was a gathering in which every voice found expression, and where membership was not limited to the educated or even literate. After all, the emerging democratic country was one in which everyone was to have freedom of expression, and this was not supposed to have any limitations based on literacy or academic underpinnings. It sufficed to be able to hold a dane gun, to have the audacity, determination and health to spend nights in a community's security vigil, without a salary for a start, but just the eventual benediction in the ranks of the official security apparatus. The rest of the benefits, like the uniform, recognition, financial remuneration, and a sense of belonging would be received after the real goal of the legal duties of public office were attained. The young men in question had been living in a sort of jobless and hopeless situation, and had started considering the whole political set-up as an egoistic and arrogant lot, that was simply creating an environment who were generally hostile to the less fortunate. They now had the chance to seek their own way to the assets and benefits that public office entails. This mentality was reflective of potential chaos in a country where security matters were supposedly institutionalised in the governmental apparatus and where the use of force is the direct preserve of the state.

The over-ambition of the AGMs and their subsequent security-related activities not only illustrated, but also equally epitomised, the characteristics of potentially conflict-prone transition societies. Cameroon, for the whole of its post-colonial history, had experienced nothing else but the one-party political monopoly and a centralised economy that choked off participatory freedom. Anyone could be forgiven for thinking that the introduction of multi-party democracy and a liberal economy was a freedom-oriented perspective that proffered political and economic empowerment for citizens. The painful reality is that Cameroon has remained a weak state, with a particularly tenacious form of unfreedom. This is the scenario that democratic hopefuls and AGMs had failed to foresee.

The circumstances under which multi-party politics were introduced in the country in the mid 1980s, the fact that it engendered the upsurge of civil militias and the issue of its timing have remained a nagging question. Some have preferred to relate the civil militias to the shortcomings of democracy, where the impression is given that everything is achievable under this system of rule. What is certain is that the Cameroon People's Democratic Movement (CPDM) took a lot of pride and self-appreciation for what they saw as the noble introduction of political and economic liberalism. They referred to themselves as the fathers of democracy, and implicitly demanded manifest recognition for this achievement. As is usually the case in quasi-dictatorial regimes like the one in Cameroon, the official press and television started their broadcast with praise singing refrains to 'the head of state and father of democracy', and this in total disregard of the threatening political tensions that loomed large. Democracy became a source of personal magnetism, and a cult of ostentation for the leaders of a country with one of the most arbitrary and cavalier political constructions and massive and intolerable levels of corruption that had emasculated young men and made self-help and self-reliance extremely difficult. Thuggery and widespread wrongdoing became a sort of youth culture. On the one hand, this created much insecurity for businesses and individuals in the country and, on the other, many quick-fix security systems to fight crimes and armed robbery. Cameroon had a priori exhibited spectacular difficulties in exercising inclusive political and economic policies, and youth unemployment was a precipitant of social exclusion and a loss of psychological health. The ruling elite had championed harsher political systems for their alleged advantages of national unity and economic development, while at the same time denying the bulk of the population the chance to take part in decisions regarding public affairs. These flawed politics formed a typical basis of state weakness and a lame security system.

With the promising advent of participatory politics in the 1980s Cameroonian young men clothed themselves with courage, determination, hope and dedication and manned the streets of every town, village or small communities in 'anti-gang' operations in a bid to get rid of thugs and other elements that operated under the cover of darkness. The oddly distorted view of democracy and the failure of the state to take timely measures and exercise control over the security situation led people to cry foul. In many communities affirmative action and the new concept of 'anti-ganging' was seen as a swift and expedient means of instituting security that could sideline the bad guys and keep their predatory behaviour in check. Their activities were mainly directed against gangs and thieves, but also against prostitutes and gamblers. In essence, these latter activities could be considered as organised crimes, but nowadays the definition of a gang is no longer limited to these groups alone, but to individuals who for one reason or another find themselves out in the streets after a certain hour that is no longer countenanced by the AGM in place. It is now commonplace for different quarters of the same town to have different hours beyond which movement is no longer allowed. Given that these AGMs are not well organised, or co-ordinated by a common network, and do not have a strong traditional ethos, there is confusion as to what hour and in which places people are allowed to move. This eventually makes their search for security even more insecure. However, the young men considered their action as pragmatism that needed no defending. In some senses, the various communities in which the movement had started operations needed this sort of assurance. The AGMs were therefore considered a yardstick for benevolence, and a readiness for service in a country where the state government was seemingly not too worried by the fact that disadvantaged people were suffering from systematic deprivation of substantive and secure opportunities.

This sudden upsurge of AGMs made the aforementioned pride the government had taken in paving the way for democracy rather short-lived. No sooner had real multi-party politics taken root, than they realised they might have opened a Pandora's Box that was to weaken their political positions and create a security crisis. Initial self-glorification also soon turned into indignation as incumbents saw their positions strongly threatened by the growing popularity of the opposition parties. As is the wont of weak states, a lot of anti-democratic measures were soon in place to challenge the awesome popularity of the opposition and those posing as alternative sources of security. The emerging centres of opposition immediately experienced massive deployments of soldiers, while the 'state of emergency' became a fact of daily life in the country. Soldiers were also deployed around university campuses, and other centres of learning. Harassment, physical, psychological and mental torture, and curfews began wrecking normal life, especially in the so-called Anglophone provinces where the opposition spirit became multi-dimensional. This was another signpost that was axiomatic of the weakness of the state. Here, it was not only a question of democracy, but also of more autonomy and self-determination. The Southern Cameroon National Conference (SCNC), which in itself was not a political party per se, also emerged in the wake of this so-called democratic era. They took advantage of the crisis around the country to campaign for an independent Southern Cameroon, as had existed prior to reunification in the 1970s. There was intense political activity at this time, and all walks of life became gradually politicised, as tensions of all sorts gained ascendancy in a continuously worsening security environment. A lot of grievances were exchanged between the government and the opposition, and democracy that was supposed to build bridges of reconciliation and understanding became ironically a divisive force. The ruling party could no longer smile at this innovation, which they now began describing as a threat to security and to national unity. The sort of state system that was being put in place was therefore replete with conflict and insecurity, a situation that strongly contradicted the original intention of the democratic social contract. The failure of the government to confine attention to the appropriate procedures for democratic transition brought about anger, rancour and many vexed questions. As is the wont of weak states, the ruling elite thought it could offer lip service with liberal paroles, but separate itself from democratic scrutiny. This was an awry move for a country faced with insecurities of sorts.

The heavy-handed policies with which the government tried to solve the problem soon became counterbalanced by massive demonstrations, civil disobedience, anti-government campaigns and militant protests. These were not carried out by organised criminals, rioting mobs, collective psychotics and loneextortionists, as the government claimed, but by a population that felt insecure and had to judge the achievements of the national government in terms of their own values and objectives. The freedom to speak became equated with the freedom to express long suppressed grievances, even at the cost of human security. The famous 'Operation Ghost Towns' became an implosive tactic of the opposition in an attempt to show their determination and indignation, and also the force the ruling party to tackle corruption and crime, and carry forth reforms of the political system. The opposition parties were calling for a national conference, a system of checks and balances, a free press and an open debate on a wide range of national issues. There was no doubt that the existing state system was not to allow for such sweeping changes, a recalcitrance that was to lead inevitably to further insecurity and dagger-drawing.

The popular calls for change alone seemed rather ineffective, especially because government action was supported by the presence of the armed forces that took special delight in raising their batons against demonstrators, especially students and intellectuals, while carrying out premeditated, deliberate and systematic torture aimed at creating fear and intimidation. This situation not only demonstrated the weakness and desperation of the state, but in fact created indignation and acute vexation in the opposing camps. The entire population was becoming wrecked with uncertainty and chagrin. As a result, and also because the opposition spirit was unbending, young people became mobilised into factions that could counteract the government forces in whatever way possible. This was another offspring for civil militantism and a basis for human insecurity in Cameroon. The embittered youth imposed and supervised the so-called ghost town operations, even though these were economically disastrous policies that further exacerbated state weakness, and neither made the national situation, nor that of these enraged youth, any better. Nevertheless, the question that was being asked here was neither philosophical nor moral. The youth thought it was time for them to stop subjecting themselves to any form of authority that did not emphasise the importance of the individual in society, rather than creating and promoting the greatest good for the greatest number of people, which for many was the essence of state, and the social contract that ensues from being part of that state. In their strongest convictions individuals had to be made active participants, consenters, and then beneficiaries of the state system. The government in power did not seem to be providing this, but on the other hand seemed to be shutting out the people from the state apparatus, with the subsequent effect that they were seen as pursuing policies which were leading more to the direction of underdevelopment rather than development, politics of personal aggrandisement rather than general welfare, and politics of the leaders, by the leaders, and for the leaders. Many people became convinced that the state was becoming exclusionist, and that it would take unwavering determination or even a revolution to bring themselves to the centre stage of politics in Cameroon. They believed they had to fight against flawed nationalisation policies that had been pursued by the one-party system of the government in place. Ironically this fight became replete with physical threats to human security.

As public outrage gained ascendancy in the entire country, local government officials, government-friendly individuals, and the dominant social classes were sent jittering. Many were condemned as traitors, and their lives and property were seriously threatened. Some Western government officials and their interests were also targeted, especially if they were seen to be supporting the government in some form. Their property and investments were threatened with arson, and there was a general boycott of their goods. This was a clear indication of the insecurity that was to ensue soon after. There was general indignation especially against the French, who were considered the backbone of the colonial mentality that the government in place could not deal with. The government was seen as ingratiating itself with the French who were giving it a longer lease of life. The greatest tendency of this cohabitation was that the Cameroonian government was seen to have become very pro - France, and consequently espoused some anachronistic and näive ideas about the goodwill of the French vis-à-vis the socio-political situation of the country. The French indeed became the number one enemy of the opposing forces at this time. There was also a general boycott of the petrol stations, since French or other foreign Transnational Corporations owned many of them. People preferred to buy illegally and cheaply produced petrol from neighbouring Nigeria, even though it endangered or even damaged the engines of their cars. Many petrol stations were attacked and looted, a dangerous adventure in which many lost their lives, and neighbouring homes were set ablaze by flames from the burning petrol tanks. This alone endangered human life and property, and the means of economic development.

The media in many weak or transition states is owned by the government or under serious censorship from it. This was unavoidably a source of friction in the troubling times of the 1980s in Cameroon. It was not so much about muckraking, but about suspicions that some journalists were unprofessional or unethical in their practice, that they were trying to be too critical of the opposition, and less critical of government, and vice versa. At this time the print media multiplied and exploded beyond recognition, each of them representing one opinion or the other, or no opinion at all. In this confused state, and for want of that which takes the population on board, those who chose to do so fabricated a lot of information. Rumours became the oil that lubricated the wheels of the political machine. Some of these rumours ignited tensions and led to reprisals from either the militias or the government forces. The organisers of the operation ghost towns were out on the watch for any 'sensitive' information, or anything that could be considered as unsupportive of the opposition spirit. Local radio stations were attacked and the lives of journalists became seriously threatened. In the light of these baffling insecurities the media became bedevilled by a lot of sabotage, and there is a generation of Cameroonian journalists from this period who were forced to abandon their profession or leave the country. They had to run for their lives, and it might be worth noting that the threat to them was not only from the opposition, but those of them who were muckraking on the government and its role in this confused state of affairs were also threatened. Many of them were arrested; they received unjustifiable prison sentences, and were never allowed any right of appeal. Some of them who were spared imprisonment had their professional licenses seized and their practise outlawed. However, a few of them who considered their job as a vocation continued reporting from opposition strongholds, and also writing articles that were critical of either the government or the opposition. These articles were either published at this time, at the risk of their lives, or came to print when the tension in the country lessened.

The student press that was normally exempt from public scrutiny was not spared in this muddling period. Most of them were banned from reporting political issues, or projecting issues outside the campus in their newspapers and magazines. It was not clear who was expected to become irritated or bewildered by their work – the government or the opposition. University professors and lecturers were highly divided on these matters, and equally represented different opinions in the political dagger-drawing. Intellectual neutrality and freedom of expression were also seriously threatened, and professors used their lectures as an avenue for attacks on colleagues of the other camp. Students were at times flabbergasted by the vehemence with which some of their professors politicised and emotionalised the lectures. Intellectual health was in the doldrums, while the impartiality of those in the learning environment became wrought with personal and academic insecurity.

The unemployed or disadvantaged youths who considered themselves the sacrificial lambs of dictatorship and state failure, and who thought they were suffering on a monstrous scale, took a special interest in the enterprise of threats and harassment. This was another foundation stone for the AGMs. It was the dawn of anarchy and lawlessness, and the creation of an environment in which certain forms of oppression were to become legitimised or even rationalised. The law of the desert or that of the jungle became the norm rather than the exception. Individuals suspected of any crimes were dealt with in the most gruesome of ways. It became commonplace for people to be set on fire in public places, sometimes out of a mere claim that they were caught stealing. People hardly sought any evidence to support such claims. Suspected criminals were never brought to the police, because many claimed they would be set free without trial or sanctions if they or their relations could bribe them out. The masses considered this as a betrayal of justice, and consequently decided to 'correct' the judicial system in these rather unruly ways.

Security at this stage, it must be noted, was not only threatened by gangs as the name of the movement above would suggest, but by both the government and the unofficial, self-declared custodians of security in towns and villages. Security was moreover threatened by the fact that many of the common folk thought they were living under a system lacking in opportunities and bedevilled by discrimination on the basis of ethnic considerations, and ruled by kleptocrats parading as leaders, but doing nothing other than practising 'politics of the belly' (Bayart, 1990). Their anger and disillusionment at this practice was to set the scene for much of the security menace that subsequently ensued around the country.

The Social Democratic Front (SDF), which, as earlier mentioned, was the first opposition political party to be formed in the country, was blackmailed by the government as a gangster group that was more interested in dividing the nation than in uniting it. This feeling or accusation was further worsened by the fact that the party slogan '*Power to the People*' or simply 'Power' became a common slogan among the AGMs. As a matter of fact many of the AGMs were actually referred to as 'Power'. Power became a word that summoned awe. People who felt threatened or maltreated by their husbands or family did not follow the official legal measures, but often took their cases to Power, which used the law of the jungle in settling family disputes. The AGMs would later thrive on this public confidence created during the tense political climate of the middle 1980s.

It is somehow hard to explain the entire circumstances under which so many people became so militant in Cameroon, and it is equally hard to suggest that it was due either to the ill-will of the government on the provision of security or enthusiasm on the part of the opposition and the youth to take part in national life. It might have been both, but what is certain is that the celebrated dawn of the democratic era in the country did set the ground for much antagonism between the government forces and other militant groups. It also produced a generation that lost many values and civility; a generation that became bred in violence and spoke only the language of force, intimidation, fear and hatred. Under these circumstances the destruction of civil society and further state collapse was becoming more likely. Many people either took the law into their own hands, or tolerated only those laws that came from the local traditional leaders who were considered at this stage as politically neutral. Those of them who were seen to be sympathetic to government policies became targets for either criticism or threats. They were no longer those untouchable royals that were beyond public criticism of any sort. The newfound democracy was not to spare royals as long as they were taking decisions of public concern. Many royal-friendly individuals considered this move as an exaggeration, since the latter took decisions that had to do with culture, and not with politics.

As the political movements, however, intensified many of the traditional leaders became actively involved, mostly on the side of the government or ruling party. It is claimed that they were 'bought over', and many could not resist the temptation for personal enrichment from public funds. It is equally claimed that they gave out sensitive information about their people to the wrong quarters, or precipitated their arrests and detention. As this trend continued and became public, these leaders lost their former deified statures and respect. Their traditional sacrifices were not attended and, in some cases, the lawless youth came around to disrupt the ceremonies, and force the participants home. It was not so much that the AGMs bore tradition any malice, but far from maintaining the traditional values or exercising political neutrality, some of the traditional leaders were becoming themselves an aberration from culture.

With the advent of this extension of force, many considered that the country had descended into the lowest levels of anarchy. Traditional rituals have long been considered in many of these settings as sacred, and it was unheard of to commit the sacrilege of tampering with this sacredness. There is a common assertion around the country that *the identity of a people is their culture*. If there is one thing over which there is unanimity, it is culture. The country has always prided itself on the diversity of its culture, the harmony and tolerance between the different cultures, and the spectacular ways through which these cultures entertain the public. Culture in Cameroon is also a tourist attraction, and this is considered as its own blessing from the mother-earth. The country has not got so much wildlife and natural parks as is the case in East Africa, even though geographers describe Cameroon as *'Africa in Miniature'*. Its different and interesting cultures are what it has to offer to the world. The fact that this section of Cameroonian life became affected was another clear indication of the disorder and chaos into which the country had descended.

The church, though in principle in favour of political reforms, was not spared the lawlessness. Like the traditional entities the church has often been considered till this stage as an institution without any political inclinations. State weakness and institutional collapse were, however, not going to spare the church. Both the government and the opposition exercised antagonism against the church. It sufficed at this point for any clergyman to say anything that sounded either pro-government or dissident for them to be threatened or actually attacked. Some people boycotted church activities, or refused to live up to their Christian obligations, and many factions, representing opposing opinions, became formed within the Christian communities. In essence the churches were being pressurised to be opposition friendly, a situation that, as we shall see later, was going to plunge the institution into very serious and tragic antagonism with the government.

At this time of intense political turmoil the same people who at night acted as the AGMs also implemented the aforementioned ghost town operations introduced by the opposition to force the government to carry on more reforms. These operations themselves were the highest demonstration of lawlessness that the country had ever experienced. There have been claims that it was second only to the pro-independence movements of the late 1950s. In the opposition strongholds, especially in the so-called Anglophone Cameroon, public as well as private life was almost brought to a standstill. Enraged youths were out on the streets to make sure that there was no movement of any kind, and that no one went to work. At this time people evaded taxes, smuggled goods through illegal channels, refused to pay water and electricity bills, or bills from any public corporations. Courts and town council halls were set on fire, and magistrates set on the run for their lives. In some towns like Kumbo, in the North West Province, offices belonging to water and energy corporations were also burnt down; their personnel sent away or forced to retire. The youth took control of the water supply, and transformed it into a community project, a situation that has actually come to stay. They claimed that this project had been granted to the area by the Canadian government as development aid that was not meant for profit-making as the government had now introduced. Till today the Kumbo Water Authority, a body that is independent of the government runs the project. The community is apparently more satisfied with this body, given that there is a regular supply of water, and lower bills.

It might have been tempting to conclude from this example that the jungle order of things was succeeding, and that a show of force was making right. This would be a dangerous illusion, because even if such an argument were logically coherent under these circumstances, it remains empirically false. Each of the connections deserves special scrutiny, but a combination of the several historical factors examined here illustrates the fact that the politics of underdevelopment and the nature of national politics led to state weakness and the subsequent radicalisation of people. The emergence of civil militias and the security threat they have posed in Cameroon can be traced back to these factors.

The *Modus Operandi* of the Anti-Gang Movements

The lack of effective national institutions for the maintenance of public order made the upsurge of alternative sources of security in Cameroon the more compelling. An overview of the historical context under which the AGMs were formed might have brought the point home. The preceding section has already suggested a lot of the ways by which the movements function, and the reason for their continued existence. Their survival as a sub-statutory security apparatus has made a mockery of state control and public reliance on the state for their protection. Their primary objective has been to fill this security vacuum and to help in reducing crime. However, they have extended this function to the ambition of promoting reforms on many sectors of public life. Like the opposition parties, they attempt (or claim) in their own way to improve human rights, and to enhance administrative efficacy by doing the job that would normally be assigned to the police force. Their claim that they are interested in an improved social welfare, a high level of administrative effectiveness in the management of public affairs, adherence to transparency, accountability, openness, and the rule of law has become a source of prolonged polemics among intellectuals. This is a group of predominantly uneducated youth who can hardly distinguish between these concepts, and who, undoubtedly, are not in a position to interpret effectively the herein enunciated sub-cultures of democracy. However, they take delight in high-sounding terminology, even when many of their critics consider or describe them as empty vessels making loud noises. The intelligentsia of the country thereby greet them with a great amount of apprehension. The movements on the other hand interpret the stance of intellectuals as cowardice, and further claim this predominantly arrogant lot is just frightened by the prospect of AGMs gaining ground, and subsequently putting their ambitions into jeopardy. For the AGMs, however, there is an old order in the country that must change into new, but should not corrupt their fortunes in the process. They too want to live with the hope that the new wind of change will send them rolling into individual and collective progress. Imagined or real, the ideas of the AGMs have come to signify an ailing and dysfunctional state security system.

What is remarkable here is the fact that, despite their enthusiasm, the AGMs are not co-ordinated into a single network, are not routinised in any identifiable framework, and are not easy to describe or analyse. Each section determines its own laws and operational methods in ways it finds fitting. They dictate their own rules of the game, frame their own willingness to provide security, and apply their principles through any coercive means at their disposal. They assume an array of functions commensurate with their ideology. They rhetorically assume these roles, but tend to cloud them with vagueness and irregularity. They are supposed to fight criminality, especially organised crimes, and to 'keep watch over the forces of night'. As earlier mentioned these powers have become extended with time, and anyone suspected of prostitution, gambling, and other 'crimes' becomes *persona non grata* to the AGMs. Gamblers are blacklisted by the AGMs because they are also alcoholics, who are given to rampant fighting and destruction of public and private property, and who either sing aloud in their drunken state at night, or curse as they pass by. They become generally associated with a lot of inappropriate behaviour.

Prostitutes are put on the same black list, not only because they are seen to be involved in the 'immoral' act of sex for money, but also because they encourage married men to cheat on their wives, or young men to get into promiscuity, which has the disastrous effect of spreading AIDS and other sexually transmitted diseases (STDs). In fact prostitutes are considered a serious threat to human security. The AGMs might not be wrong in making this conclusion. Prostitution has actually facilitated the spread of deadly diseases, which have disintegrated families through death or quarrels. Prostitutes are equally seen as particularly hampering the work of the AGMs, because they attract young men into brothels, who otherwise would have been out on security operations. Prostitutes also lure the latter into spending their hard earned and feeble income in silly, unproductive ways. They are finally seen to be responsible for the divorce of many couples, and consequently the abandonment of children, who might eventually grow up to become thugs. Linking prostitution to this eventuality gives anti-ganging a very special magnitude. If one sampled public opinion on this matter, there might be a general agreement on the case laid against prostitutes. Prostitution is not considered by this group as a way out of austerity (even if the prostitutes themselves claim that it is their own way of fighting against joblessness, since they have fewer chances of a career than the men), but as the lack of a sense of moral values. The AGMs take it upon themselves to eliminate this worm of immorality that is plaguing the society at a time when the health of the youth of the country is necessary in fighting to reshape their venerable societies, eliminating old parochial fissures and steering them up to higher levels of human prosperity and dignity. How much success these movements can register in this fight is questionable, but their actions in this domain expose the weakness of the state, because they take over an aspect that should have received serious state legislation.

As a result of these activities, which were initially seen as praiseworthy, the AGMs have received much support from the communities. They are seen as a better alternative to the corrupt and incompetent police forces, which mount roadblocks just for the sake of squeezing money from transporters and other road users, and who cannot stop crime or guarantee human security. Although operational only at night, the AGMs also make sure that people do not move around without national identification papers, or drive cars and motorbikes without the appropriate licences, a situation that the police force is seemingly incapable of arresting. Traffic offenders can tell in advance what they should pay to the police at traffic checkpoints. They only need to hand over this amount on arrival there. The AGMs claim they can radically correct this ill, and bring the traffic situation in the country beyond the generalised acceptance of bribery and corruption as practised by the police and gendarmerie.

Anyone considered by the AGM to be moving aimlessly at night, and all those without the necessary identification and traffic papers, are made to spend the night on the spot where they are caught. In some cases they are escorted to the nearest AGM station the next morning for questioning. Their parents or relatives are summoned prior to their release. Some of them are released on condition that they will perform some service to the AGM at a later date. This issue is seriously criticised, since those who are unable to produce their papers could simply render a service. This is neither a solution to the problem of non-identification, nor the right way of seeking services for the movement. The AGMs, however, claim that by doing this they make people learn the hard way. It is difficult to assess the effectiveness of this move, given the unpredictability of AGM operations in general, but more so because the AGMs can argue that there is no better security apparatus around from which a better lesson could be learned. They claim that the supposedly trained and enlightened police force also twists the laws and subjugates the people. Each of these groups could easily dwell on the perversions of the other in the context of their narrower views of security. Outlining this litany of arguments and counter arguments might be intellectually boring, because they often sound like self-pity or a miserable attempt to find excuses for unscrupulous activities by both camps. However, in this context such stereotypes are another way of telling unpleasant truths about the official security system in the country. What is equally true is that the form of punishment used by the AGMs has the foreseeable effect of bringing the real gangs closer to the Movements, and giving them an opportunity to study their weaknesses for the sake of future operations. They quickly understand the use they can make of their presence within the ranks of the AGMs. When it therefore comes to delivering the goods, most of these recruits have no more to offer than disillusionment and a hidden agenda. Like the police force they claim to replace, they are in some places nothing more than ill-meaning youth charged with ensuring the security of collectivities.

Security Provided or Insecurity Assured?

The state security apparatus in Cameroon in the 1980s was nothing but a living contradiction to all that security represents. Crime had become endimic in the country and the government forces seemingly possessed no talent at fighting it. The only genius they seemed to possess was seen to be linked to the extraction of resources and the extortion of bribes at checkpoints or from criminals who were then given a free hand to act with impunity. The standards of political control imposed were not correctly designed and were bound to falter in the face of mounting crime and armed robbery. The relevance of state security in such instances normally becomes questioned, especially if there is only rudimentary evidence that the government is serious about creating a comprehensive mechanism that could bring the chaotic situation under control. Every property owner, other defenceless people and their communities start to seek alternative sources of protection against thugs. This chiefly results in an unprecedented increase in automatic firearms and light weapons in private hands. All subsequent practical scenarios will point to a further weakening of the state and to its inability to maintain control over gun culture and the use of force.

The concept of anti-ganging was introduced under these circumstances. It is a phenomenon that has come to stay, even if in a much reduced or inconsistent form. The initial goal, or the hope that it was a springboard, or the first training camp for eventual recruitment into the armed forces has also been abandoned for the most part, and the AGMs are now a movement for their own sake. They continue to man roadblocks, control pedestrians and cars at night, meanwhile keeping special watch on their original target, the gangs or organised criminals. In some communities they are said to have been successful in fighting prostitution, gambling, rampant fighting, and the unnecessary disturbance of public order at night.

The continuous existence of these AGMs would equally seem to testify to their success and persistence and to the weakness of the state security apparatus. Service within the civil militia continues to be a voluntary and non-remunerative venture, but by no means an unpopular one, given the failure of the state forces to penetrate society and the political terrain in which the AGMs continue to operate. The motivation to join the movement might now be different, and the expectations from its membership may also have altered. However, there are people who are determined to see the movement kept alive, and there are whole communities that strongly back its existence as it is seen as filling a security vacuum. Those who have chosen to think in this way are mostly people who have either been victims of armed banditry, or have been threatened in one way or another, and did not have recourse to the services of the official police force. These sympathetic individuals have expressed open gratitude to the AGMs and also sometimes verbal encouragement and moral support to lighten up their spirits during their nocturnal operations. A police officer on the other hand is seen as a perversion to the cause of justice and an aberration to the security make-up of the generally AGM-friendly communities.

In many places the police force has lost its moral authority to the AGMs who are considered by sections of the population as a lesser evil than the men and women in uniform. People prefer some sort of force around the corner to having to depend on the police who might never turn up even if people alert them of attacks from gangs and criminals. They are equally convinced that the AGMs are a stronger source of security in their community, also because some of the guys who otherwise would have joined the gangs are now within the AGMs. They see their sacrifice, ability to disband gangs, stop or reduce prostitution, as moves worthy of praise. Women who feel they are already losing their husbands and boys to prostitutes or gambling bands welcome the idea. And it is moves such as these that have again established the AGMs strongly in some people's hearts. If this could act as a measure of success, then the AGMs have indeed succeeded. It might be worth noting here, however, that this success is not measured on a large scale, and a broader picture of the phenomenon is most often not considered in such assessments. There is no doubt that they have endangered human security in several ways.

Today, the AGMs do not exist in all the places where there had initially been one. Many of them have either sunk into oblivion, or instilled hate memories that no one could have imagined at the outset of the movements. Not only did many of them become thugs and gangs, gamblers and regular visitors to prostitute taverns, they are also known to have connived with the real gangs in their operations, and allowed those women who could pay a protection money to continue prostitution. With the introduction of the AGMs in many places, armed-robbery, rape and harassment became even more common. It is claimed that many of them have used drugs to sustain their courage and boldness, or to brave the prospect of having to spend the whole night out on the streets. Many of the innocent young men who joined the movements became schooled into such activities as drinking and drugs.

The AG norms have been unscientifically formulated, and it is no wonder that their unconventional way of thinking once cultivated will be carried forth to the families and other segments of society. In nearly every situation, like community gatherings, these people use their arguments of force, thereby irritating many people and making them act in ways that are contrary to their personal intentions or common sense. This not only brings about confusion, but also destroys the cooperative spirit and sense of commitment of some people to public welfare. This is indeed an unfortunate development, given that many communities in this country depend on individual goodwill and private contributions for the provision of some common goods like pipe-borne water, road maintenance, and the construction of community houses, churches, and health centres. Reasoned action on the part of a group that purports to represent security could lead to an avoidance of measures that strain community relationships. On the contrary the sort of irrationality that is a feature of the AGMs has strained such relations. The destruction and arson that were perpetrated by this group in another guise in the period of ghost-town operations illustrates this jungle order of things. The AGMs have not been forgotten for their role in this. The remnants of the destruction are all over the place, and speak for themselves. They remind many of an era of anarchy. Individuals who lost their relatives, property and their means of subsistence as a result thereof have carried an indelible grudge against the AGMs.

The AGMs suffer also from structural weaknesses: their criterion for recruiting new members is not based on merit, and the real intentions of the candidates are hardly taken into consideration. People with criminal records are allowed to join the movements, thereby setting thieves to catch other thieves. Although it could not always be argued that a previous criminal record is an omen for a future one, the recruitment mechanisms as practiced by the AGMs often point to the direction of a pre-programmed failure. The facts that AGMs operate in desert laws, and are accountable only to themselves, make the case even more strongly. They have no means of patrolling the quarters, but stay put in one given spot. This gives the gangs the opportunity to map the towns and communities according to which areas are protected, and which not. The AGMs also have no wherewithal to pursue the gangs, and to track them down. It is then easier for gangs to operate in such a system. They simply have to go to the unprotected areas, where probably the people have been living with a sense of false security. Worse still, the gangs or individuals can bribe their way through AG lines in some areas, and operate at will. In several places the movement actually demands a fee from any pedestrians under the pretext of seeking funding for some of the equipment they need for their operations. These include torches and guns, which in some cases are said to have been used in grandiose acts of banditry, either by the members of the AGMs themselves or by thugs to whom the equipment is rented out.

The activities of the AGMs appear more as a move against human rights, and an organised subjugation in the guise of providing security or fighting crime. They infringe on the right of movement, and take advantage of their position to settle personal scores with individuals. Their evidence against their offenders is often arbitrary, and they can claim that any person has an evil intention, is a prostitute or gambler. People so falsely accused become subjected to harassment and mob justice. The civil militias go about destroying the long African tradition of night dances, and by so doing implant much dissent that becomes the subject of conflict between those who support the AGMs and those who oppose them. Many women have accused them of rape and abuse, and of often finding excuses to keep them over night at the anti-gang lines, and using their self-ascribed powers as leverage coerce women into granting sexual favours.

Many of the AGM members see their personal failures in life as the failures of democracy or those of their society at large. They attribute their misery to the egoism of the rich of their communities, and the latter or their children and relations become targets for some members of the AGMs. These people are sometimes forced to pay protection money to the AGMs if they want their security or that of their next of kin guaranteed. In some cases the rich are given special protection around their homes, if they can pay for it. In this sense movements like AGMs can indeed become a cause for painful soul-searching. They can develop endless interpretations of what they are doing in their communities and around them, they have no constants, no fixed meanings for their action, no secure grounds for continuity, no profound secrets for the operations of the movement, no final structures and no limit to their action. They can impose their interpretation of things on others, none of them primary, and all arbitrary. All of these are a recipe for failure and a living contradiction to security.

The history of the AGMs, however, confronts us with an ambiguous story, at least from the standpoint of academic analysis. The inconsistency of the story makes it difficult to formulate any theories that can offer a firm analysis of the phenomenon. The AGMs have succeeded where they have, and failed where they have. In many communities it would be unheard of to talk of doing away with the AGMs. The common belief in such places is that not only evil acts, but also exemplary acts of humanity are brought forth by the AGMs – self-sacrifice, honour, courage, altruism on behalf of their society, and bonding with a community larger than themselves. In many other communities, however, the word AGM has become anathema. The latter believe that the AGMs have now developed different interests, have lost touch with reality, and have become prone to exaggeration. They cannot preserve individual liberty, are no longer servants of the collective will, and are in many ways an unrewarding burden. They are no longer custodians over the community's security and property, but in many ways a threat to them.

Official or Governmental Response to the AGMs

We have noted above on several occasions that the AGMs were born out of a very tense political atmosphere in Cameroon in the middle of the 1980s, and that their innovation was generally greeted with gushing enthusiasm. People considered them as appropriate in a system in which the state has demonstrated its inability to dilute a tense security atmosphere and scale down criminality. Many Cameroonians blame the government for a lot of the political and economic predicaments that made the AGMs a fact of life. As a result of the government's inability to halt political thuggery (corruption) and criminal activities, and because of its attempt to stop or halt the democratic process that had been introduced in the country, it has become generally considered as not willing to mobilise or motivate the people, not wanting to pursue a policy of inclusion, but rather that of exclusion, not wanting to bind wounds, not providing security, and not being the unifiers they are expected to be. In fact the ruling party has put itself into a suspicious position, at least from the standpoint of political reforms. Their exercise of power is not seen to be for the greater good of the country. There is no systematic effort to build a pluralistic polity, no commitment to the rule of law, and the vigorous protection of human rights, no effective management of resources, no appropriate design of policy and no efficient discharge of functions for a profitable or predictable outcome. (World Bank Report on Cameroon, 1989, p.60) There is a litany of blame against the bureaucracy and policy-making mechanisms that consequently blind Cameroonians to the negative impacts of the AGMs.

Even though many accept the axiom that the state should be the predominant and exclusive provider of the rules of the political game in society, people in Cameroon generally consider this as not being the case at the time of civil militia activity. Many think the existing constitutional principles, including the written and unwritten laws, do not provide justice, freedom and security. The fact that this government is attempting to halt the democratic process that had been introduced, discouraging or making it very difficult for political parties to mobilise their potential voters provokes feelings of ill-will towards the state. Worse still, the government imposes curfews and a state of emergency, and deploys thousands of soldiers on the streets to supervise its unpopular moves. As earlier mentioned, the AGMs are simply an extension of the civil forces that had been formed to confront the government soldiers on the streets, and which the people unwittingly welcomed. There was initial criticism on the part of the civil society, as to why such a political problem should seem to have only a military solution, but ironically some of these same critics have condoned the decision of the civil forces to counteract government action with force. A combination of these factors does not augur well for security. Not only have people become uncritically supportive of a security imposture with a lot of imperfections, but have equally come to consider the state security infrastructure as inept.

The government in Cameroon has watched the activities of the AGM with apprehension and indignation. However, it has stood by to see huge numbers of people delivered to potentially misleading faith in militias as a more trustworthy source of security. The government has never officially declared a war against any civil militias in the country, and not even against the AGMs who could have been accused of causing many security perils. There is, however, an undeclared and silent war being fought against the forces, but never to the magnitude of a civil war. This might be seen as the government's rationale in recognising the human predicament involved in the weakness or limitation of its state security system. In the absence of the state on crucial matters like security, militias are bound to compete for public attention. Security is not a desire for its own sake, but an aspect that enhances the freedom that citizens wish to enjoy. The sporadic devastation of this aspect has made human beings vulnerable to militias.

The worsening security situation has made it imperative for the government to take some action. On the political front the government promised to carry on the assignment of mobilising resources, including human resources, drawing up and implementing development plans for all parts of the country, accelerating economic growth, training skilled man-power and mobilising capital through community development techniques. Although these promises seem to address some of the grievances of the people in general, and the civil militias in particular, they are still considered as not far-reaching enough, and not addressing the political issues that had resulted in the descent in the country. The policies are simply clouded in vagueness, and seemingly make a great deal of government action appear to be concerned only with the activities of a very small number of people. In the end the people are still at daggers drawn with the government over an unimproved security system and lame democratisation process.

Historically the state has demonstrated a remarkable lack of vision on how to handle the security situation in Cameroon. The increasing numbers of demonstrations that ensue at times of political duress are met instead with an increase in the number of soldiers on the streets. Public gatherings are banned in the state of emergency; there are arbitrary, indiscriminate arrests, unjustifiable imprisonment, and the closure of universities as a punishment to the professors and students who have taken special interest in calling for reforms. This closure does not disperse the students to their different villages and towns, as the government often expects, but leaves them in their university areas with no other activity than street demonstrations and riots. In its frustration, the government becomes more aggressive.

The fact that students and professors are tortured by government forces, and the suspicion that many have died in mysterious circumstances, bring various people into the fight who otherwise would never have been committed to it. People find it incredibly annoying and intolerable that the government soldiers treat students like criminals, and close the university campuses, making the academic calendar longer and consequently more expensive for the sponsors. This anger does not, however, stop the government writing off many student benefits, and imposing fees as a means of reducing the size of the universities. Student restaurants are closed, or operated at high prices, and the city buses, which provided almost free transportation to students, have become privatised. There is a rapid shake up of the university administration, and only government supporters are appointed to academic posts of responsibility. As a further consequence campus life becomes highly politicised, as pro- and contra factions are formed. Out in the quarters, many parents and relations of students join the AGMs even if only to demonstrate their indignation at all the mishaps. They also think they are powerless as individuals, and even if they believe that civil militarism is not the best solution to the problem, they see the need to challenge the approach of the politicians to national security issues.

Also in the midst of this chaos, the government uses the bilingual nature of the country to an unfair advantage. The differences between the two language groups have become overstated. Many political parties are described as having no validity beyond the so-called Anglophone provinces. The Francophones on the other hand are deceived into thinking that the Anglophones are planning a coup against them. Anglophones are described as radicals and extremists who would subject the French-speaking part of the country to untold suffering and suppression. Naturally the latter become scared by this prospect. The Francophones form the greater part of the population of Cameroon, but there was hardly any animosity among the people because of this linguistic divide that dates back only to the colonial times. It is rather astonishing that it is the ruling party that is seen to be using this point as a tool for misinformation, and as a divisive force among the people. The fact that government seeks to sever relations between the two communities along linguistic lines is an even greater security risk than the opposition activities of the Anglophone provinces. (This same unfounded logic of linguistic conflict was also propagated by the aforementioned SCNC as a divide-and-rule mechanism, but fortunately with little or no success).

Given the fact that most of the universities are in the Francophone part of the country, English-speaking students become targeted during military reprisals. They are seen as the instigators of the riots, and as showing too much inclination and sympathy towards the opposition. The government sees their call for the decentralisation of the university system as an added voice to the call for the independence of the so-called Southern Cameroons. However, neither the determination of the students, nor that of the new opposition parties has been suppressed by these unpopular moves. The government is being forced to adopt other policies in their fight against what is considered as a threat to national integrity and their personal positions of authority. This move is justified by the argument that there is a need for the demystification of national security politics.

The crisis that is often seen to be wrecking normal life in the country is too obvious to leave anyone indifferent. Everyone seems to possess a personal opinion, or an interpretation of the policies that are being put in place in answer to these troubling times. The clergy in the country also find themselves embroiled in the chaos, either because they feel they have to show a commitment to public welfare, or because the church is that place where people still gather, the state of emergency notwithstanding. Bishops and priests could use their sermons for critical overtones against the government, and for a general sensitisation towards a better conscience in what they consider as a vulgarisation of state-society relations. Some of them also caution civilians not to take any action that could be seen as an egregious violation of civil law. Episcopal Letters are often addressed directly to government leaders in an appeal for a more humane solution to the conflicts. There can be no denying here, however, that some of the bishops and priests become too loud in their personal criticism against the government, but we have to note that even those letters which everyone considers as expressing open calls for peace become interpreted by the government as sympathy with the opposition spirit. This brings the church and the government into headlong collisions that are tainted not only with verbal accusations, but also with tragedy. Some clergymen have died in circumstances that were seen to carry a government death-stamp.[1] The fact that no official investigations are carried out into these deaths makes a strong case for those who decide to think that the priests did not die of natural causes.

The most interesting issue in this section, however, is the official approach to the civil militias that have put the government of Cameroon to the test, exposed the weakness of the state, questioned the prebendal nature of the politics practiced therein, and generally discredited its institutions. Moreover, these militias have reined in a security threat, radicalised the youth, made a mockery of the police forces, and divided public opinion. It is, however, worthwhile noting that some people, especially the government officials in Cameroon, do not take the issue of civil militias very seriously. Apart from the bloody independence struggles of the late 1950s, Cameroon as an independent country has never experienced any wars that are worth chronicling in the bibliographies of conflicts in post-colonial Africa.[2] Any knowledge of armed military confrontation between civil militias and governments that Cameroonians possess might have been gleaned from books and the experiences of other countries around the continent. Talk of civil militias would not naturally cause alarm around the country. However, the fact that thousands of people participate in political pilgrimages, go on hunger strikes and take part in demonstrations even with the gun pointing at them is enough of an indication that any other move by the militias and the opposition might be ignored only at the peril of national security, governmental efficacy and public authority. The added fact that in times of trouble many government buildings are burned down, and government officials attacked, despite the personal protection they receive, gives the government a reason not to overlook the civil forces. Added to these are the traditional sacrifices that are performed in some places, and on which occasion there are symbolic burials of some political figures. These are indeed frightful scenes for many onlookers, but more so for the officials in question, since they can hardly fall to comprehend the significance of such sacrifices. Many people indeed believe it is a real threat to the personal security of those officials being carried to the grave in this symbolic way, and they would be advised to yield to the security demands of the people.

The government was also brought to fever point when it discovered that some members of the armed forces were not in total support of the way civilians, especially students, are treated in times of political malaise.[3] Some of the soldiers are also parents, and their children might be studying at the universities or other centres of higher education. They secretly join in these symbolic sacrifices as a means of dissociating themselves from the potentially cursed government authorities.

Furthermore, the use of the linguistic divide to unleash aggression and animosity also affects the morale of the soldiers, since the army itself also reflects this diversity. Suspicion and accusations become too common among the forces, and it is rumoured that some of the Anglophone soldiers have threatened to leave the army in the event of further clashes. The suspicion here is that they might join forces with the civilian forces and recruit and train more young men into a substantial and credible force. In the wake of this threat the government reminded the soldiers once more, and publicly too, that it was illegal to quit the army for personal reasons, or to join any illegitimate factions in the country. The government is very much aware of the added threat this causes, and of the fact that the situation could get out of control if they allowed the existence of the civilian forces and the AGMs, and the prospect that their own forces might join them at some point.[4] The government has outlawed these forces, and declared its intention to take severe measures against the movement if they attempt to resist the laws that have been put in place to curtail their activities. Soldiers are deployed at some of the places where the AGMs operate at night, not for the sake of doing the job the latter does, but for keeping the AGMs off their duty stations.

This move again invites general vexation, since the communities where the AGMs have registered significant success believe that the movements are not primarily a militia group that is intent on facing the government in a war, but one that is seeking to provide much needed security around the communities. They become determined to use force in getting the soldiers off their quarters or simply making life difficult for them. The soldiers, who find themselves right inside some residential areas whose terrain they hardly know, understand the risks involved in this operation. Some of them feel that the risk they are posing to these areas and to their own lives is more than the one that could be posed by the AGMs. After all, some of them have also been victims of armed robbery, or know stories of such activity. They too begin to question the rationale behind this operation. On several occasions the government also has had to accept this deployment as a miscalculation. The soldiers are pulled back to the camps, and occasionally deployed to the streets to fight back demonstrators and rioting mobs. Despite this recognition some of the known leaders of the AGMs have been arrested and imprisoned without trial.[5] This sentencing, however, has not foretold the end of the AGMs, and has not been enough to scare potential movements away from coming into existence or old ones from continuing their activities.

It has to be noted at this point that the political situation in Cameroon has indeed stabilised, although leadership has not changed hands. The party that ruled at the time of the introduction of multi-party democracy has remained in power through undemocratic constitutional changes and amidst the usual accusations of vote rigging and electoral malpractice. Many of the political parties that were formed in the mid 1980s have remained and dominated political life in the country to same degree. They now have seats in parliament, and regularly participate in elections at all levels. The main opposition party, the Social Democratic Front, has not remained a regional party as the government initially claimed, but has made political gains in some areas. Their failure in the other parts of the country has been blamed on internal party strife and the lack of funds for more intensive and wider campaigns. The harassment they experienced at the outset has now lessened.

This 'new democratic culture' has also ushered in some economic progress. The government itself has now declared that the economic and political crisis that had held the country in bondage since the early 1970s has officially come to an end. As a further proof of this change, some government ministers have been dismissed or jailed on corruption charges.[6] (This is a situation that has been unheard of in the whole of the previous years.) The salaries of civil servants are paid regularly, and there is an evident improvement in educational and health facilities. The institutions linking the ruling elite and the masses are no longer as weak, and there is a clear indication that the government is ready to exercise social and political control. There is hardly any political intervention in the institutions of learning, and both students and professors have liberty of expression. Some university professors have actually formed political parties, or are leaders thereof.

This apparent improvement in the politico-economic situation has, however, not signalled the end of the AGMs. The new political situation has also created new insecurities against which the movements still feel obliged to fight. Small businesses have sprung up, and many other centres of commerce have been created. Many of these have to depend on the AGMs for their protection. Even if this is still a fragile state of affairs, and even if this protection from the AGMs is merely through contracts of convenience rather than real ties of loyalty and commitment, there is need for it today as yesterday. For most of the population, it no longer matters who does the job as long as it sets done.

The Fate and Future of the AGMs

Security in Cameroon is a very precious commodity, and will remain so irrespective of the different definitions and interpretations it might have. It provides one of the moral senses of value with which the state associates itself. The state has to develop a strategy on how to provide security, since this forms a pillar on which state-society relations eventually depend. For many countries in the West, for example, the provision of security by the state is part of their natural socio-political landscape. The presence of the state behind this, and many of the rules formulated to preserve that security have become so pervasive that it would be difficult to imagine the situation being otherwise. (Bratton & Nicholas, 1997, p 20) The state is always with the people through the social security system, and through uniform and broadly accepted norms about human security. People who live in this sort of system seemingly accept the rightness of the state, and its capabilities to extract, penetrate, regulate and appropriate the resources existing in their natural environment for the benefit of the entire people. Most African governments are generally unable to provide this sort of security to citizens. The existence of civil militias in nearly every African country is portentous of state weakness and the constant breakdown of law and order. The situation we have tried to establish here serves as an example of a widespread phenomenon in Africa.

The central concern of this chapter has been to probe the question of who provides security in Cameroon, and also an attempt to highlight the different strands under which some organisations have been formed with the aspiration or claim of providing security. We have explored the circumstances under which these organisations gained ascendancy in the country, and sought to interpret much of their intellectual history. We have observed that they not only claim responsibility for the provision of human security, but also for the introduction of a more charismatic view of this phenomenon in various communities. They purport to guarantee the safety of communities where the official security apparatus is very undifferentiated or lacking in cohesion. They further justify their action with the claim that political overtones about security cannot be transformed into verifiable output. The fact that the security forces provided by the government are not backed by a technological and professional superiority has given it no leverage against such arguments. The second fact that the AGMs are embodied in a mystique, and not the expression of written laws, uniforms and guns, allows them to maintain a psychological rather than concrete conceptual framework in the communities where they have successfully operated. This point helps to explain their continued relevance long after the economic and political situations of the country have changed. Many other socio-political organisations have also emerged. Some of them are centralised, and with strong bureaucracies, but many others are simply unorganised. The situation of the AGMs is therefore not unique. The argument about their disorganisation and inefficiency therefore will not hold much water, and there is every indication that these movements will continue to exist in one form or another.

Conclusion

Many intellectuals do agree to the fact that security is a contested concept, especially in the so-called underdeveloped countries, where it is at times not only about guns and rebellions, but about survival itself. Many have argued for an expansion of the concept in the context of African states, while others see weak states and prebendal politics as the major security threat. The only consensus has been that security should be based on reasoned foundations and that it should imply freedom from threats to the values that individuals and groups uphold. (Baylis, 1997) For much of its intellectual history, arguments about security have been between the ideas of individual or national security, although this concept has also taken a regional dimension in the post cold war period. In Cameroon, like the rest of the African countries, it might have been largely impossible to escape from this situation. However, there was a growing recognition in the country at the end of the 1980s that these ideologies have a powerful influence, not only on domestic stability, but also on the tactics people can choose in their fight against insecurity, or what they consider to be a threat.

The formation of the AGMs in Cameroon, as we have tried to argue here, was not prompted by thoughts about threats to national security as a whole, but most probably individual security. Personal security is considered by this group as a source of emancipation, and a foundation stone for higher goals. They are seemingly out to seek their own protection in what they have thought would become a self-help society, one in which personal and individual initiatives could get transformed into progress. This idea of security might have been too simplistic, too ethnocentric or too narrowly defined. It might also have been a demand for rights in excess of the resources available to meet them. However one chooses to interpret the phenomenon, the situation of young Cameroonians and their communities might not have allowed for anything much broader. Their intentions from the outset might have been benign, but the weak state in the transition period came to see the idea of security in military terms, and consequently considered the AGMs as a threat to those core values that must be maintained even with the fist. Their activities have been interpreted as an abrogation of the duties and obligations of the police and gendarmerie forces.

A survey of alternative ideas between the optimistic and pessimistic schools of thought would blame each of these groups for the provision of insecurity in the country. The government on the one hand had previously allowed a brutal arena in which everyone sought to achieve their own ends. The AGMs have been taking advantage of this, or merely moving on from where they feel the government has either stopped or is no longer willing to continue. No one is sure of the intentions of the other and, as potential antagonists would have it, they always find an incentive to misrepresent the moves of the opponent. These alternative ways of thinking about economic security issues have caused many social changes that have altered the balance of political power in the country, and might have created the need for interdependence in state – society relations. It might have also been a wake-up call for the government, and a time to realise that the citizens can no longer be ignored. This is the positive side of the AGM story, seen from a broader perspective.

It would be very easy to blame the AGMs for instilling a false sense of security among the populations of towns and villages in Cameroon, and for encouraging resistance against government policies. The question that we have found difficult to answer, however, is who was at the genesis of the crisis – the government or the AGMs? It has been observed here that political deprivation and poverty were a source of antagonism between the government and civil militias, and that they have created a scenario in which insecurity breeds further insecurity. If the state is weak or fails to fill a security void at any particular point in time, we should not doubt that the people would graciously accept any benevolent persons bidding to do so. This thought is what enhances the legitimacy of the AGMs, despite their ideological distortions of the security concept, and their extravagance in formulating ways of how best to achieve or maintain it. It is not to be doubted, as we earlier mentioned, that many of the youth are benign in their intentions at the time of joining the movements, even if some of them näively consider the AGMs as a stepping-stone to the armed forces or police. If democracy had turned out to be what they expected it would be, and if the government had not decided to use hard tactics in quelling what it considered as disharmonies, then membership of the AGMs might not have been a bad decision for the young men to take.

We have to note again that neither the AGMs nor the forces from which they took root have ever engaged in guerrilla warfare in the style of the 'West Side Boys' in Sierra-Leone, the Lord's Resistance Army in Northern Uganda, the Bakassi Boys in Nigeria or the Interahamwe in Rwanda, to name but a few. Cameroon is generally considered by many African states as 'a country condemned to peace'. It is claimed that the fertile nature of the soil, the easy availability of food, and the fact that Cameroonians consume great amounts of alcohol is a source of their calm nerves. This might sound too simplistic an explanation for the absence of armed struggle in this country, but peace and conflict scholars will agree that, no matter the reasons, this country has historically enjoyed peace in a sub-continent that many consider war-torn for the most part. Hunger and a desperate state of human feeling can indeed lubricate the wheels of aggression, and this is the typical stuff of which conflicts are made. Cameroon must count herself lucky for the fact that this state of affairs is overwhelmingly absent among the population, and the AGMs have not prompted an all out civil war.

The AGMs live on, presumably till that time when the people will feel confident about public security being provided by the government. This is still central to the ideological justification of the presence of the AGMs, and provides an aura of charisma, which will form the basis for the future legitimacy of the movements' activity. They have a pernicious legacy, and have undoubtedly perverted the understanding of security, but they are at times unfairly used as an easy scapegoat in deflecting responsibility for state weakness and the absence of security. Some of the charges laid against them might not be without foundation, no matter how much of a beautiful balance sheet anyone may try to draw of their activities. The scale and form of their disruption or deception might be subjective, but even where they have been generally considered as successful some of their negative consequences have been considerable. However, we can also not overlook the crushing psychological and social implications of the government's inability to live up to expectations in security matters in particular. They lay emphasis on their moral authority over these issues at the same time as the country harbours many interior areas that are virtually untouched by the government security apparatus. Many sections of the population are virtually excluded from these paternalistic and ineffective public services. People in some areas have eventually become entangled in a mesh of conflicting loyalties between the government forces, which are the official or legitimate authorities in security matters, and the 'illegitimate' AGMs, which many would consider as more approachable.

These factors, among others, have mystified the public services, and put them in a position where the indigent find them hard to reach. A police officer, even if seen around, is not considered as a source of security, but as a representative of a system that has to be placated, and not approached. This is also the feeling of some about the AGMs in some places. The fact that there is no consensus among the two about who should be responsible for security has put the people in a difficult position. In the end it is the civilian who will pay for the weakness of the state security system as well as for the depredations of the AGMs. It has become commonplace for people to build very expensive fences around their houses, and to employ security men to guard their homes with heavy guns. People want to live in security, whether provided by the government, or the AGMs and their like, and as long as the government is incapable of reversing the trend, the insecurity of the people in many communities in Cameroon will continue to be assured by whosoever chooses to do so.

Notes

[1] A very famous priest, Rev. Engelbert Mveng, who was also a professor at the University of Yaounde 1 was presumably the first to suffer this fate, but his is not the only case that is mentioned in connection with suspicious deaths among the clergy at this time.

[2] There has been a prolonged border conflict between Cameroon and neighbouring Nigeria over the oil rich Bakassi Peninsula, with sporadic fighting, and a small number of casualties. The UN International Court of Justice has now ruled the case in favour of

Cameroon. Nigeria claims not to have accepted the verdict, though they have not attempted another military confrontation with Cameroon over the peninsula since the ruling.

3   This is an understandable position, given that many of the people who suffered casualties from this repression were parents or relatives of the victims. Some of those who were deployed around the university premises actually protested to the state governors, complaining that they did not understand what warranted this move. In many of these cases senior officers were either changed or whole battalions replaced, predominantly comprising junior and younger officers. This group saw this as a chance to settle scores with the students, who they either considered as more fortunate than themselves, or to whom they wanted to show the position of authority they had attained. For one reason or another, the younger soldiers carried out the assignment from the government, namely the use of force to suppress enlightened opinions from the university campus.

4   The government was also aware of the fact that it might be unable to coerce or intimidate soldiers to stop them deserting the army despite the laws that bind them to the institution. It had to devise other mechanisms for calming the tension in the armed forces, whipping up their morale and making them stay. Their salaries were continually increased, even at a time when the country was experiencing a harsh economic crisis.

5   In Kumbo, in the North West Province, a place widely considered as the centre for the most violent type of opposition towards the government, many people were arrested, judged in military courts, and were never allowed to see any lawyers. They were finally sent straight to military prisons where they were held on the charge of carrying arms. These arms they were accused of carrying were dead-ended machetes carried in a sheath, and a spear, and used as part of costumes by men who attend a weekly traditional gathering called *Mfu*. These machetes are neither used for attack nor defence, and are incapable of cutting through a piece of cloth. These prisoners were later released, but not before they had served several years in prison.

6   The Cameroon Minister of Territorial Administration was dismissed after the 2002 legislative elections on the accusation that he mismanaged the electoral register, and manipulated the registration of voters, especially those of the opposition strongholds. It was an unprecedented move that has been greeted by many around the country as a sign of a hopeful democracy.

References

Bayart, J. (1990), *L'Etat en Afrique. La Politique du Ventre*, Librairie Atheme Fayard, Paris.
Baylis, J. (1997), 'International Security in the Post Cold War Era', in *The Globalisation of World Politics*, Oxford: Oxford University Press.
Bratton, M. and V. W. Nicholas (1997), *Democratic Experiments in Africa: Regime Transitions in Comparative Perspective*, Cambridge University Press, Cambridge.
Macpherson, C. B. (1973), *Democratic Theory: Essays in Retrieval*, Oxford: Clarendon Press.
Macpherson, C. B. (1992), *The Real World of Democracy*, Anansi Press Limited, Ontario.
World Bank (1989), *Report on the Economic Situation of Cameroon*, The World Bank, Washington D.C.

Chapter 9

Civil Militias and Militarisation of Society in the Horn of Africa

Belachew Gebrewold

Introduction

The multifaceted crisis in the Horn of Africa has become the identity card of the region. The region is known for its civil and inter-state wars, displacement, refugees, famine and hunger. The states in the region are either weak or failed or collapsed (Somalia). This problem has been discussed by various researchers seeking to explain the root causes of the continuous political and economic crisis of the region. The aim of my analysis, however, is to illustrate not only the causes and consequences of conflicts in individual states of the region, but also to discuss the correlation between the instability of one state with that of the others. Weakness, failure or collapse of a state of the Horn is influenced by the weakness, failure or collapse of the other states. The civil militias in one country are actively contributing to the emergence and/or maintenance of the civil militias in other countries. This regionalisation of civil militarism has destabilised not only the states in the region and destroyed its economy, but it is also contributing to the dilution of international peace. Political destabilisation and economic destruction have resulted not only in intra-regional displacement, but are also leading to a critical international migration. They have affected the regional economic growth, and crippled the tourism of the region. Against this background the analysis of the civil militarism in the Horn of Africa is relevant for understanding the root causes of civil militias in the region as well as for policymaking to render the weak states strong, to save failed states from collapse and to rebuild the collapsed states, if this is the wish of national and international politics.

It is against this backdrop that my analysis focuses on and examines the specific context of the phenomenon of civil militias in the situation of the war-torn Horn. The security problem in the Horn of Africa is exacerbated by the militarisation of the civilian population. Even if the people in the region do not necessarily have a war mentality, war and arms possession have become a normality of the social system in the region. The specific contexts within which the civil militias thrive are the weakness, failure and collapse of states; porous state borders; and inter-state conflicts. State-building which is considered to be the solution for political and economic problems is generally unsuccessful in the Horn of Africa. So far the political elites of the region are not ready to perceive that internal opposition and armed revolts cannot be resolved, managed or transformed by military or state supported repression. Moreover, the lack of good inter-state relationships and mutual destabilisation play a decisive role in the intra-state conflicts and arms trade. Arming civilians and supporting militant opposition in neighbouring states is usually carried out by rival states in the Horn of Africa.

For decades the politics of the Horn states has been based on 'unstable stability'. This means that stability in the region is based on artificial foundations. The first factor of instability is that the governments and the states are conflated to the extent that whenever there is a change of government (usually by force) the constitution, the flag, the anthem, regional administrative divisions, national holidays, etc. will be changed too (Carayannis and Weiss, 2003, p. 267). This creates a lack of continuity between the socio-political achievements of successive regimes. The direct consequence or concomitant of this political culture is clientelism. Since political administration cannot be stable in this atmosphere it can be stable only as long as the political positions are occupied by ethnic members and relatives of the ruling elites. Opposition groups that ultimately have the same ambitions will be suppressed and pre-empted as 'terrorists'. Labelling them as 'terrorists' legitimises any political action against them. No significant chance will be given to dialogue by revising and *relativising* the notion of so-called 'territorial integrity', which has become a 'sacred cow', inherited from the colonial period. Moreover, an obsessive myth of nation-building based on *politics of externalisation* (diverting the internal problems towards the outside by creating scapegoats) instigates more war than peace in the region wherein 'illicit' small arms and light weapons are available more than ever, and armed rebels are increasingly active.

Another factor for artificial stability of the countries in the Horn of Africa is the perpetuation of victim mentality. The brutal invasion and exploitation of the colonial powers will be re-actualised in a quasi-religious manner wherever there is a political turmoil. The speeches of the political elites on national holidays in cases of intra-state as well as inter-state wars are replenished by the memory of the suffering from the colonial past. This persistent externalisation of the enemy creates an artificial stability in unstable states. Somalia during the Siad Barre regime and Ethiopia in its long history are two good examples.

In order to cope with the centrifugal problems of Somalia, the Siad Barre regime availed itself of the ethnic clientelism. First, through the patronage network most of the political positions were occupied by the Darod-sub-clans Marehan, Ogaden and Dublahante, which Barre belonged to. Second, though the Barre government with its ambitions to create a greater Somalia in the 1970s and 1980s, by 'redeeming' all Somalis in the neighbouring states, could on the one hand offend the USSR and lose its support, on the other hand it could secure the support of many Somalis and could hold on to power. However, the lost irredentist war against Ethiopia was the beginning of the end of the Siad Barre's regime.

To a great extent the Ethiopian state is based on the re-actualisation of the memory of the brutal Italian invasion. During the wars against Somalia in the 1970s, against the Eritrean rebels until 1991, and against Eritrea between 1998 and 2000, the main strategy of the subsequent Ethiopian governments for mass mobilisation was the recalling of the victories over the Italians since the end of the 19th century. After ousting Emperor Haile Selassie in 1974 the Ethiopian socialist government reigned ironhanded by repressing all opposition. The coalition of various opposition parties ousted the socialist regime and established the present government of Ethiopia, which has ruled the country for the last 12 years. Despite the ever-growing opposition to the government of Ethiopia its repression and brutality has not abated. The independence of Eritrea, the land-lockedness of Ethiopia, the war against Eritrea, the dominance of the Tigryans in the Ethiopian politics, the revolt of the Oromo Liberation Front and other groups, high unemployment and poverty, etc have drastically discredited the present government of Ethiopia.

After the Eritrean freedom fighters fought successfully against the Ethiopian socialist government 99% of Eritreans voted for independence led by the government of Isaias Afewerki. Since then the president has lost his popularity; opposition against him is rapidly growing; the economic situation is worsening, and the people are fed up of war. The media are monopolised by the government. The president has openly discarded an essential element of democracy, which is freedom of the press. He is even planning to close the Asmara University with the argument that it has not contributed anything to the development of the Eritreans.

The failed state of Sudan is characterized by enduring violence. Islamic law and oil have become the centrepieces of the Sudanese conflict. While the war between the Sudanese government and the SPLM/A rebels seems to have come to an end after the death and displacement of millions of southern Sudanese and the destruction of its economy since 1983, in the western Sudan of Darfur region the conflict is still devastating the population and its economy. Since the outbreak of the war in early 2003 more than 70,000 civilians have died, villages are attacked, houses are burnt, the economy is destroyed, and citizens are chased away from the areas of oil exploration. So far the conflict has displaced an estimated 1.45 million people and sent another 200,000 fleeing across the border into Chad.

This event in the Darfur region has cemented the designation of the Horn of Africa as a region of permanent emergency. One of the reasons for re-focusing international attention on the Darfur crisis is the experience of the Rwandan genocide. The UN was blamed for its failure during the Rwandan genocide. Probably in order to compensate for its inaction in Rwanda in 1994 the UN Security Council passed resolutions 1547 (2004) of 11 June 2004, 1556 (2004) of 30 July 2004 and 1564 (2004) of 18 September 2004, and 1574 (2004) 19 November 2004 on the Darfur conflict. The US has described atrocities against civilians in Darfur as *genocide*. At the same time, probably against the backdrop of the experience in Somalia in 1993, the western states are not ready to send their troops into the Darfur region. They are rather materially and non-materially supporting the African Union peacekeeping troops. A 3,000-strong African Union (AU) force is due to be deployed by the end of November 2004 to monitor the ceasefire. It is planned that an AU force of 3,320 personnel, including 2,341 troops and 815 civilian police from various African countries, completes its deployment by February 2005. The deployment schedule was facilitated by airlifts of African troops provided by the EU, US, Australia, and others (HRW, 2004).

One of the factors that contribute to the emergence and maintenance of civil militias in the Horn of Africa is that the atmosphere of inter-state relations is incoducive to mutual trust. By destabilising neighbouring states and by paving the way for the destruction of their economies, the states of the Horn are destroying and destabilising themselves. In order to illustrate this security problem of the region, the cross-border arming of insurgency groups, civilians and oppositions in neighbouring states is briefly discussed in this section. This is the main source of arms flow, which leads to brutal killings, internal displacement, migration and economic destruction. However, during research it was difficult to get exact data on the arms transfer, origin and destination, and how many civil militia groups are in each country of the Horn, since this data are scarce, and the data on arms purchase are usually secret.

Since most 'state-building' in the Horn of Africa has been unsuccessful, intra-state conflicts have become commonplace. Most states in the Horn of Africa are torn by internal conflicts. The only way these internal conflicts have been managed is by repression of the opposition, the arming of civilians, the militarisation of society, high military expenditure, political distrust and distended secret security. In order to illustrate this issue the state of the states, security and violence in the Horn of Africa are discussed in the following section. Sudan (failed state) and Somalia (collapsed state), countries most affected by intra-state conflicts stirred up by the civil militias and the militarisation of the society, are discussed as case studies.

State, Security and Violence in the Horn of Africa

The political history of the Horn of Africa is characterized by armed conflicts, state violence, political repression and protracted socio-political conflicts. When states claim to be legitimate they maintain that they are able to monopolise violence, to provide and protect the material and non-material goods of the citizens within their borders. As Rotberg (2004, p. 2) discusses, states organise and channel the interests of the citizens, further national goals and values, preserve their political and economic sovereignty, compete or negotiate with international actors to keep up their cultural, political and economic interests. Wars, armed conflicts, state violence, political repression and protracted socio-political conflicts are the negation of the above mentioned dimensions. According to Rotberg, human security is on the top of the hierarchy of the political goods, which are the claims that the citizens make on states. Therefore, it is the task of the state to provide human security, to protect territorial integrity and sovereignty, to deal with internal threats to the security of the citizens, to prevent crime, and to enable non-violent conflict resolution within the state. Fundamental civil and human rights, political freedom, identification of the self with the state by supporting and respecting its institutions are other key political goods. Other political goods that are expected by the citizens and supplied by states include medical and health care, schools and educational institutions, financial institutions, promotion of civil society, environmental protection etc. (Rotberg, 2004, p. 3). According to Rotberg, these are some of the parameters that categorise states as either weak or failed or collapsed. Though violence alone does not condition failure, high levels of internal violence with enduring character are associated directly with failure and the propensity to fail (Rotberg, 2004, p. 4). Besides all other lacking aspects of political goods, the enduring character of violence in Sudan makes it a failed state. Except for the period between 1972 and 1983 the Sudanese history has been overshadowed by war since its independence in 1956. The civil wars of Sudan until 1972 and since 1983 are rooted in ethnic, religious, cultural, political and economic disparities. The tragic vicious circle of Sudanese political history is that state violence against the southern Sudanese and the Darfur people is not leading to the strengthening of the state. Through its harsh measures against the southern and western rebels the Sudanese state has become weaker and weaker, resulting in the failure of the state. Because of its failure it is not able to control the political developments within its territory or to guarantee the security of its citizens. In the face of the weakness of the state and its inability to guarantee the security of the citizens, civil militias emerge to 'secure' their people from state violence and to 'liberate' them from political, cultural and economic marginalisation. Since the marginalization of the southern and western Sudanese happened to be along ethnic and religious lines, this multi-identity based conflict generated multi-security problems based on civil militias.

In a more radical way, in the collapsed state of Somalia the political goods became completely privatised, wherein only the strong ones and those with arms can afford security, because authority does not exist. In spite of its cultural and religious homogeneity the state of Somalia collapsed. The transitional government elected in 2000 was not able to control even the capital, Mogadishu. There was no central authority to discuss with, when Somaliland declared its independence unilaterally. Various warlords who accumulated enough money and arms recruited their disciples and demarcated their territories. It is estimated that there are about 15 million arms for 8 million Somalis. The political groupings along clan lines emerged as civil militias, since the security is privatised and society is militarised, leading to multi-security problems. Another tragic characteristic of the state collapse of Somalia is that its new president, Yusuf, was elected in Kenya and cannot return to Somalia at the moment. His residence in Kenya has already been attacked.

In order to understand the issue of the civil militia and the militarisation of civil society in the Horn of Africa it is indispensable to discuss the nature of the state and security in this region. To describe it simply state-building is the coordination of the interests of people living in a certain place and time. This coordination of interests presupposes consciousness, will and participation of the members of the society to build a desired state. We can understand a secure state as an outcome of a relatively successful coordination and consolidation of common interests. The more insecure a state, the weaker is its co-ordination and consolidation. This weakness is not necessarily related to its military power; rather the economic, social and political integration of society is not coordinated, or the various interests are not compatible. An intra-state war implies that no substantial economic interdependence is developed within that political entity. That means there is no consciousness or insight that the destruction of the others' economy is an indirect destruction of one's own economy, since both economies are based on exchange and mutual interdependence.

As various happenings in the Horn of Africa show us, the state is not able to guarantee the security of its population. This is one of the reasons why civil society does not trust the police as guarantor of their security. The power monopoly of the state has become very questionable. Many people doubt the capability of the state not only regarding security, but also concerning its capability to solve political problems. As Marwa in his research paper shows us, the local people of Kuria in Kenya prefer to deal with the cattle rustlers on their own. They own guns to protect their property (cattle), and they solve the problems of cattle rustling according to their traditional system (Marwa, 2000, p. 2). Since the government is not able to solve the problem of cattle rustling it has to tolerate the possession of arms by civilians. This is an indirect militarisation of the civil society, which makes the legitimacy of the state very questionable.

Concerning conflicts and state-building we are confronted with two issues: the borders of the states are 'sacred' and the states are constructed by elites (without including the majority of the citizens). These two issues can be discussed through various examples in the Horn of Africa. If we take the example of Somalia, the Somaliland in (former) Somalia is trying to exist and function as an independent state. From the perspective of the 'sanctity' of the state-border the self-declared Somaliland state is to be rejected. But at the moment it is the only functioning part of Somalia. Maxwell Gaylard, the UN Humanitarian Co-ordinator for Somalia says, 'we can work here. The Somalilanders are setting an example for the rest of Somalia' (ARB 2003b, p. 23).

> A process of traditional grassroots negotiation involving clan elders has been key to Somaliland's success. It contrasts sharply with the string of foreign supported, failed peace initiatives in the rest of Somalia. Stability and commitment to free market economies have allowed the private sector to thrive. Telecommunications and import-export businesses compete in downtown Hargeysa. Market streets are stocked with imported goods. (ARB 2003b, p. 23)

If on the one hand the above statements are true, and on the other hand the Somaliland is not internationally recognised as a state, a relevant question is what is the essence of the state? Do we need to maintain the existing state boundary by all means and at any costs? The same bulletin says that:

> [Foreign] governments are unlikely to give Somaliland recognition as an independent state soon. The African Union (AU) is opposed to any talk of altering the borders of countries, while Western governments have indicated that they will take their cue from the AU. (ARB 2003b, p. 23)

It is evident why the members of the AU do not accept any altering of the state borders: this would mean a 'domino effect' for many states of the continent, which are already unstable. Hence, the concept of state political history is the main problem of security in the horn of Africa. Thus, borders have become absolutely irreversible, anchored in the constitution of the OAU/AU and of each state's constitution regardless of what this may cost and what the consequences of this absolute territorial integrity are.

In 2002 the border commission of the UN adjudicated Badme to Eritrea. The problem that arises here is that the people of the area are not willing to be part of Eritrea (AC, 2003c, p. 1); moreover, Ethiopia opposed the border commission's decision from the very beginning, although two years later the Prime Minister of Ethiopia seems to agree with the decision. An important question here is, is the territorial integrity of a state (in this case Eritrea) more important than the wish of the people to determine their belonging to a certain state (regardless of the Ethiopian claim)?

The second issue mentioned above is the role of elites in the political history of the Horn of Africa. As current political trends in Africa show, the building of modern state and territorial integrity seem to be conceived as a matter of course. The process of state-building is believed to require an educated class in order to implement it in a scientific way. The educated class has become de facto the legitimate architect of this project. As political history from the last century shows us, most African politicians, belonging to the educated class, tried to implement either the socialist or capitalist model of state-building; others have tried to combine these western or eastern models with the 'traditional African' models of political understanding. At the same time, many Africans, as well as non-Africans, were attacking any political model coming from outside as inappropriate for Africa. Political tendency and ideology also emerged pushing for 'back to nature', with nature meaning traditional African culture. Nevertheless, the collapse of the communist model gave a substantial basis for the arguments in favour of capitalism such as Francis Fukuyama's book *The End of History*.

In the Horn of Africa the conspicuous tensions in the process of state-building are between ethnic nationalism and territorial nationalism. Both types of nationalism are engineered by elites. Ethnic nationalism is based on the notion that 'state should be coterminous with one self-defined ethnic group' (Lesch, 1998, p. 6). Some examples for this nationalism are the Oromo Liberation Front in Ethiopia, or groups striving for a greater Somalia unifying all Somalis in Somalia, Ethiopia, Kenya and Djibouti. The separation of Somaliland from Somalia witnesses the weakness of the argument for state-building along ethnic lines. Moreover, the Oromo of Ethiopia are not as homogeneous as the Oromo Liberation Front propagates. The other extreme of political tension in the Horn of Africa is the notion of state building along territorial lines inherited from the colonial period. It is a notion of 'loyalty to a place' (Lesch, 1998, p. 7), which is mainly represented by nationalists and the unionist political elites in the Horn of Africa.

However, state building based on secessionist ethnic nationalism as well as unionist territorialism are constructs of political elites. The will of the majority of the population is not significant in determining the future and nature of the state in the Horn of Africa. This means there are no consciously coordinated common interests that substantiate politics as a way of life for people. By consciousness I mean the will of the people, coordination means an active participation of the people and common interests mean interdependence. However, neither the ethnic nationalist elites nor the unionist territorialists conceive politics in this way.

In order to understand or think over the feasibility of the state it is important to reflect on the nature of the state itself. Concerning the concept of the state Dunleavy (2000) describes some elements of the state. He maintains that a state is:

> a set of organised institutions with a level of connectedness or cohesion, justifying short-hand descriptions of their behaviour in 'unitary' terms. A state operates in a given spatial territory, inhabited by a substantial population, which is organised as a distinct 'society'. These institutions' 'socially accepted function is to define and enforce collectively binding decisions on members of society'. Their existence creates a 'public' sphere differentiated from the realm of 'private' activity or decision-making. (Dunleavy, 2000, p. 611)

In his description of a state Dunleavy talks about some central elements such as 'organised institutions' and 'socially accepted function'. However, the fundamental but neglected questions in his description are how and by whom are these institutions organised? Is the function of the institutions socially accepted? What is the contribution of the people to state-building?

A political integration, which is not based on political passion, is a mere construct of political elites. By political passion I mean 'mutual ties of one kind or another, which give the group a feeling of identity and self-awareness' (Paddison, 1983, p. 58). My key argument in this political passion building in view of state-building is that modernisation (transferring of some tribes or smaller ethnic divisions to a more all-encompassing set of social processes) (Paddison, 1983, p. 58) and state-building have become a matter of course. It has become a performance of the elites, not political evolution of the population.

Another central benchmark of the modern state is the degree of its military power. The conception that the state must be ultimately both absolute and legitimate (Held, 1989, p. 14) is one of the fatal modern myths and mistakes since Hobbes. State is not something real in itself. It is just a belief. As far as it is a mere belief, it is a weak state, which cannot monopolise power. Monopolisation of power means here a fair exploitation of resources, centralisation of military power and socio-political integration of the citizens by guaranteeing their security based on this military power. Therefore, Creveld's concept of state, which maintains that states develop a strong appeal to the emotions only as long as they prepare for war and wage it, (Creveld, 2000, p. 337) is very problematic and short sighted.

War can be the means to maintain the status quo of a state. Political elites define and determine not only the state, but its nature. Even arms are defined by the political elites as licit or illicit. In their views arms owned by the government and its security forces are 'licit', whereas those which belong to civilians or opposition groups are usually 'illicit'. 'In many African countries, the illicit arms that are in circulation started out as licit arms acquired by those entitled to them. Where governments change by means of a military coup, however, security agents also change: what was licit suddenly becomes illicit' (BICC, 2001, p. 46). The mutual negation in the political confrontation is that adversaries of respective governments call the latter *illicit* and illegitimate, each side de-legitimating the other. Hence, we must deal with a more fundamental issue: has the existence of the state itself become questionable? In this situation there are no states, since states are consciously (willingly) coordinated common interests. This de-legitimating of government and its power monopoly and the negation of the state are the main causes of arms flow and militarisation of civil society and intra-state conflict.

From the discussed theoretical background we can conclude that the Horn crisis is caused by weak states, state failure and state collapse. These states have militarised governments, the border between legislatives, executives and judiciaries is blurred; it is the super-cession of the state by the government. They are not able to guarantee the security of their citizens, to protect their borders from trans-boundary arms transfers, looting, cattle rustling etc. A publication of HRW in 2002 reports on weapons proliferation and political violence in Kenya. According to this publication there are a significant amount of illegal gun movements in Kenya happening in secret and therefore difficult to document. The traders avail themselves of the thinly populated, porous, and rarely patrolled borders (HRW, 2002, p. 11). The Kenyan police officer admits that not even all the police officers of the country, about 35,000 (2002), can prevent the flow of guns since there are so many smuggling routes. It happens that poorly paid police officers look the other way if they are given a small bribe of 3 or 4 dollars. Not only on the border, but also within its territory, Kenya is not able to control illegal arms trafficking and 'arms supermarkets'. Control has become even more difficult, since informal and illegal markets are quite mobile to avoid detection (HRW, 2002, p. 11).

Impoverished rebels, well-armed herders and corrupt members of the security forces help the illegal arms market to thrive in a weak state. When the government is not able to control the threats to the security of the citizens, people take security into their own hands. In weak states guns are openly carried not only because they are so common, but also to pre-empt various threats, and to act immediately in emergency. According to the HRW publication, in 2002 there were about 40,000 firearms held by civilians in northern Kenya, which means a significant threat to the stability of the area and national security (HRW, 2002:14). These armed civilians justify the arms possession with an argument that the government is too weak to protect its borders from attacks launched from neighbouring countries and from armed rivals, cattle rustlers, thieves, abductors who, for instance, in a February 2001 raid killed 30 people and stole 15,000 head of cattle (HRW, 2002, p. 15).

It is not only because of widespread armed violence and availability of firearms that the Kenyan government has failed to provide adequate security. The problem is cyclical and flows in both directions with failure by the government to provide adequate security leading to more armed violence and greater availability of arms for private citizens. Moreover, the lack of necessary resources, training, equipment and personnel to monitor security conditions effectively, very limited government presence and poor or non-existent roads in some parts of the country, better armed civilians and low paid security forces undermine the security of the citizens (HRW, 2002, p. 15). In some cases, the security forces not only passively let the civilians take security matters into their own hands, but even sponsor groups of armed forces. A government member in Kenya stated as imperative to give the latest model of weapons to his ethnic community living on boundaries (HRW, 2002, p. 16). Confronted by a lack of security guarantees from the government side on the one hand, and threat of armed rivals on the other, some pastoral communities organise private militia training camps. Moreover, in this northern region of Kenya it is reported that about 95% of households are armed. Even private individuals hire and organise private armed groups, especially youth. The guns distributed to community-based forces 'Kenyan Police Reservists' to protect communities, where the government is incapable of doing so, have been diverted for banditry actions; and the reservists themselves are accused of participating in banditry, which means the distinction between private militia and police reservists is blurred (HRW, 2002, p. 17).

Ethiopia is another case characterised by the symptoms of a weak state. Ethiopia is a weak state for two reasons: the conflation of state and government, and its inability to control the centrifugal forces. The current conspicuous armed challenge to the Ethiopian government is the Oromo Liberation Front, which has not only challenged the government since the 1970s, but has also paved the way for civilians to take security into their own hands in the vacuum of government security in the areas cut off from the central government.

Though the biggest ethnic group in the country, the Oromo have been, like many other ethnic groups, disadvantaged. Even those Oromo elites in the present government are complaining that the oppression of the Oromo has not yet come to an end. Armed conflict between the OLF and the government is still continuing. The OLF has been accused of various attacks in different parts of Ethiopia. Consequently, the Ethiopian government characterised the OLF as a 'terrorist' organisation and demanded that parliament adopt radical measures against it. Besides the OLF cases there are also other incidents that testify that the Ethiopian government is not able to control the situation in the country. The conflict between the Sheko-Mezengher and other ethnic groups over the political control of Tepi town in southern Ethiopia left at least 128 people dead (Hirt, 2003, p. 252). In the same way, the conflict between the Sidama and Wolayta in May 2002 left at least 24 people dead. The Sidama feel disadvantaged because Awasa, a town within their territory has been made the capital city of the Southern Peoples.

Many Oromo are revolting violently against the status of Addis Ababa as neutral national capital, and they are demanding that it should be their capital since it is within their territory. In the same way, the escalating conflict between Anyuak, resettled highlanders, and Nuer, at the Sudanese border since the end of 2003, is a further proof that Ethiopia is a weak state. Nearly 200 people had been killed and 10,000 were displaced at the end of January 2004. One of the main causes of the conflict is that for more than two decades the population has been steadily increasing, and overcrowding has become a serious issue in the Gambella region. Since the 1980s, many highlanders were resettled in this fertile western part of the country. Moreover, the influx of Nuer refugees from eastern Sudan has contributed to population overcrowding in the area. However, the conflict is not only between the Anyuak and resettled highlanders/Nuer; the Anyuak are accusing the Ethiopian government of helping the resettled highlanders who control both politics and economic resources in the area. Besides that, the Ethiopian government is planning oil exploration in the region. Because of all these factors the Anyuak feel that they have been gradually displaced from their traditional lands (Plaut, 2004). Moreover, in December 2003 when the highlanders turned on the Anyuak about 300 people were left dead. The problem of the Ethiopian Somalis is not solved but just repressed. Complaints against the Ethiopian government are increasing concerning silencing opposition voices and critics, jailing of journalists etc. (Hirt, 2003, pp. 252-253). The Ethiopian Free Journalists Association is threatened by criminal sanctions. An imposed ban by the government overthrew the leadership of the association by its own members in January during a meeting organised by the justice ministry.

Eritrea is another weak state in the Horn. All news media is controlled by the government, which does not tolerate any criticism. Criticism is banned as endangering the national security. Eritrea is one of many countries in Africa infamous for jailing journalists and for suppressing freedom of the press. The Eritrean government dashed the hope of the Eritreans, who were very optimistic after achieving independence from Ethiopia. After their independence the Eritreans expected that the Eritrean state would be one of the most democratic and prosperous countries in Africa. In the first half of 2003 the grievances and disappointment of the Eritreans led an alliance of 13 Eritrean opposition groups to set up a military wing to topple President Isaias Afewerki. Moreover, the Eritrean Islamic Jihad Movement is another factor that challenges and characterises Eritrea as a weak state.

The other cause of crisis in the Horn of Africa is state failure. The first symptom of a failed state is the inability of a state to control criminal networks and its territories. Furthermore, state failure means when an internal strife ends up in humanitarian crisis. As Crocker says, state failure is characterised by the victory of guns over normal politics (Crocker, 2003, p. 35). The intensity of a conflict, the quality of a regime change and the propensity to state failure are essentially interdependent. This means, the higher the intensity of a conflict, the lower the quality of the regime change (regime change by military force) and the higher the propensity to state failure. As Crocker maintains, 'when state failure sets in, the balance of power shifts ominously against ordinary civilians and in favour of armed entities operating outside the law' (Crocker, 2003, p. 36). As the case of Darfur region in Sudan shows us, state failure is the absence of a state with the legitimacy and authority to manage its own affairs, and when armed militias determine the destiny of civilians. This is usually preceded by intra-state conflict and the militarisation of society.

Intra-State Conflict and the Militarisation of Society in the Horn of Africa

Small ethnic confrontations and civil war have become the main source of civil militias in the Horn of Africa. The huge number of small arms and light weapons are the big threat to peace and stability in the region. The lack of consolidated states in the Horn of Africa is the main cause of the easy transfer of small arms and light weapons. This means the states are neither able to control their borders nor to create societies willing to live together. The uncontrolled availability of small arms and light weapons exacerbates violence, criminality and internal conflicts and thereby threatens not only the political stability, but also the socio-economic development (MOFA, 2000).

In the previous section we have discussed briefly the problems of state-building. The unfulfilled project of state-building is the main cause of the destabilisation and the militarisation of the peoples in the Horn of Africa. The question for many people in the Horn of Africa is why they belong to a certain state and why they are governed by a certain regime. In this context, militarisation of the society goes hand in hand with the issue of political legitimacy. Since regime change in most of the Horn states happens with armed violence, the weapons left behind after regime change provide civilians with a weapons source and direct access to arms. Moreover, as Wassara says, weapons get into the hands of civilians through the intentions of parties to armed conflicts to seek allies who could help in prosecuting war, or interested community members join armed movements deliberately to have access to weapons (Wassara, 2001, p. 5).

In the early 1990s, before the socialist government of Ethiopia was ousted from office, president Mengistu announced that Ethiopia had enough weapons for all Ethiopian citizens to defend themselves against the EPRDF fighters. Luckily the distribution of the weapons did not happen. However the fleeing Mengistu forces left substantial quantities of weapons that fell into the hands of various groups within, as well as outside, Ethiopia.

As Wassara says, the schisms within various fighting groups in the Horn of Africa are another source of weapons for civilians who are either allies of various factions or use these weapons for private 'self-defence'. The number of weapons and the number of actors in a state cannot be separated from the political nature of a state itself. The weaker the state, the more militarised it is in order to repress internal revolts.

Another aspect of the militarisation of societies in the Horn of Africa is how small arms serve as instruments for the earning of livelihoods in communities (Wassara, 2001, p. 6). This is especially the case among the nomadic peoples in the Horn of Africa. Light weapons and small arms are necessary means to occupying grazing land and to rustling cattle. 'If I do not carry a gun, the men despise me as a defenceless woman; if you kill a government soldier, you keep the gun and use it for buying cattle…you can get six cows for one gun – when it used to cost ten' (ISS, 1999, p. 1). A parliamentary conference organised jointly by AWEPA (European Parliamentarians for Africa) and the UNDP Small Arms Reduction Programme for the Great Lakes Region, Kenya 26–28 November 2003, reports on an estimated distribution of firearms in Sub-Saharan Africa that civilians (643,000,000, i.e. 79% of the population) possess 23,000,000 firearms. The estimated number of insurgents in sub-Saharan Africa runs to 237,000, possessing about 600,000 firearms (2% proportion of firearms). According to this estimation the military is 1,900,000, strong equipped with 4,850,000 firearms controlling 16% of firearms. 800,000 police equipped with 800,000 firearms possess 3% of all available firearms (AWEPA, 2003:8). Thokozani Thusi in *Africa Security Review*

12(2), 2003 estimates about 5,000,000 small arms in the hands of 189,000,000 inhabitants of the pastoral areas of eastern Africa and the Horn (Thusi, 2003, p. 20). State collapse in Somalia has exacerbated weapons circulation in the Horn of Africa. Ethiopia accuses the Transitional National Government of Somalia of directly and indirectly supporting the *Al Itihaad*, which allegedly transfers arms as far as Ethiopia (Thusi, 2003, p. 20).

Arms have become guarantors of personal security and a symbol of bravery in societies where bravery has a special value for men (Marwa, 2000, p. 15). This is one of the reasons for *masculinisation of weapons*. 'A man without a gun in zones of conflict is often not considered a 'real man'. Masculinity and femininity are defined in a way that supports patriarchal military states and nationalist movements while at the same time subordinating women' (Jack, 2002, p. 53). In this *masculinisation* of weapons a kind of labour division emerges: men as protectors of women and land *by violence,* and women as producers of children and living (Jack, 2002, p. 53).

Some governments understand the possession of arms by their citizens as a means of self-protection and protection of their properties against rivals (BICC, 2002, p. 13). In Uganda it is reported that the Karamoja are highly armed. This has become a major threat to neighbours as the so called Local Defence Units and vigilantes in the neighbouring districts are often government armed. This move again increases the proliferation of small arms and heightens tension across borders. One of the main sources for acquiring light weapons since 1979 has been the collapse of successive regimes in Uganda, which provided opportunity to the Karamojong. In Kitido, among the Acholis, guns are mostly owned by the *young warriors* of different ethnic groups. These arms are either captured in battle or transferred from Sudan.

Another aspect of the militarisation of civil society is caused by cattle rustling in some areas in the Horn of Africa. However, this is not considered to be problematic. Issues connected to the availability of weapons among the civilian nomads are not only cattle rustling or self-defence. In some areas, as a symbol of social status, the people are more armed than the security forces, and in the face of massive unemployment and poverty this leads to a threatening criminality and looting. As Marwa says, colonial police, tribal police and the armed militia have made the access to arms easier for civilians in Kuria/Kenya.

Ayalew Gebre, while discussing the conflict between different Oromo pastoralist groups in Ethiopia, maintains that there is a permanent inflow of firearms into the region. In the face of the fact that land scarcity is growing rapidly and government officials are not capable of solving the problem the conflicting parties resort to arms for attack or defence purposes. Even arbitration is successfully conducted only by the traditional authorities (Gebre, 2000, p. 18). Therefore, it is important to understand the civil militias in the Horn of Africa not only from the point of view that governments in the Horn of Africa are neither capable of controling their territories, solving their internal political problems, arbitrating inter-ethnic conflicts nor coordinating collective interests (which is state-building), but also from the perspective that governments *actively* arm the civilians. It seems these are the pillars of the continuous inflow of arms in the region, which will be illustrated by the Sudanese and Somalian cases.

Sudan

The Sudanese case shows us a very important development in the militarisation of civil society in the war history of this country. Both the government and the rebels in the south militarise the civil population under the disguise of self-defence. The real motivation behind 'maintaining security and self-defence' has been to organise an allied-armed tribal militia.

> This has a long history dating back to 1960s when the government launched civilian national guards (Haras al-watan) and the Anya Nya created civilian armed groups that they referred to as scouts. But the current civil war has given rise to several self-defence groups. There are the Arab, Dinka, Ferit, Mandari, Murle Nuer and the Toposa militias among others. Most militia formations are politically motivated. (Wassara, 2002, p. 12)

Since the beginning of the civil war in Sudan, many political as well as militant groups emerged such as Azania Liberation Front, Southern Sudan Defence Force, Southern Sudan Freedom Front, Southern Sudan Independence Army/Movement, Southern Sudan Liberation Front/Movement, Southern Sudan United Army, Southern Sudan Political Association, Sudan People's Liberation Movement/Army, Sudanese Allied Forces, Southern Sudan Independence Movement, United Democratic Salvation Front, Sudan People's Democratic Front, Equatoria Defence Force, SPLA-United, SPLM/SPLA Bahr El Ghazal, United Democratic Front, Sudan Liberation Movement/Army, Justice and Equality Movement etc. The concomitant phenomenon of these insurgency groups is an emergence of civil militias.

The three main causes that contributed to the militarisation of Sudan are: the civil war following independence in 1956, the militarisation of the country after the discovery of oil in 1983 and the militarising Islamisation of the country since 1989. These events have led to the death of more than 2 million and displacement of more than 4.5 million between 1984 and 2000 (Jack, 2002, p. 52). Moreover, the problem of Sudan is characterised by various features: the discrepancy between the Islamisation of the north and Christianization of the south, Arabisation of the north and Africanisation of the south, privileges of the north during the colonial period and the pauperised south despite its rich natural resources (Maxted and Zegeye, 2001).

It is estimated that there are at least 25 government-backed militias in Sudan. Civilians are armed either to fight the respective 'enemy' with the argument of self-defence, or they are armed to attack and pre-empt the alleged supporters of the Sudanese government or of the SPLA. These militias have adopted tactics aimed at denying a civilian base of support for the adversary. Wherever there is a suspicion of civilian support, the civilian population will be looted of its property, houses burnt, women kidnapped etc.

Since 1985 the government of Sudan has created an Arab civil militia against the population of southern Sudan. When the SPLA killed unarmed Arab residents of Gardud in 1985 the government responded brutally by arming the Baggara Arab militias (Muslims of Arab descent and considered racially acceptable to the regime), which perpetrated a catastrophic retaliation (Lesch, 1998, p. 91). The Baggara militias were created to counter the SPLA, after the SPLA made its first incursion into the Nuba Mountains in July 1985. According to *New Internationalist,* the Baggara had stolen cattle and burnt Nuba villages and consequently more than 60,000 people were displaced from the oil rich area. More than 10,000 children from this area were kidnapped, kept in military training camps and indoctrinated in Islamic fundamentalist principles (New Internationalist, 1992). Moreover, the Murahaliin militia was created as a pro-government force against the SPLA. Around the middle of the 1980s the Misiriya militia was reorganised into a paramilitary force. Towards the end of the 1980s the NIF-government, in effect, legitimised the Murahaliin militia (World Bank, 2004). Early 2002 Arab Paulino Matia militia and more than one hundred mounted Arab horsemen, supported by the MI-24 gun-ships, attacked the SPLA positions and committed atrocities including rape, murder, burning and looting against the local villagers in Bentiu during withdrawal after fighting with the SPLA (Sudan Care, 2004).

In the view of the southern population the Sudanese government is not simply arming the Arab pastoralists, but also orchestrating ethnic cleansing, which leads to the forming of alliances and the purchasing of arms in the south. Coordinated destruction of villages, attacks on travellers, persecution, arrest of educated people, hanging, amputation and stoning to death are being perpetrated by Arab Islamic militias (AC, 2002c, p. 7). The same magazine reports that the government tries to cover up the assaults against the people as ethnic conflicts exacerbated by weapons flowing in from Chad and Libya. Moreover, in April 2002 the Arab militias burned over 600 homes, killed 17 civilians. The government forces knew but did not want to intervene or act on behalf of the people (AC, 2002c, p. 7). *Africa Confidential* reported that a ship loaded in Tunisia with some 680 tons of explosives and 8,000 detonators was heading for Sudan intended for both civilian uses as well as artillery shell manufacture (AC, 2003b, p. 3).

In 2000 Bulgaria and Sudan had signed a secret arms deal worth hundreds of millions of dollars, which the Bulgarian government neither denied nor confirmed. Since 2000 Omar al-Bashir has been planning to create a national armaments industry, which will be funded by oil revenues. The main aim of the industry is army building and the manufacture of small arms under a Chinese license. Furthermore, there are secret contacts with Iraq and Iran and with military experts of Kazakhstan. In the first half of 2001 Sudan concluded a deal with Russia, estimated to be worth more than $600 million, to manufacture battle tanks (ARB, 2001c, p. 31). Oil revenues have also enabled Sudan to acquire surface-to-surface missiles in its war against southern rebels (ARB, 2001e, p. 26). Oil in Sudan is not only a means for financing war, but also the object of the warring factions that leads them to abuse human rights, militarise the civilians and recruit child soldiers. In March 2001 UNICEF airlifted more than 2,800 demobilised child soldiers away from the frontlines in southern Sudan (ARB, 2001b, p. 25).

The politics of the civil militias and the militarisation of the civil society was exacerbated after the creation of the Popular Defence Force (PDF) in 1990, which became the 'school for national and spiritual education' in order to 'remould the mind' and enhance 'religious consciousness'. Arab tribal militias and NIF volunteers were two of the decisive components of the militia (ARB, 2001b, p. 25). Another strategy of militarising the population by the Sudanese government is the method of dividing the opposition. In the first half of the 1990s the SPLA disintegrated into SPLA-Nasir and SPLA-Torit, which led to mutual destruction supported by the government. Moreover, the NIF-government covers up the conflicts in order to orchestrate a scenario between the Nuer and Dinka and portray these conflicts as interethnic; although it strives for subjugating all Sudanese people under the Islamic religion. As part of the Popular Defence Force, NIF-students are mobilised and armed beside the Arab militia for the 'purity of religion', the 'integrity of the homeland' and to intimidate the 'foes of Allah'. The people of the Upper Nile area continue to be attacked and displaced by government-backed militias because of oil exploration in the area. In the south various militias that consist of the government's Popular Defence Force, press-ganged youths, Islamist zealots, government-paid Arabic speakers, etc attack and chase civilians (ARB, 2001c, p. 2).

In order to smash the rebels in Darfur region the Sudanese government supports the brutal measures of the Janjaweed militias. The Janjaweed militias are armed and mobilised by the Sudanese government to strike back against the *Fur*, Zaghawa and Massalit peoples, who are collectively accused of supporting the rebellion in the Darfur region.

> *Janjaweed* soldiers' salary comes from what they can grab and the promise of land cleared of those now living on it: in other words, the booty captured in raids on villages. The government has thus handed the *Janjaweed* a license to terrorise the population of Darfur and given them the means to do so (Prendergast, 1999).

In the south, as well as in Darfur region, the government arms Arab nomads and criminals with the pretext of self-defence, and gives them the green light to shoot, loot, burn alive and rape. When the government of Sudan is accused of igniting conflicts by arming civil militias, it maintains that the conflicts were about land or cattle though they are helped out with intelligence and uniforms by the government, which on its part drops bombs and supports the militias with helicopters. Not surprisingly, the government denies controlling the militias. It describes the incidents as an unruly 'local conflict' resulting from the proliferation of arms in the region (The Economist, 2004, p. 32). This militarisation of the civilians and the obstruction of the process of coordinating common interests and peace is a fundamental aspect of the political history of the Horn of Africa. This phenomenon can be further illustrated by an analysis of Somalia.

Somalia

The phenomenon that intensifies state collapse in Somalia is the emergence of numerous factions with their own militia groups. When this research was conducted (early 2004) various parts of Somalia were controlled by different clan-based militia groups. The self-declared state of Somaliland consists of the United Somali Front (drawing support from the Issa clan armed with small arms and commanded by Abdurahman Dualeh Ali), the Somali Democratic Alliance (supported by Gadbursi clan), the Somali National Movement (supported by 5 000 to 6 000, drawn from the Tur, Dhegaweyne and Kahin clans equipped with 5 or 6 medium tanks, 15-20 Fiat armoured personnel carriers, artillery, mortars, anti-aircraft weapons and naval patrol vessels based at the port of Berbera and of the United Somali Party (supported by Midigan and Tumaal clans commanded by Ahmed Guure Adan). In other parts of Somalia, the Somali Salvation Democratic Front (3,000 militiamen drawn from the Darod clan and commanded by Abdullah Yusuf Ahmed), the United Somali Congress (drawn from Hawiye clan and commanded by Hussein Mohammed Aideed and Osman Atto), the Ali Mahdi Faction (10,000 drawn from Abgal clan commanded by Ali Mahdi), the Somali National Front (2,000 to 3,000 militiamen drawn from the Darod sub-clan of the Marehan commanded by Gen. Omar Hagi Mohammed Hersi and equipped with mortars, anti-aircraft weapons, recoilless rifles), the Somali Democratic Movement (drawn from the Rahenwein/Digil) and the Somali Patriotic Movement (2,000 to 3,000 drawn from the Darod clan commanded by Ahmed Omar Jess) are operating (ISS, 2004). Contrary to the agreement of January 29, 2004 six faction leaders signed a statement accusing Kenya and Djibouti of mismanaging the talks and of bias in favour of the Transitional National Government during the Somali national reconciliation conference, which took place in Nairobi, Kenya in February 2004. Signatories to the statement are the Jawhar-based faction leader, Muhammad Habib; Shaykh Adan Madobe of the Rahanwein Resistance Army; Gen Muhammad Sa'id Hirsi Morgan; Abdullahi Shaykh Isma'il; Mahmud Sayyid Adan of the Somali National Front; and Abdiqadir Abdi Hasan. The six belong to the SRRC (Somali Reconciliation and Restoration Council) a group, which opposes the TNG (All Africa, 2004).

The fall of Mengistu and Siad Barre has been one of the main reasons for an abundant supply of weapons in Somalia since the beginning of the 1990s. Somalia is the best case to question the nature and value of the state and the meaning of state boundaries.

> Almost everyone got hold of guns... Armours are empty. Police have no weapons. There is no army as such. The elders of the clans do not seem to be able to control many of their armed youth, and there are conflicting inter-clan interests, which prevent their elders from acting jointly to improve security (Woodward, 2003, p. 73).

As HRW reported, the consequences of the militarisation of Somali civil society is that the fighters steal and extort from rival clans or groups, and their leaders do nothing to discourage them (HRW, 1993). Since there is no central authority that monopolizes power and guarantees the security of citizens, rival militias often fight for control of toll collection, which is a major source of revenue for militia leaders.

> The looting and banditry prevalent in Somalia is not solely due to individual looters and bandits, but is a direct result of the manner in which the armed factions choose to recruit their forces and wage war. In fact, many observers argue that without the implied promise of fruitful looting, few factions would be able to summon any sizable military support (HRW, 1993).

The militarisation of the civil society happens when either secessionist ethnic elites or unionist nationalists instrumentalise and militarise the civil population in order to create a state. The two fatal errors here are: first, that state building is engineered by the elites; and second, that this is done with the help of weapons. The formation of the Somaliland movement, its resort to violence, the suppression of the opposition by the Siad Barre regime, etc. indicate that the state had already failed. Even international law, which presents the state border as sacrosanct, is incapable of solving the problem of the nature of the state and resorts instead to mere suppression.

> During the reign of Siad Barre, the government of Somalia stockpiled arms with the intent of using them in the armed struggle to create a 'Greater Somalia', which was to include parts of Kenya, Djibouti and Ethiopia. In the course of its armed struggle, the SNM [Somali National Movement] distributed a lot of weapons to sympathizers and auxiliary forces supporting its cause with the help of Ethiopia. Militias, which were loyal to different clans, sprang up. A lot of arms also got into civilian hands as the government began to disintegrate in 1980s. (Omar, 2002, p. 18)

Those civilians who own arms in Somaliland see the arms as a necessary means for defending themselves, their property, and their 'nation' against Southern Somalia (Omar, 2002, p. 19). A dangerous qualitative jump in this society (as it is in many parts in the Horn of Africa) is the sudden transition from traditional weapons to modern firearms. In the face of the scarcity of economic resources, firearms have become the most efficient means to appropriate wealth as well as defending it. Moreover, firearms have become a symbol of high social status and wealth. Thousands of militiamen, supporting either the SNM (Somali National Movement) or the Siad Barre regime, play a central role by destabilising society (Omar, 2002, p. 21).

The repression of the Siad Barre regime could not solve the political problems. Instead, it enkindled devastating conflicts in which militia attacks by various factions began to disrupt normal economic activities and caused insecurity, starvation and flow of refugees (Project Ploughshares, 2001). Towards the end of the 1980s the government began to sponsor some militia forces in order to crush the SNM (Shinn 2003, p. 3). One of the causes of the creation and consolidation of the SNM was Siad Barre's strategic concentration of political control and power in the capital city by ignoring the rest of the country. This was one of the reasons for SNM support in Somaliland. After the Siad Barre regime was ousted, anarchy and war were exacerbated by various militia groups that controlled the top political positions because of their military power (Woods, 1997, pp. 1-2).

Besides the politics of allegiance, the Siad Barre regime was famous for stirring up competition among sub-clans and clans by manipulating them in order to create inter- and intra-clan conflicts as we have seen in the case of the Sudanese government. Looting and selling of the spoils of war in the markets of Mogadishu by Barre troops was openly allowed during this regime. These same troops later joined various militia groups (HRW, 1993).

On November 15th 2001 Susan Rice, the Clinton administration's Africa policy maker, in her speech to the House of Representatives, called Somalia a 'terrorist haven', the 'continent's proverbial black hole, an ungoverned lawless, radicalised, heavily armed country with one of the longest undefended coastlines in the region' (ARB, 2001f, p. 2). The fight between the pro-government militia and Hussein Aideed's on May 11th and 12th 2001 was the bloodiest fighting in the last few years (ARB, 2001d, p. 25). Kiflemariam says that more than 350,000 guns are owned by civilians in Somaliland (by about 80 percent of able-bodied males), and every second household in northeastern Kenya owns a gun (Gebrewold, 2002, p. 20). Because of the increased tensions in various regions of Somalia the demand for weapons is growing and the prices are going up. Moreover, it was reported that various types of weapons were arriving from Ethiopia. Since the interim government of Somalia is not recognized by various factions, there has been fighting between its forces and the forces of two warlords; Musa Sudi Yalahow and Mohamed Dhereh (Somali Reconciliation and Restoration Council – claimed to be backed by Ethiopia) (ARB, 2002a, p. 23). For counter attack the TNG (Transitional National Government of Somalia) received weapons from Djibouti, Libya, Eritrea and Yemen.

Power struggle and internal schism is leading to civil militias and the militarisation of civilians. For example, in the month of June 2002, the rivalry in self-declared autonomous Puntland, between two rival leaders Abdullahi Yusuf and Jama Ali Jama, led to the mobilisation of their forces and to a renewed fighting between the two sides (ARB, 2002b, p. 26). Another power struggle that led to the militarisation and suffering of civilians is that of the Rahanwein Resistance Army, which declared southwestern Somalia as autonomous in late March 2002. The fight between the faction of Muhammad Nur Shatigadud on one hand, and the faction of Shaykh Ada and Muhammad Ibrahim Habsade on the other claimed the lives of over 40 people. In the face of the fight, the mediating elders decided upon the dissolution of the self-declared autonomous state of southwest Somalia (ARB, 2002c, p. 25). Since the beginning of 2003 the number of people killed more increased rapidly because of the clan affiliation of the civilians. People have been unable to harvest their crops. It has become difficult for the humanitarian organisations to have access, such as to the town of Baydhabo (Baidoa), because of the fight between the Shatigadud faction of the Rahanweyn Resistance Army and the Madobe/Habsade faction, which is probably allied to the TNG in Mogadishu (ARB 2003a, p. 26). Since the TNG is challenged by inter-faction wars, it has admitted that it cannot disarm various militias on its own. Moreover, the proliferation of militias has reached such high proportions that it has asked foreign troops to help disarm these militias. The Information Minister of the government asked only 'friendly countries with no political or military agenda in Somalia' (ARB, 2002c, p. 25), are quest which is apparently phrased to underline that Ethiopia, in particular, is being accused of destabilizing the TNG.

The Somali society is flooded by militiamen fighting for clan warlords and working for private businessmen as a consequence of the state collapse. Somalia has become a highly militarised and divided society with various warlords and authorities controlling various parts of the country. Children and minorities are most affected by the consequences of state failure. Children are forcibly recruited by militias; they become addicted to alcohol and drugs; sexually abused; have jobs hazardous to their health and seek volatile protection joining urban gangs (Global IDP, 2004). Besides children, minorities bear most the consequences of state failure and militarisation of civilians. Internally displaced persons from minority groups such as Rahanwein, Bantu, Ajuran, Jarso, Madhiban and Ashraf lack political representation; they are discriminated against, targets of attacks, displaced and dispossessed by militias. Since competition for political power goes hand in hand with the grabbing of resources, minorities on fertile lands disproportionately suffer from killings, destruction, discrimination, land alienation, obstruction of humanitarian relief, and forced displacement. Moreover, since the strategy of Siad Barre was divide-and-rule, he armed the Galgala minority against the Abgal. Later this led to retaliation against the latter when the regime fell. The Bantu minorities, who ultimately suffered and were despised as slaves, were displaced from their lands in the Gosha area by Majerten and Habargedir militias who fought over control of resources in 1991 and 1993 (Global IDP, 2004).

Neither the case of Somalia nor of the region as a whole can be understood, regarding civil militias, if the trans-boundary arms flow from neighbouring states or other states that transfer arms to Somalia in particular and to the Horn of Africa in general is not discussed. Moreover, this inter-state arms transfer leads us to another very important issue of the atmosphere of relationships among the states of the Horn.

Transboundary Arms Transfer and the Militarisation of Civilians in the Horn of Africa

Due to porous and expansive borders, weak governments, and ineffectual national security systems, SALW [Small Arms and Light Weapons] are difficult to control or account for as they move within the region from one conflict to another. They filter far beyond armies and police forces to criminal organizations, private security forces, vigilante squads, and individual citizens. For example, among cross-border pastoralist communities, arms are acquired overtly for security purposes but become facilitating instruments in traditional practices of livestock raiding. The use of such modern weapons has turned such traditional practices into lethal warfare. Also, as pastoral areas get saturated with arms, pastoralists themselves become suppliers of arms to non-pastoral rural areas and urban centres. Inadequate policing makes it easy for these illegal arms to circulate without being detected by law enforcement authorities. As a consequence armed criminality in urban, rural and border areas is on the increase. (Griffiths-Fulton, 2002)

The Horn of Africa is characterised by fragile inter-state relations. This situation is maintained not only because of the war between Ethiopia and Eritrea between 1998 and 2000, but also because of the war between Ethiopia and Somalia in the 1970s. The states in the Horn of Africa are characterised by mutual destabilisation and distrust.

> The war between Ethiopia and Eritrea has led both governments to increase their military support to rival proxies in Somalia, thus igniting new rounds of deadly conflict, spreading instability to northern Kenya, re-legitimizing warlords and destroying hopes for internal peace efforts. At the same time, Ethiopia and Eritrea have reduced their support for the Sudanese opposition, thus strengthening the hand of the Khartoum regime and reducing the likelihood of progressive change in Sudan. In addition, Sudan supports insurgent groups in Ethiopia, Eritrea, and Uganda; Somali militias have launched cross-border attacks into Ethiopia and supported Ethiopian oppositionists, while Ethiopian troops have launched assaults into Somalia to create a protective buffer zone; and Uganda has supported the main rebel groups in Sudan. With each new act of violence, with each cross-border arms transfer, the regional dimensions of these conflicts deepen. (Prendergast, 1999)

The Siad Barre regime used to arm the Ogaden National Liberation Front and Oromo Liberation Front in Ethiopia, whereas the Ethiopian government used to arm the SNM. As a response the Siad Barre regime began to arm local militia in Somaliland to counter the SNM activities (Gebrewold, 2002, p. 19). The arms build up in Sudan has not only escalated Africa's largest twenty year civil war, but has also acted as a launching pad for insurgencies, which have recently emerged in neighbouring Uganda, Eritrea and Ethiopia (Achieng, 1998).

Conflicts that spill over borders and the availability of light weapons are interconnected (ISS, 1999, p. 1). The *Newsletter* of the ISS (Institute of Security Studies) says 'it is estimated that the Mengistu government in Ethiopia inherited thousands of weapons that flooded into Somalia. These same weapons, and additional ones from the war in Sudan, are now in Kenya and other parts of East Africa. Renewed fighting between Eritrea and Ethiopia, and its spill-over effect on Somalia, has promoted fears of another arms race in the Horn of Africa' (ISS, 1999, p. 2). In the second half of the 1990s Ethiopia and Eritrea began to support the opponents of the Sudanese NIF-government, which was helping the Islamic groups both in Ethiopia and Eritrea.

Regional security complexes and the spillover of civil wars into neighbouring states are exacerbated by the support of some of the states of the Horn for the armed opposition groups in other countries. According to the Ethiopian government, the collapsed state of Somalia has become a haven for militant opponents of Ethiopia such as ethnic Somalis in eastern Ethiopia, and the OLF in eastern, southern and western Ethiopia. Hence, the Ethiopian government has pretexts to persecute these groups even within Somali territory.

The Oromo Liberation Front is an ethnic separatist guerrilla group, which has been fighting against the Ethiopian state since around 1973, operating from within Ethiopia, Eritrea, Somalia and Kenya. The goal of the guerrilla group is to carve out a separate homeland for the Oromo people estimated to make up about 40% of Ethiopia's population and more than half of Ethiopia's territory, including Adis Abeba. Since the start of the war between Eritrea and Ethiopia in 1998 and the Ethiopian support for SRRC (forces fighting the Somali transitional government), parties from the neighbouring countries of Somalia and Eritrea are suspected of supporting the OLF in an effort to weaken Ethiopia. Since 2000 the OLF has been blamed for many casualties. Its attacks on trucks and railways on March 22, 2000 and June 24, 2002 respectively killed 28 people. On September 11, 2002 a bomb exploded in Tigray Hotel in Adis Abeba, which again the OLF was blamed for. A hand-grenade attack on May 2, 2004 that killed one and injured three others in Bishoftu, Ethiopia, and another hand grenade attack on May 5, 2004 at a teachers college in southern Ethiopia that damaged property but without injuries and fatalities are blamed on the OLF which is alleged to be supported by and operating mainly from Eritrea and Somalia. In the face of this security complex, in order to retaliate against the Somali transitional government for its active support and/or passive tolerance the Ethiopian government has been supporting the SRRC materially (militarily) as well as non-materially (diplomatically). For its part the Somali transitional government has been enabling the OLF to import weapons from and through Somalia. The OLF and the SRRC have become proxy armies of Somalia and Ethiopia respectively.

If national boundaries are rarely recognised by communities at the border and the rebels take advantage of this opportunity, respective governments have good pretexts for incursion into foreign territory and to arm rebels and even the civilians of that country. The support by Ethiopia for the Eritrean National Forces Alliances during the Ethiopian-Eritrean war (1998-2000) is a good example. In the same way Eritrea continues active support by arming and training Ethiopian opposition movements such as the Oromo Liberation Front, whereby it could reinforce Ethiopian concerns and as a consequence a number of violent incidents have made the Ethiopian government nervous (AC, 2003c, p. 2). Many Ethiopians are already unhappy with the secession of Eritrea from Ethiopia. This unhappiness has been exacerbated not only by the war between Ethiopia and Eritrea since 1998, but also by this destabilising act by Eritrea. Angered by the administration of the Ethiopian government and by the International Court of Justice's adjudication of the disputed Badme region to Eritrea various militant groupings are challenging the Ethiopian government. Paradoxically, though groups such as the Ethiopian People's Patriotic Front (EPPF) and the Tigray People's Democratic Movement (TPDM) are against the decision of the International Court of Justice (against adjudication of Badme to Eritrea) they are supported by Eritrea in attempt to weaken the Ethiopian government. EPPF is being extensively armed by Eritrea and claims to have killed or wounded over 150 government soldiers in various operations (AC, 2002a, p. 6).

A UN-report by the Security Council Committee reported on 27 January 2003 regarding the situation in Somalia and the regional arms-related destabilisation. Ethiopia, Eritrea, Yemen, Djibouti, Sudan and Egypt are all said to have violated the embargo over the last decade by giving arms, equipment, militia training and financial support to Somalian factions (AC, 2003a, p. 8). In 1999 two Mogadishu faction leaders (Ali Mahdi Mohamed and Hussein Mohamed Aideed) called Ethiopia 'the enemy' trying to disintegrate Somalia, interfering in its internal affairs and obstructing the formation of a central government by giving arms and ammunitions to Somali factions (Somali Salvation Democratic Front, United Somalia Congress Peace Movement and Rahanwein Resistance Army) (ARB, 1999a, p. 3).

The situation in Somalia is a combination of proxy war and inter-state war. In 1999 a ship from Eritrea carrying arms for Aideed and purchased by OLF docked at Marka port in southern Somalia, which caused Ethiopia to plan to bomb if more arms were offloaded there (ARB, 1999b, p. 6). Despite the UN arms embargo on Somalia in 1992 there are arms supplies for various factions from the usual suspects: Anti-TNG such as Muse Sudi supported by Ethiopia, and the TNG and its allies backed by Eritrea, Yemen and Libya. On the other side, the OLF and ONLF can purchase their weapons on the Mogadishu market (AC, 2002b, p. 7). Even the UN is concerned, although it cannot independently verify it, over the persistent reports that Ethiopia is militarily present in Somalia. Somalia demands that Ethiopia 'withdraws' from its territory, stops reviving the civil war and arming factions opposed to the interim government (ARB, 2001a, pp. 24-5).

Conclusion

Without redefining politics, the state and the role of political elites, the crisis in the Horn can neither be understood nor solved. Modern politics and state building as constructs of the political elites have not solved the political, economic and social problems of citizens in the Horn. On the contrary, they have led to the de-politicisation of the people and professionalisation of politics for the benefit of those who are in the state apparatus. Any sound political change in the Horn of Africa demands active participation, decentralisation of political administration, and weakening of elitism and its militarisation of politics.

Since no politics can be successful by repressing the political passion of the people, any political unity and identification of the self with a given state can be possible only if people are willing to and convinced of belonging to a certain state. Any enforcement of citizenship on people will lead, sooner or later, to the destruction of the state. Therefore, the sanctity of borders, as anchored in international law as an irreversible political dogma, has to be revised for the sake of peace. People must belong to a state freely and willingly, whereupon if necessary state disintegration has to be made possible by international law. The self-declared independence of Somaliland from Somalia, the question of the Ethiopian Somalis and of the Oromo Liberation Front, etc. cannot be solved by military power and by dogmatising the issue of territorial integrity.

Another important aspect regarding states in the Horn of Africa is to develop inter-state cooperation and confidence. Inter-state conflicts and proxy wars are the main sources of weapons inflow, civil militias and the militarisation of society. If inter-state confidence building and cooperation are materialised, and if there is no military incursion into the territories of the neighbouring states, one of the main sources of arms flow for civil militias can be curbed.

The recent developments in the Horn could be the beginning of the stabilisation of the region. The election of the Somali parliamentarians, state President and Prime Minister in the second half of 2004 and various Sudanese peace agreements since May 2004 could alleviate the political and economic crisis of the Horn. Whereas the developments of the Somali Peace Process still remain uncertain and even disappointing, the agreement between the Sudanese government and the SPLA towards the end of May 2004 seems to be a decisive step to end the activities of the government supported civil militias and the militarisation of society. Following the killing of approximately two million people, there were scenes of jubilation when the deal between the Sudanese government and SPLA on power and resources sharing, and the sharia issue was signed in Kenya. Accordingly, the south will be autonomous for six years and sharia remains in the north. Whereas this peace achievement was celebrated not only as a victory of the people of Sudan, but also of the entire continent, the Arab militias supported by the Sudanese government are persecuting the civilians in the Darfur region. As long as the main causes of killings, displacements and insurgencies, the social, political, cultural and economic marginalization, is not taken seriously, the militarisation of societies in the Horn of Africa will never end. Hence, the central issue involved in solving the problem will be rethinking the nature and aim of state territory and the project of state building for the sake of peace and security of the civilians.

References

Achieng (1998), Judith, Horn of Africa: Flow of weapons fuels conflict:
    http://www.oneworld.org/ips2/sept98/12_52_040.html
Africa Confidential (2002a), V.43, No.11, May 31st.
Africa Confidential (2002b), V.43, No.12, June 14th.
Africa Confidential (2002c), V.43, No.23, November 22nd.
Africa Confidential (2003a), V.44, No.5, March 7th.
Africa Confidential (2003b), V.44, No.13, June 27th.
Africa Confidential (2003c), V.44, No.15, July 25th.
Africa Research Bulletin (1999a), V.36, No.2, March 22nd.
Africa Research Bulletin (1999b), V.36, No.5, June 21st.
Africa Research Bulletin (2001a), V.38, No.1, February 22nd.
Africa Research Bulletin (2001b), V.38, No.2, March 29th.
Africa Research Bulletin (2001c), V.38, No.3, May 2nd.
Africa Research Bulletin (2001d), V.38, No.5, June 22nd.
Africa Research Bulletin (2001e), V.38, No.8, September 21st.
Africa Research Bulletin (2001f), V.38, No.11, December 20th.
Africa Research Bulletin (2002a), V.39, No.5, June 27th.
Africa Research Bulletin (2002b), V.39, No.6, July 25th.

Africa Research Bulletin (2002c), V.39, No.7, August 29th.

Africa Research Bulletin (2003a), V.40, No.1, February 24th.

Africa Research Bulletin (2003b), V.40, No.6, July 24th.

All Africa, Somalia: Six-Faction Leaders Demand Postponement of Peace Talks: http://allafrica.com/stories/200402230023.html

AWEPA bulletin (2003), Vol.17, No.4.

Bonn International Centre for Conversion (2001), *Small Arms in the Horn of Africa*, Bonn.

Carayannis, Tatiana and Weiss, Herbert F. (2003), 'The Democratic Republic of Congo, 1996-2002', in Boulden, Jane (ed), *Dealing with Conflicts in Africa: The United Nations and Regional Organizations*, New York: Palgrave, pp. 253-303.

Creveld, Martin van (1999), *The Rise and Decline of the State*, Cambridge: Cambridge University Press.

Crocker, Chester A. (2003), 'Engaging failing states' in *Foreign Affairs* September/October 2003 V.82, Nr.5, pp. 32-44.

'Displaced children lack protection': http://www.db.idpproject.org/Sites/idpSurvey.nsf/wViewCountries/05A658225C529027 C1256D44005A7B8A

Dunleavy, Patrick (2000), 'The state', in Robert E. Goodin and Philip Pettit (eds.), *A Companion to Contemporary Political Philosophy*, Oxford: Blackwell.

Ethiopia: Human Rights Watch accuses government of harassing journalists. http://www.irinnews.org/report.asp?ReportID=39478&SelectRegion=Horn_of_Africa& SelectCountry=ETHIOPIA

Gebre, Ayalew (2000), 'Conflicts over natural resources and institutional mechanism for their resolution and management: the case of the Karrayu and their neighbours', in *Curbing the Demand for Small Arms, Lessons in East Africa and the Horn of Africa*, Conference, Nairobi, Kenya, 12-16.

Gebrewold, Kiflemariam (2002), 'Understanding the demand for small arms in the Horn of Africa', in *Bonn International Centre for Conversion, Small arms in the Horn of Africa*, Bonn.

Griffiths-Fulton, Lynne (2002), 'Small arms and light weapons in the Horn of Africa', Ploughshares Monitor: http://www.ploughshares.ca/CONTENT/MONITOR/monj02a.html

Held, David (1989), *Political theory and the modern stat*, Stanford: Stanford University Press.

Hirt, Nicole (2003), 'Äthiopien' in Rolf Hofmeier and Andreas Mehler *Afrika Jahrbuch 2002*, pp.252-257, Hamburg: Leske+Budrich.

Human Rights Watch (7. March 1993), Somalia, Vol. 5, No. 2.

HRW (2004), 'Playing with Fire: Weapons proliferation, political violence, and human rights in Kenya': http://www.hrw.org/reports/2002/kenya/

HRW (2004), 'International Response to the Crisis in Darfur', November: http://www.humanrightswatch.org/backgrounder/africa/darfur1104/8.htm

Institute of Security Studies (1999), 'Small arms proliferation and Africa', *Newsletter* 3 April-June.

Jack, Amani El (2002) 'Gender perspectives on the management of small arms and light weapons in the Sudan', in Bonn International Centre for Conversion, *Small Arms in the Horn of Africa*, Bonn.

Lesch, Ann Mosely (1998), *The Sudan – Contested National Identities*, Oxford: James Curry.

Marwa, Peter (2000), 'SALIGAD', in *Curbing the demand for small arms. Lessons in East Africa and the Horn of Africa*, Nairobi, Kenya, 12-16.

Maxted, Julia and Zegeye, Abebe (2001), 'Human stability and conflict in the Horn of Africa', in *African Security Review*, Vol.10, No.4, Pretoria.

MOFA (2000), 'Armed Conflicts around the World':
www.mofa.go.jp/policy/un/disarmament/weapon/conflict.html.

Mohamed Suliman, resource access (2002), 'A Major Cause of Armed Conflict in the Sudan. The case of the Nuba Mountains':
http://www.worldbank.org/wbi/conatrem/Sudan-Paper.htm.

New Internationalist (1992), Issue 238, December.

Norbury, Frank (2002), Field Report from Sudan, Western Upper Nile Area. Available from: http://www.sudancare.org/ICI-Feb02.htm

Omar, Mohamoud Jama (2002), 'Management and control of small arms: the Somaliland experience', in Bonn International Centre for Conversion, *Small Arms in the Horn of Africa*, Bonn.

Paddison, Ronan (1983), *The Fragmented State*, Oxford: Basil Blackwell.

Plaut, Martin (2004), 'Ethiopia faces new rebellion':
http://news.bbc.co.uk/1/hi/world/africa/3483531.stm

Project Ploughshares Monitor (2001), 'Horn of Africa: Building sustainable security':
http://www.ploughshares.ca/content/MONITOR/monm01e.html

Prendergast, John (1999), 'Building for Peace in the Horn of Africa. Diplomacy and Beyond':
http://www.usip.org/pubs/specialreports/sr990628.html.

Rotberg, Robert I. (2004), 'Failed states, Collapsed States, Weak States', in Rotberg, Robert I. (ed), *State Failure and and State Weakness in a Time of Terror*, Cambridg: World Peace Foundation, pp.1-25.

Shinn, David H. (2003), 'The Horn of Africa: How does Somaliland fit', Umea, Sweden (unpublished).

Somalia: security information. http://www.iss.co.za/AF/profiles/Somalia/SecInfo.html#top.

The Economist, January 10th-16th 2004.

Thokozani Thusi (2003), 'Assessing small arms control initiatives in the East Africa. The Nairobi Declaration', in *African Security Review 12(2)*.

Wassara, Samson, 'Conflict and state security in the Horn of Africa: Militarisation of civilian groups':
www.aaps.co.zw/Publications/AIJP/Wassara.html

Woods, Emira, 'Somalia':
http://www.somaliawatch.org/archivejuly/000907605.htm

Woodward, Peter (2003), *The Horn of Africa:. Politics and International Relations*, London: Tauris.

Chapter 10

Protracted Civil War, Civil Militias and Political Transition in Uganda since 1986

A. Byaruhanga Rukooko

Introduction

The issue of militias in the whole of Africa may be worrying, but, generally, not as much as it is in Uganda today. In its history, Uganda has had numerous militias,[1] both in the opposition and those supported by government, but those that have evolved under President Museveni's Movement government are of a new genre. Not only are they numerous, but they are also an encapsulation of repressive politics, mismanagement, and abuse of power, contrary to the wind of optimism blowing across Africa.[2] This repression has led to the formation of various militia groups opposed to government causing a race of armed groups' formation on the side of both government and opposition, the consequences of which undermine against stability and sustainable development. This paper examines the regime-supported militias and their effect on democratic processes, and their shadowy existence.[3] Like rebel militias, they are private and numerous and it would not be proper to describe them as government militias because the Ugandan government is established by constitution and these militias are often not established this way.[4] However, their creation and activity suggest a security problem for Uganda, which must be explained.

Conceptualising the Militia

A militia is a group of citizens organised to provide military service. It is usually a supplementary or reserve army, composed of non-professional soldiers and not necessarily supported or sanctioned by the government, thereby making it distinct from the regular army of a nation. It can serve to supplement the regular military as an irregular reserve, or it can oppose it, for example, to resist a military coup.[5] Consequently, militias are often of a less professional character and intended to carry out emergencey tasks of a military nature. But this definition is not satisfactory for, in many cases, even when a specific militia is less professional, in a military sense, some of its members well trained and either retired or expelled soldiers or warriors, but who have formed a force to accomplish a task before disbanding as a regular, professional force takes over.

The proliferation of both pro-government and the anti government militias in Africa have originated in the anti-colonial liberation struggles since the late 1950s the purpose of which was the contesting of power by use of violence. For this reason, they manifested themselves as extra-democratic, illegitimate formations, suitable for sustainable peace and development; in spite of being referred to as progressive or revolutionary or democratic forces. But whereas most of the anti-colonial militias were against the colonial state, those that have emerged since independence have either been anti or pro-government. In most cases, anti-government, militias seek to overthrow the sitting government much as the pro-government militias seek to protect the sitting government, its ideology, and property. In general, although the anti-government militias are is often painted in the most negative sense, the government militias are functionally no better, in terms of levels of legitimacy or criminality.

Consequently, when talking about the militia, issues of state formation and democratic processes are also at stake. Militias are raised for the purpose of settling an otherwise failed non-violent political process because the democratic channels are distrusted and perceived as helpless, unsatisfactory weapons for accessing or retaining power.

Additionally, militias are also a cheaper means of recruiting and maintaining a military force which would be loyal to it commander. Whereas the professional army may be based on contracts, the army is recruited and privately managed even though it is hardly privately disbanded, for very often, at the stage of disbanding or winding up, other international forces are called in because such forces become uncontrollably murderous. Hence, the 'short cut' of raising the militia becomes expedient. Unfortunately, due to their illegitimacy, they are often criminal and unaccountable, even though they are described as 'democratic forces', or 'progressive forces'.

How does one explain African regimes creating militias, which, in most cases lack specific laws to back them? How do we explain their deliberate abuse of the same population they are purported to protect? How do we account for the deliberate mismanagement of the militias in both function and welfare? How, after all, can we explain the existence of militias outside government, if democracy is working, or if the nation-state is functional? How can the state accomodate sustain a force of men, ill-equipped, half trained, illiterate, and fighting to take over an established government? In short, how can a functioning state fail to defeat a vicious, mystical, fiendish group such as the LRA, whose target is women and children? What other logical consistency can be predicated of primitive war if it is not a primitive struggle for power? What sort of democratic nation-state can be constructed out of a society, which is dominated by one group which is intent on excluding, by violence, other legitimate democratic political interests? Uganda goes beyond ordinary limits in most of the above cases; it has probably the highest known number of government supported militias, and it has experienced the most virile rebel groups in recent times, with as many being created as are being defeated. Indeed, little hope remains with the idea that President Museveni is anxious to change the Constitution in order to secure a limitless period for him self to remain in power. Consequently, for purposes of specificity, in this paper we shall restrict our discussion to government militias since 1986.

NRM Guerilla Warfare and the Auxiliary Forces

After the controversial elections of 1980, Mr. Museveni, one of the contenders who had lost, declared a guerilla war against Milton Obote's victorious Ugandan People's Congress (UPC) government. Museveni's strategy of war was, among other things, designed to integrate the military into the democratic process by involving as much of the population as possible, and hence, creating his so called popular resistance. His own army was a militia and was in all aspects one, but, of significance to this paper is the Local Defense Forces that were created following the above, mentioned military strategy.

When the National Resistance Movement/Army secured territory from the enemy soldiers of Milton Obote, elective local governing councils would be established to take charge of their own affairs. These councils would be accountable to the National Resistance Movement/Army, and although they would provide general administration, because of the war, they were also used to gather intelligence and give general support, whenever they could, in carrying out military operations.

However, it was LDUs that were useful in military formations and functions. Firstly, instance, they were given some military training, which made them more 'amenable' to war. Much of their work involved acting as a back-up force for the National Resistance Army as well as for the Local Councils. For the NRM/A, they collected intelligence, and helped transfer the wounded, the sick, children, pregnant women, and others to safety. It is interesting to note that during the war some local people refused to leave from their homes, and for their own safety, they were forced out, sometimes being carried. They also acted as a rear force, in as much as they searched for food, and protected people who were going to collect food.

Additionally, the Local Defence Units (LDUs) supported the Local Councils in the mobilize action of the population against Obote's forces and politics. They also ensured law and order and discipline, and checked 'excesses', like when individuals refused to do public service, or investigated robberies, and supported the population in economic activity. During the Bush War, the LDUs were, understandably, not paid, but this persisted after the war ended. They were under the control of Moses Kigongo, Gertrude Njuba, and Kakoza Mutale all of whom have remained close to Museveni.

In short, the LDUs were a political tool or a branch of the movement political system dynamic that was meant to secure political gains and defend political programmes. They pursued this activity until NRM assumed power in 1986. And this, character has helped to shape the pro-government militias in Uganda since then.

Consolidation of NRM

When the NRM took over the reigns of power, they abandoned all the police and nearly annihilated all the soldiers of the former government and other rebellious groups who did not join NRA, like Uganda Freedom Movement (UFM). According to one source, referring to the absence of UNLA soldiers in Uganda: 'Have you seen any of these soldiers? We really killed them'. It is also reported that it is the LDUs who slowly but surely annihilated Andrew Kayira's remnants of the UFM, a sister rebel group, which fought Obote's government. As a rear force, the LDUs made it safe for the army to forge ahead with minimum infiltration and risk of ambush.

As NRM consolidated its power, the LDUs were being recruited across the country, to support the NRA which, among other things, was doing police work. However, much more importantly, LDUs were created for the purpose of countering insurgence that to developed because the NRM had come to power by means of violence. Violence seemed to be the only tactic, which the NRM leadership understood, and so they created the LDUs to support them. Their role, therefore, was to supplement the military inexpensively and to protect the homes and their residents. People were expected to be part of the security system and therefore security was everyone's responsibility. Also, their role was political; to defend government against insurgency fighting, and later, to support the regime against the opposition.

In terms of functions, apart from patrolling villages and sometimes molesting suspected criminals, the LDUs complemented the official and professional forces, eg police, military intelligence, and the army when there were operations in their area. Indeed, LDUs were supportive in this regard and, not surprisingly, to date they continue to do this work. They were also recruited as cadres or mobilizers of youth and for general security of the areas in which they were located. Others were absorbed into the regular army, then called the NRA (now Ugandan Peoples' Defence Forces), Internal Security Organsation, and, by this time, they were being paid. But although they were security personnel, they have never lived in barracks.

It should nonetheless, be noted that one of the most significant political innovations of the NRM was the introductions of the Resistance Councils we referred to above. During the process of consolidation, the most significant activity, apart from physical fighting, was establishment of political structures whose major character was the resistance council, operating in the village, the parish, sub-county, county and, finally, at the national level. Much emphasis was put on the lower levels. Councillors were elected, the higher levels virtually dominated by the President and his military leaders in the High Command and Army Council. Ideological schools (popularly referred to as mchaka mchaka) were put in place to bolster these structures and widen support for government political programmes and war strategies. It is now acknowledged that these measures were a deliberate attempt to undermine existing structures, especially the political parties, which potentially constituted a challenge to the presidents nascent power structure. For this reason, Legal Notice No. 1 1986 suspended the activities of political parties and, to date this position has not changed. Effectively, this meant that the social, political and economic space was only accessible to the NRM government.

Unfortunately, violent conflict did not stop after Museveni assumed power; not only did the remnants of the armies NRA defeated fight back from northern and eastern Uganda, but also other rebellious forces (read rebellious militia) rose up in the West Nile, and Central and Western Uganda. (It is likely that war will continue unless drastic measures to address current unanswered political questions are taken.) In response, the government continued recruiting and training soldiers but also, recruited LDUs to support the NRM government in the manner reminiscent of the period before the take over.

However, the posturing of the LDUs in the country depended on the prevailing situation. That is to say, different areas required different postures from the LDUs. If the situation were violent, the LDUs would act usually as a rear force, but sometimes in front line combat. If it were relatively peaceful, the LDUs would support development programmes, keeping law and order, and still gather intelligence for the security organizations. When NRA was involved in national combat or other operations, the LDUs would be helpful in capturing deserters, recruit for NRA, and check illegal recruitment of rebel groups from villages as well as deny establishment of rebel groups in areas of their control. In this context, they were labeled according to the territory as well as the fragility or stability of the region.

In times of peace, they would simply be called LDUs but, in times of violence, they would be labeled according to the territory in which they were established, the time and task they were confronted with. For instance, the vigilantes in the Eastern Uganda and Kitgum, Home Guards in Gulu, Amuka (rhino) in Lango, Mountain Defense Brigade in Rwenzori mountains, the Reserve Force (soldiers in transition to retire), Anti-Stock Theft Unit in Karamoja, Arrow Boys in Soroti, Kalangala Action Plan for 2001 Presidential and Parliamentary elections. In the East, they were called the vigilantes, and these were people who killed Odhiambo and Ojongole, the leaders of Force Obote Back (FOBA), a group that was killing Local council leaders in the late 1980s and was bent on bring back Obote to power by force. In Western Uganda, they were simply called LDUs because there was no war and then the Reserve force, which is a transitory stage for the retiring soldiers.[6] In the contemporary Uganda, the number of militias and the categories of the militias as much as the security agencies in Uganda are more than can be easily memorized and their functions and impact hardly estimated. We examine a few, if only to offer their effect in terms of political processes in Uganda since 1986.

Kalangala Action Plan (KAP)

Probably the most significant and most notorious militia in recent Uganda is the Kalangala Action Plan. It was in October 2000 when President Museveni launched the militia and it became clear to the public that there was a group of people being trained for purposes of forceful influencing of the 2001 presidential and parliamentary elections.[7] This was another informal group of LDUs without legislative mandate that was created and organized in the Kalangala District, an

Island in Lake Victoria, with the view to supporting President Museveni's candidature and Movement parliamentary candidates by *deliberate use of violence and intimidation.* It was to be headed by Senior Presidential Political Advisor, Maj. Ronald Kakoza Mutale.[8]

Its members were mainly recruited from retired and unemployed soldiers, and other non-professional half-trained categories of people. The core group was Major Kakooza Mutale's former rebels. Although it was claimed that the group was taken to Kalangala for 'mchaka mchaka' courses and for the design of a campaign strategy for President Museveni, they were in fact being instructed on how to use violence to undermine and demobilize the opposition, as well as boost and mobilize supporters of President Museveni.

As the election campaigns progressed, and as Museveni realized that he was facing a stiff challenge from his former physician and serious high ranking soldier, Retired Colonel Dr. Kiiza Besigye, members of the Kalangala Action Plan were mobilized to roam the country in yellow buses clad in yellow, which were symbols of Museveni and his Movement system. If it was understood that a specific area was opposed to Museveni's candidature, they would travel to that region and literally beat people with sticks and gun butts. Not only would KAP members beat the opposition members, they would also kidnap and torture the opposition leaders. Members of the KAP committed arbitrary arrests, detained people without legal authority, and committed violent attacks, according to reports in both government and independent newspapers based in Kampala, and eyewitness testimony to Human Rights Watch (Human Rights Watch Report, 2003).

However, they would organize to welcome and entertain Museveni at the political rallies by playing a band and drumming in the streets, and, therefore, help to demobilize opposition and mobilize Museveni supporters.

Even though it may be claimed that the UPDF is funding KAP as a Special Operations Unit, it is probable that it is President Museveni who permits and sponsors their activities, and arms them. Former Minister of State for Security, Muruli Mukasa, pointed out, Mutale, as a Presidential Advisor, draws his salary from the President's Office, while those working under him, most of whom are soldiers, are paid by UPDF. Earlier in 2001 KAP is public relations officer of KAP claimed that President Museveni was chairman of KAP; an accusation that is often made but is neither denied by Museveni his spokesman. Clearly, it was Musveni who launched KAP's operations and that in return KAP supported his Presidential election bid, and continues to do so for candidates who follow his political inclination. Two cases among many, reveal, the repressive intentions and character of President Musveni's regime. In one, Museveni tried to undermine the election of Ms Winnie Byanyima as a member of parliament for Mbarara Municipality, and in another, he tried to violently rig the election of Francis Runumi as the LC V chairman for Kabale Municipality.

In addition, in February 2000, two by-elections were held in the Bushenyi district and Kabale municipality, but it is the one in Bushenyi that was most illuminating. As the campaigns progressed it appeared that the opposition candidate was becoming stronger. Accordingly, by his own revelation later, President Museveni sent armed people suspected of being KAP to intervene for 'security reasons'. To quote Museveni, at his candidate Mary Kaooro's victory celebrations, held at the Nile Hotel, Kampala in February, 2004: *When I heard that there were people dishing out money, I sent there my boys and I think they did a good job*. Meanwhile, one campaigner for the opposition candidate, Emanuel Ndyakira, was shot, causing panic and fear among the voters. Ndyakira died but, surprisingly, the boys who did what the president called a good job, have up to now failed to give a report regarding his death.[9]

In any case, KAP exists, and is generally perceived as, a repressive force against the opposition and perhaps the most dreaded tool of the government, to the extent that the media presents it as a national scare. For example, the Monitor News, paper (2004), reported: 'Mutale sighted in Mbale' (May 25th). At this point, one needs to understand why a newspaper should announce that Kakooza Mutale has been sighted! It is reported that Mutale recently advised President Museveni to barricade Kampala City with tanks in case some people wanted to overthrow the government, after a court ruling that declared the Movement illegal.[10] In general, KAP remains a private but illegitimate force for President Museveni to deploy when there are real or imagined threats to his power, under the guise of providing security. Its management remains inaccessible to the public much as its accountability, because it was never intended to be transparent, even when the money for its existence is derived from Ugandan citizens.

Anti-Stock Theft Unit (ASTU)

This group was made up of home guards or local vigilantes and was created, firstly, to protect the lives of the Karamajong and their property, especially cattle, from raiders from neighbouring regions.[11] It replaced the Vigilante Program which was started in June 1993 (Muhereza, 1999, p.1). As the raiding of cattle and killing of people grew worse in the early 1990s, in spite of sustained military operations, it became clear that the army alone could not halt the raiding menace. Not only had the region accumulated unknown quantities of guns, but the skills with which to use them had also increased. Not only had guns become easily accessible, but they had also become a way of life, making the region highly unstable.

Therefore, the government introduced a strategy, which would involve the concerned communities by recruiting some of the Karimajong warriors into a force that would, under the control of government, help in the fighting of raiders in their region as well as offering support to government programmes. Specifically, they would protect cattle, organize local defence in the kraals, monitor and maintain security of cows, the population and property, and stop gun-trafficking which was originating in the troubled horn of Africa in countries such as, Sudan and Somalia. They were also supposed to back-up political and military programmes in Karamoja, including the securing disarmament of illegal guns, supporting local council decisions, keeping law and order, gathering intelligence and backing-up military operations (Muhereza, 1999, p.2).

To some extent, this force had significant achievements including facilitating reconciliatory meetings, returning of raided property and animals, and coordinating security activities in the region. Indeed, quite a number of guns were recovered and a semblance of peace seemed to exist. However, although much more could have been attained practical problems on the ground; meant agreements were hardly sustainable because they were premised on good will and enforcement could not be achieved because internal rivalry was not as yet resolved. Additionally, the traditional leaders had lost their authority and could not enforce the so-called 'good will agreements'. Perhaps the adage that 'Trust is good but Control is better' is a phrase that the government should have heeded, for, after setting up the Anti-stock Theft Unit, they scaled down the presence of the Army personnel, and soon after the raids began. Also, the reward, which was used to pay for the return of a gun, was no longer forthcoming, either because it was embezzled or because it was no longer available to government. Instead, government decided to fight Kony's LRA (IRINNEWS.ORG, UN Office for the Coordination of Humanitarian Affairs, September 9th, 2003).

However, the management of this force left a lot to be desired and it seems to have been a deliberate attempt to keep these forces less organized and, therefore, less effective as a democratic force. In fact, it was not generally respected by the central authority, as shown by the conditions under which members were recruited and maintained. For example, recruits do not have clear terms of service; they are not part of a regular force, yet when they are involved in disciplinary problems, they are judged under martial law, which is often very harsh. Worse still, even the little money or any benefit due to them either delayed, reduced further or never delivered. As a consequence, the discipline in this force has deteriorated to the extent that a good number of these militiamen are criminals who are known to abet gun- trafficking, rape, cattle rusting and other common crimes. In fact, as I write now, it has been reported that gun trafficking is probably at its highest peak ever. But like other militias, they were not properly controlled, and lacked legality. In some cases this force is still operational as the home guards, in other cases they have been absorbed into the regular UPDF.

Worse still these forces are mixed and integrated within the political Movement system and militarization of politics, or, should we say, militarization of democracy?[12] It is extremely difficult to explicate these problems unless one deals with the organization of the movement and its attendant politics. For example, if opposition was allowed, it would highlight these problems, demand accountability and offer solutions. For instance, it was reported that Lt. Colonel 'Fearless' Obwoya, a commander was able to build a hotel in Kitgum out of the money meant for militia, and yet, nothing could be done tomake him accountable. Who could hold anybody to account, especially if he is a high-ranking soldier acting on behalf of a corrupt, exclusive regime like the Movement?

Nyekundiire

In the 2001 Presidential and parliamentary elections the role of the militia was quite remarkable. Of particular importance was the Nyekundire[13] group, which brought together different categories of people including serving soldiers, local political leaders, and other secret security organizations, to support Museveni's candidature for Presidency. According to one source, the English variant of 'Nyekundire' is the Popular Intelligence Network, whose leaders include the President's brother, Salim Saleh, his wife, Jovia Akandwanaho, and Captain Bashaija, the Director of the Ngabo Secondary School in Mbarara.[14] But according to another source, Nyekundiire emerged very late in the 2001 elections after realizing that all was not well for Museveni's presidential campaign. It was, according to this source, a brain-child of the 'kitchen power' wielders, including the President wife, Janet Museveni, Mrs. Muhwezi, and Mrs. Kutesa, but mainly Mrs. Jovia Akandwanaho and her husband Salim Saleh. It is also claimed that former Army Commander, Lieutenant General Elly Tumwine, was behind the operations of this organization. It is claimed that they used state resources including vehicles, money, and state controlled houses like State House, Nile Hotel and the Conference Centre in Kampala, and other regional structures, like the office of the RDC and the Movement leadership for their activities.

They complemented the work of other similar security organizations (like Internal Security Organisation (ISO), Chieftaincy of Military Intelligence (CMI), External Security Organisation (ESO) and militias like Kalangala Action Plan), to form a strong, but violent campaign machine which unleashed unprecedented electoral violence on the population in Western Uganda but also working in other regions. It is a security network, which has spread across Uganda which, according to one source, was largely responsible for the support Museveni garnered during the 2001 Presidential elections, particularly in Western Uganda. It is further alleged that this network superintends torture chambers in Kampala where victims are terrorised by snakes, crocodiles and other methods. Nyekundiire is financially supported and armed by Saracen (a private security company owned by Salim Saleh) and whenever there is a violent threat, another source is revealed.

This network is national and is already being resuscitated most especially, the nation anticipates, for the 2006 presidential and parliamentary elections (http://www.iss.co.za/pubs/Monographs/No99/Chap5.htm). The same Captain Bashaija who was involved in the Nyekundire in 2001 has announced the founding of another organisation whose name is the Action Implementation and Reconciliation Programme (Orumuri, (2004) 'Nyekundiire Kugaruka', June 7-9th June).

According to Bashaija, it will be directed by army generals, government ministers, and other freedom fighters. Ostensibly it will undertake to reconcile the people with Museveni and the Movement, creating the space for the former to speak to the latter. It will also address the mistakes of the Movement.

Interestingly, while the announcement was made in Mbarara Municipality, it was revealed that this military–cum civilian formation would set up its headquarters at Kyengera in Kampala. Its offices would cost 400 million Uganda shillings and its target would be the whole of Uganda (Orumuri, 2004) 'Nyekundiire Kugaruka', June 7-9th June). This is yet another indication that it has a national agenda. Moreover, another parallel effort is being organized in Kampala under Nava Nabagesera. She is reportedly convincing motor cycle cyclists, 'bodaboda' and other categories of people who are unemployed, to organize themselves so that the state house can give them *entandikwa* (initial capital). At the same time, there is effort to politicize the bodaboda cyclists not only in Kampala city but also in Mbarara to support the 'Third Term'.[15] For instance, I personally heard the MP for Kampala Central, Capt. Francis Babu telling the Bodboda cyclists not to receive a leading opposition member and a good mobiliser of the Democratic Party, Hajji Nasser Sebagala, on his returning from the UK. It is widely alleged that within the 'bodaboda' groups, there are government spies, retired soldiers, and others, all of whom are beneficiaries of the Musevenist Movement. At the centre of their mobilization are the government functionaries.

Related to this announcement however, was another Musevenist Movement group, which has also been formed and is called Nkore Cadres Association, led by Captain Steven Rwakanuma and Tabaaro of Kashari, for the mobilization of cadres for development. According to varied sources, these groups have one goal: to support the 'Third Term', or 'Sad Term' as other critics have pointed out. It is also expected that more violence will characterize the 2006 elections because of these formations. Tthese announcements were made at the time the Movement/Musevenist National Political Commissar met district Movement leaders in the Western region (Orumuri, (2004) 'Nyekundiire Kugaruka', June 7-9th June).

Therefore, Nyekundire must be seen in the wider context of Movement politics and in particular in relation to Museveni's wish to retain power and disregard democratic processes. This also explains the violent elections in recent the past, and the ever-widening corruptive practices associated with Museveni government. For example, how does a group use its money without authorization and hope to secure money from the government? How does anybody organize an armed group without a legal backing and still secure funding from the brother of the President? Under what conditions do army generals get involved in partisan politics?

Arrow Boys and Amuka (Rhino) Militia

As the Lord's Resistance Army became more aggressive and expanded its area of operation to Eastern and North Western Uganda in mid 2003, the army proved less equipped to fight the enemy.[16] Many battles were fought between the UPDF and LRA but the situation got worse, forcing nearly 400,000 in the Teso region and 300,000 in Lango to become displaced. In all, more than one million people in northern Uganda were displaced by September 2003. (IRIN News Org., 19th July 2004). Simultaneously, some incidents of rebellion were also reported in Tororo and Busia in September 2003 and it has recently become clear that the intention was to cut off the Kenya-Uganda border supply line. In response local leaders and ministers, like Capt. Mike Mukula, Grace Akello, and Juventino Akaki, supported the Movement government and mobilized the population against the LRA's aggression. Among the local leaders, the Resident District Commissioner (RDC) of Kasese District, Mr. Musa Ecweru was the most vigorous, having been a rebel himself under UPDA. Basically, two strategies were designed, one military and the second, political, but executed simultaneously.

From the military standpoint, they undertook to raise the Arrow Boys and Amuka militias for the respective regions, but the political strategy was also designed ethnicize the war, mobilizing the spirit of the Iteso and the Langi against the Acholi and eliminating the opposition's resistance against recruiting the militias. In short, the Movement leadership sought to bring the population onto their side (www.iss.co.za/pubs/Monographs/No99/Chap5.pdf).   So, while the Movement leaders went on radio and used other media to call for recruits, other ethnic forces took the opportunity to point out that the LRA war was an Acholi affair which was intended   to   bring   disaster   to   the   people   of   Iteso   and   Lango. (www.iss.co.za/pubs/Monographs/No99/Chap5.pdf). It was, for instance, claimed by some leaders in Lango and Soroti that the Acholi living in those areas should be killed. Indeed, in spontaneous rage, a number of innocent Acholi innocent people were killed within a short time (http://www.thestar.com/static/archives/search.html). It would appear that this killing would have continued, had the Acholi Religious leaders, led by Archbishop of Gulu, John Baptist Odama, not gone to Lira to plead for the life of the innocent Acholi. In comparison, although the President camped in both war-affected areas of Lango and Soroti, he never condemned any thing against this ethnic killing of innocent Acholi. Instead, he thanked both the Iteso and Langi for rejecting the rebellion, and did not comment on keeping quite about whether the Acholi supported it or not.

From a military tangent, a number of willing people were recruited amidst opposition by both northern and north eastern parliamentarians who argued that such an act was unconstitutional and bound to lead to more bloodshed, robberies, and   further   insecurity   (http://www.thestar.com/static/archives/search.html). Consequently, a number of willing recruits come forward and remain in service today.

Be that as it may, by 26th June, 2003, 2000 veterans of the defunct rebel Ugandan People's Army (UPA), retrenched soldiers, the unemployed, retired policemen, and other able-bodied people were said to be ready to fight the LRA after 45 days training. By January 2004, the number of militias had peaked at 12,000. The Iteso, were commanded by Musa Ecweru, supported by MPs like John Eresu and Mike Mukula. They came under the command of the UPDF. Indeed, the President joined them and was stationed with them for a couple of months to oversee the fighting. By the beginning of July 2004, the activities of the LRA in Soroti had been extensively reduced, and for many reasons, the number of militias had been reduced to 9,000.Their numbers are probably less by now. The UPA reduced robberies within the community, recovered arms from the hands of criminals and LRA collaborators and informers, and somewhat re-assured the population giving them a sense of security. They enjoyed the support of the local population, who offered free food and money, as well as morale. They positively saw them as their saviors who fended off the LRA.

With similar military and political tools, the leaders in Lango tried to fight the LRA. Like the Itseo, the Langi raised a militia called Amuka totaling 8,000 men and women. The Langi approach, however, was slightly different in the sense that many political leaders were recruited alongside the militia (The New Vision (2003), Amuka Militia Trains, 24th December). The political leadership in Langi seemed enthused and encouraged by the Soroti experience and leadership especially Mike Mukula who visited the Amuka training camps. Arriving before the President, he assured the force that the government would provide uniforms, gumboots, food, medicine, and a token salary of 60,000 Uganda shillings (slightly less than 40 dollars). He also ordered that a health unit should be erected in the camp to treat the trainees (The New Vision (2003), Amuka Militia Trains, 24th December). However, the Amuka have not been as successful as the Arrow Boys because the former were less equipped, loosely committed, poorly trained and poorly remunerated. (http://www.thestar.com/static/archives/search.html).

In all fairness, the Arrow Boys and Amuka militias achieved the purpose for which they were established even though the latter did not do so well. Most of these militias were already militarily trained and had been rebels in the same area, which was not the case with the UPDF. This means that they could, as well, obtain more accurate intelligence information since they knew the local language. As Z. Lomo, et.al., point out, the name 'Arrow Boys' comes from the image of the straight movement of the arrow as if 'it knows' where it is flying (http://www.iss.co.za/pubs/Monographs/No99/Chap5.pdf). Also, they already had military skills and could easily be mobilized. As such, they were given jobs and promised payment by the government. It seems too, that the militia was imbued with courage and charisma, knowing that they were better fighters as compared to the UPDF who were used to a soft life (http://www.iss.co.za/pubs/Monographs/No99/Chap5.pdf).

In 2003 (the Arrow Boys and Amuka), were paid from the Defense vote but it is now being proposed that they should be paid from the Ministry of Internal Affairs budget. If they were to be construed as serving security purposes, they should be catered for under Statutory Instruments 2000, no. 80, The Security Organisations (Terms and Conditions of Service) Regulations, 2000. Yet, these oragnisations mentioned above, are not legally part of the organizations referred to in the Statutory Instruments. This leaves victims of their violations with great difficulty in seeking redress. Another concern is the question of chain of command and reporting and accountability of Local Defence Units (sometimes referred to as home guards). LDUs are officially under the Ministry of Internal Affairs, yet receive their orders from the UPDF and may be deployed by the UPDF far from home, but the army does not accept responsibility for the activities of LDU members (see below). Instead, their existence seems to depend on President Museveni's private decisions and payment, hence they can be seen as private organizations.

Further, it has been alleged that many recruits die either due to poor hygiene, or poor food and other harsh conditions. It is also reported that some of the recruits are children, and rather than being convinced to go to school and study, they are encouraged to join the militia. As a consequence, the members of this group have turned into criminals, misusing arms to settle trivial grudges among themselves, shooting at others and extorting contribution, the robbing civilians and committing rape. Others, like the Amuka and Arrow Boys, are supported by the local population, which provides encouragement and food. The local population saw these militias as their saviours. They seemed to be the ones who fought off and defeated the LRA.

Thus, whereas the Amuca and Arrow Boys could have helped the UPDF to check the marauding LRA fighters, and although they were supposed to be protecting Internally Displaced Persons in the camps, other long-term grave problems are foreseen. For instance, most of the people who have left school for Amuka have probably left it for good, and because of poor health conditions and poverty, diseases and among them, HIV/AIDS are easily spread. The cause of most of these is derived from the national repressive framework of President Museveni; it is feared that this is yet another army to be deployed against the opposition in order to stop them from freely choosing their leaders.[17]

The ethnicization of the LRA war and the corresponding recruitment of Amuka and Arrow Boys was an unprincipled strategy. Not only did this cause loss of life of innocent lives, but it was also wrong in itself, and has had long term conflict implications. It may call for revenge and suspicion for instance. Besides, that the method of recruitment and maintenance of the militia was poor; not only did they recruit criminals but they also absorbed children. For this reason, the force has already caused its own insecurity in the region. It is absurd that they have been prooly fed, if fed at all, and poorly paid, if paid at all.

Since the Arrow Boys defeated the LRA, they have been encouraged to rise to the occasion when faced with their old-age problem of Karimajong cattle rustling, now been 'coined' 'Konymojong' among the Iteso. It is argued that since they were able to defend themselves against Kony, and especially after the UPDF failed to do so, they should also be left with guns and supported to fight off the Karimajong raiders. If this view was accepted or if government failed to retrieve all the guns, then another war front and a culture of acquisition of arms would be encouraged and hence creating further regional insecurity and instability.

Yet another danger derives from the fact that all these forces have been recruited from opposition areas and, if properly mobilized against the Movement government, it would be very difficult to sort out the security issues. According to one source, there are rumours in Soroti that there are tensions between the UPDF and Arrow Boys, resulting from the debate over who actually defeated the LRA and over poor pay and management. The recent celebrations to mark the founding of the militia were also confronted with challenges and indeed, as I write, they have been postponed. Whereas the Commander of the Arrow Boys wanted to celebrate such a function in the town of Soroti and have the celebration presided over by the President, others, especially MPs, rejected the idea insisted that such celebrations, should take place in Obalang, where much of the fighting had taken place.

Labeca Group

Like the KAP, the Labeca group (also spelt Labeja) is a paramilitary group active in the Gulu municipality of northern Uganda and named after a retired UPDF field commander, Labeca. This group is supplementary to the home guards in the countryside, although most people are now living in the Internally Displaced camps. The question of northern Uganda and the militia is old and evolving. In the early years of the LRA rebellion LDUs were always used as previously explained but as it became clear to the local population that the government would not easily win the war they asked for guns to protect themselves. The government refused because it suspected their intentions as much as the northern politicians distrusted the government.[18]

Reserve Force

This is a reservoir force created from the professional soldiers who were either retired or expelled from the force, the so-called the veterans, partly due to Structural Adjustment Programmes, which had insisted that the government should reduce the number of soldiers. Indeed, with the help of the IMF and the World Bank, the soldiers were retired and organized into a national force under the command of the President's brother popularly known as 'Salim Saleh', but whose actual name is Caleb Akandwanaho. A former Army Commander and generally popular because he is the President is brother and is therefore capable of accessing resources for easy which he would then distribute to the soldiers, Saleh has remained a 'strong man' of the army. In fact, he is considered the de facto Army Commander whose decision is seldom contradicted by the President.

Ironically, he is also known as one of the most notorious high level criminals of the regime, enjoying his brother's (President Museveni) protection.[19] He has been associated with large financial frauds and military adventures, yet, he has commanded the reserve force for an unknown period but at least, not less than 10 years. Most, if not all soldiers who retire, are always controlled under the reserve force for three years, and after which, they are allowed to retire fully. This category of soldiers is attached to the Ministry of Defense and control by government is essential for the stability of the country. Soldiers in the transition to retirement could easily be lured into rebel groups whose presence has never waned since President Museveni came to power in 1986. Although it is reasonable to have organized those soldiers they should have been given benefits, which could enable them to live a fully settled civilian life. It is not exactly known where they located; some may be in security companies, others may be in petty trade supported by government, others may be re-deployed in intelligence work or any other temporary military programme that the government may lave designed.[20] For instance, it is alleged that they are currently involved in political mobilization for Museveni's support for the amendment of the constitution. This is can be sesn in the State House support of a bizarre campaign by the commercial motor cycle (bodaboda) cyclists (mostly veterans) against payment of taxes to the city authorities.

Emerging Issues

It has already been pointed out that nearly all these above militias have lacked legal law or contract backing for formation, their activities, and general management that, for this reason, they could be seen as illegitimate or even criminal formations. The absence of this basic requirement affected commitment in terms of their payment, general welfare, compensation, and retirement benefits (The New Vision (2003), Press Statement, 27th August). Moreover, there was no specific authority from which by were supposed to be paid. According to one source, whenever they sent their claims to the Ministry of Finance, they would be rejected because it was not clear where the money should come from to pay them. For example, the UPDF, which is responsible for their payment has often failed to pay them in time if ever. Even senior civilian and military authorities seem to have different information about who is responsible for which organization.

Suspected supporters of the political opposition, as well as civilians at large, have been subjected to arrests and detention by the UPDF, LDUs (home guards), the Presidential Protection Unit (PPU), the Chieftaincy of Military Intelligence (CMI), and the Internal Security Organization (ISO). The former Director General of the ISO, Brig. Henry Tumukunde, at the time of internal controversy over role of these private security organizations, made it clear, in a statement issued in September 2002, that the authority of the security and paramilitary agencies was restricted and that only the police had the authority to arrest people. No other security organ, he said, including ISO, was allowed to arrest suspects (http://www.hrw.org/wr2k3/africa13.html). Yet, nearly, those same organizations do so.

Another important issue is the absence of a specific law under which the militias are recruited, maintained and discharged and/or compensated. What is to be done with such an army when the overt purpose for which it was created is over? What happens to those who are maimed or lose their lives in the war? When they are aggrieved by the organization, where do individuals get redress?

Nonetheless, the greatest fear derives from the experience of the violent roles armed groups have played in electoral processes in the past, as mentioned earlier. It is, for example, feared that they may be used to intimidate the opposition and rig the elections in 2006. This view has given credence, due to the fact that the commanders of the Arrow Boys militia are most the aggressive Movement leaders in that region. The fear derives It is not only from the fact that other African countries like Rwanda, Mubutu's Zaire (DRC), Zimbabwe, and Kenya have used militia as to subvert a fair and free election, but that Museveni used them already in 2001. This is likely to be reported because the popularity of President Museveni has waned and yet he seems to be desperate to retain power even beyond his second, but last constitutional tenure.[21]

Lastly, it is important to remember that the LRA was formed as a result of remnant, armed, but uncontrolled forces of the UNLA, and if seen vis-à-vis disarmament and post-conflict reconstruction phases, worrying scenarios can be anticipated. That is to say, if the conflict is resolved, how will former militia personnel behave especially with increasing poverty, unemployment, conflict prone experience societies, and unsettled political questions? If disarmament has failed in Karamoja with little military experience, and with the UNLA, how easy will it prove in relation to a wide range of various and sometimes antagonistic militias?

Conclusion

All in all, it is clear that inside the dynamic of recruitment, deployment, retention and management of the militias lies the political contest between the Musevenist Movement and other possible contenders for power. Such contenders could be multi-party advocates, former followers, potential challengers, or presidential subordinates who imagine they could wield power. Hence, the questions of 'how' and 'who' are the central. To what extent will the militias become a tool for maintaining or capturing power? This obviously raises the issue of the legitimacy of President Museveni's Movement. Consequently, a smooth democratic transition under President Museveni is unlikely, given such conditions. Unfortunately, the Movement has become corrupt, dictatorial, unpredictable and overly militaristic, and therefore, the role of the militias in Uganda leaves little hope for sustainable peace; once again creating pessimism for Africa. This is especially so as President Museveni mobilizes for removal of a constitutional presidential term limit.

Notes

1   The usage of the term 'militia' in Uganda is suppressed; instead the word 'auxiliary forces' is preferred because it confers a form of legitimacy. They are forces supporting regular forces.

2   For example, President Milton Obote established and abused General Service Unit (GSU), Amin established and abused State Research Bureau (SRB), when Obote ruled again, he established and badly abused the National Security Agency (NASA).

3   They are as numerous as they are unknown. They include Arrow Boys, for Soroti, 7000, Amuka, for Lango, 8000, Anti Stock Theft Unit for Karamoja, 6000, Gulu Local Defense Forces, 4th Division, 7000, Labeja Group for Gulu Municipality (unknown), 7000 LDUs for Gulu 5th Division, for Pader 6800, making a total of 33600 persons in northern Uganda. But there are many others like Nyenkundiire. Kalangala Action plan, Popular Intelligence Network, Violent Crack Unit, Special Investigation Bureau, Reserve Force, Special Presidential Operatives, the Presidential Army Brigade, and many others possibly unknown, both in number and identity. This adds to the official organisations like Internal Security Organisation (ISO), External Security Organisation (ESO), and Chief of Military Intelligence (CMI) of course, these forces work with a state controlled police and the regular army Uganda Peoples Forces (UPDF).

4   The militias cannot be referred to as 'government' because they lack a specific law supporting them and some of them are officially denied by government officials even though they are aware of their existence and are benefiting from their actions. In legal terms, they are supported by article 3 of the National Resistance Army Statute, 1992. Probably, more specifically article 3 c, which states that, 'such other officers and militants attached to the Regular Force under arrangements made by government.' By all legal accounts, this is a very vague law that is bound to be abused as it has indeed,

been so. It would be better to define the arrangements. What, if, as is in the Ugandan case, the 'Regular Force' is heavily involved in politics and such a militant group is deployed against the opposition?

5   (http://www.wordiq.com/definition/Militia).

6   It is however, seen by the public as a standing army that could be deployed any time President Museveni's Movement felt threatened either politically or militarily. It is indeed, 'a reserve army'.

7   One source has told me that during the Presidential Campaign, members of the official security organizations (Internal Security organization, External Security Organization and Chief of Military Intelligence) advised President Museveni to withdraw Kakooza Mutale from the campaign process but Museveni refused to do. The security agencies argued that even without beating people, President Museveni would still have won the elections.

8   It is alleged that when Y. Museveni went to the Bush in 1981, Major Roland Kakooza Mutale was already there with his own rebellious group known as 'Vumbura', but largely less professionally than the NRA. In time, Museveni's NRA arrested Kakoza Mutale due to indiscipline and kept him captive before his group was absorbed by NRA. Major Kakooza Mutale is currently serving President Museveni as his Presidential Advisor as well as the de facto commander of the dreaded Kalangala Action Plan.

9   Having had a tension gripped election, and having had one of their members killed, the voters would have been relieved if his 'boys' said something about the killing of this person, since they were sent on national duty using the tax payer's money. What exactly, did these boys do?

10   On Thursday 24th, the Constitutional Court ruled that the Movement system was illegal because the referendum Act under which the citizens are alleged to have chosen the Movement system was nullified, implying that there was no such choice. See, the *New Vision*, Friday June 25th, 2004, the *Monitor Newspaper*, June 25th, 2004. Kakoza Mutale reasoned that the Constitutional Court judgment signified a military coup. See also *The Red Paper*, July, 2-5th, 2004.

11   'Themselves' because Karimajong are made of small sub-groups and these groups often fight against, and raid cattle from each other.

12   President Museveni's Movement is described as democratic but behind the scenes, the role of the military is inordinately preponderant as evidenced by the role of the militias and statements and activities of the army generals during elections.

13   Nyenkundire is a Kinyankore word for 'Voluntary', but in effect it meant those supporting Museveni's candidature and his programmes willfully, even though it means that in spite of the fear of Museveni, we still support him.

14   The owners of this school are associated with the military and power wilders of the state of Uganda especially the military establishment.

15   There have been running battles between central government and urban authorities of Kampala over whether the 'bodaboda' cyclists should be taxed; whereas the urban authorities insisted on taxing them (now have given up. See Monitor, July 10th, 2004), because it is within their mandate, the central government (supported by Museveni) has barred the urban authorities from taxing them. There are tendencies to buy them off by giving them money or fuel to get them involved in Movement programmes including protesting the court ruling that de-legitimized the Movement system. Earlier on they were given fuel and other support to receive the President at the airport and ironically in all these cases, they were wearing dry banana leaves, the current symbol for the 'Third Term'.

16   Until May 2003, the war was mainly concentrated in Gulu, Kitgum and Pader districts and a few districts in the West Nile. Soon after however, the LRA spread the activities to Soroti, Kaberamaido and Katakwi in Eastern Uganda, and Adjumani, Lira and Apach in North Western Uganda.

[17]   As already mentioned, such a militia becomes useful in terms of rigging elections, intimidating the population, and orchestrating violence. They are part and parcel of a failed democratic state in Africa.

[18]   This is a very important indication terms of understanding the LRA rebellion which is about political power. Suspicions between government and the northern Uganda politicians have always informed efforts. Whereas the government wants to win this war by militarily defeating the LRA, the political leaders from the northern region have always pushed for a negotiated settlement. Consequently, the northern war should never be understood.

[19]   Not only was he involved in the fraudulent sale of a public bank (UCB) but he was found identified by the United Nations body of experts as one of those who looted the Democratic Republic of Congo's natural resources.

[20]   For instance, when the violent robberies in Uganda became intensified, a reckless paramilitary force code-named 'Operation Wembley' was established by the government. Its members were both military and civilian, but it included half-trained people. Although it significantly reduced the incidence of robberies quite a number of the human rights of innocent people were violated. It really acted as a terrorist organization, because it mainly lacked a law and procedure.

[21]   If there were debates in the political history of Uganda since 1986, for example whether the Movement was a system or not, or whether Uganda should federate or not, or whether Kony should be fought or fought, or any other debate, there has never been such a time when the country has been gripped with fear, anxiety and confusion over the change of the constitution to remove Presidential Term Limits. It is understood that this is meant to offer President Museveni a 'life presidency' package on silver platter.

References

Government of Uganda (1992), *The National Resistance Army Statute*, Kampala.
http://www.wordiq.com/definition/Militia
http://www.hrw.org/reports/2003/uganda0703/p/024_173430.
http://www.iss.co.za/pubs/Monographs/No99/Chap5.htm
http://www.iss.co.za/pubs/Monographs/No99/Chap5.pdf
http://www.hrw.org/wr2k3/africa13.html
http://www.thestar.com/static/archives/search.html
Human Rights Watch Report, 2003.
IRINNEWS.ORG, UN Office for the Coordination of Humanitarian Affairs, September 9th, 2003.
IRIN News Org., 19th July, 2004.
Muhereza, F. (1999), 'Violence, and the State in Karamoja, Causes of Conflict and Initiative for Peace', in *Cultural Survival*, Issue No.22.4, Jan. 31st.
Orumuri (2004), Local biweekly Newspaper in Western Uganda, 'Nyekundiire Kugaruka', June 7-9th June.
Rwanyarare (2003), Uganda People's Congress National Secretariat, Press Statement, Kampala.
The Monitor (2004), 'Mutale Goes to Mbale', May, 25th May.
The Monitor (2004), 'Ex-Rebels Cry Over Jailed colleagues', 25th June.
The Monitor (2004), 'Army Commander Summons Kayanja', 10th July.
The New Vision, Daily Newspaper (2003), Amuka Miltia Trains, 24th December.
The New Vision (2004) 'Amuka Gets', 25th June, 2004,
The Red Paper (2004), 'Mutale tells Museveni to Deploy Army on Kampala Streets after Court Ruling', 2-5th July.
Toronto Star, February 29th 2004.

Chapter 11

Mayi Mayi and Interahamwe Militias: Threats to Peace and Security in the Great Lakes Region

Macharia Munene

Introduction

The name Congo conjures up adventurous myths regarding contacts between Europeans and Africans. Those contacts were beneficial to Europeans and dangerous to Africans and are the root cause of the chaotic condition that Congo continues to find itself in. Broadly, the term Congo has the geo-political connotation of referring to a number of territories through which the waters of the Congo River flow and end up in the Atlantic Ocean. Amongst these are the Republic of Congo, whose headquarters are in Brazzaville, the Democratic Republic of the Congo whose official headquarters are in Kinshasa, Northern Angola, Gabon, Central Africa Republic, Rwanda, Burundi, Western Tanzania, Northern Zambia, Sudan, and Uganda. These political entities were the outcomes of European interaction with Africans, and more importantly, European rivalry over African resources. In more recent times, this area has come to be termed The Great Lakes Region.

The region is also one that symbolises the worst in terms of the different phases of the colonial experience in Africa. The scramble for the partition of Africa officially began in this region and ushered in classical colonialism in the 1880s. Classical colonialism, in which countries from Europe officially ruled territories in Africa, gave way to neo-colonialism in which control and exploitation were through leaders on behalf of the master states. Again it was in this region that the worst manifestation of neo-colonialism first became evident in 1960 through proxies such as Joseph Mobutu who became the best exemplification of neo-colonialism in Africa; he did what the master state wanted and the master state kept him in office until he outlived his usefulness in the 1980s. As the Cold War came to an end, neo-colonialism gave way to postmodern colonialism in which control is through a myriad of institutions that are hardly accountable to any state but which answer to the sponsoring or master state. Once again, the region is a good example of postmodern colonialism.

The continuing warfare in the Great Lakes region, therefore, can be explained in terms of rivalry over who should own and control extensive resources and for what purpose (de Waal, 2000, p.15). The nature of that control has varied with time and the prevailing ideological conditions. It has often meant the use of militias as proxies, the most prominent in recent times being the interahamwe in Rwanda and the Mayi Mayi in Kivu, Eastern Congo. They were not the first militias, the tradition goes back to the beginning of classical colonialism. Whatever the nature of external control, the people of the region were caught in the fighting mostly as victims, occasionally as soldiers for particular regimes, and as militia.

Colonialism and the Menace of Civil Militias in the Congo

Classical colonialism in the region can be traced to the activities of four white men representing the interests of four Western countries, namely Portugal, the United States, Belgium, and France. The first of these was a Portuguese voyager named Diego Cao who, in 1482, planted a Portuguese limestone pillar at the mouth of the Congo River to symbolise Portuguese claims. More than planting a pillar, he abducted a few people to take to Portugal and thereby started a process of enslaving people (Hochschild, 1999, pp.7-8; Forbath, 1977, pp.71-77; Croegaet, 1999, pp.144-145). Although Portuguese slave trading had started in West Africa in 1441 (Forbath, 1977, pp.50-54; Duffy, 1961, p.8), it was the creation of large plantations at the Sao Tome island and across the Atlantic in the Americas that institutionalised slavery and the slave trade as a way of supplying needed labour to those plantations. Other Europeans, particularly the Spanish, the British and the French, who also established plantations in the Americas, also cashed in on the slave trade. In this way, African slave labour was used to build what later became the United States of America (Ewans, 2002, pp.23-25; Hochschild, 1999, pp.21-32; Forbath, 1977, pp.112-114, 133-134; Croegart, 1999, p.163). It was fitting that the second white man to drastically affect the region would be an American.

The American was British born Henry Morton Stanley, a man whose identity appeared to fluctuate between being American and being British and one who had fought on both sides of the American civil war. He attracted the attention of *New York Herald* Publisher James Gordon Bennett who commissioned him to look for a lost Scottish missionary in Africa named David Livingstone. Starting from Zanzibar in the Indian Ocean, Stanley found Livingstone at Ujiji on the shores of Lake Tanganyika in 1871. He then proceeded westwards along the Congo River and came out on the Atlantic Ocean side at the mouth of the great river in 1877. A man who liked publicity, stories of his exploits attracted the attention of the King of Belgium (Forbath, 1977, pp.226-245; Munene, 1995, pp.9-10; Ewans, 2002, pp.47-54).

The King of Belgium, Leopold II, was the third white man to affect the region. He had a big ambition to have an empire but since Belgium was a tiny, weak country that was created in 1830 with the help of the British, he had to look elsewhere and Stanley's activities gave him the opportunity. Stanley was to create a personal empire for Leopold in Africa and so the king sent the American back to the Congo to persuade various African chieftains to agree to be ruled by Leopold's representatives. Stanley agreed to serve Leopold's interests and headed back to the

Congo, only to find a French representative already in the region planting the French flag (Ewans, 2002, pp.14-20, 35-38, 52-54, 64-67; Hochschild, 1999, pp.70-72).

The French representative was the fourth white man to affect the future of the Congo, and his name was Pierre Savorgnan de Brazza. Like Stanley, although born in Rome, de Brazza's nationality was at times confusing as to whether he was Italian or French. He had been funded by the French Minister for Education, Jules Ferry, whose interest was in securing potential sources of raw materials for French industries as well as potential markets. In sending de Brazza, Ferry's objective was to thwart Leopold's dreams by having de Brazza beat Stanley to the Congo. Operating on the northern banks of the Congo River, de Brazza was busy collecting thumbprints from an assortment of African chiefs for France. Stanley's complaints that he had prior claims made no sense to the Frenchman and so Stanley crossed the river and set camp on the southern bank facing de Brazza'a camp. (Forbach, 1977:334, 347-348; Ewans, 2002, pp.64-67, 78-81; Hochschild, 1999:70-72). The northern camp later became Brazzaville while the southern camp became Leopoldville and the two camps, facing each other across the river, symbolised the first division of the Congo by the Europeans.

The confrontation between the Belgians and the French attracted the attention of other Europeans who did not want to be left out of a potentially lucrative market and source of raw materials at a time that industrialisation was in high gear. The Portuguese, in particular, complained that they had been in the Congo first and that the French and the Belgians were intruders (Ewans, 2002: 78-81; Hochschild, 1999:71). For a while, it appeared as if white people might start killing each other in tropical Africa and since it would not look good for white people to kill each other in front of Africans, a solution had to be found. This was a time when the doctrine of Social Darwinism that seemingly justified cutthroat competition also justified the supposed superiority of white people over all others with Africans being at the bottom of the human social hierarchy. It was German Chancellor Otto von Bismarck who then suggested a meeting in Berlin to be attended by representatives of all the white powers that were interested in Africa's potential. (Munene, 1995a, pp.8-10; Ewans, 2002, pp.88-94; Hochschild, 1999:84)

The meeting at Berlin in 1884-1885, known as the Berlin Conference on the Partition of Africa, set out to determine the rules of grabbing African lands in order to avoid fighting in front of Africans. Those in attendance ranged from the United States of America in the west to Turkey in the east. At the end of the conference, the Europeans shared the Congo amongst themselves with Portugal, France, and Leopold taking most of it. Portugal took the area south of the mouth of the Congo River as part of what became Angola and France took the area north of the Congo River as their colony. The French also retained the little enclave of Gabon as a separate colony. The British ended up claiming Northern Rhodesia in the south and Uganda in the west. Leopold, with access to the Atlantic Ocean, got the rest of the Congo stretching all the way to Uganda, wherever the Congo waters flowed. Leopold's territories came to be called Leopold's Congo and, with that, the notion that Congo was a private personal property to be contested by various claimants crept in. And, for his effort, Bismarck got Cameroon. He succeeded in averting war among the Europeans over African territories by helping to fragment the Congo and dishing its pieces to European powers.

Leopold reaped a lot of profit from his property in Africa but he also attracted unfavourable publicity that threatened to dispossess him and so he avoided dispossession by selling the Congo to his kingdom in 1908. The unfavourable publicity was because he had turned the Congo into a huge slave camp from which he extracted profits from rubber using cruel means. The atrocities committed by his agents, such as cutting off limbs, aroused the wrath of the anti-slavery movement led by D.H. Morel and the media. The likelihood that the powerful states of Britain or France might intervene in the Congo led Leopold to organise for his own kingdom to buy him out at a huge profit. The territory, therefore, changed name from being Leopold's Congo into being Belgian Congo; from being a personal property to being the property of the kingdom of Belgium and the profit reaping continued (Munene, 1995a, p.20; Ewans, 2002, pp.88-94; Hochschild, 1999: 257-259; Forbath, 1977, pp.359-383).

From 1908 to 1960, therefore, the Congo was the property, or rather the colony, of Belgium and in that context got involved in Belgium's international activities that tended to raise the Congo's profile. In World War I, Belgium was invaded by Germany, which became the official reason for Britain to get into the war. After the war, the British, the French, and the Belgians shared German colonies with Belgium acquiring the provinces of Rwanda-Urundi from German East Africa as League of Nations mandates. The territory under Belgian control and exploitation was thus expanded (Nzongola-Ntalaja, 2002:216). Rubber, even after the change of ownership from Leopold to Belgium, continued to be extracted and in very much the same manner with the difference being that the profits were not said to belong to one man. And rubber was not the only source of wealth to be exploited.

There were also minerals that made Belgium rich and among those minerals was uranium. Uranium became a strategic mineral during World War II because it was necessary for the making of a new weapon associated with the splitting of the atom. In the 1930s, scientists in Germany were working on how to split the atom, a fact that worried the scientists in Britain, Canada and the United States because of Adolph Hitler's warlike behaviour. At the outbreak of World War II, Germany occupied Belgium and ships carrying uranium in the high seas were diverted to other destinations such as New York instead of being allowed to fall into Hitler's hands. When the United States President Franklin Delano Roosevelt decided to support the atomic project in full during the war, the Congo uranium lying in the New York harbour became very useful. It was the uranium from the Congo that was used to make the atomic bombs that were dropped on the Japanese cities of Hiroshima and Nagasaki in August 1945 and thereby ended World War II (Nzongola-Ntalaja, 2002: 259).

The Cold War between the United States and the Soviet Union that had been simmering during World War II became open by 1947 and the Congo became an issue because of the strategic minerals. The future of former Italian colonies in Africa was the point of reference since the Soviet Union was interested in becoming a trustee of at least Tripolitania. In this, the Soviets initially had the support of the United States but the exigencies of the Cold War led the United States to change its position with regard to the Soviets in any part of Africa. The new position by the United States was that the real intent of the Soviet Union in seeking a United Nations Trusteeship in Africa was so that it could have access to the minerals in the Congo. To permit a Soviet UN Trusteeship, therefore, would be to open up strategic minerals in the Congo to the potential enemy and that could not be allowed (Munene, 1995a, pp.91-95). In this way, the control of the Congo became the centre of discussions on matters atomic because of the large deposits of uranium. And that control was to remain Belgian because Belgium was an ally of the United States and could be trusted more than the African anti-colonialists (Munene, 1995a, pp.80-85).

Anti-colonial agitation by Africans went back to the establishment of colonialism in Congo arising from the mistreatment that Africans suffered at the hands of Leopold's men. In that suffering, there were Africans who were the pawns and instruments of enslaving others and selling them. Most active in this were those conscripted into, or recruited in, the Force Public from within the Congo and from West Africa (Nzongola-Ntalaja, 2002, pp.44-47). The conscripts or recruits were often the most ruthless and sadistic and from the remotest of regions (Egerton, 2002: 188). Irrespective of where they were recruited from, Africans were divided into three categories that were subordinate to the Europeans. These were the actual soldiers who fought and subdued other Africans and could rise up to the rank of a sergeant, the military workers, and the porters who carried luggage for whites. They were all mistreated by white officers, many of whom were psychopaths and treacherous (Nzongola-Ntalaja, 2002, p.45).

In reaction to mistreatment and treachery, a series of resistances to the imposition of colonial rule, as well as revolts, took place as early as 1890 when Tippu Tipp refused an appointment as governor of Eastern Congo, a region he already controlled. In April 1891, Msiri of the Wanyamwezi refused to accept Leopold's flag as he asserted, 'I am master here ... and so long as I live the kingdom of Garenanze shall have no other' (quote in Nzongola-Ntalaja, 2002, p.44). There was a revolt within the Force Public in 1893, after the execution of Ngongo Lutete who had previously worked for Leopold, that lasted over a decade, led by Lutete's bodyguard, a sergeant Kandolo. In this revolt, the conflict between conscripts from the Congo and conscripts from West Africa was brought out as the 'Hausa' were used to suppress the Congolese (Nzongola-Ntalaja, 2002, pp.44-47).

After suppressing the rebellion, the Belgians then started thinking of their colony as a model colony but this was plagued by intermittent rural and urban uprisings that, especially after World War II, became part of the dominant Cold War calculations. The Pende uprising of 1931 left one thousand Congolese dead while the mine workers general strike of 1941 was crushed by African soldiers leaving 100 people dead. The soldiers then mutinied against their superiors in 1944 and attracted other African groups (Nzongola-Ntalaja, 2002, pp.52-53). These disturbances had been during World War II, at a time that the uranium from the Congo had taken strategic value because of the atomic bomb project that had given the United States a controlling interest in how that uranium would be accessed and used. The safety of uranium became critical after the World War, and with the onset of the Cold War, due to the activities of African anti-colonialists in the Congo (Munene, 1995a, pp.173-174).

The Congolese, therefore, were caught up in the post-World War II developments pertaining to the worldwide decolonisation movement. For Africa, the signal had been given in a 1945 meeting of potential African leaders at Manchester, better known as the Fifth Pan-African Congress although no Congolese attended that meeting. The participants sent fraternal greetings to anti-colonialists in Algeria, Malaya, and Indochina and called for intensified anti-colonial activities involving mass movements, labour strikes, and, if necessary, bloodshed (Munene, 1995a, pp.58-60). One of the participants at Manchester, Kwame Nkrumah, returned to the Gold Coast and led intensified political movements ending with self-government in 1951. Another participant, Jomo Kenyatta, was responsible for arousing political radicalism in Kenya that led to the Mau Mau War in 1952 and for which he was sent to jail. And in the Congo, there were reported disturbances in the mines that led the United States to recommend the stationing of white troops in strategic places (Munene, 1995a, pp.173-174). The general impact of anti-colonial activities was to destabilise colonial comfort in Africa and Congo was affected. It was a Kenyan political activist, Tom Mboya, who took Patrice Lumumba to the All Africa People's Conference in Accra in 1958 where Lumumba's anti-colonial credentials were enhanced by meeting the likes of Kwameh Nkrumah of Ghana and Abdel Gamal Nassir of Egypt (Nzongola-Ntalaja, 2002, p.84). Classical colonialism ended in June 1960 when Congo officially became independent from Belgium; it gave way to neo-colonialism.

Cold War Politics, Anti-Colonial Struggle and the Use of Militias

Neo-colonialism in Congo was a Cold War phenomenon as the build up for independence required the devising of new methods of control. Once it was clear that anti-colonial activities would force the Belgians out, the machinery for neo-colonial relationships to counter serious nationalism were mobilised. In the process, the Americans and the Belgians identified Joseph Mobutu as their man and started grooming him to be the instrument of their wishes. This eventually meant perpetual chaos as the two sides, forces of neo-colonialism and those of serious nationalism, competed for the control of the Congo. In the process, all sorts of militias were engaged in a period that was dominated by that perfect symbol of neo-colonialism – Mobutu.

Anti-colonial activities in Belgian Congo started coming into serious public focus in the 1950s and the machinery for countering nationalism activated. The American Secretary of Defence, George C. Marshall, in 1951 wanted the Central Intelligence Agency, the CIA, to mount counter-sabotage plans for the mines, increase the number of intelligence agents in the Congo, and increase the number of reliable white troops to protect the mines (Munene, 1995a, p.173). This did not stop a Belgian professor, A.A.J. van Bilsen, arousing the wrath of the colonialists by suggesting the possibility of Congolese people governing themselves in thirty years. Joseph Kasavubu, leader of the 'Association des Bakongos' or ABAKO, had reacted by rejecting gradualism and by demanding immediate self-government for Africans (Nzongola-Ntalaja, 2002, pp.81-82). Other activists came up and among them was Lumumba who formed the Congolese National Movement or MNC with one of his supporters being Joseph Desire Mobutu. Lumumba's MNC had a national, as opposed to tribal, appeal and it was in that context that he attended the All African Conference in Accra in December 1958 organized by Nkrumah. In the following year, following political riots in Leopoldville, the Belgians decided to leave rather unceremoniously. And the CIA was closely watching these developments and took the necessary steps to ensure that its interests in the Congo would be protected, if not by Belgium through classical colonialism then through neo-colonialism.

Congo's independence was shrouded in neo-colonialist intrigue and struggle that plunged the country into chaos. To start with, the new Congolese government was a split one in a federalised system designed to check Lumumba's nationalistic drive and to entrench Belgian interests. Before leaving, the Belgians created a three-way division of power and emphasisd tribal and regional differences as their legacy to the new regime. Regions were supposedly relatively autonomous and held together in a federal format with a non-executive president in the person of Kasavubu. The regional interests were represented in the Senate that was hostile to Lumumba while the parliament represented the Congolese. At the same time there was to be a prime minister who believed in a national unitary system in the person of Lumumba.

What were more, many politicians were not committed to the nationalist cause and took the earliest opportunity to start lining up their pockets. They awarded themselves huge pay hikes, ignored the electorates (Nzongola-Ntalaja, 2002, pp.88-89) and became regular visitors to foreign embassies rather than their constituencies. It was from the embassies, they believed, that 'power and money' seemed to flow (Weiss, 2000). They became willing tools of neo-colonialism.

The looming conflict between the forces of neo-colonialism and 'radical nationalism' was evident in the tension during the independence ceremony on June 30, 1960. King Badouin was symbolic of neo-colonial forces as he talked of Belgian benevolence towards the Congolese people and paternalistically said they were on their own. The King said, 'It is now up to you, gentlemen, to show that you are worthy of our confidence' (Quote in Hochschild,1999, p.301). Prime Minister Lumumba, representing radical nationalism, responded by telling the King 'we are no longer your monkeys' (Forbath,1977, p.395). Lumumba's radical 'move towards independent nationhood,' wrote Indar Jit Rikhye, who served as military adviser to the UN Secretary General, 'was contrary to the intentions of Belgians and other interested parties, who wanted to retain power and influence in the Congo. Thus there was no place for Lumumba in this setting, and he had to be removed' (Rikhye, 1993, p.318).

Trouble for Lumumba, therefore, was inherent in his belief that Congo's political independence had to be accompanied by economic independence (Depelchin, 1992:85-86), which meant opening up trading links with areas that had previously been excluded. Making Congo's resources available to all countries including the Soviet Union aroused the animosity of the Americans who conspired with the Belgians to get rid of Lumumba. The process started less than a week after independence with a Force Public commander, General Emile Janssens, provoking the Africans. Having, Rikhye wrote, 'planned to organize resistance to the successor government headed by Patrice Lumumba,' Janssens insulted African troops by writing on the blackboard that 'After Independence=Before Independence' and then went on to make the situation worse by declaring that 'The Force Public continues as before' (Rikhye,1993, p.1). White officers mocked the soldiers, telling them 'independence is not for you' (Forbath, 1977, p.395). The results of such provocation were military mutinies that gave the Belgians an opportunity to undermine the new government. And the Belgians intervened militarily on July 10, 1960 supposedly to safeguard Europeans and their properties (Nzongola-Ntalaja, 2002, p.99).

The Belgians were not alone in the effort to frustrate Lumumba for they had the support of the British, the French, the South Africans, and most importantly that of the United States (Nzongola-Ntalaja, 2002, p.101; Rikhye, 1993, pp.1-2), which controlled the United Nations (Weiss, 2000). Considering Lumumba to be a threat to its interests, the United States decided to remove him. As a result, claim Marq de Villiers and Sheila Hirtle, 'an unholy alliance of Western forces (South Africa, the CIA, and the Belgians) went into action to overthrow Lumumba' (de Villiers and Hirtle, 1997, p.186). The United States ambassador to Kinshasa decided that Lumumba had to go (Egerton, 2002, pp.191-192) and he was not alone.

At that time, the President of the United States was Dwight D. Eisenhower who believed that Lumumba was a 'radical and unstable Congolese prime minister,' a probable 'soviet tool' and 'a communist sympathizer if not a member of the Party' (quoted in Lyons, 1974, p.820). With such beliefs, Eisenhower wondered whether 'we can't get rid of this guy' (quote in Nzongola-Ntalaja, 2002, p.107) and so the machinery for getting rid of Lumumba was activated. The instrument for removing Lumumba was Mobutu, a man whom Lumumba had appointed Chief of Staff of the Congolese army but who was in the pay of the Central Intelligence Agency, (CIA) of the United States (Wrong, 2000, pp.63-65, 76-79). By September 1960, Lumumba had become a fugitive, captured and sent to Katanga where Moise Tshombe, the leader of the Katanga province who worked closely with Belgian mining companies to fragment the Congolese state (Rikhye, 1993, pp.1-2), was waiting. Lumumba was assassinated in Katanga in January 1961. He was reportedly cut into small pieces that were thrown into sulfuric acid (Egerton, 2002, p.196).

Part of the Belgian and American plot to destabilise Congo in order to undermine and overthrow Lumumba entailed secessionism in two places and Tshombe was a willing instrument for that. The only politician of import to participate in the pre-independence Economic Round Table Conference in Brussels, April 26-May 16, 1960, he was part of the Belgian conspiracy to strip Congo of resources while, argues Nzongola-Ntalaja, 'leaving virtually all the public debt to the new state' (Nzongola-Ntalaja, 2002, p.88). After the Belgians provoked army mutinies and then intervened militarily, Tshombe declared his secession of the Katanga province on July 11, 1960 and, immediately, the Belgians started disarming non-Katangese soldiers, expelling them from the province, and went on to establish diplomatic relations with Katanga (Nzongola-Ntalaja, 2002, p.99; Forbath, 1977, pp.397-398).

Another man who fell into the neo-colonialist trap has Albert Kalonji. With a big ambition to become a chief somewhere, Kalonji was assisted in his ambition by Tshombe and the Belgians. They supported his decision to declare the secession of the Kasai province from Congo. Kalonji declared the secession of South Kasai on August 8, 1960 and then proclaimed himself 'king' of the Luba (Nzongola-Ntalaja, 2002, p.105). Their independence, however, could be tolerated only for as long as Lumumba and his followers were considered serious threats in the Congo.

With Lumumba out of the political picture, Congo remained in political turmoil but secessionism was no longer attractive to the forces of neo-colonialism and so Katanga had to be crushed. Unity in Congo became paramount as symbolised in the person of Joseph Mobutu, the instrument of neo-colonialism, who had to deal with the secessionists and those trying to regroup and perpetuate Lumumba's ideals. With American/UN support, secessionism was defeated but the Lumumbist movement thrived. There was Pierre Mulele who started guerrilla warfare in 1964 and whose anti-government exploits made him a legend in his own time. He was assassinated in October 1968 and became some kind of patron saint of anti-Mobutu forces (Nzongola-Ntalaja, 2002, pp.128-130). There was also another group that came to be referred to as *Simba*, lion, that claimed to comprise disciples of Lumumba, who were said to be Marxists and mounted a protracted struggle against the central government.

It took time before Mobutu entrenched himself and initially engaged in shifting leaders while he remained in the background. In one of those shiftings, Moise Tshombe, the Katanga chieftain, was induced to become prime minister of Congo, as part of the deal to end his secessionism, in 1964 (Marsden, 1999, p.164) and he subsequently became involved in negotiating with the Simba and other rebel groups. This was in keeping with the aspirations of the newly created Organization of African Unity (OAU), formed in 1963, to try to reconcile various factions but there was little success. Amongst these were the efforts of Jomo Kenyatta, Kenya's prime minister, who brought different sides together in Nairobi only to have his efforts sabotaged by the United States and Belgium when they sent paratroopers into Congo supposedly to save white lives. The Nairobi peace attempt flopped and so fighting continued with Mobutu increasingly taking control (Woronoff, 1970, pp.270-274; Nzongola-Ntalaja, 2002, p.260). In 1965, Mobutu took power for himself and with American backing, materially and financially, he was able to establish himself as Congo's absolute ruler. He, Herbert Weiss claimed, 'became for decades the West's favorite dictator in Africa' (Weiss, 2000).

As the absolute ruler, Mobutu transformed the Congolese army into a private outfit for his relatives and cronies (Nzongola-Ntalaja, 2002, p.157) and turned the country's resources into his private property (Reno, 1998, p.153) He went on to decree the doctrine of authenticity in which he changed the country's name to Zaire and ordered all to drop European names. His changed his name from Joseph Desiree Mobutu to Mobutu Sese Seko Kuku Ngbenda Wa Za Banga and he went to the extent of demanding deification. After ordering that his name, Mobutu, be substituted for 'God' in church hymns the Roman Catholic Cardinal of Kinshasa 'was forced to flee the country in fear of his life' when he opposed Mobutu's decree. Authenticity, other than feeding the vanity of a megalomiac, was also a cover for American Cold War interests in southern Africa against Soviet operations (Marsden, 1999, pp.166, 289-290).

Mobutu's absolutism, however, was not absolute because he continued to be challenged from different quarters from 1965 to 1997 when he was eventually ousted. Although the Mulele movement subsided after the leader, Mulele, was assassinated in October 1968, remnants of Simba, among them a man called Laurent-Desire Kabila, continued to be a problem for Mobutu and the west and their fortunes improved with changing times (Nzongola-Ntalaja, 2002, pp.128-130; Marsden, 1999, p.165). Such remnants joined various liberation movements and, with Mobutu being identified as a kleptocrat in sympathy with racist regimes, their numbers increased. In 1978, Mobutu barely survived an attack mainly by groups associated with former Katangese secessionists operating from Angola. He survived due to military support from the United States, France, Belgium, and Morocco, (Marsden, 1999, p.189; Nzongola-Ntalaja, 2002, pp.181-184; Weiss, 2000).

Mobutu survived military onslaught as long as the United States considered him what US President Ronald Reagan considered a 'voice of good sense and good will' (quote in Marsden, 1999, p.289). Reagan's successor as president, George H. Bush, had worked closely with Mobutu in setting up a regional headquarters for the CIA in Kinshasa, and thought of Zaire under Mobutu as 'America's oldest and most valued friend' (Marsden, 1999, pp.167-168; Egerton, 2002, p.218). With the end of the Cold War that ushered in what Bush called a New World Order, however, neo-colonialism in which leaders of client states were important to the interests of the master states became irrelevant. Subsequently, Mobutu stopped being a 'valued friend' or a 'voice of good sense' because he was no longer needed as a neo-colonial instrument; and he instead became what the New York Times, in April 1990, called 'a repellent dictator' (quoted in Egerton, 2002, p.218) to be dumped. A new mode of control that does not need individual leaders or states to protect and advance the interests of the master states, postmodern colonialism, had replaced neo-colonialism and thus Mobutu had become irrelevant.

Interahamwe and Mayi Mayi Militias: Postmodern Colonialism and 'Africa's First World War' in the Congo

The forces of postmodern colonialism in the Great Lakes confused many people. Postmodern colonialism does not need specific individuals as presidents or leaders. All that postmodern colonialism needs is an environment in which to impose dictates without the actual manipulator being blamed for anything that might go wrong. Such an environment, at times, implies the existence of socio-economic and political chaos whose gravity is portrayed as relative. In a chaotic situation, a lot of organisations, countries, and institutions make a lot of money and take no responsibility for the mess that they help to create (de Rivero, 2001, pp.51-52).

The emergence of postmodern colonialism can be traced to failures in the American led western anti-communist crusades in the Third World. As a result, the United States, in particular, was forced to adopt changes in its international outlook with regard to the Third World countries (Munene, 1995b, pp.25-49). 'Shaken by disillusionment with the Vietnam experience,' wrote former US Secretary of State Henry Kissinger, 'many supporters of Cold War policies either retreated from the field of strategy or, in effect, rejected the essence of postwar American foreign policy' (Kissinger, 2001: 29). In rejecting postwar American foreign policy that had led to disaster, Americans abandoned their client regimes and, as Kissinger observed, abetted 'a civil war in Zaire ... in the name of democracy' that 'has led to the disintegration of much of the central authority' (Kissinger 2001, p.204). Zaire and the Great Lakes Region had been plunged into postmodern colonialism.

Postmodern colonialism in the region can be seen in terms of two phases; before 1997 and the period after 1997. The first phase deals with the war associated with the dumping of Mobutu and his replacement by Yoweri Kaguta Museveni of Uganda as the point man for American interests in the region. Considered one of the 'new leaders' of Africa who acquired power through the gun, were beholden to the United States, accepted the 'American agenda' and were 'accorded special status' by the Clinton Administration (Lyon, 2001, p.41), Museveni had grabbed power in Uganda in 1986 with the help of Rwandan Tutsi exiles. The second phase comprises the wars arising from conflicting interests that involved numerous countries that were competing to control one aspect or another of the region.

In both phases, the plundering of the region and its resources was associated with two notorious civil militias, the interahamwe and the Mayi Mayi. Of the two, it was the interahamwe that played pivotal roles in wreaking havoc and plunging the region into war. First, as a government supported militia in Rwanda, it was an instrument for genocide in 1994. Second, it precipitated Rwanda's war with Zaire that led to the oustimg of Mobutu from power and the installation of Laurent Kabila. Third, its activities rejuvenated the other militias in Eastern Congo, particularly the Mayi Mayi and together they continued to make the Great Lakes region unsafe.

The Interahamwe

The rise of the interahamwe can be traced to the conflict in Rwanda over who, between the Hutu and the Tutsi, should take over political power from the departing Belgians. Between 1959 and 1961, the Hutu managed to send the Tutsi into exile. Some of them ended up in Eastern Congo but many went to Uganda where they got involved in local political upheavals. With their dreams of returning to Rwanda fading as different Rwandan governments, particularly the regime of President Juvenal Habyarimana, making it clear that the Tutsi were not welcome, many became 'warrior refugees' and joined different warring factions in Uganda. They joined Museveni's camp when he launched his movement and together Museveni and the 'warrior refugees' grabbed power in Uganda in 1986. The most important of these 'warrior refugees', Fred Rwigyema and Paul Kagame, helped to organize the Rwanda Patriotic Front, a new militia aiming at overthrowing the government in Kigali.

While the existence of the Rwanda Patriotic Front put pressure on the Rwandan government, it was not the only source of concern. There was also the changed attitude of the donor community, which, through the IMF and the World Bank, forced the Habyarimana regime to impose structural adjustment programmes that hurt people at the very time that Rwanda was going through climatic and agricultural disasters. Unable to deal with the IMF/World Bank and having surrendered sovereignty to these institutions, Habyarimana's regime shifted the blame for its problems to the enemies of 'Hutu Power', meaning the Tutsi (Pottier, 2002, pp.22, 33-34).

Preparations to defend 'Hutu Power' had led the government to start condoning and arming vigilante groups that targeted the Tutsi. Amongst these vigilante groups were the interahamwe or 'those who attack together'. Starting as a sports youth movement, they were often rowdy, drugged and intoxicated as they were diverted from sports into enforcing social and political desires of the 'Hutu Power' elite. Other than having access to intoxicants and drugs, these youth were paid, provided with uniforms to identify them and were given military training (Sibomona, 1997, p.51). The training of these interahamwe intensified after the Rwanda Patriotic Front launched an invasion in October 1990 but Habyarimana was saved by the intervention of France, Belgium, and Mobutu's Zaire (Nzongola-Ntalaja, 1998, p.7).

The RPF invasion and the rescue of Habyarimana, claimed Rwandan journalist Andre Sibomana, 'was a gift to the government. It derived a new legitimacy from the real or imaginary threat which the war had cast over the country. The argument of national defence was over-exploited .... The government deliberately created an atmosphere of confusion, turning every opponent into an accomplice of the rebellion and every Tutsi into a secret RPF soldier.' Subsequently, the government staged a fake 'battle' in Kigali, in which no one died, which became an excuse for detaining 6,000 men for the crime of being Tutsi (Sibomana, 1997: 42-43).

With this self legitimation in which every Tutsi was an enemy soldier, the hate campaign and killings and the training of the interahamwe intensified. In Bugesera region in March 1992, the militia massacred 300 Tutsi with a message that they should return to their mythical homes in Ethiopia. Anyone opposing Habyarimana, Leon Mugesera, Vice-President of MRND told the Tutsi in November 1992 would be wiped out as he added: 'Your country is Ethiopia ...and we shall soon send you back via the Nyabarango ... on the express journey .... And I repeat, we are quickly getting organized to begin this work' (quote in Pottier, 2002, p.22) And helping the Hutu Power 'to begin this work' were the French who were busy training the interahamwe killing machine as well as other militias (Pottier, 2002, pp.35-36; Dunn, 2003, p.161).

While the hate campaign and the training of the militia intensified, a civil war raged in Rwanda between the RPF and the Habyarimana government and this led the OAU to push for peace talks in Arusha that the government was not eager to maintain. Consequently, two telling events took place in 1993. First, there was a settlement, called the Arusha Accords, that allowed the RPF and other groups to be involved in a reconstituted government. Despite having signed the Accords, however, Habyarimana undermined the settlement and he had French support in doing so (Nzongola-Ntalaja, 1998, p.7). Second, information about the intended government-orchestrated slaughter of the Tutsi was passed to the United Nations and, in December 1993, *Le Flambeau*, a newspaper in Rwanda, made the information public. It reported: 'that 40,000 interahamwe have just completed their training in several centers in the Akagera Park ... are about to carry out a plot which the instigators will portray as a civil war ... their leader ... decided to apply the 'final solution' to their compatriots who are seen as enemies of the regime' (quoted in Sibomana, 1997, p.51). As the parties were signing the Accords which the Hutu Power had no intention of honouring, the interahamwe were well prepared to start sending the Tutsi to Ethiopia through the Nyabarongo River.

The thoroughness with which the Forces Armées Rwandaises (FAR) and the interahamwe had prepared to slaughter the Tutsi revealed itself in April 1994 after Habyarimana died in a plane crash. They were well prepared not only in training but also in the availability of killing tools. FAR had given a gun to every *nyumba kumi*, or ten houses, and thereby made available at least 150,000 guns to the interahamwe (Pottier, 2002, p.31). Within a period of three months, FAR and the interahamwe had killed roughly 800,000 Tutsi and moderate Hutu. Many moderate Hutu were forced to prove they were good 'Hutu' by killing their Tutsi friends (Sibomana, 1997, p.104; Pottier, 2002, p.61).

The slaughter ended only after Paul Kagame's RPF decisively defeated the FAR, captured Kigali and sent FAR and the interahamwe into exile. The French, in their 'Operation Turquoise', had tried to forestall Kagame's victory in 1994, as they had done in October 1990, but they failed. They succeeded, however, in protecting high level government officials and other members of the Hutu Power structure, the FAR, and the interahamwe who escaped to Eastern Zaire (Dunn, 2003, p.161). The French helped the killing machine to escape, notes Nzongola-Ntalaja, 'with virtually all the weapons at its disposal into the Congo and regroup for future attacks on the newly established RPF regime in Rwanda' (Nzongola-Ntalaja, 1998, p.7)

The disappearance of the FAR and the Interahamwe, collectively referred to as *genocidaires*, into Eastern Congo led to the second phase in which the region's geopolitics was reorganized and helped to give prominence to the Mayi Mayi. The new regime in Rwanda was effectively led by another 'new leader,' Paul Kagame. Kagame, previously a 'warrior refugee' became a key player in the reorganisation as he warned the United Nations of the dangers posed by the genocidaires masquerading as refugees in Eastern Congo.

Using the refugee camps, which they controlled, and with support from Mobutu's regime, the FAR and the interahamwe reinforced their 'Hutu Power' in Eastern Zaire by suppressing those Tutsi that they found in Zaire, also known as the Banyamulenge. To make matters worse, Mobutu decided to expel the Banyamulenge from Eastern Congo using the Interahamwe (Reno, 1998, p.149; Cilliers and Malan, 2001, p.21; Dunn, 2003, pp.2-3). They continued with their rhetorical incitement against the Tutsi, calling them cockroaches and in the process recruited some Zairians to join the anti-Tutsi campaign. They also mounted a protracted campaign to overthrow the new regime in Kigali that lasted roughly two years before their actions could be stopped through a well orchestrated invasion of Zaire (Dunn, 2003, pp.149-151; Evans, 1997, p.9).

Interahamwe activities reactivated the Mayi Mayi in Kivu whose desire was to get rid of both Mobutu and the Banyarwanda. They had been active in the 1960s supporting Mulele's Simba rebels, then had disappeared first into the Ruwenzori Mountains, and then to the forests around Beni. They were driven into the underground only to reappear early in 1993 when they tried to make Kivu free of 'foreigners'. With the *interahamwe* and the FAR exporting Rwandan problems into Kivu, the Mayi Mayi were by 1996 terrorizing both Mobutu's FAZ and the Banyarwanda, whether they were Hutu or Tutsi (Pottier, 2002, pp.29, 41, 214n).

Other than giving a new lease of life to the Mayi Mayi, the activities of the interahamwe intensified the security threat for Rwanda coming from Mobutu and the genocidaires. This provided Kagame with a justification to invade Zaire and to drive Mobutu out of office. This decision pleased the Mayi Mayi who then downplayed their hostility towards all Rwandans in order to join Kagame's forces in bringing Mobutu down. There was a realignment of the militia; one side were FAR and the interahamwe fighting for Mobutu and his FAZ, and on the other were the Banyamulenge and the Mayi Mayi fighting for Kagame's RPA.

With their hostility diverted from the Banyamulenge to Mobutu and the interahamwe, the Mayi Mayi acquired a kind of temporary respectability because they were part of a coalition that Kagame had built in order to oust Mobutu. That coalition included Museveni of Uganda as well as the United States of America. Together they created an army named the Alliance for Democratic Forces (Marsden,1999, pp.37-46, 155-161, 185-189). They, claimed former United States Assistant Secretary of State for African Affairs Herman Cohen, 'recruited, trained, and armed Congolese fighters who formed an army of liberation. They also selected a leader of this army and government-in-waiting named Laurent Kabila' (Cohen, 2000). The Mayi Mayi, therefore, appeared to be part of a respectable team.

Kabila, however, had additional supporters, other than the United States, Uganda and Rwanda and these included those who had gripes against Mobutu and/or shared his revolutionary credentials. There was, for instance, Angola whose Marxist government had suffered from UNITA insurgencies encouraged and supported by Mobutu in cahoots with racist South Africa. There was also Zimbabwe whose leader, Robert Mugabe, had known Kabila in Dar es Salaam as a comrade. Kabila was, therefore a beneficiary of external forces that for different reasons wanted Mobutu out. They succeeded in May 1997 when Mobutu fled Zaire and Kabila declared himself president of the renamed Democratic Republic of the Congo. And for a while, the Rwandans and the Ugandans made sure he was safe in power.

With the ousting of Mobutu, the region's geopolitics changed as allies turned on each other and once again the Mayi Mayi were involved in the developing commotions. Although the Mayi Mayi had joined hands with the

Banyamulenge and with Kabila in order to get rid of Mobutu, they had very different political agenda and they were bound to collide once their common objective was achieved (Pottier, 2002, pp.85, 91).

Having defeated Mobutu, the alliance started disintegrating because of the political agenda that each group had. Among the first to be shunned were the Mayi Mayi with their reputation for roughness and desire to drive the Banyarwanda out of Kivu. Given that the new government in Kinshasa had a lot of suspicious Banyamulenge in the top positions, containing the Mayi Mayi became one of the first things that the new regime tried to do as a way of asserting its authority against an unruly militia. When ordered to disarm, the Mayi Mayi refused, tried to kill the government official who gave the order, and fighting broke out between the Mayi Mayi and the ADFL (Pottier, 2002, pp.93, 100, 221n).

The unsuccessful effort to disarm the Mayi Mayi, however, was only one part of the disintegrating alliance and the fallout that followed between Kabila and his Banyamulenge supporters. Kabila wanted to survive as president and reshape the Congo to his liking but not to practice democracy or to share power. He at the same time did not have effective control of the country and was subjected to internal pressure to reduce the presence of the Banyamulenge in his government (Weiss, 2000, p.1). Suspicious of his benefactors, who had become his lobbyists in Washington, Kabila ordered his two former allies (Rwanda and Uganda) to remove their troops and advisors (Cohen, 2000). And since he wanted to free himself from the image of being a puppet of Rwanda and Uganda, he failed to control anti-Rwandan and anti-Ugandan insurgencies (de Waal, 2000, p.31). And these included the interahamwe.

Having broken with his former allies, Kabila behaved like Mobutu in inciting rebels against both Rwanda and Uganda. He supported the interahamwe and the FAR remnants against the 'Tutsi' in Eastern Congo and this was a threat to Rwanda. With the spectre of the interahamwe getting a new lease of life, Rwanda and Burundi started supporting an anti-Kabila militia that struggled to portray Kabila as a neo-Mobutu (Dunn, 2003, p.156). On its part, Uganda considered the presence of the Lords Resistance Army (LRA) and the Allied Democratic Front (ADF) within Congo to be a threat (Cilliers and Malan, 2001, pp.23-24). Both Uganda and Rwanda quickly moved into large parts of Congo and effectively annexed Eastern Congo.

Their invasion was considered a threat to other previous allies, such as Angola, Namibia, and Zimbabwe whose troops managed to stop Ugandan and Rwandese forces from capturing Kinshasa and ousting Kabila (Cohen, 2000, p.1; Nkiwane, 2003, p.68). Angola worried about Rwanda's and Uganda's possible capture of a region, Kitona, that Luanda considered to be too close to home. It also suspected that the two American surrogates supported the UNITA rebels and therefore felt justified to support Kabila (Weiss, 2000, p.II). The most important of these Kabila supporters, however, was Zimbabwe and it had three reasons. First, it considered Kabila as part of its wider anti-imperialist struggle that had come to be represented by Museveni who looked like an American surrogate. Second, it was a way of asserting its influence as a regional power in Southern Africa, especially in competition with South Africa through SADC. South Africa was losing mining and economic influence under the Kabila regime and Zimbabwe was ready and eager to fill in by supporting Kabila when it mattered. Third, there were economic interests in the form of mining commitments to top level Zimbabwean officials (Cilliers and Malan, 2001, pp.21-22; Weiss, 2000; Nkiwane, 2003, p.68).

Although they stopped the ousting of Kabila, they could not stop Rwanda and Uganda from continuing to occupy and exploit Eastern Congo which they considered to be their security zone (Cilliers and Malan, 2001, pp.23-24). Thus Congo, in reality, became fragmented into zones of foreign interest although no one wanted to have the country officially divided (de Waal, 2000, p.31).

The situation became worse than before when the original 'new leaders', Museveni and Kagame started fighting over Kisangani in Eastern Congo. The two, noted Nzongola-Ntalaja, were 'fighting over turf and resources' with Uganda seemingly getting the short end of it (Nzongola-Ntalaja, 2002, p.237). Subsequently, the anti-Kabila movements that they had sponsored also became split between a pro-Museveni RCD-Kisangani led by Ernest Wamba Dia Wamba to serve Kampala interests and a pro-Kagame RCD-Goma led by Emile Illunga to cater for Kigali's concerns (Nzongola-Ntalaja, 2002, pp.230-232). The net effect was to fragment Congo with foreign troops, whether supporting or opposing Kabila or turning on each other, controlling different regions. These troops from various African countries, with their Congolese surrogates, helped to siphon all types of wealth in collaboration with international dealers and major corporate bodies safely headquartered in Europe and North America (Nzogola-Ntalaja, 2002, pp.235-237; Marsden, 1999, pp.455-478).

There were various attempts at peace making that led to the Lusaka Accord in July 1999 signed by key players in the war that included Congo itself, Zimbabwe, Namibia, Angola, Rwanda, and Uganda. The Accord called for a cessation of hostilities, withdrawal of foreign forces from Congo, national dialogue and reconciliation, disarming of militias, formation of a national army, establishing administrative machinery throughout the Congo, and securing the borders between Congo and its neighbours (Cilliers and Malan, 2001, pp.30-31). The problem with this agreement was that it seemingly catered for the interests of other countries but not the factional groups and militias within the Congo that were fighting in collaboration with foreign troops.

Some of these militias had developed in reaction to external presences in the Congo and the ineffectiveness of the central government and were not willing to be bound by the Lusaka agreement. A number of them were not disciplined soldiers and, particularly the kadogos, had joined Kabila in excitement and were not willing to conform. Yet they were Kabila's key supporters, as his bodyguards, and they killed him in January 2001 only to have Kabila's son, Joseph take over leadership. Kabila had also armed the interahamwe to fight the Rwandans and these were similarly not willing to lay down the arms.

And there were the Mayi Mayi who considered it their patriotic duty to fight both Uganda and Rwanda without necessarily paying attention to what Kinshasa said because as far as they were concerned Kinshasa was very remote. It was this kind of scenario that produced rebel commanders such as General Laurent Nkunda in Eastern Congo, who seemingly pays little attention to his superiors. And as each of the factions continues to fight, it also continues to give mineral concessions to various international dealers who provide the necessary ammunition and money for them to continue fighting.

Conclusion

Civil conflict in the Great Lakes seems to be a constant that can be traced to European greed for African resources in the 19th Century. It started its classical colonial period as personal property of Leopold who then sold it to his kingdom of Belgium in order to escape international censure. In that period, the militia was in the hands of the Belgians who treated the Congolese as of their property, as slaves, despite the claim that Congo was a model colony. The Belgians were unable to resist the post-World War II anti-colonial movement that forced them to beat a hasty retreat in 1960 but before leaving they laid the ground work for neo-colonialism in Congo. As a Cold War phenomenon, neo-colonialism required pliable leaders who would make their countries serve the interests of master states. Such a leader was Mobutu who privatised and plundered his country while serving the master state, the United States of America.

Once it became clear that neo-colonialist instruments like Mobutu could not safeguard the interests of master states for long, they became expendable and new instruments that did not depend on individual leaders were devised. This led to postmodern colonialism that coincided with the end of the Cold War and with the promotion of an economic faith called globalisation through all powerful institutions that are protected by the master state. Widespread chaos was subsequently unleashed in the region.

Among the perpetrators of chaos in the region were the two notorious civil militias of interahamwe in Rwanda and the Mayi Mayi in the Eastern Congo area of Kivu. These two greatly affected the turn of events in the region for the worse. The Mayi Mayi appeared to be older as a rag tag rebel movement that disliked central authority in Kinshasa and had fought against Mobutu in the 1960s. Suppressed into the underground, it strangely re-emerged with ferocity in early 1993 as a result of land pressures in the area and also as a response to developments in Rwanda, which had a habit of 'exporting' disorder to Kivu. The disorder being exported from Rwanda was, first, the Tutsi refugees who were absorbed into the existing Banyamulenge community and, later, advocates of Hutu Power who ran away from Kagame's forces after committing genocide. Whether Hutu or Tutsi, as far as the Mayi Mayi were concerned, they were all 'foreigners' to be removed from Kivu.

The interahamwe, in contrast, arose as a militia designed as an instrument for maintaining Hutu Power in Rwanda and attracted attention with the thoroughness with which they slaughtered almost a million people in three months. Driven out of Rwanda, despite the help they got from France and Zaire, the interahamwe had taken over refugee camps in Kivu, which they turned into bases for attacking the new regime in Kigali.

The relationship between these two militias, interahamwe and the Mayi Mayi, was one of strange realignment and constantly affected the Great Lakes Region. What they had in common was that they espoused deep hatred of others and their rank and file comprised mainly riff-raff promoting a Hutu Power agenda in the case of the interahamwe or displaying fear of 'foreign' presence in Kivu in the case of the Mayi Mayi. They started their relationship awkwardly as the Mayi Mayi sought to remove all Rwandans from Kivu. Since the interahamwe allied itself to Mobutu, whom the Mayi Mayi hated, the Mayi Mayi entered into an alliance with Kagame, Kabila, and the Banyamulenge. Upon victory, however, the alliance broke down as the Mayi Mayi and the Banyamulenge turned on each other to settle separate political scores that led to Kabila and Kagame also trying to settle other political scores. The alliance system switched again and curiously brought the interahamwe and the Mayi Mayi onto the same side with Kabila against Kagame and Museveni.

The Great Lakes region today, therefore, is as it was in the 1880s, only that there is a twist to it. The Europeans and Americans are still attracted to the region's wealth and are still determined to avoid killing each other in that region. As they ensure that they have access to, and control of, the wealth they are careful not to be seen openly to be doing it as they did in the days of classical colonialism. And since there is no Cold War to worry about, they are not interested in neo-colonialist tools of control in the name of individual heads of state since the control can be through agents of postmodern colonialism such as the World Bank and the International Monetary Fund. Unlike the 1880s, the twist is that there exist states in Africa that are willing to be surrogates and to do the dirty work for the international community, meaning Europe and North America. It is this situation that has given rise to the claim that the war in the Congo is an African war.

The reality, however, is different because as Africans fight in the region and such militia as the interahamwe and the Mayi Mayi become catalysts for fighting, minerals and other resources are siphoned to North America and Europe. The Great Lakes region, therefore, was and still is a place of adventure where the white people could/can make great wealth at the expense of the Africans. It is today a postmodern colony, not quite united and not quite decimated, but quite exploited with most of the wealth being siphoned out. As in Leopold's Congo, 1885 to 1908, African militias are killing Africans for profits that end up outside Africa. And what is more, Africans get blamed and the exploiters look innocent.

References

Amnesty International, (2002), 'Democratic Republic of Congo: Making a Killing, The Diamond Trade in government-controlled DRC':
    http://web.amnesty.org/library/Index/engAFR620172...\DEMOCRAT+REPUBLIC+OF +CONGO (October 2002).
Cilliers, J. and Malan, M. (2001), *Peacekeeping in the DRC: MONUC and the Road to Peace*, Institute of Peace Studies, Pretoria.

Cohen, H. J. (2000), 'The Agony of the Congo,' *American Diplomacy*, Vol. V, Number 3, Summer:
[http://www.unc.edu/depts./diplomat/AD_Issues/amdipl_16/cohen_agony_prt.html]

Croegaet, L. (1999), *The African Continent: An Insight Into Its Earliest History*, Paulines Publications, Nairobi.

Depelchin, J. (1992), *From the Congo Free State to Zaire, 1885-1974: Towards a Demystification of Economic and Political History*, Codesria, Dakar.

Diamond, L. (1995), 'Promoting Democracy in Africa: United States and International Policies in Transition', pp.193-219, in Munene, M., Adar, K. and Nyunya, O. (eds), *The United States and Africa: From Independence to the End of the Cold War*, East African Educational Publishers, Nairobi.

Duffy, J. (1961), *Portuguese Africa*, Oxford University Press, London.

Dunn, K. C. (2003), *Imaging the Congo: The International Relations of Identity*, Macmillan, N.Y.

Egerton. R. B. (2002), *The Troubled Heart of Africa: A History of the Congo*, St. Martin's Press, N.Y.

Evans, G. (1997), *Responding to Crises in the African Great Lakes*, Oxford University Press, N.Y.

Ewans, M. (2002), *European Atrocity, African Catasrophe: Leopold II, the Congo Free State and Its Aftermath*, Routledge Curzon, London.

Forbath, P. (1977), *The River Congo: The Discovery, Exploration and Exploitation of the World's Most Dramatic River*, E.P. Dutton, N.Y.

George, E. (2003), 'Private Security Companies and Postmodern Colonialism in Africa,' *M.A Thesis; Peace and Development Program*, Universitat Jaume I, Castellon, Spain.

Hochschild, A. (1999), *King Leopold's Ghost: A Story of Greed, Terror, and Heroism in Colonial Africa*, Macmillan, London.

Khadiagala, G. M. and Lyons, T. (eds) (2001), *African Foreign Policies: Power and Process*, Lynne Rienner, Boulder, Co.

Kissinger, H. (2001), *Does America Need a Foreign Policy? Toward a Diplomacy for the 21st Century*, Simon & Schuster, N.Y.

Luttwak, E. N. (1996), 'A Post-Heroic Military Policy', *Foreign Affairs*, Vol. 75, No. 4, July/August, pp.43-44.

Lyon, P. (1974), *Eisenhower, Portrait of the Hero*, Little Brown and Company, Boston.

Lyons, T. P. (2001), 'US Diplomatic Strategies to Resolve Conflicts in Africa', in Morrison, J. S. and Cooke, J. G. (eds), *Africa Policy in the Clinton Years: Critical Choices for the Bush Administration*, The CSIS Press, Washigton DC, pp.33-54.

Marsden, W. (1999), *Genocide and Covert Operations in Africa, 1993-1999*, The Edwin Mellen Press, N.Y.

Munene, M. (1995a), *The Truman Administration and the Decolonisation of Sub-Saharan Africa*, Nairobi University Press, Nairobi.

Munene, M. (1995b), 'Cold War Disillisionment and Africa', in Munene, M., Nyunya, J. O. and Adar, K. (eds), *The United States and Africa: From Independence to the End of the Cold War*, East African Educational Publishers, Nairobi, pp.25-49.

Nkiwane, T. C. (2003), 'The Quest for Good Governance', in Baregu, M. and Landsberg, C. (eds), *From Cape to Congo:Southern Africa's Evolving Security Challenges*, Lynne Rienner, London, pp. 53-71.

Nzongola-Ntalaja, G. (2002), *The Congo: From Leopold to Kabila: A People's History*, Zed Books, N.Y.

Pottier, J. (2002), *Re-Imagining Rwanda:Conflict, Survival and Disinformation in the Late Twentieth Century*, Cambridge University Press, Cambridge.

Rikhye, J. I. (1993), *Military Adviser to the Secretary-General: U.N. Peacekeeping and the Congo Crisis*, St. Martin's Press, N.Y.

Reno, W. (1998), *War Lord Politics and African States*, Lynne Rienner, Boulder, Colorado.

Rivero, O. (2001), *The Myth of Development: The Non-Viable Economies of the 21st Century*, Zed Books, London.

Sibomana, A. (1997), *Hope for Rwanda: Conversations With Laure Guibert and Herve Deguine*, Pluto Press, London.

Villiers, M. and Hirtle, S. (1997), *Into Africa: A Journey Through the Ancient Empires*, Phoenix Giant, N.Y.

Waal, A. (2000), *Who Fights? Who Cares? War and Humanitarian Action in Africa*, Africa World Press, Trenton, N.J.

Weiss, H. (2000), 'War and Peace in the Democratic Republic of the Congo, Part I, Part II, Part III,' *American Diplomacy*, Vol. V, Number 3, Summer: [http://www.unc.edu/depts./diplomat/AD_Issues/amdipl_16/weiss/weiss].

Williams, D. (2000), 'Aid and Sovereignty: Quasi-states and the International Financial Institutions', *Review of International Studies*, No.26.

Woronoff, J. (1970), *Organizing African Unity*, The Scarecrow Press, Metuchen, NJ.

Wrong, M. (2000), *In the Footsteps of Mr. Kurtz: Living on the Brink of Disaster in the Congo*, Fourth Estate Ltd, London.

Zacarias, A. (2003), 'Redefining Security', in Mwesiga Baregu and Christopher Landsberg (eds), *From Cape to Congo:Southern Africa's Evolving Security Challenges*, Lynne Rienner, London, pp.31-51.

Zeleza, P. T. (1997), *Manufacturing African Studies and Crises*, CODESRIA, Dakar.

Chapter 12

Civil Defence Forces and Post-Conflict Security Challenges: International Experiences and Implications for Africa

Jeremy Ginifer and Hooman Peimani

Introduction

African conflict-prone states and war-torn and post-conflict transition societies frequently face severe challenges relating to CDFs (Civil Defence Forces), not least in their capacity to undermine human and national security, the development of justice, good governance and democracy, as other chapters in this volume elaborate. There is a tendency perhaps to regard the challenge of CDFs as in some sense peculiar, or distinctive, to Africa. However, as this chapter demonstrates, many other countries and societies have been through conflicts where CDFs have played a central role in armed violence and have emerged as a post-conflict challenge. International experience suggests that there is nothing distinctively African about the emergence of CDFs as a post-conflict challenge; indeed, they have sometimes proved to be equally problematic in other countries.

This chapter examines the types of generic challenges that CDFs have posed through looking at four contexts and how these experiences might be factored into post-conflict recovery in African contexts. These countries can all be described as primarily conforming to the war-torn and post-conflict transition model elaborated in the introduction, rather than being conflict-prone societies, although many do remain conflict-prone.

This chapter primarily concerns itself with the human and state security dimensions of CDFs both during and following armed violence. In particular, it examines how the circumstances in which CDFs are formed and operate during conflict, where they are both victims and perpetrators of armed violence and human rights abuses, almost inevitably leads to an erosion of the state's monopoly on the use of legitimate force and reconfigures the contract between the state, CDFs, and civilians.

In particular, this chapter, in moving beyond the conflict phase into post-conflict recovery, focuses on issues of integration and regulation relating to CDFs, including security sector reform (SSR), as a key challenge in accommodating CDFs into civilian or military frameworks where they do not pose a threat to human or state security. At the same time, it recognises that during conflicts they sometimes acquire a legitimacy, constituency, or power, that cannot be readily ignored, particularly in the absence of a credible or legitimate state authority. International experience shows, in fact, that CDFs are frequently sidelined by governments. Unlike mainstream rebel and government forces, CDFs rarely have political representation or involvement in peace negotiations and subsequent settlements. They are often regarded as little more than adjuncts to government forces, and SSR programmes, for example, tend to pay scant attention to CDFs.

However, CDFs are often potent post-conflict actors in the 'private' security sector with considerable military experience and expertise often painfully gained, ready access to arms, persisting command structures and also political ambitions. They also frequently have grievances – both 'real' and 'imagined'. They represent a challenge to the monopoly of violence that states are presumed to accrue following conflict endings. Indeed, some CDFs are not just seeking to defend their interests or those of their community, or assist national armies in repelling rebels, rather they may be seeking to deconstruct the legitimacy of the state. In this undertaking, they may have the support, implicit or explicit, of some communities or sectors of society. However, the case studies demonstrate that other communities are often highly negative, or at the least ambiguous, regarding the legitimacy of CDFs both during and following conflict. At the same time, CDFs may have private economic interests, such as the exploitation of mineral resources, which they developed with the erosion of state authority during conflict, and which they are unlikely to relinquish willingly. This has implications for state recovery as well as communities where these resources are located.

The contexts examined here represent a cross section of experience across several regions. The approach adopted is to highlight areas where CDFs seem to have posed particular difficulties during the conflict phase from a human and state security perspective, and which also created dilemmas in terms of the reassertion of state authority, civil society and an accountable and democratic security sector in the post-conflict or recovery phase.

These are, first, the often-negative human security impacts CDFs have had on civil society and on post-conflict recovery, as well as negative relations with state security forces, which, among other things, make integration and regulation often problematic. Second, their frequent to act as an effective back-up to the state in countering rebel challenges to the state. Third, their negative impact in terms of humanitarian and human rights abuses, and last, their sometimes detrimental impact upon development. In three of the case studies (Peru, Guatemala, and Sri Lanka), these problematic elements were quite marked, but less so in Sierra Leone where CDFs were held in higher esteem by large swathes of the population.

Having explored these issues, the chapter will move on to consider how these challenges might be met by states and war-torn societies that are passing through often unstable post-conflict phases. Finally, it will suggest how these might be related to African contexts.

International Experience of CDFs: Case Studies

Although CDFs have sprung up in many African countries they are by no means a phenomenon peculiar to Africa. They have also existed in South America and Asia to a very significant extent, while operating on a smaller scale in other regions, including the Balkans. The following four case studies elaborate on the experience of CDFs in two South American states (Guatemala and Peru), an Asian state (Sri Lanka) and an African state (Sierra Leone).

Guatemala, Peru, and Sri Lanka are all war-torn society contexts, which share in common major flare-ups in conflict between government and rebel forces in the 1980s, which, to a greater or lesser extent, are continuing or have yet to be fully resolved. Amongst other things, they have in common governance issues, poor progress in terms of development, and to varying extents 'ethnic' fault-lines. In all three countries, governments have been able to amass fairly substantial military forces, but these have been unable conclusively to defeat rebel movements (even with the support of CDFs), which have drawn some popular support in the face of genuine grievances over issues such as land reform, and the often brutal conduct of the state security sector. Sierra Leone differs from the above case studies in being a conflict that has, for the moment at least, resulted in a clear end and a defeat for rebel forces, while post-conflict reconstruction is well-established and the state's monopoly on the legitimate use of violence is to an extent restored. Further, unlike Peru and Sri Lanka, Sierra Leone benefited from extensive external intervention to end the conflict and CDFs linked strongly at certain key conflict points with external forces as well as with the state.

The case studies show that, in broad terms, governments have established CDFs in order to defeat or counter rebel movements challenging the legitimacy of the state in circumstances where their own security forces (military and police) have proved unable to do so on their own. In some contexts, CDFs have been mobilised and set up by civilians, rather than governments, as in some communities in Sierra Leone during the civil conflict, but this has been less common. A central objective of governments has been to mobilise the very same population from whom insurgents often recruit and receive support, to decrease the security forces' burden, and to end conflicts by denying the armed opposition safety and support, mainly in rural areas.

The *modus oprandi* of CDFs has tended to follow similar lines across conflicts. In Peru, for example, the rondas campesinas described their function as the defence of communities from terrorists and support of the police and army. Similarly, the role of the Home Guard in Sri Lanka was to reduce the burden of community defence for the army and police near rebel-controlled areas. However, in Sierra Leone the role of the CDFs was less clearly defined and fluctuated over time. In certain areas, and at points in the conflict, CDFs fought army elements. They also cooperated widely with external forces intervening in the conflict. Further, they came to take on offensive operations but, as elsewhere, their primary role was essentially community defence, with, or without, the co-operation of the national army.

The Emergence/Constitution of CDFs

Peru

As the civil war was expanding in 1983, Peru's government established the self-defence committees (comités de autodefensa) or civil defence committees (comités de defensa civil) to suppress the main armed leftist opposition groups, the Communist Party of Peru (Partido Comunista del Peru) also known as the Shining Path (Sendero Luminoso), and the Tupac Amaru Revolutionary Movement (Movimento Revolucionario Tupac Amaru or MRTA).[1] The CDFs' establishment coincided with the creation of emergency zones where many constitutional freedoms, including those of movement and assembly, were suspended in an effort to curb the civil war's destabilising affect.[2]

Throughout the 1980s-1990s, the Peruvian government established urban and rural civil defence committees in Peru's civil war affected areas,[3] but only their rural units (rondas campesinas) served as armed counter-insurgency entities in the countryside, which was the main arena of the civil war. Reorganised and expanded to function as a counter-insurgency force,[4] the Peruvian army largely controlled and armed them throughout their operational life.[5]

They were composed of poor and poorly-educated male adult peasants, including 'native tribes' (e.g., the Asháninkas)[6] and in some cases women and children.[7] In the early 1990s there were about 4,732 armed rondas campesinas with about 370,000 members.[8] Their declared purpose was to 'exercise self-defence in their communities, prevent infiltration by terrorists, defend themselves from the latter and support the Peruvian Army and the police.'[9] The rondas campesinas developed into the major armed CDF, which, in many instances, fought along with the military.[10]

The apprehension of many high-ranking figures of MRTA and the Shining Path during the early 1990s[11] prompted the government to begin disbanding the self-defence committees. However, most of them are yet to be disbanded despite the end of the civil war.[12]

Guatemala

The Guatemalan government created in 1982 the rural civilian defence groups called Patrullas de Autodefensa Civil (PAC), or the Civilian Self-Defence Patrols with the declared objective of restoring law and order.[13] As the armed Guatemalan National Revolutionary Unity (URNG) was growing in the countryside, populated by impoverished peasants, the PAC's main role was to defend villages against the armed rebels and ease the security forces' military burden through independent operations and/or joint ones with the army against the rebels.[14] Having mainly impoverished and poorly-educated male peasants as recruits, the PAC served as the 'civilian agents of the army' to eliminate rebels and their sympathisers in the countryside.[15] Guatemala's Minister of Government, in charge of the police, which shared responsibility for internal security with the army, officially controlled the

PAC.[16] The PAC units worked along with security forces (police and the army) in counter-insurgency operations as well as on their own.[17]

In 1996, the government disbanded the PAC as part of its peace accord with the rebels[18] when its membership was about 250,000.[19] However, there are reports that it has been reorganised,[20] although the civil war is over. The extent of this reorganisation was unknown late in 2004.

Sri Lanka

In 1984, the Sri Lankan government created a civilian defence force, the Home Guards.[21] They were stationed in the vicinity of Tamil villages in the locations hostile to the Liberation Tigers of Tamil Eelam (LTTE), an armed group seeking the independence of Tamils. They were composed of Sinhalese villagers initially,[22] while the Sri Lankan government embarked on setting up units of Tamil-speaking Muslim villagers in 1990.[23] The Home Guards' mandate was 'self-defence': to provide security for Muslim and Sinhalese villages near LTTE-controlled areas and to reduce the military burden of the security forces (police and the military) in their counter-LTTE operations.[24]

The majority of the Home Guards were impoverished and poorly educated Sinhalese and Muslim villagers.[25] With a short pause in 1987,[26] the force, which was armed and trained by the Sri Lankan military, continued its growth throughout the 1980s, the 1990s, and reportedly even after the conclusion of the February 2002 ceasefire agreement between the LTTE and the Sri Lankan government.[27] Its strength rose from 12,000[28] in 1987 to the current estimate of 15,000,[29] or more than 20,000[30] or 23,000,[31] according to some estimates. Lack of progress in the peace negotiations increased the possibility of the resumption of hostilities late in 2004, as in November the LTTE explicitly made a threat to that effect to express its 'frustration' with the situation.[32] As the civil war is not yet over, the force is still operational.

Sierra Leone

The CDF emerged in Sierra Leone in the early 1990s in response to attacks on communities by the Revolutionary United Front (RUF). They were not, in many instances, formed and trained by the government, as in many other civil conflicts. As well as fighting the RUF, they also on occasions fought army elements, which committed extensive human rights abuses against civilians. However, the CDF also co-operated with Sierra Leone Army (SLA) units during phases of the conflict. Government support for the CDF under President Kabbah, for example, during the conflict was sporadic and at times half-hearted. The government only provided logistical support to the CDF irregularly and most of that went to the Kamajors.

The CDF, and in particular the Kamajors which was the largest group within the CDF, started to make a significant impact against the RUF from 1993-4 onwards with the mobilisation of a mass civil defence movement that often had the military advantage of knowing the terrain better than the RUF and enjoyed the support of many civilians. Kamajor groups tracked and countered RUF attacks and interfered with their supplies and freedom of movement. The CDF also saw one of its key roles as rooting out RUF, and RUF sympathisers, within local communities.

These CDF forces, with the aid of military intelligence supplied by the private security group, Executive Outcomes (EO), in some locations, allowed combined army-Kamajor units to surround the main RUF camps during the latter half of 1996.[33] This military pressure contributed to the conclusion of a comprehensive peace plan in 1996. The Kamajors, in particular, received formal military training from EO and Economic Community of West African States Monitoring Group (ECOMOG) troops. The SLA also used the CDF as scouts.

The CDF expanded during the Armed Forces Revolutionary Council (AFRC) Junta rule, 1997-1998, when President Kabbah was deposed and exiled, and was engaged in fighting junta forces, thus gaining credibility with the government and some civilians. By mid-1998, the CDF numbered between 25,000-30,000 personnel and was concentrated in the Bo, Kenema, and Pujehun districts in the south and west. It was not until later in the conflict that many northern CDF units were formed.

However, the RUF managed to make inroads during 1998-2000 controlling large parts of the country and Freetown at times until external forces, in conjunction with the CDF, managed to finally defeat the RUF in 2000. The CDF drew upon traditional institutions and customs. This gave it substantial prestige and support in many communities that the RUF, nor for that matter the SLA, could not achieve. It also gave it considerable internal solidarity.

CDF Negative Relations with Communities and/or with Government Forces and Impacts upon Human Security

A clear finding that emerges in the case studies is that CDFs were involved in numerous human rights abuses and provoked hostility in many communities. Rather than acting as security providers – either in consort with state forces or independently – they frequently diminished aspects of human and group security through community violence, pillaging, score-settling, and establishing new power structures built upon exploitation. Many CDF members were poor, under-privileged, and in some instances regarded as socially or ethnically inferior, and some used their new position of power to seek revenge or advance their position. All this resulted in polarisation within some communities and the prolongation of armed conflict by pushing many people towards co-operation with the armed. Further, in many cases, relations between state security forces and CDFs were poor and ex-members of the CDFs resorted to anti-government activities after their disbanding.

Peru

In Peru, the rondas companies inflicted heavy casualties on the armed opposition groups and denied them a safe haven in the countryside, their hoped-for stronghold.[34] This reality forced them, especially the Shining Path, to shift their focus from rural guerrilla operations to urban guerrilla activities, although the impoverished countryside was potentially a more promising arena for their growth.[35] However, against a background of economic inequalities, harsh treatment at the hands of the security forces, the rondas companies, landless farmers, and the indigenous people helped the armed groups and, in many cases, joined them. Abuses included forcible recruitment of poor peasants, including women and children, for unpaid and dangerous combat duties as CDF members for which death threats were even used.[36] By alienating the very social group that the government needed the support of to combat the armed rebels, the rondas companies' abuses contributed as a factor to the prolongation of the civil conflict. The counter-insurgency operations of the security forces and the rondas companies worsened Peru's social polarisation along ethnic lines pitting the indigenous people, who accounted for 75% of the civil war's victims, against Spanish-speakers.

Guatemala

Guatemala's PAC units were theoretically voluntary organisations of peasants.[37] However, while volunteers accounted for the majority of their members, forced membership also existed.[38] Army officers and PAC leaders, according to some reports, pressurised male peasants to 'become and remain members or extorted a fee from individuals in exchange for permission to resign,' while those who refused to serve in PAC units 'suffered threats and other abuses.'[39] In fact, many victims of the PAC were peasants suspected of being members or sympathisers of the armed opposition since they refused to join the voluntary force.[40] As a discriminated against social group, the Guatemalan landless indigenous people faced additional abuses during the civil war for their real or perceived sympathy for the armed opposition. The PAC's abusive policy towards the peasants helped the armed opposition recruit in the countryside from among the dissatisfied landless and/or poor peasants who also became a target of ill-treatment. The atrocities committed by the PAC contributed to the growth of a dissatisfied population in the countryside and undoubtedly alienated the indigenous people accounting for about 60% of the population. This situation helped the armed opposition survive and recruit and, along with other factors such as poverty, to prolong the bloody civil war.[41]

Sri Lanka

The Home Guards contributed to social polarisation in the countryside in Sri Lanka by increasing the hostility between the Tamils and Sinhalese. In addition to their committing human rights abuses against Tamil villagers, a factor has been their settlement in the 'Tamil territories' captured by the Sri Lankan army to replace the local Tamil villagers who have been forced to leave.[42] Moreover, the formation of Muslim Home Guards and their abusive behaviours towards Tamil peasants have worsened conflicts between the LTTE and Muslims damaged by human rights abuses committed by both sides and by the security forces.[43] The cycle of violence created by the atrocities of LTTE against Muslim villages in the east escalated when the Muslim Home Guards began reprisals, which further damaged Tamil-Muslim ties.[44] Home Guards' operations have also resulted in large-scale displacements of civilian Tamils especially in the eastern part of Sri Lanka.[45] Thus, the deterioration of ethnic ties has been a direct byproduct of Home Guards' operations. Moreover, the creation of Home Guards acted as another incentive for the LTTE to attack non-Tamil villagers for their housing of Home Guards, causing civilian casualties.[46]

Sierra Leone

In Sierra Leone, the CDF was popular in many parts of the country and to have belonged to or to have supported the CDF still carries weight in the post-conflict phase. However, it committed atrocities during the conflict, in particular in its attempts to root out alleged RUF sympathisers or spies. It was also involved in instances of rape, abduction, and forced labour. The CDF were particularly strong in southern Mende areas and less strong in the north. The SLA in the mid-1990s was mainly comprised of northern ethnic groups and the civil conflict has led to lasting resentment over SLA human rights abuses in Mende communities. Further, there is a strong perception in Mende areas that the south has suffered under northern-dominated All People's Congress (APC) governments.

However, elsewhere the CDF is alleged to be less popular. Some people in Freetown, for example, reportedly considered the Kamajors as bad as the RUF, and a threat to peace. In May 2001, for example, it was reported that Kamajors based at Makoloh were removed by the United Nations Mission in Sierra Leone (UNAMSIL) to Moyamba for encampment, bringing relief to local villagers unhappy with their behaviour. Further, the CDF can be said to have had an impact on the power of Paramount Chiefs and traditional leaders, although the CDF regarded itself as a traditional organisation espousing traditional values and generally displayed outward respect to traditional hierarchies (unlike the RUF who killed or drove out many traditional leaders in areas under their control).

CDF Effectiveness as Security Providers

As well as exploiting communities and diminishing human security, CDFs have sometimes proved ineffective in military terms due in part to a lack of training, poor equipment, and the adverse environments they have had to operate in. This runs contrary to one of the main rationales behind their creation, namely helping the security forces to meet the challenge of rebel forces. In instances where they did manage to hold back or defeat rebel forces this has often been at the cost of heavy casualties. This lack of professionalism frequently has considerable implications when it comes to the post-conflict phase and considerations of engaging CDFs in reconstituted national armies.

While CDFs were relatively effective in Peru and Sierra Leone, in the case of Peru this was achieved at the expense of heavy casualties on both sides to the conflict in addition to grave human rights abuses targeting indigenous peasants. In the case of Sierra Leone, the CDF managed to protect some communities, and eventually played a significant part in the defeat of the RUF. However, the latter still managed to hold large swathes of Sierra Leone at certain points of the conflicts and without external military intervention may well have prevailed in Sierra Leone.

Peru

In Peru, throughout the 1980s and the early 1990s, the rondas companies fought alongside the army units conducting anti-insurgency operations.[47] To a significant extent, the rondas companies decreased the Peruvian security forces' military/security burden.[48] Their assistance helped those forces to suppress the Shining Path and the MRTA as they inflicted heavy casualties on the latter despite their poor training and equipment, while forcing them to leave the countryside where they sought to expand among the dissatisfied poor rural population.[49] This forced the rebels to shift their focus from rural guerrilla operations to urban guerrilla activities, which ultimately proved unsuccessful.[50]

Guatemala

The PAC assisted Guatemalan security forces in their anti-insurgency operations. Yet, unlike in Peru, the end of the civil war in Guatemala was not due to the neutralisation of the armed opposition, but because of a political and military stalemate, which forced the government and the armed opposition to end the 36-year civil conflict through a negotiated settlement. The Guatemalan military commanded, trained, armed and controlled the PAC units.[51] However, their recruits were poorly paid, trained and equipped and lacked the discipline needed for a law enforcement force.[52] Added to their lack of training and discipline, a lack of supervision contributed to their extensive human rights abuses and led the Inter-American Commission on Human Rights to demand their abolition in June 1993.[53] Added to a general sense of dissatisfaction among the rural population, their abusive behaviour helped prolong the armed conflict. The PAC proved unable to ensure the defeat of the armed opposition by the government security forces. That reality forced the Guatemalan government to conclude a peace treaty in 1996.

Sri Lanka

There is no indication that the Home Guards played a pivotal military role in changing the pace of military events in favour of the Sri Lankan government. In fact, the Sri Lankan government's acceptance of a Norwegian-brokered cease fire in 2002 and its engaging in a peace process clearly indicated its inability to crush the LTTE. Poorly-paid Sinhalese and Muslim Home Guards villagers, with little or no military training, who lacked military discipline, failed to develop into an efficient auxiliary of the Sri Lankan military capable of meeting the LTTE challenge.[54] Home Guards often took severe casualties in combat against the LTTE because of their military deficiencies.[55] In 2002, such deficiencies prompted Sri Lankan Interior Minister John Amaratunga to announce future additional training for the force.[56]

Far from changing the tide in favour of the Sri Lankan government, the Home Guards have contributed to the expansion of the civil war by intensifying the ethnic conflict between the Sinhalese and Muslims, on the one side, and the Tamils, on the other side. Their reprisal attacks on unarmed Tamils were a factor in the increasing radicalisation of the Tamil population.[57] Their brutality has been matched by the LTTE in its indiscriminate attacks on unarmed Sinhalese and Muslim villagers, which further alienated the Tamils and pushed them towards the LTTE. This has enabled the LTTE to justify its brutality and to recruit by capitalising on the anger of the Tamils, which has helped it survive as a 'legitimate' Tamil force.[58]

Sierra Leone

In contrast to many CDFs elsewhere, the CDF turned into a major military force in parts of Sierra Leone. The Kamajors, in particular, became an effective fighting force, moving from their hunter origins and being armed with hunting rifles and shotguns to a well-armed force that developed effective ambush tactics to counter the RUF. Some Kamajors received formal military training from EO and ECOMOG troops. The SLA also used the CDF as scouts. As a consequence, the Kamajors developed a cadre of trained fighters.

Elsewhere, in the north for example, CDFs were less strong and in places like Makeni, which became an RUF stronghold in the late 1990s, the CDFs were quickly over-run and a number of CDF combatants joined the RUF once Makeni fell to them. The CDF played a major role in ensuring that the RUF, even at the height of its military fortunes in the late 1990s, could not take control of the whole country. In the central town of Bo, for example, CDFs surrounded the RUF, which was laying siege to the town. They contributed to the eventual near starvation of the RUF, which could never fully take Bo Town.

CDF Human Rights and International Humanitarian Law Violations

CDF units, like national armies and rebel elements, committed extensive human rights abuses in the countries surveyed. These were directed not only at rebels, but also many civilians. A lack of serious government or any other form of supervision of their activities, or meaningful accountability, underpinned such abuses. Governments tolerated, if not sanctioned, such abuses as in many cases they took place with the knowledge of, in the presence of, and in co-operation with government security forces. This lack of oversight and accountability has further raised doubts as to the legitimacy of CDFs as security providers. Addressing the grievances of victims and their families abused or killed by CDFs has been a major source of tension for governments in the post-conflict era and a barrier to reconciliation. Further, without CDFs, along with other elements, facing truth and reconciliation commissions or criminal tribunals, attempts to achieve post-conflict justice are likely to be hollow. However, trying CDF members suspected of, for example, war crimes is fraught with difficulties.

Peru

The rondas companies committed extensive human rights abuses during the civil war. According to the United Nations and Human Rights Watch, such abuses included 'extrajudicial, summary or arbitrary executions' of unarmed civilians independently and in cooperation with or with the knowledge of security forces.[59] Most of the victims were peasants, mainly indigenous ones, 'suspected of being members or sympathisers of the armed opposition' because of their refusal to join the voluntary rondas companies.[60] Thus, forced recruitment, including women and children, was also another form of human rights abuse as the rondas companies on occasions demanded that peasants, indigenous or Spanish-speakers, including the displaced, join them or face prison sentences for suspected ties with the Shining Path, intimidation (e.g. death threats) and even extra-judicial killings.[61] In addition, Peru's indigenous peasants became the targets of forcible displacement. The rondas companies' confiscation of peasants' lands after, in many cases, falsely accusing them of sympathising with the armed opposition and their 'counter-insurgency' activities resulted in the forced displacement of mainly landless indigenous peasants whose numbers were estimated at 600,000 in 2002. In 1994, the rondas companies grave human rights abuses forced the United Nations to express fears about them becoming 'another factor contributing to the spiral of violence in Peru'.[62] This further alienated the already-dissatisfied poor indigenous peasants who suffered disproportionately from such abuses and turned them against the Peruvian government. In particular, the brutality of the rondas companies, including massacres of real or perceived pro-rebel villagers helped the Shining Path justify its atrocities as responding in kind to the Peruvian government's atrocities.[63]

Guatemala

During the course of the civil war (1982-96) the PAC committed numerous grave abuses of human rights. At least one-fifth of PAC members were involved in massacres and other human rights abuses during the civil war, according to the Guatemalan Catholic Church.[64] The Guatemalan security forces and the PAC are implicated in the disappearance of about 45,000 and killings of about 100,000 Guatemalans suspected of supporting the armed opposition between 1960 and 1991.[65] Also, they are held responsible for 18% of the massacres of unarmed civilians during the civil war.[66] At least 2,100 men, women and children lost their lives in 25 documented massacres orchestrated by the PAC and the army.[67] The PAC also committed numerous instances of extra-judicial, summary or arbitrary trials and executions of mostly peasants suspected of being members or sympathisers of the armed opposition for their refusal to join the PAC as well as the lynching of mainly Mayans.[68] The indigenous people were the main target of 'violent counter-insurgency reprisals' by the military and the PAC. PAC abuses included acts of genocide, harassment and intimidation, forcible displacements and appropriations of lands, extorting money, and general criminal activity, such as burglary and assault.[69] Forced internal displacement of peasants resulted in the creation of a large internally displaced population whose numbers have been estimated at 750,000[70] or 1,000,000.[71] The PAC's other abuses include child abuse,[72] physical abuse, arbitrary arrest and detention and death threats,[73] and killings of foreign and domestic journalists critical of human rights abuses.[74]

Sri Lanka

The Home Guards have committed a wide range of human rights abuses. They have done so with impunity, often in co-operation with security forces.[75] Their abuses included indiscriminate killings and massacres of unarmed Tamil villagers,[76] massacres of Tamil refugees displaced from their homes,[77] extra-judicial killings in reprisals against civilians for LTTE attacks,[78] and the killing of children.[79] In April 2002, the Home Guards' abuse of power resulted in the Sri Lankan security forces decommissioning of the weapons issued to 1,000 Home Guards as they were allegedly used for 'crime, lawlessness and violence'.[80]

The Home Guards' mandate was to fight armed LTTE units in self-defence, but their military operations have gone far beyond this with the effect of exposing non-combatant civilians to intentional and unintentional violence and hardship. To avenge LTTE attacks on military and non-military Sinhalese and Muslim targets, the Home Guards targeted unarmed Tamil villagers in reprisal attacks resulting in further LTTE retaliatory attacks on unarmed Muslim and Sinhalese villagers.[81] This has created a vicious circle of violence.

The Home Guards' rampant human rights abuses have contributed to the expansion of the civil conflict. Their ill-treatment of unarmed civilian Tamils, including kidnappings, killings and rapes, has radicalised them to accept violence as an appropriate instrument.[82] Such ill-treatment has made the Tamils inclined to join the LTTE.[83]

Sierra Leone

The CDF committed numerous human rights abuses, as did all parties to the conflict. Discipline among combatants was sometimes poor, and further, violence was sometimes a policy instrument to ensure the compliance of civilians in areas under CDF control. The CDF was said to have engaged in extortion and to have harassed communities. There is also evidence that CDFs raped women accused of being rebel sympathisers, and they also engaged in kidnappings, including aid workers and journalists. CDF efforts to root out RUF and alleged supporters from local communities also involved human rights abuses. However, the CDF killed fewer civilians than the RUF.

During the conflict the CDF, like all other groups involved in the fighting, did not adhere to international humanitarian law pertaining to civilians. Captured combatants and suspected civilian sympathisers, were frequently tortured and executed, and child soldiers were frequently used. The CDF tended to regard children as legitimate soldiers under traditional customs. However, the CDF did not generally drive civilians into supporting the rebel cause as occurred in the other case studies.

Detrimental Impact on Development

With respect to development, the impact of CDFs was largely negative. Their involvement in armed violence and extensive human rights abuses, including mass displacement of the rural population, impeded, if not completely stopped, rural development in many areas. Their contribution to an insecure environment for civilians in the countryside also hampered developmental efforts by decreasing the rural population's incentive to stay in certain areas and to engage in farming and other economic activities. This insecurity contributed to dissuading aid and development assistance in conflict-affected areas. In Sierra Leone the impact of the CDF seems to have been less negative than in the other case studies – there is evidence that development continued in some communities where the CDF operated. However, Sierra Leone in 2004 was still to recover and fully return to pre-conflict levels of development.

Peru

The establishment of the armed rondas companies decreased the availability of human resources capable of improving the rural areas whose under-development helped stimulate the civil war. The rondas companies perceived themselves as having certain 'social and economic cooperation' tasks to perform, but their role as armed civilian defence units practically ended those limited development functions. Reports suggest that the Peruvian military accused those rondas companies, which 'demanded social and economic reinsertion as well as recognition of their rights as ethnic minorities', e.g., the Asháninkas in Satipo and Río Tambo, of having an 'affinity with the Shining Path'.[84] Moreover, the massive displacement of peasants, especially the indigenous ones, and the confiscation of their lands to safeguard the economic interests of large landowners, worsened relations between the poor peasants and the large landowners, which were already damaged because of land disputes.

Guatemala

Land disputes have been a major source of conflict and violence in the Guatemalan countryside pitting the majority of poor landless peasants and those having inadequate land against a minority of large landowners. Among other factors, the efforts of the ruling elite to preserve the unfair *status quo* created a suitable climate for the rise of armed groups advocating the interests of the impoverished peasants. As in Peru, the use of military means to maintain this destabilising situation through the suppression of the peasants has blocked 'agrarian reform'. Grave human rights abuses by the PAC, including killings, as a means to force the indigenous peasants to leave their smallholdings has only helped to prolong a situation, which impedes, if not totally prevents, rural development. The result has been the perpetuation of rural underdevelopment.

Sri Lanka

The conflict in the northern and the eastern parts of Sri Lanka has been a major impediment to assistance in those regions. In 1996 and 1997, for example, there was a total halt of humanitarian assistance in Jaffna, which was the scene of an extensive military operation. However, human rights abuses by the Sri Lankan government's forces prompted foreign donors such as Canada to consider a suspension of bilateral assistance to Sri Lankan government projects in 1992 and a reallocation of funds to other programmes in Sri Lanka, a policy already followed by the Nordic countries.[85]

Sierra Leone

The CDF did not as a rule pursue a policy of hampering development or humanitarian assistance. Within communities under its control, it allowed continued farming, for example, both for the benefit of the community and to sustain its fighting capacity. CDF combatants were embedded in communities so it was in their interests to maintain a degree of normalcy in terms of activities such as agriculture, although the impact of the civil conflict in general terms put a huge strain in terms of development in destruction of infrastructure and transportation, and shortages of commodities.

CDFs and Post-Conflict Issues

The impact of CDFs potentially extends well beyond the end of armed conflict. It is evident in all the case studies that CDF activities during conflicts will endure, both locally and nationally, in the post-conflict phase. Those who have suffered at the hands of the CDF, for example, will probably demand justice and, given the direct involvement of government and security forces in the creation and operation of CDFs, justice cannot be confined to ex-CDF.

At the same time, many ex-CDF find themselves unpopular with their national governments and sectors of the population particularly if they have engaged in criminal actions (e.g. banditry and hostage-taking), anti-government protests (e.g. occupation of government facilities), and if they attempt to regroup and assert their perceived rights through rioting and armed violence. In short, whether they like it or not, governments and societies will have to live with the consequences of CDF activities for a long time despite the end of armed conflicts.

Below is a brief summary of some of the challenges faced by Peru, Guatemala, Sri Lanka and Sierra Leone in dealing with CDFs in the post-conflict era.

Peru

The social, political and economic consequences of the rondas companies' abuses have created a barrier to national reconciliation in the post-conflict era, begun around 2000 when the Shining Path and MATR ceased to exist as fully-functional groups capable of destabilising Peru.[86] Peru's Truth and Reconciliation Committee has since sought to deal with the grievances of the civil war era, including atrocities against the rural population.[87] Most of the perpetrators – ex-ronderos – are yet to be called to account, a source of continued discontent and destabilisation in a country with a large rural population. The Peruvian government has recognised the necessity of addressing the injustices faced by the indigenous population, including their forcible displacement. However, its 'Project in Support of Repopulation' (PAR), which has focused on the resettlement of the internally displaced population, has not yet fully addressed the problem.

Guatemala

The atrocities of the PAC during the civil war have complicated the process of national reconciliation in the post-conflict era. The Guatemalan government and security forces have made efforts to ensure ex-PAC members have immunity, a cause of anger for many Guatemalans victimised by the PAC.[88] According to an Inter-American Commission on Human Rights report, years after the end of the civil war the Guatemalan government is yet to initiate a serious investigation and wide-ranging punishment for those responsible for human rights violations.[89] While cases have been brought against some ex-PAC members, prosecutions in many cases have been halted as judges, prosecutors and witnesses have received death threats.[90] The continued atrocities of ex-PAC members and former military personnel are causing concern. For example, during the 1997-99 period, at least 18 individuals fell victim to their extra-judicial killings.[91] There were credible reports in July 2002 regarding the reorganisation of ex-PAC members, which had the capacity to lead to killings on an even greater scale.[92] The extent of their reorganisation was unknown late in 2004. PAC's brutal policy towards the indigenous people, the majority of the Guatemalans, created a climate of fear and insecurity among them during the civil war. This still persists, as the government is yet to honour its commitment under the 1996 peace accord to help return the displaced indigenous peasants. Indeed, some ex-PAC members resumed their atrocities against the indigenous people, as it was reported in late 2002, for example.

In June 2002, ex-PAC members occupied roads, an airport, and an oil refinery and detained tourists in the Province of Peten demanding cash payments for services rendered to the army during the armed conflict.[93] In October 2002 they resorted to hostage-taking for similar ends.[94] The government's conciliatory response and promises to consider monetary compensation outraged many Guatemalans.[95] The PAC has become a political liability for the Guatemalan government, which seeks to reconcile its divided nation.

Sri Lanka

In February 2002, the LTTE and the Sri Lankan government signed a ceasefire agreement brokered by the Norwegian government as a prelude to finding a peaceful negotiated settlement to the two-decade long civil war.[96] The two sides have refrained from resuming war although they have violated the ceasefire on many occasions such as in August 2003.[97] Despite this, on 17 June 2002 Sri Lankan Interior Minister John Amaratunga denied any plans for disbanding the Home Guards, while announcing their future increase in strength.[98] Late in 2004, it is not yet certain whether the current ceasefire will lead to a permanent end to hostilities and the impact of the Home Guards on the post-conflict era is not yet clear.

Sierra Leone

CDF elements remain a potent political force nationally and locally in the post-conflict era. They still have power and influence in areas they controlled during the civil conflict. However, they are not currently regarded as militarily active, although command structures are said to be intact and it is thought they could be reconstituted as fighting forces quite readily in parts of the country. CDFs are thought to have hidden weapons in arms caches, but the condition of these is uncertain. However, re-supplying the CDF would not appear to be a problem given the ready availability of arms in West Africa and poorly policed borders.

Given the poverty of many ex-CDF members and their resentment at a lack of recognition for their role in 'winning' the conflict and protecting communities, it is not inconceivable that they might engage in unrest or violence, particularly if developments in Sierra Leone take an unfavourable turn. A mobilising factor might be the Special Court trials that were taking place in 2004 in which CDF commanders are among the indicted. For many CDF members, and indeed large sectors of the population, CDF commanders are regarded as heroes or community defenders who should not be on trial. Guilty verdicts and heavy-handed policing of possible subsequent demonstrations could quite readily lead to violence among ex-CDF.

In the post-conflict era finding a role for ex-CDF combatants both as a stabilising factor and to reflect the role they played in the conflict is a key issue. It was envisaged that the CDF might form the basis of a 'Territorial Army'. Plans for this were developed by the UK International Military Advisory and Training Team (IMATT), which is currently training the RSLAF, and by the Sierra Leone Ministry of Defence. During consultations it became apparent that the CDF did not want to be modelled into a Territorial Army, but appeared to want to remain independent of MoD/Republic of Sierra Leone Armed Forces (RSLAF) control.

Politically, being associated with the CDF during the conflict carries kudos among much of the population and the ex-CDF cannot be under-estimated as a political or military factor in Sierra Leone politics.

Post-Conflict Challenges of CDFs in Africa

The contexts analysed above have the capacity to inform post-conflict recovery frameworks in Africa where CDFs or civil militia have been a factor. They demonstrate that any attempts to accommodate, assimilate, or disband CDFs in Africa and reassert the authority of the state, will have to take account of the following.

First, the issue of the constitutional and legal status of CDFs is important, but it was not properly defined in any of the case studies analysed. Governments tended to keep the status of CDFs poorly-defined, in part so that the government's scope for manoeuvre was not restricted, but also because many governments were wary of allocating CDFs legal or constitutional status. However, this sometimes backfired and CDFs within certain communities or areas threatened to usurp the state's constitutional responsibility to provide security and protect civilians and indeed became an oppressor of some civilians. In Africa, redefining and re-asserting the role of the state in community protection is likely to be a key post-conflict challenge.

Second, it has been asserted that civil militias in general terms have the capacity to threaten peace and national stability, undermine democratic governance, and replace the rule of law and the ballot box with armed violence and the rule of the gun. The case studies examined do not fully bear this out. While the CDFs examined certainly have the potential capacity to cause trouble locally, particularly if some of their core demands in terms of opportunities for economic and social development are not met, in the main they do not seem presently to threaten national stability and peace. An exception might be ex-CDF elements in Sierra Leone, who at their height numbered tens of thousands. Given the key role they played in defeating the rebels, their dissatisfaction, economic marginalisation, easy access to arms, and their hostility to the trial of their leaders by the Special Court, it would not take much for them to be remobilised. Further, while CDFs did engage in armed violence within communities and terrorise citizens, they were not noticeably more abusive than state or rebel forces. Whether they in any singular way represent a threat to democratic governance also remains open to question, particularly when the state governments in question mainly have a poor record in upholding democratic values. It would seem that African states, in assessing the positioning of CDFs in post-conflict situations, need to address issues of law and order, democratic governance, and military reform in relation to the state, as well as in relation to non-state actors, such as CDFs.

Third, CDFs have been said to have the capacity to polarise already bitterly divided and war-torn societies and to undermine the monopoly of the state to control the use of force. It is said that they also have often been subverted by diverse interest groups, for example, for private economic interests. The former was certainly the case in many of the contexts examined. Indigenous people in Peru and Guatemala were persecuted by CDFs and ended up in some instances assisting or joining rebel movements. Their marginalisation still remains a potentially explosive issue. However, this was not the case to any significant extent in Sierra Leone.

  Moreover, the monopoly of the use of force by the state was challenged locally but has been largely reasserted in the post-conflict period in most of the case studies.

  Finally, the hijacking of CDFs by private interests is apparent in the case studies, but, once again, this is not a unique phenomenon with corruption widespread in government and across societies in all case studies. Of the above factors, the divisive impact of CDFs (and for that matter the national security sector) in terms of ethnic mobilisation and associated tensions may be one of the most significant in the African context.

The Importance of SSR and Assimilation/Regulation of CDFs

The above analysis suggests that African states in war-torn and post-conflict situations need to renegotiate and re-orientate their relations with non-state actors, such as CDFs, and civil society, if they are to have credibility as security providers and reclaim their legitimate monopoly of the use of force within the state following conflict. This can be worked towards through measures such as justice reform, good governance, and social and economic development. However, a strategy that has assumed considerable importance in post-conflict reconstruction in Africa is Security Sector Reform (SSR). Not only does a reformed security sector open up the way for halting the abuse of civilians by security forces during complex political emergencies, it also opens up the possibility of foreclosing the development of rebel movements and also CDFs.

  SSR as experienced internationally has characteristically sought to bring about: the reform of military and police forces through professionalisation; the development of civilian control; respect for human rights; and the development of skills and internal structures of accountability and technical modernisation, as well as greater functional competencies. Further, SSR has attempted to reform judicial and penal structures to underwrite or guarantee the rule of law and thus improve the security of civilians.[99] The main engagement in these processes has been with former state actors and to a more limited extent rebel forces. SSR has sought to address these kinds of issues through a largely statist institutional perspective. SSR thinking, and other approaches to integration and regulation, on CDFs is poorly developed and has either ignored CDFs or has not put in place procedures to address the challenges they present or their needs and concerns. This has been demonstrated, for example, by the following. Firstly, Disarmament, Demobilisation and Reintegration (DDR) programmes do not provide for a meaningful engagement of CDFs. In particular, the fact that CDFs are often not asked or earmarked to surrender arms during formal DDR thus leading potentially to the persistence of Small Arms, Right Weapons (SALW) in civil society following conflict. Further, many CDF fighters are left outside or fail to enter reintegration programmes and drift into criminality or pose potential rallying points for future conflict.

  Secondly, the record of integrating CDF into reconstituted national armies is poor. There is evidence that national governments are often reluctant to integrate

CDF units into national armies, both on account of their alleged lack of professionalism, but also because they are seen as a potential disruptive element that may, for example, mutiny. This exclusion often has serious security ramifications.

Thirdly, CDFs are only sparsely represented in reconstituted police forces following conflict. Their involvement in human rights abuses, the often partial roles they have adopted in protecting communities, and their low levels of education have frequently excluded them from police programmes.

Fourthly, they have little representation or stake in oversight bodies.

Finally, CDFs run the risk of becoming 'enclave' groups, groups apart from the security sector, the state or even civil society – often poor and living at the margins of civil society, but proud of their achievements in defending communities and resisting rebels, and alert to remobilisation in the event of perceived threats or challenges.

As Bourne notes:

> CDFs...may be...accountable to the populations in the areas in which they operate, but security provision is fragmented and the perceptions of the legitimacy of the state may be diminished. While such actors may be accountable to their clients or communities, if left unregulated they are not accountable to the executive, legislative or wider civil society except when their provision of security takes the form of illegal action.[100]

Options for Reform

Fresh thinking is required to reframe the role of CDFs within SSR and strengthen integration and regulation options if post-conflict difficulties of the sort described above are to be avoided in African contexts. There seem to be three core SSR approaches that might be pursued within this framework.

First, to strengthen the capacities of national security bodies to fill or take on roles that CDFs undertook during conflicts at the community level; second, to assign to some CDFs security roles while reconstituting CDFs to make them more acceptable in terms of accountability, representation and human rights observance. A further option is to seek to forcibly dismantle CDFs but this is a far from straightforward process. Of these integration may be a particularly relevant approach to forestall post-conflict insecurity.

CDF Post-Conflict Roles

International experience demonstrates that CDFs are usually untrained, or poorly trained, not just in war-fighting or insurgency skills needed to fight rebel forces but, more importantly, they have few skills that might be applied to post-conflict peace-time roles. If CDFs are to play a post-conflict role in Africa, they will probably need to acquire both conventional military competences and training in post-conflict roles where they are operating in support of the state and society, rather than according to their own, government, or factional interests. This kind of training is already being undertaken in some African countries but is still not fully acknowledged as a priority. Those elements that are not to be reintegrated or returned to civilian life will need to be incorporated into, or associated in some way with, a reformed national army. A key element in this integration will be training. It is not advisable to allow untrained CDF combatants, some of whom are likely to have retained their weapons, to operate in and around communities in the post-conflict period; not least to protect civilians from human rights abuses and to avoid the emergence of armed criminality. Special training out of area is likely to be a prudent policy option as part of a national army reform programme. However, persuading ex-CDF combatants to undertake training or sign up to reformed national armies has often proved to be problematic in Africa, not least in the Sierra Leone case study that was examined.

A further approach to bring CDFs post-conflict into a SSR reform framework may be to address their claims to have regional or local legitimacy by forming local national army units. However, experience shows this will require some innovative thinking and therefore recruitment will be particularly important. There should be ethnic diversity within such units, as far as is practical, and recruits should be acceptable to the community, while criminal elements should be kept out of local units and also those who have been associated with human rights abuses. To this end, communities should be consulted, including traditional leaders and civil society, to secure community support for any CDF-based units that are constituted. Further, there will be a need to publicise in communities and nationally, the rationale of such units and seek to assuage fears regarding human rights, particularly through civilian oversight. More broadly, human rights mechanisms should be developed, perhaps drawing on NGOs and international organisations as well as government authorities, to specifically monitor ex-CDFs. This draws attention to the need, highlighted above, for African governments to engage with human rights and human security issues following conflicts.

Accountability and oversight will be another key element in the forming of regional units. This should be monitored by accountable civilian authorities and national army officers or civilians might be seconded or placed within regional units of CDFs. Close co-operation should be established between regional units and national army units in the field.

Integration into national armies of ex-CDF or other 'irregular' units has proved to be highly problematic both in Africa and elsewhere. Attempts to achieve an integrated national army in the Democratic Republic of Congo (DRC), for example, are indicative of the kind of problems that the integration of 'irregulars' poses. Following the 'withdrawal' of foreign forces in 2002 and the setting up of a transitional period of power-sharing, there were attempts in the DRC to form a national army constituted of rebel and Congolese units. However, this quickly broke down when rebel units mutinied in and seized the eastern Congolese city of Bukavu claiming that the Banyamulenge minority in the east had been victimised by government forces. In Sierra Leone, CDF elements have declined to join a national reconstituted army. There are fears that CDF leaders on trial in the summer of 2004 in Freetown in connection with the Special Court will, if found guilty, spark unrest or renewed fighting. Without the presence of the United Nations Mission in Sierra Leone (UNAMSIL) and a strong international stake in Sierra Leone it is perhaps likely that the impoverishment of many CDF, their sense of a lack of recognition for their achievement in countering the RUF, and their distaste for the abuses committed by some elements of the army might spill over into violence.

More generally, many CDFs seem to have developed an aversion to serving in national armies, which they perceive – often with justification – as having exploited them and as having often regarded them with disdain due to their lack of military and formal education. Overcoming these suspicions is a major challenge in the post-conflict period, particularly when civilian oversight bodies seem to take little account of CDFs and fail to incorporate them into their work and structures, thus increasing their sense of isolation and exclusion.

A parallel problem area is the DDR of ex-CDF combatants and the continued post-conflict existence of semi-mobilised or easily mobilised ex-CDF combatants. These often have easy access to arms and sometimes use them for armed robbery, intimidation, and other purposes. CDFs are rarely included in formal DDR processes, in part because of the often low-priority accorded to them by national armies and governments during conflict and during peace negotiations. CDFs are also often reluctant to see their units disbanded for a variety of motivations including losing power, a reluctance to see the conflict as over, and a realisation that their post-conflict prospects are often poor. CDFs have sometimes handed in weapons as part of community arms collection and weapons for development programmes outside of the formal DDR process, but have also hidden arms in caches and retained their command structures. All this points to the need for regulation options to include follow-up weapons collection programmes and in particular to formulate confidence-building and incentive strategies to bring CDFs on board. DDR programmes have been traditionally weak in reintegrating ex-combatants into society with many ex-combatants becoming outcasts in their former communities, drifting from former rural to urban livelihoods that are not sustainable and becoming more impoverished. Reintegration options for ex-CDF will probably need to focus on building livelihoods in the communities where they were based during the conflict. However, this is a challenge when they have committed human rights abuses and when they are sometimes mistrusted. There will be a need to involve ex-CDF combatants in schemes, which build trust between them and their communities, such as joint work schemes and micro credit. Where the CDF has been broadly trusted or regarded as protectors of communities this will be simpler – as in parts of Sierra Leone – but, at the same time, this may lead to problems of its own: ex-CDF combatants may acquire undue influence in civil affairs.

One approach to engaging ex-CDF combatants both at a community level and nationally may be to consider how they might be retrained to enter police forces. CDFs have often had better relations with the police, than with armies in Africa. This may open up opportunities to engage with local communities provided they can be demonstrated to have taken on the impartial ethos of a democratically-controlled constabulary.

More broadly, some ex-CDF leaders in Africa may need to be engaged or absorbed into the political process following conflicts to avoid future governance challenges and to secure key constituencies. This is not just a matter of securing stability, but also recognition of the support they sometimes have in communities, or even nation-wide, and the role they have played in countering rebel movements, provided they are not in breach of international humanitarian law or under investigation by criminal tribunals.

Reformulating Government Security Sector Representation Regionally

The alternative to a continued engagement of CDFs in the security forces is for national governments in Africa to address more seriously the difficulties that led to the outbreak of conflicts and the formation of CDFs and to avoid future recruitment of CDFs when confronted by conflict outbreaks. If progress can be made in this direction, it may be possible to re-establish the authority and legitimacy of state security forces and governments in communities that have been caught up in conflict. This may allow the decommissioning of CDFs and their command structures. For this to happen, they will need to have confidence that national security forces will be accountable and sensitive to the concerns and needs of communities, as well as not posing a threat to ex-CDF combatants.

Key approaches are likely to emphasise: the regional character of national army units; human rights and accountability; investment in development; and emphasis on community engagement. African governments might negotiate with CDFs and community leaders to, for example, set up regional national army units which draw upon local recruits who have local knowledge of geography, terrain and conditions, as well as customs and contexts. They would also need to ensure that these regional units, if formed, are recruited from groups that are likely to be accepted in communities and will not be swayed by 'ethnic' considerations. This can assist in building community confidence and support.

Further measures might include: setting-up civilian community involvement for these regional units in terms of community works programmes; publicising in communities and nationally the community protection rationale of regional army units and stressing their community links and civilian oversight. This may imply a less offensive posture and doctrine – for community and confidence-building purposes – than national armies might adopt elsewhere.

Finally, African governments should consider ensuring that communities where ex-CDF combatants live have developmental support as far as is possible within the constraints of government resources. This is likely to erode dissatisfaction. Key constituencies within communities should also be supported to win over communities, which may be hostile to the national government and the army.

Further, if national army regional contingents, with or without CDF elements, are to build support in communities emerging from complex political emergencies during which atrocities have been committed, they will need to respect human rights. This may imply co-operation with international human rights bodies and NGOs, as well as government bodies, in terms of training. There should also be mechanisms for ensuring that national army contingents are accountable to local and national civil authorities, as well as military commands.

In short, if CDFs are to be fully dismantled, and this has rarely been attempted in a systematic way in Africa or elsewhere, this will need to be done in co-operation with CDF commanders and combatants, probably in a phased way, with external facilitation or assistance, and with incentives being offered such as weapons for development, micro credit schemes, and other confidence-building and developmental approaches. The option of forcibly dismantling CDFs, a tempting approach when they are frequently engaged in criminality and abusing local communities with fall out for national governments, is a highly risky strategy that could reignite conflict along new fault-lines, particularly in post-conflict contexts where the legitimacy of the state is still in question and conflict grievances are not resolved.

Conclusion

African states considering meeting rebel challenges during conflict by forming or supporting CDFs will need to bear in mind the longer-term costs this may involve, as well as the potential shorter-term benefits. The case studies, with the exception of Sierra Leone, point to the overall no connection cost of forming CDFs during conflicts in terms of the abuse of local communities, increasing support for rebel movements and consequently running the risk of prolonging conflict, and the costs for ex-CDF members themselves in human security terms. The expediency of recruiting or supporting CDFs in terms of easing the burden on national forces, saving costs, and allowing them to take the burden of casualties, often rebounds in the post-conflict phase when CDFs are likely to prove difficult to dismantle, may harbour grievances, and ultimately have the capacity to resort to violence or re-start conflict. There is also the possibility of CDFs emerging with a new political awareness and a sense of empowerment post-conflict with both positive and negative impacts for governments.

It is tempting for governments in Africa in the post-conflict phase, often with a democratic mandate, to exclude, marginalise, ignore, or persecute ex-CDF combatants. However, this is ultimately likely to rebound on state authorities unless CDFs wither away of their own volition and cease to exist as organisations or entities that can be readily resurrected. In the case studies examined, this has not happened and CDFs have tended to persist. African governments and the African security sector will need to engage with ex-CDF combatants. This implies not only incorporating them in the security sector in terms of representation in civil and military structures, but perhaps in a few instances allocating them regional roles when they can be incorporated into accountability and oversight frameworks to acquire local acceptance and legitimacy. There will also need to be programmes of social and economic development targeted at both ex-CDF combatants and the communities they are situated in who have often suffered greatly as a result of CDF, rebel and government fighting. Ultimately, the challenge that CDFs present in Africa is one of reintegration rather than exclusion.

Notes

[1]   Foreign and Commonwealth Office, Foreign and Commonwealth Country Profiles: Peru (http://www.fco.gov.uk/servlet/Front?pagename=OpenMarket/Xcelerate/ShowPage&c=Page&cid=1007029394365&a=KCountryProfile&aid=1020338161701). Accessed on 17 December 2003.

[2]   United Nations Economic and Social Council, Commission on Human Rights, Fiftieth Session, Item 11 (a) of the provisional agenda, Distr. General, E/CN.4/1994/38, 2 February 1994: (http://www.unhchr.ch/Huridocda/Huridoca.nsf/0/b76d2813680101b380256738003b75c 0?Opendocument). Accessed 24 December 2003; United States Department of State, 'Guatemala', Country Reports on Human Rights Practices – 2000, Released by the Bureau of Democracy, Human Rights and Labor on 23 February 2001, (http://www.state.gov/g/drl/rls/hrrpt/2000/wha/775.htm). Accessed on 2 January 2004.

[3]   USAID, USAID Civil-Military Programs: Country Programs: Peru, 12 May 2003 14:38:52 EDT: (http://www.usaid.gov/democracy/cmr/peru.html), Accessed on 20 December 2003.

[4]   Ibid.

[5]   Ibid.

[6]   United Nations Economic and Social Council, Fiftieth Session.

[7]   Human Rights Watch, Human Rights Watch Report 1992, 1992, (http://www.hrw.org/reports/1992/WR92/AMW2-06.htm#P384_137680). Accessed on 29 December 2003.

[8]   United Nations Economic and Social Council, Fiftieth Session.

[9]   Ibid.

[10]   USAID, USAID Civil-Military Programs.

[11]   *Prevent Genocide International News Monitor* for November 2002: http://www.preventgenocide.org/prevent/news-monitor/2002nov.htm). Accessed on 4 January 2004.

[12]   USAID, USAID Civil-Military Programs.

[13]   United Nations Economic and Social Council, Commission on Human Rights, Forty-ninth session, Item 11 (a) of the provisional agenda, Distr. General, E/CN.4/1993/34, 28 January 1993. Accessed on 24 December 2003.

[14]   United States Department of State, 'Guatemala', Country Reports on Human Rights Practices – 1996, Released by the Bureau of Democracy, Human Rights and Labor on 30 January, 1997: (http://www.state.gov/www/global/human_rights/96hrp_index.html). Accessed on 2 January 2004; United Nations Economic and Social Council, Fiftieth Session.

[15]   United Nations Economic and Social Council, Fiftieth Session.

[16]   United States Department of State, 'Guatemala', 1996.

[17]   Ibid; United Nations Economic and Social Council, Fiftieth Session.

[18]   United States Department of State, 'Guatemala', 1996.

[19]   CAFOD, CAFOD fears democracy in Guatemala is under threat, 31 July 2003: (http://www.cafod.org.uk/latinamerica/guatemalademocthreat20030731.shtml). Accessed on 21 December 2003.

[20] Human Rights Watch, World Report 2003, 2003:
(http://www.hrw.org/wr2k3/americas6.html). Accessed on 21 December 2003.

[21] Federal Research Division of the Library of Congress, Sri Lanka: A Country Study Washington, DC: Library of Congress, October 1988:
(http://memory.loc.gov/frd/cs/lktoc.html). Accessed on 17 December 2003.

[22] 'Sri Lanka to Expand Paramilitary Auxiliaries', *TamilNet*, 21 June 2002 10:03 GMT
(http://www.tamilnet.com/art.html?catid=13&rid=2002062102). Accessed on 21 December 2003.

[23] University Teachers for Human Rights, Jaffna, Sri Lanka, Briefing No 1: Human rights and The Issues of War and Peace, August 1992:
(http://www.uthr.org/Briefings/Briefing1.htmhttp://www.uthr.org/Briefings/Briefing1.ht m). Accessed 18 December 2003; United Nations Economic and Social Council, Forty-ninth Session.

[24] United States Department of State, 'Sri Lanka', 2002; Federal Research Division.

[25] Federal Research Division; 'Sri Lanka to Expand Paramilitary Auxiliaries'; 'Sri Lanka to Expand Paramilitary Auxiliaries'.

[26] Federal Research Division.

[27] 'Sri Lanka to Expand Paramilitary Auxiliaries'.

[28] Federal Research Division.

[29] http://www.sinhaya.com/srilanka.htmhttp://www.sinhaya.com/srilanka.htmMILITAR.

[30] United States Department of State, 'Sri Lanka', Country Reports on Human Rights Practices–2002.Released by the Bureau of Democracy, Human Rights and Labor, 31 March 2003:
(http://www.state.gov/g/drl/rls/hrrpt/2002/18315.htm Sri Lanka). Accessed 19 December 2003.

[31] 'Sri Lanka to Expand Paramilitary Auxiliaries'.

[32] Voice of America, 28 November 2004.

[33] See: Ibrahim Abdullah and Patrick Muana, 'The Revolutionary United Front of Sierra Leone', Christopher Clapham (Ed.) in *African Guerrillas,* James Currey; Oxford, p. 187.

[34] United Nations Economic and Social Council, Fiftieth Session.

[35] United States Department of State, 'Peru', Country Reports on Human Rights Practices 1994. Released by the Bureau of Democracy, Human Rights and Labor, Released on February 1995:
(http://dosfan.lib.uic.edu/ERC/democracy/1994_hrp_report/94hrp_report_ara/Peru.html) Accessed on 26 December 2003.

[36] United States Department of State, 'Guatemala', Country Reports on Human Rights Practices for 1997. Released by the Bureau of Democracy, Human Rights and Labor 30 January 1998:
(http://www.state.gov/www/global/human_rights/1997_hrp_report/peru.html). Accessed on 31 December 2003; United Nations Economic and Social Council, Fiftieth Session; Human Rights Watch, 1992; Human Rights Watch, 1992.

[37] United States Department of State, 'Guatemala', 1996.

[38] Washington Times, 8 May 1992, p. A9, quoted in CIA Support of Death Squads, 9 October 1999:
(http://www.serendipity.li/cia/death_squads.htm). Accessed on 31 December 2003.

[39] United States Department of State, 'Guatemala', 1996.

[40] Washington Times, 8 May 1992, p. A9; United Nations Economic and Social Council, Fiftieth Session; United States Department of State, 'Guatemala', 1996.

[41] Ibid; United Nations Economic and Social Council, Fiftieth Session.

42 'Sri Lanka's Dirty War: the Home Guards'. *TamilNet*, 6 August 1997 23:59 GMT (http://www.tamilnet.com/art.html?catid=13&artid=46). Accessed on 5 January 2004.
43 University Teachers for Human Rights, Briefing No 1.
44 Ibid: Federal Research Division.
45 University Teachers for Human Rights, Briefing No 1.
46 University Teachers for Human Rights, Jaffna, Sri Lanka, Information Bulletin No. 16, 5 February 1998:
    (http://www.uthr.org/bulletins/bul16.htm). Accessed on 27 December 2003.
47 United Nations Economic and Social Council, Fiftieth Session.
48 Ibid.
49 Ibid.
50 United States Department of State, 'Peru', Country Reports on Human Rights Practices 1994.
51 United States Department of State, 'Guatemala', 1996.
52 United Nations Economic and Social Council, Fiftieth Session.
53 Ibid.
54 'Sri Lanka to Expand Paramilitary Auxiliaries'; Federal Research Division.
55 'Sri Lanka's Dirty War: the Home Guards'.
56 'Sri Lanka to Expand Paramilitary Auxiliaries'.
57 Federal Research Division; University Teachers for Human Rights, Briefing No 1.
58 University Teachers for Human Rights, Briefing No1.
59 Human Rights Watch, 1992; United Nations Economic and Social Council, Fiftieth Session.
60 United Nations Economic and Social Council, Fiftieth Session.
61 United Nations Economic and Social Council, Fiftieth Session; Human Rights Watch, 1992.
62 Ibid.
63 *Prevent Genocide International News Monitor* for November 2002.
64 CAFOD, CAFOD fears democracy in Guatemala is under threat.
65 United Nations Economic and Social Council, Fiftieth Session.
66 Neue Zürcher Zeitung (Switzerland), www.nzz.ch ,28 Nov 2002, reprinted in *Prevent Genocide International News Monitor* for November 2002:
    (http://www.preventgenocide.org/prevent/news-monitor/2002nov.htm). Accessed on 31 December 2003; United States Department of State, 'Guatemala', Country Reports on Human Rights Practices – 2002. Released by the Bureau of Democracy, Human Rights and Labor, 31 March 2003, (Url). Accessed on 28 December 2003; Human Rights Watch. Guatemala: Political Violence Unchecked – Human Rights Watch Guatemala Mission Findings. August 18-22, 2002:
    (http://www.hrw.org/press/2002/08/guatemission.htm). Accessed on 23 December 2003; United States Department of State, 'Guatemala', 2000.
67 Jill Replogle, 'Defense Stand or Presidential Office?', *Latinamericapress.org*, 7 January 2004:
    (http://www.lapress.org/Summ.asp?lanCode=1&couCode=10). Accessed 7 January 2004.
68 Washington Times, 8 May 1992, p. A9. United States Department of State, 'Guatemala', 2001; United Nations Economic and Social Council, Fiftieth Session.
69 Neue Zürcher Zeitung (Switzerland), www.nzz.ch ,28 Nov 2002; Human Rights Watch, Guatemala: Political Violence Unchecked; United States Department of State, 'Guatemala', 2000; United States Department of State, 'Guatemala', 1996.
70 Ibid.

[71] *UNWire.* 'Guatemala.' 12 November 2002: UNDP Supports Plan For Reparations To War Victims, reprinted in *Prevent Genocide International News Monitor* for November 2002:
(http://www.preventgenocide.org/prevent/news-monitor/2002nov.htm). Accessed 31 December 2003.

[72] United States Department of State, 'Guatemala', 1996.

[73] United Nations Economic and Social Council, Fiftieth Session.

[74] United States Department of State, 'Guatemala', 2000; United State Department of State, 'Guatemala', 1997.

[75] Amnesty International, 'Sri Lanka: Government forces kill eight civilians – justice needed now', *News Service 18/98*, AI INDEX: ASA 37/2/98, 3 February 1998:
(http://web.amnesty.org/library/Index/ENGASA370021998?open&of=ENG-LKA). Accessed on 18 December 2003.

[76] Ibid; Federal Research Division; 'Sri Lanka to Expand Paramilitary Auxiliaries'; University Teachers for Human Rights, Briefing No 1.

[77] 22 December 2003; University Teachers for Human Rights, Briefing No. 1.

[78] United States Department of State, 'Sri Lanka', 2002; University Teachers for Human Rights, Jaffna, Briefing No 1.

[79] Amnesty International, 'Sri Lanka: Government Forces Kill Eight Civilians – Justice Needed Now'. University Teachers for Human Rights, Briefing No 1.

[80] 'Home Guards Bound for Warfront', *TamilNet*, 09 April 1998 23:59 GMT (http://www.tamilnet.com/art.html?catid=13&rid=98040906   ). Accessed on 20 December 2003.

[81] University Teachers for Human Rights, Briefing No 1; Federal Research Division.

[82] Ibid.; Federal Research Division.

[83] University Teachers for Human Rights, Briefing No 1.

[84] United Nations Economic and Social Council, Fiftieth Session.

[85] University Teachers for Human Rights, Briefing No 1.

[86] United States Department of State, 'Peru,' Country Reports on Human Rights Practices – 2000, Released by the Bureau of Democracy, Human Rights and Labor on 23 February 2001, Guatemala (http://www.state.gov/g/drl/rls/hrrpt/2000/wha/775.htm). Accessed on 2 January 2004.

[87] CAFOD, Truth Commission in Peru Reports on War That Led to 70,000 Deaths, 2 September 2003:
(http://www.cafod.org.uk/news_and_events/news/september_2003/peru_truth_commissi on). Accessed on 5 January 2004.

[88] Ibid; United States Department of State, 'Guatemala', 1996.

[89] Human Rights Watch, World Report 2003.

[90] United States Department of State, 'Guatemala', 2001.

[91] United States Department of State, 'Guatemala', 2002.

[92] Human Rights Watch, World Report 2003.

[93] United States Department of State, 'Guatemala', 2002.

[94] Amnesty International. Public Statement, *News Service* No: 248, 28 October 2003, AI Index: AMR 34/062/2003 (Public):
(http://www.amnestyusa.org/countries/guatemala/document.do?id=80256AB9000584F6 80256DCD006979E8). Accessed on 2 January 2004.

[95] United States Department of State, 'Guatemala', 2002; Human Rights Watch, World Report 2003.

[96] 'Text of Sri Lanka Truce Deal', *BBC News online*: World: South Asia (http://news.bbc.co.uk/1/low/world/south_asia/1836198.stm). Accessed on 17 December 2003.

[97] 'Muslims Gunned Down in Sri Lanka', *Aljazeera.NET*, 18 August 2003, (http://english.aljazeera.net/NR/exeres/B1B82CEB-851F-4FE8-97FF-058D5BB83F7B.htm). Accessed on 19 December 2003.
[98] 'Sri Lanka to Expand Paramilitary Auxiliaries'.
[99] See Mike Bourne, 'Security Sector Reform and the Challenges and Opportunities of the Privatisation of Security', in Damian Lilly and Michael von Tangen Page, *Security Sector Reform: The Challenges and Opportunities of the Privatisation of Security* (London: International Alert, September 2002).
[100] Mike Bourne, p. 25.

References

Abdullah, Ibrahim and Patrick Muana, 'The Revolutionary United Front of Sierra Leone', Christopher Clapham (Ed.) in *African Guerrillas,* James Currey; Oxford, pp. 172-193.
Amnesty International. Public Statement, *News Service* No: 248, 28 October 2003, AI Index: AMR 34/062/2003 (Public):
(http://www.amnestyusa.org/countries/guatemala/document.do?id=80256AB9000584F6 80256DCD006979E8). Accessed on 2 January 2004.
Amnesty International, 'Sri Lanka: Government forces kill eight civilians – justice needed now', *News Service 18/98*, AI INDEX: ASA 37/2/98, 3 February 1998:
(http://web.amnesty.org/library/Index/ENGASA370021998?open&of=ENG-LKA). Accessed on 18 December 2003.
Bourne, Mike. 'Security Sector Reform and the Challenges and Opportunities of the Privatisation of Security', in Damian Lilly and Michael von Tangen Page, *Security Sector Reform: The Challenges and Opportunities of the Privatisation of Security* (London: International Alert, September 2002).
CAFOD, CAFOD Fears Democracy in Guatemala Is under Threat. 31 July 2003, (http://www.cafod.org.uk/latinamerica/guatemalademocthreat20030731.shtml). Accessed on 21 December 2003.
CAFOD, Truth Commission in Peru Reports on War That Led to 70,000 Deaths, 2 September 2003:
(http://www.cafod.org.uk/news_and_events/news/september_2003/peru_truth_commissi on). Accessed on 5 January 2004.
Country Reports on Human Rights Practices 2002.Released by the Bureau of Democracy, Human Rights and Labor, 31 March 2003:
(http://www.state.gov/g/drl/rls/hrrpt/2002/18315.htm Sri Lanka). Accessed 19 December 2003.
Federal Research Division of the Library of Congress, Sri Lanka: A Country Study (Washington, DC: Library of Congress, October 1988):
(http://memory.loc.gov/frd/cs/lktoc.html). Accessed on 17 December 2003.
Foreign and Commonwealth Office, Foreign and Commonwealth Country Profiles: Peru: (http://www.fco.gov.uk/servlet/Front?pagename=OpenMarket/Xcelerate/ShowPage&c= Page&cid=1007029394365&a=KCountryProfile&aid=1020338161701). Accessed on 17 December 2003.
'Home Guards Bound for Warfront', *TamilNet*, 09 April 1998 23:59 GMT, (http://www.tamilnet.com/art.html?catid=13&rid=98040906). Accessed on 20 December 2003.
Human Rights Watch. Guatemala: Political Violence Unchecked – Human Rights Watch Guatemala Mission Findings. August 18-22, 2002:

(http://www.hrw.org/press/2002/08/guatemission.htm). Accessed on 23 December 2003.
Human Rights Watch, World Report 2003, 2003:
(http://www.hrw.org/wr2k3/americas6.html). Accessed on 21 December 2003.
Human Rights Watch, Human Rights Watch Report 1992, 1992:
(http://www.hrw.org/reports/1992/WR92/AMW2-06.htm#P384_137680). Accessed on 29 December 2003.
'Muslims Gunned Down in Sri Lanka', *Aljazeera.NET*, 18 August 2003,
(http://english.aljazeera.net/NR/exeres/B1B82CEB-851F-4FE8-97FF-058D5BB83F7B.htm). Accessed on 19 December 2003.
Neue Zürcher Zeitung (Switzerland), www.nzz.ch ,28 Nov 2002, reprinted in *Prevent Genocide International News Monitor* for November 2002:
(http://www.preventgenocide.org/prevent/news-monitor/2002nov.htm). Accessed on 31 December 2003.
Prevent Genocide International News Monitor for November 2002:
(http://www.preventgenocide.org/prevent/news-monitor/2002nov.htm). Accessed on 4 January 2004.
'Religious Tensions Rise in Sri Lanka', NEWS: Global, *Aljazeera.NET*,
(http://english.aljazeera.net/NR/exeres/94922116-1838-45AD-8E70-C6D40E0A6D68.htm.) Accessed on 22 December 2003.
Replogle, Jill, 'Defense Stand or Presidential Office?', *Latinamericapress.org*, 7 January 2004:
(http://www.lapress.org/Summ.asp?lanCode=1&couCode=10). Accessed 7 January 2004.
'Sri Lanka to Expand Paramilitary Auxiliaries', *TamilNet*, 21 June 2002 10:03 GMT:
(http://www.tamilnet.com/art.html?catid=13&rid=2002062102). Accessed on 21 December 2003.
'Sri Lanka's Dirty War: the Home Guards'. *TamilNet*, 6 August 1997 23:59 GMT:
(http://www.tamilnet.com/art.html?catid=13&artid=46). Accessed on 5 January 2004.
'Text of Sri Lanka Truce Deal', *BBC News online*: World: South Asia:
(http://news.bbc.co.uk/1/low/world/south_asia/1836198.stm). Accessed on 17 December 2003.
UNDP Supports Plan For Reparations To War Victims, reprinted in *Prevent Genocide International News Monitor* for November 2002:
(http://www.preventgenocide.org/prevent/news-monitor/2002nov.htm). Accessed 31 December 2003.
United Nations Economic and Social Council, Commission on Human Rights, Fiftieth Session, Item 11 (a) of the provisional agenda, Distr. General, E/CN.4/1994/38, 2 February 1994:
(http://www.unhchr.ch/Huridocda/Huridoca.nsf/0/b76d2813680101b380256738003b75c0?Opendocument). Accessed 24 December 2003.
United Nations Economic and Social Council, Commission on Human Rights, Forty-ninth session, Item 11 (a) of the provisional agenda, Distr. General, E/CN.4/1993/34 28 January 1993. Accessed on 24 December 2003.
United States Department of State, 'Guatemala', Country Reports on Human Rights Practices – 2002. Released by the Bureau of Democracy, Human Rights and Labor, 31 March 2003: (http://www.state.gov/g/drl/rls/hrrpt/2002/18273.htm). Accessed on 28 December 2003.
United States Department of State, 'Guatemala', Country Reports on Human Rights Practices 2000, Released by the Bureau of Democracy, Human Rights and Labor on 23 February 2001, Guatemala: (http://www.state.gov/g/drl/rls/hrrpt/2000/wha/775.htm). Accessed on 2 January 2004.

United States Department of State, 'Guatemala', Country Reports on Human Rights Practices for 1997. Released by the Bureau of Democracy, Human Rights and Labor 30 January 1998:
(http://www.state.gov/www/global/human_rights/1997_hrp_report/peru.html). Accessed on 31 December 2003.

United States Department of State, 'Guatemala', Country Reports on Human Rights Practices 1996, Released by the Bureau of Democracy, Human Rights and Labor on 30 January, 1997):
(http://www.state.gov/www/global/human_rights/96hrp_index.html). Accessed on 2 January 2004.

United States Department of State, 'Peru, Country Reports on Human Rights Practices 2000, Released by the Bureau of Democracy, Human Rights and Labor on 23 February 2001, Guatemala (http://www.state.gov/g/drl/rls/hrrpt/2000/wha/775.htm). Accessed on 2 January 2004.

United States Department of State, 'Peru', Country Reports on Human Rights Practices 1994.Released by the Bureau of Democracy, Human Rights and Labor, Released on February 1995:
(http://dosfan.lib.uic.edu/ERC/democracy/1994_hrp_report/94hrp_report_ara/Peru.html). Accessed on 26 December 2003.

United States Department of State, 'Sri Lanka', Country Reports on Human Rights Practices 2002. Released by the Bureau of Democracy, Human Rights and Labor, 31 March 2003:
(http://www.state.gov/g/drl/rls/hrrpt/2002/18273.htm). Accessed on 28 December 2003.

UNWire. 'Guatemala', 12 November 2002.

University Teachers for Human Rights, Jaffna, Sri Lanka, Information Bulletin No. 16, 5 February 1998:
(http://www.uthr.org/bulletins/bul16.htm). Accessed on 27 December 2003.

University Teachers for Human Rights, Jaffna, Sri Lanka, Briefing No 1: Human rights and The Issues of War and Peace, August 1992:
(http://www.uthr.org/Briefings/Briefing1.htmhttp://www.uthr.org/Briefings/Briefing1.htm). Accessed 18 December 2003.

USAID, USAID Civil-Military Programs: Country Programs: Peru, 12 May 2003 14:38:52 EDT: (http://www.usaid.gov/democracy/cmr/peru.html), Accessed on 20 December 2003.

Voice of America, 28 November 2004.

Washington Times, 8 May 1992, p. A9, quoted in CIA Support of Death Squads, 9 October 1999: (http://www.serendipity.li/cia/death_squads.htm). Accessed on 31 December 2003.

Index